COPYFIGHT

The Global Politics of Digital Copyright Reform

Widespread file sharing has led content industries – publishers and distributors of books, music, films, and software – to view their customers as growing threats to their survival. Content providers and their allies, especially the United States government, have pushed for stronger global copyright policies through international treaties and domestic copyright reforms. Internet companies, individuals, and public interest groups have pushed back, with massive street protests in Europe and online "Internet blackouts" that derailed the 2012 US Stop Online Piracy Act (SOPA). But can citizens or smaller countries really stand in the way of the US copyright juggernaut?

To answer this question, *Copyfight* examines the 1996 World Intellectual Property Organization Internet treaties that began the current digital copyright regime. Blayne Haggart follows the WIPO treaties from negotiation to implementation from the perspective of three countries: the United States, Canada, and Mexico. Using extensive interviews with policymakers and experts in these countries, Haggart argues that not all the power is in the hands of the US government. Small countries can still set their own course on copyright legislation, while growing public interest in copyright issues means that even the United States might move away from ever-increasing copyright protection.

(Studies in Comparative Political Economy and Public Policy)

BLAYNE HAGGART is an assistant professor in the Department of Political Science at Brock University.

Studies in Comparative Political Economy and Public Policy

Editors: MICHAEL HOWLETT, DAVID LAYCOCK (Simon Fraser University), and STEPHEN MCBRIDE (McMaster University)

Studies in Comparative Political Economy and Public Policy is designed to showcase innovative approaches to political economy and public policy from a comparative perspective. While originating in Canada, the series will provide attractive offerings to a wide international audience, featuring studies with local, subnational, cross-national, and international empirical bases and theoretical frameworks.

Editorial Advisory Board

For a list of books published in the series, see page 371.

Copyfight

The Global Politics of Digital Copyright Reform

BLAYNE HAGGART

UNIVERSITY OF TORONTO PRESS
Toronto Buffalo London

© University of Toronto Press 2014
Toronto Buffalo London
www.utppublishing.com
Printed in Canada

ISBN 978-1-4426-4664-3 (cloth)
ISBN 978-1-4426-1454-3 (paper)

Printed on acid-free, 100% post-consumer recycled paper with vegetable-based inks.

Library and Archives Canada Cataloguing in Publication

Haggart, Blayne, author
Copyfight : the global politics of digital copyright reform/Blayne Haggart.

(Studies in comparative political economy and public policy)
Includes bibliographical references and index.
ISBN 978-1-4426-4664-3 (bound). – ISBN 978-1-4426-1454-3 (pbk.)

1. Copyright and electronic data processing – North America.   2. Copyright – Electronic information resources – North America.   3. Internet – Law and legislation – North America.   4. Copyright – North America.   I. Title.   II. Series: Studies in comparative political economy and public policy

K1420.5.H33 2014   346.704'82   C2013-907497-X

This book has been published with the help of a grant from the Federation for the Humanities and Social Sciences, through the Awards to Scholarly Publications Program, using funds provided by the Social Sciences and Humanities Research Council of Canada.

University of Toronto Press acknowledges the financial assistance to its publishing program of the Canada Council for the Arts and the Ontario Arts Council.

Canada Council   Conseil des Arts
for the Arts   du Canada

ONTARIO ARTS COUNCIL
CONSEIL DES ARTS DE L'ONTARIO
50 YEARS OF ONTARIO GOVERNMENT SUPPORT OF THE ARTS
50 ANS DE SOUTIEN DU GOUVERNEMENT DE L'ONTARIO AUX ARTS

University of Toronto Press acknowledges the financial support of the Government of Canada through the Canada Book Fund for its publishing activities.

Contents

Acknowledgments

Having spent my life on the other side of the Acknowledgments racket until this very moment, I've tended to treat these laundry lists with a mixture of envy and resentment ("I'd like to thank George Clooney, the Dalai Lama, and Nelson Mandela for the late-night spitball sessions"), with just a touch of condescension (Prof. So-and-so's not listed here? Why should I read this *obviously* incomplete "book"?) thrown in for flavour. Now, of course, I realize that I was completely mistaken, and that acknowledgments sections are an invaluable means for thanking those who helped shepherd a fundamentally collaborative enterprise into existence, the people without whom … And if they just happen to drop the names of well-known and brilliant superstars and superstars-to-be, well, what can you do?

It's a burden.

Studying copyright, especially if you're not a lawyer, is akin to stepping into a madhouse where things barely adhere to any internal logic, let alone traditional standards of what makes good public policy. As an economist *cum* political scientist, I found recent calls for "evidence-based" copyright policy to be a bit stunning: it's a three-hundred-year-old policy and only *now* we're starting to ask for evidence? That's the copyright debate in a nutshell. Copyright and intellectual property lawmaking often involve the exercise of power and influence justified in terms of foundational Western concepts like the individual and property. No wonder Cory Doctorow and others refer to the "copyfight."[1] It's politics laid bare.

---

1 If you're interested in where the term "copyfight" came from, the good folks at the Copyfight blog (with which I am not affiliated) have you covered: http://copyfight .corante.com/archives/2005/07/30/what_does_copyfight_mean.php.

All of this makes copyright wonderful fodder for a political scientist, so thanks to Keith Serry for suggesting over dinner in September 2006 that copyright might be something I'd find interesting. That ended up being something of an understatement. Sometimes I think if he'd mentioned that copyright would turn into an obsession – a not-uncommon occurrence among copyright scholars and lobbyists – I might've gone and studied something less inflammatory, like euthanasia. Thanks also to Simon Doyle for being my first guide into the weird, wonderful world of Canadian copyright policy, and Sara Bannerman for helping me make sense of copyright in general.

One of the things that studying copyright has taught me is that Jessica Litman is right: the notion of originality – and thus, I think, the individual author – is a "conceit."[2] It's humbling to think of how many people helped me along the way, through interviews, manuscript comments, previously published work, and informal discussions. So, I'd like to thank George Clooney, the Dalai Lama … Kidding! George had very little to do with the book. Unlike Laura Macdonald, Melissa Haussman, Jeremy de Beer, and Sheryl Hamilton, all of whom provided invaluable guidance from the very beginnings of this project. When I think what this manuscript would have looked like without their extensive revisions and discussions, well, there's no way that it would've been even remotely publishable. Three anonymous reviewers also provided very helpful comments. On the actual getting-the-book-out side of things, I'm grateful for the efforts of Daniel Quinlan and everyone at University of Toronto Press. And special thanks to Stephen Clarkson, who indirectly helped me select the book's case studies at a conference back when I was a mere master's student. I told him I was thinking of concentrating my studies on Canada-US politics, to which he responded that I should probably focus on Mexico as well. That suggestion has made all the difference to my entire academic career.

We stand on the shoulders of giants.

I'm also humbled and thankful for the time my interview subjects, in all three countries, took to walk a neophyte through the tangled world of copyright politics. If this book makes any sense at all, it's thanks to them. But if that's true, what if the book doesn't make sense? This is usually the point in the acknowledgments when the author claims sole responsibility for any errors, but if sole authorship truly is a conceit, where does that leave us?

2 Jessica Litman, "The Public Domain," *Emory Law Journal* 39.4 (1990), 1019.

One of the best parts of researching this book was the travel, which took me to Washington, DC, and Mexico City for fieldwork, and to Canberra, Australia, where I worked on significant parts of the manuscript. In Washington, I was fortunate enough to work out of the Kluge Center at the Library of Congress as an intern (thanks to the Washington Center and the Kluge Center's Mary Lou Reker for arranging that, and to Kay Kaufman Shelemay for the recording pedal). There is simply no better place for a researcher to work in DC than that centre and that library. In Mexico City I was hosted by the Centro de Investigaciones Sobre América del Norte at the National Autonomous University of Mexico (UNAM). My seriously fantastic Spanish teacher, Monica Riquetti, made it possible for me not only to conduct my fieldwork, but to get to and from a part of Mexico City that isn't served by the metro in order to attend the 2010 Division 2 World Hockey Championship (Spain has a surprisingly good team). Thanks also to Esteban Nicholls for transcribing those Mexico interviews. Finally, its collegial interdisciplinary atmosphere made the Regulatory Institutions Network at the Australian National University an ideal place to polish the final versions of this text. Thanks especially to Peter Drahos for his comments on an early version of this book. And this has nothing to do with copyright, but thanks to Cynthia Banham for introducing me to Australian Rules Football. Go Swans!

Beyond these cathedrals of learning, substantial portions of this book were written in pubs, cafés, and restaurants around the world. Much of the Mexican case study was composed in a Starbucks in Mexico City's Zona Rosa (corner of Calle Genoa and Calle Londres). It's on a pedestrian street, with a patio that's perfect for people watching. And it has a strong wifi signal. If you're feeling homesick for bad Canadian food, just around the corner, near Londres at Florencia, La Casa del Dragon has an affordable Chinese food buffet. El Péndulo, a beautiful bookstore/café in the more upscale Polanco neighbourhood (Alejandro Dumas 81), also did the trick: great food, beautiful patio, free wifi. I didn't do a lot of café writing in DC, but I can recommend Afterwords Café & Grill (1517 Connecticut Ave. NW, at Dupont Circle), which is attached to the charming Kramerbooks. Unfortunately, their peanut butter pie is no longer on the menu, so you'll have to make do. In Ottawa, afternoons at Chez Lucien (137 Murray St), fuelled by the incomparable Frida and Diego Burger (served with salad and home-cut fries), were always productive. The Canberra café and restaurant scene, unfortunately, isn't exactly setting the world on fire, but you can get the world's best laksa at the Asian Noodle House (49 Northbourne Ave.).

One of the most important lessons I learned in my political science classes at Carleton University was that home is the base from which we engage in public life. Others provided the conceptual spark for this enterprise, but no one was more instrumental in moving it from idea to book than my partner, Natasha Tusikov. She copyedited this entire document at least three times and endured endless rants about copyright, international relations theory, and policy windows. In the process, she's become almost as obsessed with intellectual property as I have, which makes for scintillating conversations around the dinner table, as you'd no doubt imagine. Publishing a book has been one of two lifelong goals (hosting the overnight show on CKCU-FM being the other). Without Natasha's intellectual, emotional, and financial support – including gamely going along with my insistence that I really do write better at the pub (Diet Coke only during working hours) – I would not have been able to get there. This book is for you.

Blayne Haggart
St Catharines, Ontario
30 May 2013

PS: George, call me!

COPYFIGHT

The Global Politics of Digital Copyright Reform

1 A Most Unlikely Debate

Introduction: A Dress Rehearsal for History

Historically, copyright had been thought of – by those who could be bothered to consider such an obscure subject at all – as a dry, technical area of interest primarily to professional creators, copyright lawyers, and the companies – the recording, motion picture, publishing, and software industries, collectively referred to here as the content industries – that employed them. Copyright was not the type of issue to inflame the general public. That was almost certainly the point of view of Canada's Conservative government in November 2007 as it prepared to introduce a bill that would reform the country's copyright law for the first time in a decade and implement two World Intellectual Property Organization (WIPO) treaties. These treaties, concluded in 1996, were designed to help member countries update their copyright laws to deal with the increasing ubiquity of digital reproductions of creative works like movies, books, and music.

Instead of engaging in an insiders' debate, the Conservatives ended up being blindsided by one of the first-ever successful social-media-driven grassroots political campaigns. As chapter 6 details, it is not an exaggeration to say that the December 2007 creation of the Facebook page "Fair Copyright for Canada" changed the terms of the Canadian debate, politicizing copyright among the general electorate. The movement effectively delayed the passage of any legislation and was directly responsible for the introduction of new user rights in the government's eventual bill, passed five years later. Before Barack Obama's "Yes We Can" 2008 US presidential campaign, before the 2009 Iranian protests, before the 2010 WikiLeaks release of over 200,000 US diplomatic cables, before the 2010–11 Arab Spring revolutions, there was the 2007 Canadian Facebook Uprising.

That copyright, a subset of intellectual property (IP) that covers literary, artistic, and dramatic works,[1] could excite such public passion and help to inaugurate a new type of social movement was a revelation to many, not least to those in government. For all of copyright's reputation as a complex, arcane area of commercial law, Canadians were right to be concerned with the future direction of their copyright law. Copyright law, by its very nature, affects who can access what information and cultural works, and on what terms. It influences who gets paid, and how much, favouring some groups over others. It determines whether a purchased song is actually "owned" by the buyer, or merely loaned by the copyright owner (who, it should always be remembered, is usually not the song's creator). It influences the very process of creation, enabling some types of writing and art while effectively outlawing others or pricing their creation out of existence. Most important, these biases are not the result of anything inherent in the creative process – there is nothing "natural" about copyright – but rather they are the outcome of political decisions dating back hundreds of years. Since the first modern copyright statute in the United Kingdom in 1709, the scope of copyright has expanded to cover new forms of expression such as computer programs and actions tangential to creation (i.e., broadcasts and performances, referred to as "neighbouring rights," which function similarly to copyright). In the 1990s and 2000s, copyright's extension, through international treaties and domestic laws, to digital media and the Internet, has turned copyright into a law that directly affects the daily lives of billions of individuals and strikes at the very heart of the global economy and democratic society. With such an obvious stake in the debate, many new groups have become involved in copyright politics for the first time.

The Complex World of Global Copyright Reform

Global copyright policy is currently in a drawn-out moment of transition in which digital technologies are challenging long-standing copyright-based business models and providing previously marginalized groups with the tools to engage substantively in copyright debates at home and abroad. Increasingly, copyright has become politicized among the general population. In 2012, tens of thousands of Europeans took to the streets to protest the US-driven Anti-Counterfeiting Trade Agreement (ACTA), a copyright-focused treaty that they felt would impair basic human rights such as expectations of privacy and access to knowledge and culture.[2] That same year, copyright exploded as a domestic US concern, as millions of US citizens engaged in an online protest against two copyright bills in an event that became known as the "Internet blackout."[3] These events will have important ramifications for the development of global copyright laws for years to come.

This book is about the first phase of the global battle to define copyright in the digital age, of which the Canadian Facebook Uprising was but one front. This battle centred on the negotiation and implementation of these two WIPO treaties – dubbed the "Internet treaties." These treaties set the terms of the global digital-copyright debate and established the actors – some veteran players, others newly minted, all with strongly held views about how copyright law should be reformed – who would drive copyright reform in the twenty-first century. Understanding the dynamics unleashed by these treaties is a crucial step towards understanding how copyright policy is made in the digital age and the extent to which citizens can shape the copyright laws under which they live.

This book is interested in understanding who influences copyright rulemaking in the twenty-first century, how these rules are made, and to what end. More specifically, this book represents an attempt to answer two questions of great importance. First, in a world where economic giants – the United States, the content industries – drive copyright reform, are smaller countries able to exercise copyright-policy autonomy and implement policies that reflect their citizens' economic and cultural needs? Second, and no less important, when it comes to making copyright policy, whose voices matter, and how do they matter?

Although copyright has been rising in economic and political importance, the politics of copyright remains surprisingly understudied.[4] Existing studies tend to focus on copyright's (admittedly important) global dimensions, on a single country, or on the relationship between a single country and the international regime.[5] While useful in and of themselves, they cannot fully capture the complexity of global copyright politics. Embedded in a dense network of domestic regimes, regional and international agreements, intergovernmental relations, and national and transnational businesses and interest groups, copyright policymaking challenges our traditional divisions between domestic politics and international relations. Digital technologies and the mass politicization of copyright have only complicated the situation.

A study that captures the multilayered complexity of copyright policymaking – its domestic and international dimensions, from treaty negotiation to domestic implementation – is useful in allowing us to understand better the limits and potential effectiveness of political engagement. In a system of overlapping institutional responsibilities, it can be difficult to locate areas in which one can best affect policy outcomes. Designing such a study presents significant challenges. Focusing on just one country inhibits our ability to generalize to other countries, to say nothing of understanding the international dimensions of copyright policymaking. Large-scale analysis, such as Carolyn Deere's 2009 study of developing countries' implementation of the 1995 Agreement on Trade-Related Aspects of Intellectual Property Rights (TRIPS), provide us with a good picture of the general forces that shape how countries decide to implement international treaties. Such "large-n" statistics-focused studies, however, sacrifice depth for breadth. Understanding the global politics of copyright – where policies and ideas come from, how they are propagated internationally, and how they are interpreted in international agreements and domestic law – requires understanding the institutions, actors, and ideas that drive this debate, both globally and in their specific domestic contexts.

This book argues that the intersection between the domestic and international/global politics of copyright requires particular attention. As Deere's study reminds us, the way in which a country implements a treaty depends on both domestic and international political and economic factors. Whether or not any given country implements or enforces a treaty, to say nothing of the way in which that country decides to implement it, are open questions and can only be understood in reference to its domestic politics.

Domestic implementation goes hand in hand with treaty negotiation. This book argues that domestic convergence towards or divergence from international norms or the preferred policies of large-state actors like the United States can be driven by domestic as well as external factors. Furthermore, domestic politics can also serve as the incubator for policies that are then disseminated internationally. Domestic politics are thus the key to understanding both how individual countries implement their international copyright obligations and the future direction of global copyright policy itself.

With these challenges in mind, this book takes a novel approach to the analysis of the global politics of copyright. Starting from the assumption that policy is made by purposeful actors interacting within historically specific and contingent institutional contexts, it examines three closely related countries' experiences with the Internet treaties – the United States, Mexico, and Canada. More specifically, it examines how these countries approached the regulation of "technological protection measures" (TPMs) – digital locks that regulate the use of digitized works like eBooks and MP3s – and the liability of Internet Service Providers (ISPs) for the potentially infringing actions of their customers. TPM protection, the most controversial part of the final treaties, touches on the central issue of who controls how creative works are used. ISP liability (which in this book also covers the liability of content-hosting sites like YouTube and search engines like Google), meanwhile, highlights the key question of how and by whom copyright law is enforced, and who pays.

This project, then, has two related goals: understanding global copyright policymaking and the sources (and significance) of variation in the implementation of these global rules. It begins with the observation of the Internet treaties' uneven global implementation. A 2003 survey by the World Intellectual Property Organization on the implementation of the treaties by the thirty-nine states (both developed and developing) that had acceded to or ratified one or two of the Internet treaties before 1 April 2003 (including Mexico and the United States but not Canada), found that the treaties had been implemented differently by the member countries, while several countries had not yet implemented various treaty provisions.[6] In particular, the survey found that only twenty-two of the thirty-nine implementing countries had implemented any rules in this area, and of those that had, "the range of language and coverage varie[d] widely."[7]

Similarly, only ten of the thirty-nine countries surveyed expressly addressed the issue of ISP liability.[8] That variation exists is not surprising in and of itself: Carolyn Deere's comprehensive study of developing countries' implementation of TRIPS and Andrew Mertha's fascinating 2005 study of China's intellectual property regime[9] are explicitly focused on just such variations. They also serve as a general reminder of how easy it is to overreach in discussions of "global governance." That international agreements are implemented domestically means that our accounts of global governance regimes must take into account the agency of domestic actors, even – as the significant variance found by the WIPO survey suggests – in those smaller developing countries often thought to have little agency and underdeveloped domestic IP institutions. By offering an account of how three different countries have struggled with and (to differing degrees) implemented the Internet treaties, this project offers a template for understanding how all these countries fit into the global political economy of copyright.

Overview

The remainder of this chapter outlines the topic at hand. It begins by considering the choice of North America as a representative sample of the global copyright-governance regime, as well as providing a brief overview of copyright itself and the challenges it faces in the digital age. It then introduces the WIPO Internet treaties and the resulting policy outcomes in the three countries, which this book seeks to explain. It also provides further background on the book's two main policy focuses: technological protection measures, or digital locks, and ISP liability. From there, it briefly introduces the book's theoretical framework, historical institutionalism, which will be developed in chapter 2, outlines the book's argument in greater detail, and presents this study's methodology.

Why North America?

Sketching a full picture of the global copyright governance regime would be a tall order for any book. One of the interesting things about copyright politics is how this global regime is interpreted somewhat differently in every country or region. To take the most obvious example, in the United States copyright is treated as an explicitly economic issue, whereas other countries in the "Continental European" tradition, such as France or (arguably) Mexico,[10] emphasize its role in guaranteeing the human rights of the author (e.g., by protecting the integrity of the work itself). The strength of the domestic institutions protecting and promoting copyright also vary by country. The Canadian government, for example, has a substantial bureaucracy devoted to copyright; the same is not true for an island country like Vanuatu, which also engages in global copyright negotiations.[11] Similarly, in some countries the domestic creative industries are more politically powerful than in others. In the face of these differences, an exhaustive account of the global politics of copyright, to say nothing of the connections among the various levels, would be beyond the scope of any one text.

That said, the three case studies presented here fulfil two important objectives. First, and most generally, they offer a template for thinking about the global governance of copyright. By laying out a framework that incorporates domestic, regional, and international actors and institutions, some of which differ dramatically in their economic power, this book offers a way to think about global copyright politics that can be used to analyse how other countries with different domestic and regional politics affect and are affected by global copyright debates. Second, on its own merits the North American experience provides us with a useful lens that allows us to consider the wider question of global copyright policymaking in the digital age. That it includes the global copyright superpower, a small developed country, and a key developing country allow us to make inferences about the current state of global copyright politics. Studying the three together provides us with a means to examine fully the interplay of domestic, regional, and international institutions, hegemonic powers, developing and developed countries, powerful multinational content industries, and newly empowered users taking advantage of new social-networking technologies that drive copyright politics in the twenty-first century.[12]

No account of global copyright policymaking would be complete without accounting for the role of the United States. As the state behind both the Internet treaties and the overall global push for stronger copyright protection, its domestic politics have an influence well beyond its own borders.[13] The current global copyright environment is characterized by a global convergence in copyright policies and laws on the particular US approach to copyright, which sees copyright as an economic right to be maximized in favour of copyright owners. The United States has been remarkably successful in using a mixture of coercion and persuasion via bilateral, plurilateral, and multilateral agreements in various fora to convince other countries to adopt its particular view of copyright even when it is not in their direct material interest to do so. Such treaties and bilateral actions by the United States suggest a near-unstoppable drive towards global harmonization in copyright laws, a harmonization that events such as the Canadian Facebook Uprising suggest is not necessarily welcome by citizens in other countries.

Although the United States drives the global copyright debate, its own copyright politics are no less contentious than those of other countries.[14] Treating the United States merely as a force that acts on other countries can obscure the reality that the aggressive US international copyright position is not as monolithic as it appears. US copyright politics are shaped by the particular idiosyncrasies of the domestic US copyright policymaking regime. These idiosyncrasies shape not only domestic US copyright law, but also influence the content and negotiation processes of treaties like the WIPO Internet treaties. Most important, they can be challenged successfully, under certain conditions. Not all US-based actors support the official US position, and this position is not immutable.

US attempts at copyright imperialism raise important issues regarding the potential for smaller countries to implement copyright laws that respond to their own domestic interests, rather than those of the United States. Canada and Mexico are particularly appealing choices to consider this policy-autonomy question, for two reasons. First, each occupies a different position in the global-economy hierarchy. Canada is a small, high-income, developed economy. As a net importer of copyrighted works, its material interests differ from those of the United States. Mexico, meanwhile, is a developing country whose citizens cannot easily afford copyrighted works.

The consequences of copyright reform are particularly serious for developing countries, where access to information is key to developing a modern economy. At the global level, the debate over intellectual property and copyright pits developing countries against developed countries, with developed countries usually arguing for stricter protection and developing countries arguing that IP amounts to a trade barrier designed to protect developed countries' competitive advantage and access to technology. Since the beginning of the 2000s, developing countries in particular have become increasingly aware of how copyright and IP laws affect their place in the global economy.[15] The institutional capacity of developing countries varies widely, from small island states, in which copyright institutions are relatively underdeveloped and copyright royalties contribute little to the country's economy, to countries like Mexico, with relatively well-established copyright institutions and a significant cultural sector. The specific experiences of these countries are different, although they all have an acute material interest in promoting economic development, a policy goal that strong copyright laws can sometimes adversely affect. Consequently, an examination of the Mexican debate over the Internet treaties helps to illuminate the nature of the interaction between developing and developed countries in the wider IP debate.

Second, the close relationship among the three countries (or, rather, Mexico and Canada's close relationships with the United States) makes North America a telling case study for small-country copyright-policy autonomy. If one were to think of two countries that would be most vulnerable to US influence, Canada and Mexico would not be unreasonable choices. They are neighbours of the hegemonic regional and global power, and their economies are deeply integrated with that of the United States under the North American Free Trade Agreement (NAFTA). Transnational corporations (TNCs) have long treated North

America as "a single production, distribution, and marketing zone": in 1989, US-based TNCs accounted for 69 per cent of total US exports to Canada (65% of which was intra-firm trade); the corresponding numbers for Mexico were 46% and 52%.[16] Just under half (48.6%) of NAFTA exports in 2010 were intra-NAFTA, far below the 65.3% of intra–European Union exports, but well above the 25.1% and 15.6% registered for intra-region trade within the ASEAN (Association of Southeast Asian Nations) and MERCOSUR (Mercado Común del Sur, or Southern Common Market, in South America) areas, respectively.[17] As tables 1.1 and 1.2 indicate, in 2010, the United States was overwhelmingly the primary destination and source of Canadian and Mexican merchandise exports and imports.[18]

Few, if any, other countries share such tight economic linkages with the dominant global power. How they handle their copyright policies under pressure from the United States offers a critical case study of the potential for autonomy from US copyright pressures. Any finding of divergence from the US position would be a clear signal that such divergence is possible among countries characterized by looser economic relations with the global hegemonic power. Finally, studying North America also allows us to consider the effect of regional trade agreements on copyright policymaking, in this case NAFTA. Australia's experience with the Internet treaties offers a useful example of the importance of considering these types of relationships. In 2000 it implemented one version of its Internet treaties obligations with respect to TPMs, only to change the law in 2004 because of a trade agreement the government had negotiated with the United States in which copyright and IP featured prominently.[19] Although the specifics of particular trade agreements may differ, a complete analysis of copyright policy requires that they be taken into account.

Copyright in the Digital Age

Copyright law has a deserved reputation for being ridiculously complex, but at heart it is simply a way in which governments regulate the market in creative works, such as books, CDs, digital music, motion pictures, computer software, and DVDs. While the regulation of this market has "existed from time immemorial," different societies have regulated this market in different ways. In Ancient Greece, the concept of "author" did not hold. "Greek writers such as Aristotle and Plato regarded themselves as teachers or philosophers rather than authors,"

Table 1.1. Top five export markets, Canada, Mexico, United States, 2010

Canada		Mexico		United States	
Country	Share (%)	Country	Share (%)	Country	Share (%)
United States	**74.9**	**United States**	**79.9**	**Canada**	**19.4**
United Kingdom	4.1	**Canada**	**3.6**	**Mexico**	**12.8**
China	3.3	China	1.4	China	7.2
Japan	2.3	Brazil	1.3	Japan	4.7
Mexico	1.3	Colombia	1.3	United Kingdom	3.8

Sources: Canada and United States – author's calculations from Industry Canada, Trade Data Online, http://www.ic.gc.ca/eic/site/tdo-dcd.nsf/eng/Home; Mexico – Secretaría de economía, Información Estadísticas y Arancelaria, http://www.economia.gob.mx/comunidad-negocios/comercio-exterior/informacion-estadistica-y-arancelaria.

Table 1.2. Top five import sources, Canada, Mexico, United States, 2010

Canada		Mexico		United States	
Country	Share (%)	Country	Share (%)	Country	Share (%)
United States	**50.4**	**United States**	**48.1**	China	19.1
China	11	China	15.1	**Canada**	**14.5**
Mexico	**5.5**	Japan	5.0	**Mexico**	**12.0**
Japan	3.3	South Korea	4.2	Japan	6.3
Germany	2.8	Germany	3.7	Germany	4.3
		Canada (6)	2.9		

Sources: Canada and United States – author's calculations from Industry Canada, Trade Data Online, http://www.ic.gc.ca/eic/site/tdo-dcd.nsf/eng/Home; Mexico – Secretaría de economía, Información Estadísticas y Arancelaria, http://www.economia.gob.mx /comunidad-negocios/comercio-exterior/informacion-estadistica-y-arancelaria.

more concerned with recognition than remuneration. As a result, these works were protected mainly by "misappropriation [laws] rather than property laws."[20]

The modern institution of copyright dates from the British 1709 Statute of Anne. While the scope of copyright has expanded dramatically since this date, this original law has influenced all subsequent copyright laws in the Anglo-American tradition.[21] Then, as now, copyright denotes a form of property that is a subset of IP rights, "rule-governed privileges that regulate the ownership and exploitation of abstract objects in many fields of human activity."[22] Like all forms of property, copyright is defined in the final instance by the state, which determines what is protected by copyright and the extent of this protection. Like other forms of property, copyrights are alienable, meaning that they can be bought and sold.[23] In the moment of fixation (e.g., the writing of a book or recording of a song), a creator receives copyright protection in the work. In practice, copyright rarely remains with the creator, who usually assigns it to a publisher and distributor (in return for compensation); these intermediaries hold and benefit from these assigned copyrights. The alienable and tradable nature of copyrights allows them to function as intangible assets for the content industries that hold them.[24]

Intellectual property involves a set of protections not provided to other types of property. All property involves a monopoly right of use, subject to certain conditions. This right seems "natural" in the case of physical objects because this monopoly is partly the consequence of the physicality of normal property: if one person is eating an apple, no one else can eat it. Because copying creative works does not require that the possessor of the work relinquish the original, this scarcity must be created completely through the law. Consequently, copyright owners are given the extra right to prevent unauthorized parties from copying, adapting, distributing, performing, or displaying their work.[25] Copyright thus creates a monopoly in the good: the copyright owner is able to avoid competition from unauthorized copiers. As a result of this right, the copyright owner has the legal market all to herself, preventing others from "using information that they want to use in the way they want to use it."[26]

All copyright laws involve a paradox related to what Bruce Doern and Markus Sharaput call its "protection" and "dissemination" roles, terms that this book also adopts.[27] Copyright laws are justified on the assumption that without their protection, creators would lack sufficient incentive to create, the marginal costs of copying being too low to allow a creator to recover her investment in the initial act of creation.[28] "Stronger" copyright, by which is meant more extensive "protection" from copying and unauthorized uses of a copyright owner's work, in theory provides a greater incentive to create. The paradox emerges with the realization that this protection diminishes the flow (or "dissemination") of creative works by making them more difficult and costly to obtain, and restricts future creation, since all creative works are built upon that which has come before.[29] This restriction can have substantial negative effects on the quality of life in a democratic society, whose existence depends on the presence of a well-informed electorate.

In practice, all copyright laws express a particular balance between these two roles: providing sufficient protection to encourage production while limiting their damage to dissemination.[30] The monopoly rights enshrined by copyright are limited in duration, scope, and use. After a certain period of time has elapsed, the copyright expires and works enter the "public domain," meaning anyone is free to copy the works without authorization from the original copyright owner.[31] Originally limited to fourteen years (renewable once for an equal period),[32] copyright terms have expanded worldwide, reaching the life of the author plus fifty years in Canada, life plus seventy-five in the United States, and a world-leading life plus one hundred years in Mexico.[33] In terms of scope, some things, such as "facts" and ideas, are considered uncopyrightable and thus are available to be used by anyone. Furthermore, where reproduction has been determined to have a positive social effect – for example, quotations for the purposes of criticism, education, and research – users are often granted exceptions without seeking permission of the copyright holder. This limitation is "a judicial safety valve that allows copyright to be fine tuned so that it may better achieve its utilitarian objectives."[34] In the United States, this right takes the form of an open-ended "fair use" right.[35] In Canada this user right takes the form of a "fair dealing" right, which enumerates the specific instances under which someone can reproduce a copyrighted work without permission.[36] Mexico's Ley Federal del Derecho de Autor (Federal Copyright Law, LFDA) recognizes a similar right to that of Canada, although it is "particularly strict and rigid in [its] application."[37]

ECONOMIC AND MORAL RIGHTS

In addition to economic rights (*derechos patrimoniales* in Spanish) related to copying, copyright is sometimes also discussed in terms of "moral rights" (*derechos morales* in Spanish), which provide authors with a "right to attribution, integrity, disclosure and withdrawal."[38] While copyright as an economic right originated in eighteenth-century Great Britain as a pragmatic, utilitarian way to fulfil the societal goal of encouraging the creation and dissemination of creative works, copyright as an author's right originated around the same time in Continental Europe (notably France) and is based on a discourse of human rights. As a form of human rights grounded in article 27 of the Universal Declaration of Human Rights,[39] moral rights are taken to be inalienable, in contrast to the contractual and alienable economic rights of "copyright." Discussions of copyright are often needlessly complicated by the conflation of these two types of rights under the label of "copyright."

Clarifying the differences between the two systems is particularly important in North America. The Canadian and US approaches to copyright emerged mainly from the "copyright," or Anglo-American, tradition, while Mexican law is descended from the Continental, or moral rights, tradition. Consequently, the three countries legitimize copyright by appealing to different concepts (maximization of production, or the human rights of the author, for example), which in turn can affect the development of a country's copyright law. In practice, however, copyright regimes in both traditions contain elements of both approaches and differ more in "emphasis and degree" than in kind.[40] Canadian copyright, reflecting the country's French and British colonial roots, explicitly refers to both moral and economic rights. Mexico, especially since the 1997 changes to its copyright law as a result of its adherence to NAFTA and TRIPS, treats copyright as an economic right despite its long-standing emphasis on copyright as a moral right. Even the United States, which more than any other country treats copyright as an economic right, provides creators with rights equivalent to moral rights, although not necessarily in its Copyright Act. For example, false attribution is against the law, and publication without authorization similarly can be considered illegal.[41]

THE IMPORTANCE OF COPYRIGHT

Since its emergence in its modern form in early eighteenth-century England, copyright has gone through three phases.[42] These phases have been driven by technological change and the creation of linkages to other issues, even as copyright itself has remained recognizable as a limited property right granted to creators in their works. In its initial phase, which lasted until the late nineteenth century, copyright was largely a national affair. Violating the copyright of other countries' citizens was a way of ensuring inexpensive access to cultural products and to the technological information and knowledge that could help countries modernize and develop.[43] Then, starting in the mid-1800s, copyright began to be internationalized to a significant degree, first through a series of bilateral treaties of reciprocal protection and then through an international treaty, the 1886 Berne Convention.

The current period, dating to the mid-1980s, is characterized by the aggressive pursuit of ever-stronger global copyright laws. These changes have been driven primarily by the United States. US content industries, interested in protecting and expanding their own global economic position, successfully linked US government officials' concerns about declining US global economic dominance to their self-interested calls for increased IP protection as a means of arresting this perceived decline.[44] This period has witnessed attempts (often successful) to commodify what was once seen as a common resource (knowledge and information), creating, in effect, "new enclosures"[45] in which every use of a copyrighted material would require payment to the copyright holder. Whether or not this era of ever-stronger copyright will continue or is coming to an end is the central issue of the digital-copyright battle.

A country's copyright laws can have important economic and cultural implications. In addition to their already noted effect on future creation, stronger copyright protection can raise the cost of acquiring information needed for countries to modernize. The global spread of strong copyright protection in effect acts as a barrier to development.[46] Just as the most-developed states advocate or impose liberal free-trade policies because they provide them with a competitive advantage while ignoring the historical reality that their own economic development depended on protectionist measures,[47] strong copyright is being pursued by those firms and countries, such as the United States, that currently enjoy a lead in information production and information technology.

DEALING WITH DIGITIZATION

Current global copyright trends have been favourable to the interests of large corporations.[48] Driven by technological changes that have made information copying and transmission increasingly simple – including the popularization of personal computers and the Internet – content industries generally have sought and received "tougher" copyright protection in the form of longer-term protection and the extension of copyright to cover more forms of knowledge and information, like computer software. The US government has been the main regional and global state proponent of stronger protection. Since the mid-1980s, it has made strong IP protection (including copyright) an integral part of its international-trade agenda.

The Internet treaties are a response to the challenges posed by digital-copying technologies to existing business models. Their rules and the way they have been implemented by Canada, Mexico, and the United States therefore reveal a great deal about who makes copyright law, and to what purpose. As chapter 3 details, the reactions of individuals, firms, and governments to technological change have often driven changes in copyright laws, and the arrival of the digital age has been no different. The digital age's main effect on copyright policy stems from two interrelated developments. First, newly ubiquitous personal computers provided individuals with an easy way to copy digital works. Second, the Internet has provided individuals with an easily accessible global distribution system for these works.

These new technologies are potentially revolutionary. Where previously only large corporations were able to reproduce and distribute informational goods on a commercial scale, individuals and small groups can now easily act as producers and distributors. This has allowed not only for a huge spike in unauthorized downloads and file sharing of music, movies, books, and anything else that can be digitized, but also has made it easier and relatively inexpensive for artists to create and distribute their works on a global scale. Faced with the loss of their monopoly on the means of production and distribution, these corporations face extinction. However, because laws are the outcome of political processes, rules governing digital distribution will not necessarily favour individuals or artists over corporations, no matter the inherent technological biases. One of the primary objectives of this book is to understand how copyright laws in Canada, Mexico, and the United States have changed in response to these technological and political pressures.

The Puzzle

THE WIPO INTERNET TREATIES

On 20 December 1996, members of the World Intellectual Property Organization, including Canada, Mexico, and the United States, adopted the WIPO Copyright Treaty (WCT) and the Performances and Phonographs Treaty (WPPT).[49] These two treaties, known collectively as the WIPO Internet treaties, largely mirror each other: only their subjects (authors in the case of the former, performers and record producers in the latter) differ.[50] They responded to concerns, particularly from the United States, that existing copyright laws regulating the production and dissemination of physical reproductions of creative works were not well suited to regulate digital works, which can easily be copied and distributed. Their most controversial provision, WCT Article 11 (mirrored in WPPT Article 18), commits contracting parties to providing "adequate legal protection and effective legal remedies" against digital locks or technological protection measures (TPMs), protecting copyrighted works. They also tangentially address the issue of the liability

Internet and online service providers would have for the actions of their customers with respect to infringing uses of copyrighted materials.[51]

As the first copyright treaties negotiated following the implementation of 1995 TRIPS agreement, they offer a glimpse into the dynamics of copyright policymaking in a post-TRIPS world.[52] Even more important, as the first treaties to address the pressing question of how copyright should respond to the challenges (and opportunities) posed by digital technologies and the Internet, they have acted as the normative baseline for states considering how to reform their copyright laws in the digital age. International treaties, which often lack binding dispute-resolution mechanisms, tend to set the parameters for the future debate over whatever issue they address. A government looking to modernize its copyright laws to respond to the challenges of the digital age will tend to look towards international standards – in this case, the Internet treaties – for guidance. For policymakers, "digital-copyright reform" tends to be synonymous with "implementation of the WIPO Internet treaties," even though these treaties represent only one possible way in which copyright laws could be reformed.

The leeway provided by the Internet treaties allows members to decide how, or even if, to implement them. This makes the treaties' implementation a useful entry point to the study of the potential for convergence or divergence in North American (and global) copyright policies.[53] For example, the terms "adequate legal protection" and "effective legal remedies" are, by design, nowhere defined in the treaties. This vague language has provided the grounds upon which the debate over the implementation of TPM-related rules has been fought.

TECHNOLOGICAL PROTECTION MEASURES
AND THE PRIVATIZATION OF COPYRIGHT LAW

TPMs have emerged as the central issue in digital-copyright reform and the main lightning rod in debates over implementation of the WIPO Internet treaties. A TPM is

> a technological method intended to promote the authorized use of digital works. This is accomplished by controlling access to such works or various uses of such works, including copying, distribution, performance and display. TPMs can operate as safeguards or "virtual fences" around digitized content, whether or not the content enjoys copyright protection. Two common examples of TPMs are passwords and cryptography technologies.[54]

TPMs and digital rights management (DRM) systems[55] predate the 1990s and the Internet treaties,[56] although the Internet treaties brought them into the mainstream of political debate. Depending on how they are used and regulated, TPMs have the potential to shift the balance of power between copyright owners and users in subtle ways related to authorization and access, effectively overturning any legislated balance set in copyright laws. TPMs effectively transfer control over a work from the purchaser of a work to whoever put the lock on the work. In the absence of digital locks, a user can exercise her statutory rights without having to seek anyone's authorization. If a work is locked, however, the purchaser effectively must seek the permission of the content owner (or whoever locked the content) in order to exercise her legal rights. As a result, TPMs can allow owners to impose restrictions more onerous than are available to them in the non-digital world.[57] They can even restrict basic human rights such as freedom of speech and the "transfer of information and knowledge,"[58] partly because TPMs are not yet sophisticated enough to distinguish between situations in which it is legal or illegal to copy, access, or use a work.[59] While copyright law is the outcome of a public debate, a TPM allows a single individual or company to set the terms of access.[60]

TPMs can regulate activities far beyond copying.[61] A TPM can prevent an individual from copying a work, but it also prevent perfectly legal uses such as playing a DVD bought legally in Canada on a DVD player from a different "region," such as Australia or Mexico, and thereby restrict competition and trade.[62] Anti-competitive uses of TPMs include locking consumers into company-specific platforms. For example, videos sold through Apple's iTunes service are locked by the FairPlay DRM system. FairPlay, in addition to limiting the number of computers to which a video could be copied, makes the videos unplayable on other platforms, such as an Xbox 360. As a result, Apple can use FairPlay to exercise market power over video-playback devices and the online video market. TPMs also raise privacy issues, as they often require a degree of monitoring of consumers' activities in order to ensure that the locks are not being broken.[63]

TPMs can also affect existing general property rights.[64] Just as the monopoly right in copyright affects a purchaser's ability to use a creative work any way she sees fit, so do TPMs allow the copyright owner to retain much of the control over a work.[65] The issue is best illustrated with the oft-repeated "locked house" analogy. From the copyright owner's perspective, a TPM is like a lock that someone places on her house, to keep her property from being stolen. However, in the case of a legitimately purchased work, this analogy does not quite hold. The problem arises from who is placing the lock. In the case of an actual house, homeowners place the lock on the house they own and are legally allowed to use their house as they see fit. If they do something illegal with their property, the police can intervene legally. TPMs are like locks, but more like locks that *someone else* places on your house and that require you to get permission to use the thing you have purchased, even for legal purposes.

Beyond legal overreach, TPMs have an even darker side. TPMs exploded into the public consciousness in 2005, with the "Sony Rootkit" debacle. In order to prevent people from copying CDs, Sony BMG shipped several titles with a copy-protection TPM that would install itself on a user's computer (those with the Windows operating system) and limit CD copying and completely prevent people from "ripping" CDs into the MP3 format.[66] However, this TPM was hidden by a "rootkit" – a program that allows basic access to a computer system – that also installed itself (by design and without requiring consent) on people's computers. Unfortunately, Sony did not tell people that this program (which doubled as "spyware," secretly contacting Sony when the CD was being played), making things exponentially worse. It turned out that the rootkit could be exploited by hackers to gain control of unsuspecting users' computers. What's more, as security expert Bruce Schneier remarks, even "trying to get rid of it damages Windows." This vulnerability was publicized on 31 October 2005 by security researcher Mark Russinovich. The outcry was so great that by 14 November Sony had pulled their copy-protected CDs and were offering "to replace customers' infected CDs for free."[67]

TPMs represent the embodiment and logical conclusion of a view of copyright that overemphasizes the rights of the copyright owner. Under this approach, copyright owners control all access and approve all uses of their works, while the needs and rights of users of copyrighted works, which include future creators, are neglected. The great danger posed by TPMs is that they threaten to replace negotiated copyright law, which balances the interests of several groups, with rules set in the lock itself by whoever controls the lock. TPMs raise the spectre that copyright law could be overridden and effectively privatized by whoever controls the locks. This owner-centric perspective also elides the central contradiction in copyright, which is that all works build on previously existing works, and that the continued creation of works depends on ensuring that the rights of "authors" do not overwhelm those of "users," a group that, again, includes future artists.[68] It is for these reasons that TPMs represent the apotheosis of the current strong-copyright era. How they are regulated can thus tell us much about the future direction of copyright itself.

A Legal Remedy? The appeal of TPMs to content owners (who are not necessarily creators) is obvious. Faced with a situation in which their products can be copied and distributed easily by their customers, TPMs offer protection for existing business models, which are based on the artificial, legal construction of scarcity, via technological means and the downstream control of their products beyond that allowed by current copyright laws.[69]

However, while TPMs offer copyright owners the possibility of vastly expanded control over creative works, all TPMs share the same Achilles heel: they can be broken, often quite easily. As a result, copyright owners – especially the content industries – have sought to enshrine in law the protection of TPMs. Such protection is entirely new in copyright law. Copyright has traditionally dealt with the protection of authors' rights and the conditions under which works could be copied. These new provisions introduce what de Beer and others have called "paracopyright," an additional layer of legal protection above copyright that protects the lock, not the underlying work.[70] The implications of paracopyright laws related to TPMs vary depending on the breadth of the law in question. A "minimalist" law would make it illegal to break a digital lock only for the purposes of infringing the underlying copyright. This approach, while redundant to existing copyright law, would not create any new rights. A "maximalist" law, however, would make it illegal to break a digital lock under any circumstances. Such an approach has the potential to interfere with existing user rights under copyright law and to impair the functioning of other laws including, for example, those related to competition policy.

Typically, this maximalist prohibition against breaking a TPM is accompanied by a prohibition on the traffic in devices (i.e., computer programs) that could break these locks, on the grounds that lock-breaking devices (also known as circumvention devices) can be used for both legal and illegal purposes. Effectively making circumvention devices illegal, however, also makes it hard, if not impossible, for regular individuals to break a TPM for perfectly legal, non-copyright-related reasons, thus restricting their legitimate uses. As a result, such a provision would tilt the balance in copyright law almost completely towards owners, at the expense of everyone else.

TPMs and the Purpose of Copyright Copyright laws reflect a balance among different groups, interests, and activities because they are the outcome of negotiation processes. The philosophy behind TPMs, however, proposes something different: that TPMs and copyright are about protecting the interests of one group – the copyright owner – rather than those of, for example, individuals and future creators. How governments and societies respond to the debate over TPMs reveals a great deal about their view of the future of copyright and the creation and sharing of information and culture. To anticipate the discussion of historical institutionalism in chapter 2, today's choices influence tomorrow's decisions. Tilting the copyright playing field in one direction today can legitimize a particular view of copyright at the expense of other perspectives, setting copyright policy on a particular path that would be difficult to reverse in the future.

ISP LIABILITY AND THE COPYING CONUNDRUM

The digital age has made telecommunications companies such as Verizon in the United States, Telmex in Mexico, and Bell and Rogers in Canada, and Internet companies like Google increasingly central to economic activity and social interactions.[71] It has also brought them into direct contact with copyright law. While these companies, in their roles as Internet service providers, are not exactly broadcasters, rights-holders have successfully argued these companies are similar enough that they should be covered by copyright law.[72] Unsurprisingly, ISPs' interests can conflict with those of the content industries. Where content industries wish to control the transmission and use of their works, ISPs and computer manufacturers have tended to emphasize network and product speed, information dissemination, and storage capacities and to be indifferent to whether the content on their networks or stored on their computers violates copyright laws.[73]

Computers and the Internet function by making copies of files. This poses a challenge for copyright law, which is based on the assumption that copying must be controlled. Under copyright law, telecommunications companies, ISPs, search engines like Google, and content hosts like YouTube face a legal problem regarding their potential liability for their clients' actions on their networks.[74] At the heart of the issue lies the question of how to ensure that copyright law does not impede the development of these now-indispensable technologies.[75]

As with TPMs, addressing ISP liability raises questions of balance and fairness. The treatment of copying that occurs as a result of the normal functioning of a network has generally been exempted. With respect to hosted content, in the main period covered by this book (the 1990s to 2010, although subsequent developments are also considered), countries chose between two general approaches to ISP liability. Under a "notice-and-notice" regime, ISPs are exempt from liability if, when they receive a notice of infringement from a copyright owner, they pass it on to the alleged infringer. Under a "notice-and-takedown" regime, they are required to remove the allegedly offending content. While both provide a straightforward way to shield ISPs from liability, the former is friendlier to users than a notice-and-takedown regime. As it requires the removal of materials based on claims and not findings of infringement, a notice-and-takedown approach can interfere with users' rights, as it places the onus on them to show that they are not infringing copyright.

While these two ISP-liability regimes continue to be dominant worldwide, political pressure from content industries seeking to offload enforcement costs onto ISPs has led to the emergence of more extreme approaches since mid-2007.[76] In these approaches, ISP clients accused repeatedly of infringement are banned from using the ISP. The most infamous of these policies, France's "three strikes" HADOPI law, required that individuals accused of unauthorized downloading of copyrighted works would be cut off from the Internet. This highly controversial law was replaced in July 2013 by graduated fines for repeat infringers, with the French government claiming that the three strikes approach was a "totally inappropriate punishment.[77] Despite this rollback, similar policies remain in place elsewhere, most notably the United States, where several large ISPs and the content industries implemented a voluntary "six strikes system" in February 2013.[78] While the effects of the US system on users and unauthorized downloads were unclear as of December 2013, these developments have the potential to affect significantly not only copyright but also communications policy, specifically the principle that computer networks should be neutral in terms of how they treat content. That said, this book focuses primarily on the main established approaches to ISP liability that emerged in the immediate aftermath of the Internet treaties, namely, notice-and-notice and notice-and-takedown.

DIFFERENT IMPLEMENTATION OUTCOMES IN NORTH AMERICA

US-based content industries are active and important in all three countries. NAFTA itself includes copyright provisions that were essentially written by the United States. These provisions placed the three countries within a common regional orientation for the countries' copyright laws. In the case of Mexico, it required a wholesale rewriting of its copyright law. While the orientation of Canada's copyright law was already substantially similar to that of its US neighbour, and while NAFTA Annex 2106 exempted Canada from implementing NAFTA's copyright obligations, Canada nonetheless changed its copyright law as a result of NAFTA.[79]

And yet, a closer examination of the intertwined domestic, regional, and international politics of copyright – the subject of this book – suggests that despite an uneven economic relationship, despite similar legal copyright regimes and adherence to the same copyright treaties, and in the face of US attempts to advance the economic interests of what it perceives as a key industry, Canadian and Mexican copyright debates continue to be driven by domestic institutional, ideational, and political factors, not all of which favour harmonization. As this book elaborates in the three case studies that form the heart of its analysis, the three countries have alternately converged and diverged in their interpretation of various parts of the Internet treaties, and both convergence and divergence outcomes can only be understood fully in relation to domestic factors.

Despite strong and consistent lobbying by the United States and its US-identified content industries[80] in favour of a particular (US) style of implementation of the Internet treaties, the three countries have approached the implementation of the Internet treaties quite differently. The United States, the main proponent of the treaties, quickly implemented the treaties with the 1998 Digital Millennium Copyright Act (DMCA), which went far beyond what the treaties required. The DMCA became the preferred model of the United States and its allied content industries (in particular the motion picture and music industries) in their campaign to persuade other countries to implement the Internet treaties. As will be discussed in chapter 6, the DMCA extended strong legal protections to digital locks, which allow copyright owners (or, rather, whoever controls the locks) to set the terms under which someone can access a work. These terms often go far beyond the rights that traditional copyright protection provides to copyright owners. It also provides a regime for limiting the liability of ISPs that requires ISPs to remove a user's content from their network upon reception of an accusation of infringement (no due process necessary) in order for the ISP to avoid liability for its customer's alleged infringements.

The WIPO Internet treaties' status in Canada and Mexico is more fluid and complex. Even though the treaties' implementation is a major economic concern for the United States, Canada delayed introducing any implementing legislation for nine years, finally implementing the treaties in mid-2012. Mexico has yet to implement fully the treaties. In Canada, the actions various federal governments have taken suggest the potential for both convergence on and divergence from the US standard. Successive governments have proposed implementing policies in ways that did not always follow the US example. A 2005 attempt by a minority Liberal government would have made overriding a digital lock to access a work a crime only if it were done for the purposes of infringing an underlying copyright, while legislation proposed by subsequent Conservative governments, including the version that was finally passed in 2012, followed the US lead on TPMs. All Liberal and Conservative bills, however, consistently eschewed the US notice-and-takedown approach to ISP liability in favour of the more moderate notice-and-notice approach.

In Mexico, full implementation of the Internet treaties, as of December 2013, has not yet happened. Mexico currently does not have an ISP-specific liability-limitation regime; on TPMs, it only provides (US-style) protection to those digital locks protecting computer programs. Whether and how Mexico will implement the treaties is an open question. While Mexican society contains several interest groups favouring stronger copyright protection, the Mexican Senate in 2011 effectively rejected the US-led, pro-stronger-copyright Anti-Counterfeiting Trade Agreement (ACTA), the same agreement that drove tens of thousands of Europeans into the streets in 2012. This move, sparked by an anti-ACTA Twitter-based protest reminiscent of the 2007 Canadian Facebook Uprising,[81] marked copyright's politicization in Mexico and suggests that the future direction of Mexican copyright policy is very uncertain.[82] Given that inaction is as much a policy decision as a specific action, both the reasons for this delay and the forces that will influence Mexico's ultimate decision on the treaties deserve serious attention.

Historical Institutionalism: Linking the Domestic and the International

Studying a complex issue like copyright requires a theoretical framework that is able to focus on the international-domestic intersections that characterize modern copyright policymaking. This study uses historical institutionalism as an analytical framework to trace the sources of constancy and change in the domestic and international copyright debates covered in the following chapters. As chapter 2 shows in greater detail, although it is typically applied to domestic and comparative case studies in political science, historical institutionalism can also be used to study international relations.[83] It has also been used in studies of international political economy,[84] but usually not in a way that covers the entire cycle of domestic-international linkages between both treaty negotiation *and* implementation. Associated with theorists such as Kathleen Thelen, Sven Steinmo, and Paul Pierson,[85] historical institutionalism argues that policy developments must be understood in terms of ideas, institutions, and interests (i.e., actors). Institutions and policies are characterized by "path dependence," in which initial choices and conditions can constrain the future development of policies and institutions. These can be located at the domestic, regional, international, and global "levels" depending on the subject being addressed. While change can occur, institutions tend to persist over time. As a result, policy outcomes are likely to be contingent on specific institutional, political, and social factors.

This study adopts the view that copyright policy is politically made and reflects the distribution of power among interested actors. While state power is important (the very existence of copyright depends on state power), the state is both a battlefield for societal interests and a quasi-autonomous actor,[86] and is both shaped by and shapes its society. This study argues that historically specific conjunctions of domestic political considerations allow for the maintenance of distinctive copyright regimes in the three countries. The prospects for, and shape of, distinctive policies depend on the relative power of domestic and regional/transnational groups, history (including cultural factors), and the distinctive nature of the relevant state and non-state institutions.

Explaining Outcomes

This book argues that copyright policy in North America represents a battle between national path-dependence and regional/international convergence, or as Banting, Hoberg, and Simeon might write, between "inexorable pressures for convergence" and "domestic pressures for divergence."[87] In each case, domestic politics have a strong influence over the ultimate direction of a country's copyright policy, and even have the potential to negate pressure exerted by a more powerful (in the conventional sense) country. In certain cases, most notably the United States, changes to domestic policy have the potential to lead to further changes at the international level, and thus in other countries.

Table 1.3a. Copyright institutions in North America

Institutions	Description
Regional: NAFTA	Sets and reinforces the orientation for copyright along US-determined lines; emphasizes economic nature of copyright
International: WIPO Internet treaties	Sets parameters for debate (i.e., digital-copyright reform should address ISP liability and TPMs); vague on specific rules
International: TRIPS	Largely mirrored by NAFTA copyright provisions internationally

Pressures for convergence come from several sources. In all three countries, advances in information technology have changed the parameters of the copyright debate, increasing both the stakes facing the public and the ability of civil society to affect the debate over copyright. The overall effect of this change in each county depends on the amount of technological change experienced. That Mexican digital-copyright reform efforts, for example, have lagged behind those of its neighbours partly reflects its relatively low level of technological development (digital-broadband penetration rates, for instance, lag those in Canada and the United States). Technological changes have also led to greater civil-society involvement in the debate, although their effectiveness varies according to the possibilities and constraints offered by the institutional contexts within which they operate.

Tables 1.3a and 1.3b provide an overview of the main institutions, interests/actors, and ideas driving North American copyright policy that will form the basis of the case studies that constitute the heart of this study. As already noted, the main international institutions are WIPO and TRIPS. The WIPO Internet treaties provide leeway for countries to determine how to implement their provisions. Member countries also retain the right not to implement or ratify the treaties. As well, all three countries are members of the TRIPS agreement. Regionally, NAFTA Chapter 17 has given all three countries a roughly similar orientation regarding copyright (primarily through its effect on Mexican copyright law), while NAFTA's overall creation of a more-or-less integrated economic space also makes it difficult to link domestic copyright reform to improved market access. Chapter 3 explores these international and regional institutions in greater detail.

The United States has worked to impose its view on copyright on its neighbours. However, NAFTA's particular institutional form, lacking a decision-making mechanism to easily alter copyright law on a regional basis, means that any convergence on a "North American" standard

Table 1.3b. Copyright institutions, influences, actors in North America

	United States	Canada	Mexico
Domestic bureaucratic institutions	Unified approach to copyright; bias towards maximizing copyright protection for copyright owners	Divided approach: two departments with opposing (user/owner) mandates; prime minister plays decisive role	Unified approach to copyright; bias towards maximizing copyright protection for creators and owners
Domestic political policymaking	Pluralistic inter-industry negotiations; some industries more powerful than others, but all groups' interests met to some degree; low-to-moderate politicization for DMCA (1998)	Contentious inter-bureaucracy negotiation; presence of parliamentary majority or minority influences degree of effective politicization; high degree of politicization	Inter-industry negotiation (corporatist); low level of politicization and little general public interest
Ideational and material influences	Copyright as economic right; copyright exporter	Copyright as primarily economic right; copyright importer	Copyright as primarily economic right (post-NAFTA), legitimized by traditional approach to copyright as author's human right; self-image as cultural superpower
Dominant interests and role of public	Domestic content industries; domestic telecommunications sector increasingly important; public increasingly active	US content industries; domestic telecoms sector increasingly important; public-interest groups increasingly active, along with musician and new-technology groups	Authors' collection societies; US government; domestic and US content industries; domestic telecoms sector increasingly important; increasing public involvement in the debate

will be shaped by the domestic political processes in the three countries and their relative balance among involved actors/interests.

All three countries also currently share the view of copyright as primarily an economic right. This view is strongest in the United States, although it has become stronger in the other two countries since the 1980s. Canada's status as a net importer of copyrighted works reduces its objective material interest in strengthening copyright laws, while, as chapter 8 will discuss, Mexico's adherence to the economic view of copyright is sustained partly by its previous tradition of copyright as an author's human right and reinforced by Mexico's self-image as a cultural superpower.

Differences among the three countries are driven by the configuration of each country's domestic political institutions and related interests/actors. The relevant bureaucratic institutions in Mexico and the United States tend to share a similar outlook that favours copyright's "protection" function over any role in encouraging the dissemination of creative works.[88] In Canada, formal responsibility for copyright is divided between two departments whose mandates fall on opposite sides of this division. However, the highly centralized nature of the Canadian federal political system has allowed the Prime Minister's Office to drive policy, and the prime minister in recent years has taken full advantage of this fact, as chapter 7 discusses in detail.

Regarding interests – the actors involved in the copyright debate – in the United States the content industries are the most entrenched drivers of copyright reform, although "user" groups, and increasingly the telecommunications sector, also make their voices heard. At the time of the DMCA's enactment, groups and individuals representing a "public interest" separate from the interests of traditional stakeholders were beginning to become involved in the policymaking process. In Canada, the primary drivers of copyright reform are the United States (through domestic channels and legislative tools such as its Special 301 process, which "names and shames" countries with IP laws of which the United States disapproves) and the largely foreign-based content industries. They are often supported by domestic creators' groups. As in the United States, user groups and the telecommunications industry are also involved. Since 2007, copyright reform has become an issue of public concern. In Mexico, there was less evidence of significant public involvement before 2011, although copyright-critical voices have since become more prominent. In their absence, the copyright debate has been driven largely by *sociedades de gestión colectivas* (collection societies), representing creators, and by foreign- and domestic-based content industries. The United States also plays a significant role promoting Mexican copyright reform.

Methodology

Copyright policies are constantly evolving. This book focuses on the period of negotiation of the Internet treaties: roughly from 1989 to 1996 (though the most important action occurred near the end of this period) to 2010. At the beginning of this period, each country had yet to implement the treaties; given this "blank slate," we can then compare policy developments over the next decade or so. The choice of 2010 as the artificial end point in this analysis can be justified by the fact that fourteen years (from the conclusion of the treaties in December 1996) represents a sufficiently lengthy period within which to observe the implementation dynamics in the three countries. By 2010, the United States had implemented the treaties and the eventual Canadian response had largely been determined; Mexico as of August 2013 had yet to implement the treaties.

While this book focuses primarily on the Internet treaties, it also addresses the three main post-treaty developments in global copyright reform:

- the conclusion and subsequent firestorm over the Anti-Counterfeiting Trade Agreement, the US-led sequel to the Internet treaties, including its July 2011 rejection by the Mexican Senate;
- the commencement of negotiations for a Trans-Pacific Partnership (TPP) among the United States and several Pacific Rim countries, including Canada and Mexico; and
- potentially most significant, the 18 January 2012 US "Internet blackout," a hugely successful civil-society protest against US copyright legislation that may portend a fundamental shift in US and international copyright policy.

Each case followed the political patterns established by the Internet treaties debate, even as they pushed the debate further into the realm of mainstream politics.

This project employed a combination of semi-structured interviews with experts, policymakers, and business and civil society representatives from all three countries and an examination of primary legal and governmental documents related to the negotiation and implementation of the Internet treaties. In the case of Canada and Mexico, these sources were complemented by media and blog sources that were covering the ongoing debate over the implementation of the Internet treaties. Over fifty formal interviews were conducted in the three countries. Subjects were selected for their representativeness of the perspectives in the debate, which continues to be focused mainly around policy experts. Consequently, elite interviews were the most appropriate means of approaching the subject. Questions were modified depending on the expertise of the subject and for any developments in what remains an ongoing issue. Most participants agreed to participate in on-the-record, for-attribution interviews, although some asked that their comments be not for attribution.

In certain cases, I was unable to interview those directly involved in the debate. In Canada, entreaties to the Canadian Recording Industry Association and the Canadian Motion Pictures Distribution Association, the two main players in the Canadian debate, were never acknowledged. In Mexico, I was unable, after eight months of rescheduled meetings, to interview the head of the Mexican delegation to the WIPO Internet treaties. This was a particularly disappointing development, as Mexico is mentioned rarely on its own in the negotiations' official records. Almost all the primary and secondary sources for the Mexican case study were in Spanish, and several of the interviews with Mexican citizens and officials were conducted in Spanish. Spanish-language citations were translated by the author.

Book Overview

This book is based around three interrelated case studies, one for each country. While these case studies will hopefully help people understand the institutions, forces, and processes that shape copyright policymaking, there is also some value in pulling back the curtain to discuss the model I use here to think about copyright politics. Chapter 2 outlines the book's historical-institutionalist framework. While much of this will be familiar to political scientists (although I think it does present a novel argument for considering ideas and change within historical institutionalism), copyright and IP politics – as Haunss and Shadlen have noted – remain under-theorized. This chapter represents an attempt to address this gap in our understanding of intellectual property and copyright. That said, less theoretically inclined readers who skip this chapter will still be able to follow the book's argument. Chapter 3 uses the theoretical approach developed in the previous chapter identify the relevant actors, ideas, and institutions active in the debate over the Internet treaties, and how they affect the overall course of the debate.

Chapters 4 through 8 present the book's case studies. Because of the intimate, organic connection between the US domestic policy debate and the negotiation at WIPO of the Internet treaties, the two are treated as one inseparable account. Chapter 4 provides an overview of the political economy of the US copyright policymaking regime, and Chapter 5 discusses the beginnings of the US digital-copyright debate and the international-institutional context and outcomes of the WIPO negotiations. Chapter 6 covers the final debate that led to the DMCA, assesses its outcome, and addresses the relevant US-focused post-DMCA copyright developments, notably US attempts to negotiate the WIPO-plus ACTA agreement. The Canadian case study is presented in chapter 7, focusing on the three unsuccessful attempts to implement the WIPO Internet treaties between 2005 and 2010, as well as the ultimate, successful attempt in 2012 that finally ended the Canadian implementation debate. Chapter 8 considers Mexican inaction on the Internet treaties and assesses the current state of Mexican copyright policymaking, particularly in light of the ACTA negotiations and the Senate's 2011 rejection of ACTA. The book then concludes with a discussion of the lessons learned from the case studies for the making of domestic and international copyright policy, particularly in light of rising US public activism against stronger copyright and the ongoing Trans-Pacific Partnership negotiations. It also assesses the potential for copyright reform that better addresses the societal need to spur both the creation and dissemination of creative works.

2 A Historical-Institutionalist Framework for Analysing Copyright Policymaking[1]

Copyright law is the outcome of historically contingent processes and cannot be understood outside of the political forces that shape it. Because copyright is perpetuated by the exercise of power, understanding the power relations of copyright – who makes the rules, how they do so, and who wins and loses – is essential to our understanding of what IP is, how it is perpetuated, and even if it is necessary. Providing a complete picture of the linkages among copyright-reform efforts in three countries is complicated by the fact that a country's copyright law is embedded within domestic political institutions, regional agreements, and international treaties, some of which originated in the late nineteenth century. It encompasses domestic and transnational actors, and is often the subject of bilateral diplomacy. To make things more interesting, as mentioned in the introduction and developed in chapter 3, copyright itself embodies two often conflicting mandates: encouraging both the creation and dissemination of creative works. Any theoretical framework for analysing such a policy must also account for its longevity, the particular way it has developed, and how it has persisted even as technological changes – notably the development of digital-communications technologies – have challenged its very raison d'être.

Copyright is a policy influenced by many moving parts. Understanding how copyright policy is made, and how decisions at various "levels" and times and in different countries influence each other, requires a theoretical approach that can incorporate these parts. This chapter outlines a specific approach – historical institutionalism – that can contribute to our understanding of IP's development and potential future changes. Historical institutionalism focuses on the changes over time in the relationship among the ideas underpinning IP, the actors involved in policymaking, and the institutions structuring their interactions. After a brief overview of historical institutionalism itself, the chapter provides an overview of each of these factors – institutions, ideas, interests (or actors), and change and continuity – as seen from a historical-institutionalist perspective. In particular, it argues for an "unstable institutions" model of institutional or policy development, in which actors constantly either reproduce or change institutions. The remainder of the book applies this framework to the analysis of North American copyright policymaking.

Historical Institutionalism

Drawing on classical political economy, particularly Marx's historical materialism and Weber's comparative institutional history,[2] historical institutionalism emerged from the comparative politics subfield of political science as one of the (now-not-so-) "new institutionalisms" of the 1980s and 1990s.[3] HI offers a middle ground between overly structuralist theories in which actors have no agency and overly atomistic behaviouralist theories that "often obscured the enduring socioeconomic and political structures that mould behaviour in distinctive ways in different national contexts."[4] It focuses researchers' attention on the interaction of three key variables – institutions, interests (or actors), and ideas – and how they change over time.[5]

Perhaps unsurprisingly, historical institutionalism, more than other neo-institutionalist approaches, emphasizes timing and history in shaping policy and institutional outcomes. In an HI analysis, "causal relations of elements and variables always are patterned by context and circumstance, and ... historical developments are contingently shaped by choices taken by actors about the content of the institutional links connecting state, economy and society at key moments of historical indeterminacy."[6]

Institutions

Humanity lives within a world of institutions, both formal and informal. Institutions can be thought of as semi-persistent "formal or informal procedures, routines, norms and conventions embedded in the organizational structure of the polity or political economy." Institutions in this catholic view "can range from the rules of a constitutional order or the standard operating procedures of a bureaucracy to the conventions governing trade union behaviour or bank–firm relations."[7] Copyright can be thought of as an institution, in that it provides us with rules and norms for how we should create and disseminate creative works and knowledge.

Institutions are "meso-level" structures that provide the crucial link between social structures like capitalism, class, and the nation-state system and individuals or groups.[8] Consequently, even homogeneous global forces or technological changes (such as the rise of digital technology and the Internet) can produce heterogeneous results.[9] Institutions structure these broader social forces, effectively "constrain[ing] and refract[ing] politics."[10] Different institutional set-ups can lead to different outcomes, even when they face similar external pressures, such as technological change.[11]

In HI, institutions both constrain strategic actors with formal and informal rules while also influencing their preferences. Actors' preferences therefore are not wholly exogenous to institutions, but rather are endogenous to institutional structures.

While institutions (and policies) are created and sustained by the purposeful actions of actors to achieve various objectives, they do not necessarily represent efficient, unique equilibria, or objective "best practices." They are created, sustained, and changed by purposeful actors with varying degrees of resources, and under conditions of imperfect information and less-than-perfect foresight; they can also persist beyond the situation that they were created to address. Institutions always favour some groups and policies over others. Outcomes depend on actors' skills and resources, and technical expertise deployed in public and private debates.[12]

Neither are institutions wholly self-contained, internally consistent entities. They exist within a universe of other institutions, some with overlapping jurisdictions that may complement or contradict the rules set forth in the particular institution being studied. Inter- and intra-institutional rules often conflict, with significant effects on policy development. Furthermore, the institutions in a given policy area can be located on any "level," from the subnational to the global. Just as, for example, US copyright policymaking institutions can have a disproportionate effect on international IP treaties,[13] so can international institutions influence domestic policy outcomes, maintenance, and change in other countries.

Interests/Actors

Historical institutionalism holds that actors are purposeful agents acting under conditions of constrained agency. Actors act strategically,
seeking to realize complex, contingent, and often changing goals, in a
context that favours certain strategies over others, and they must rely
upon incomplete (possibly inaccurate) perceptions of context, seen primarily in institutional terms. In other words, actors' strategic actions
are limited cognitively by the ideas and identities promoted by their
institutional context.[14] Actors exhibit a "situated ... rationality," "operating within relational structural fields that distinguish the possible
from the impossible and the likely from the less likely."[15]

Actors both shape and are shaped by the institutions within which
they operate, institutions that they either sustain or change (often in
unforeseen ways) through their actions. Institutions can affect actors in
two ways. First, they provide the rules governing their interactions,
based in the "background" ideas discussed below. At their most basic,
institutions divide actors into insiders and outsiders, operating within
either preset or self-defined boundaries. These boundaries "divide persons and activities inside the institution from persons and other institutions outside; boundaries array institutions in society, bringing their
activities to bear on one another or keeping them more distant."[16] This
insider-outsider dynamic can create a tension between those wishing to
defend an institution and those wishing to change it.

Institutions also provide actors with a "logic of appropriateness,"[17]
partially constituting actors' identities. Institutions "create categories and
'realities' that seem natural," comprising "actors with particular identities, values, interests, and strategies – that is, preferences – who seek to
manage and solve problems."[18] An actor's "behaviour is governed by
standardized and accepted codes of behaviour, prescriptions based on a
logic of appropriateness, and a sense of obligations and rights derived
from an identity, role or membership in a political community and the
ethos and practices of its institutions."[19]

In an HI approach, "goals, strategies and preferences" are "something to be explained."[20] Researchers cannot take an actor's rationality
for granted; they must demonstrate how preferences of similar actors
do or do not differ across institutions.[21] In keeping with this insight, one
of the main points of this book is the extent to which the institution of
copyright has shaped not only the way that authors and publishers, for
example, have pursued their self-interest, but also the way they have

identified their well-being with the intermediate objective of maintaining control over property in their work, rather than maximizing revenues, which does not necessarily require this property right.[22]

Because actors can also remake institutions, one must also investigate actors' influence on institutional rules. Unintended consequences, and actors' reactions to them, are an important driver of change in historical institutionalism. Even though actors try to shape institutions and rules to favour their perceived interest, that they lack perfect foresight means that institutions can (and do) develop in ways that the original designers failed to anticipate. As a result, small decisions taken in one period can end up having unintended results down the road.[23]

Actors vary not only in their objectives, but also in their access to material and ideational resources: better-resourced actors, all else being equal, will have a greater effect on institutional and policy outcomes than those lacking resources, as will those privileged by an institution's rules. As a consequence of this state of affairs, institutions, themselves shaped by actors with different resource levels, will favour some actors and policies over others; as noted above, institutions do not represent socially optimal equilibria.

Ideas

Although theorists such as John Campbell have argued that the role of ideas in HI has remained underdeveloped, HI's incorporation of their constraining and enabling effects represents one of its primary contributions to policy studies.[24] Ideas play two important roles in the policymaking process, along the lines of what Campbell refers to as "background" and "foreground" ideas.[25] "Foreground" ideas are those that are linked to specific policy proposals. Lying behind these foregrounded ideas are what Campbell refers to as "background" ideas. Background ideas are the assumptions about how the world works that constrain the range of acceptable policy solutions available to policymakers and, in a democracy, the public. Even more interestingly, actors often internalize background ideas; these ideas become the lens through which they view policy and politics, predisposing them towards some solutions over others, and shaping their policy preferences.

Background ideas represent the primary link between institutions and the deep structures that undergird the political and economic system. Ideas are embedded within institutions, which are maintained by "a powerful supporting idea ... generally connected to core political values which can be communicated directly and simply through image and rhetoric."[26] While whatever are considered to be the "best" ideas will differ from society to society, investigating which are the fundamental ideas underpinning institutions and policies, both as they are and how they ebb and flow over time, provides a way to highlight dominant social structures.

The effectiveness of foregrounded ideas depends not only on the material resources deployed by actors to support them, but also on the fit between these foregrounded ideas and background ideas, which Campbell divides into policy paradigms (elite ideas) and public sentiments (public ideas). For example, foundational concepts like "freedom," "individuality," and "property" represent powerful concepts embedded within institutions and which policymakers will seek to use to frame their proposals.

Just as institutions can embody sometimes-conflicting rules, foundational background ideas rarely exist uncontested. Institutions can embody conflicting paradigms. *Liberté, égalité, fraternité* may be foundational ideas in French society (and in Western society generally), but they exist in tension with each other. Often, a successful challenge to a dominant institution will involve reworking dominant paradigms, including a redefinition of an issue, expressed in a way that deploys powerful symbols. Policy proposals do best when they are linked to a "strong" paradigm[27] that makes institutions seem natural, rather than "socially constructed arrangements."[28] Copyright, as the following chapter develops, is anchored in core Enlightenment ideas of property and individuality: powerful ideas that are often deployed to defend copyright as a policy. However, the positive idea of ownership is in tension with the negative idea of copyright as "monopoly" (i.e., copyright prevents someone who has lawfully acquired a work to do whatever they wish with it), which can be used by those who do not benefit from copyright law to challenge it.

Similarly, institutional challengers can succeed by redefining an issue and linking it to a strong counter-paradigm: "'Losers' can often redefine the basic dimension of conflict to their advantage, thereby attracting previously uninvolved citizens."[29] The extent to which actors (including losing actors) can challenge existing policies is shaped by the nature of the institutions in which they operate. These institutions structure the opportunities to introduce new ideas and challenge old ones. Actors who control institutions and definitions can control both the type and the amount of change in a political system.[30]

In order to effect change in a crisis (i.e., a situation in which the legitimacy, usefulness, or validity of an institution is being challenged), alternative ideas must be available. These ideas must be credible (fitting the dominant paradigm), effective ("insofar as it promises a reasonable solution to a decision-making problem"), and legitimate (resonate with public sentiment).[31] "Public" in this usage, it should be noted, refers to that subset of the population whose opinion matters to decision-makers, since the public at large will not be interested in every decision made by, for example, a government. The task of the researcher is to identify the various types of ideas that are at play in a given situation. Classifying ideas in this way helps one to understand the effect that they have on the debate.[32]

Consistency and Change in HI

"CONSTRAINED INNOVATION": PATH DEPENDENCE

HI scholars continue to debate the conditions under which change happens in HI, and the mechanisms that drive it. In most accounts, existing institutions structure and shape the direction of reform along a certain "path." Change in HI is thus the "consequence (intended or not) of strategic action (intuitive or instrumental) filtered through perceptions (informed or misinformed) of an institutional context that favours certain strategies, actors, perceptions over others. Actors, then, appropriate a structured institutional context which favours certain strategies over others by way of the strategies they formulate or intuitively adopt."[33] While this view tends to be associated with sociological/constructivist institutionalisms,[34] its account of constrained agency within institutional frameworks allows it to exist comfortably within the HI tradition. Because actors, pursuing their own partial interests, lack perfect information, resulting institutions do not represent societally optimal results.

These postulates lead to HI's famous notion of "path dependence," which is based on the observation that institutions, once established, are difficult to change, and can outlive their objective utility. Institutions structure future actions, resulting in "constrained innovation"[35] and institutional persistence: "preceding steps in a particular direction induce further movement in the same direction."[36] "Path dependence," in other words, involves much more than the banal claim that "history matters."[37] The concept of path dependence is incredibly useful in explaining how and why policies like copyright have persisted, in some recognizable form, over several centuries. While it has changed over time, what we know as copyright today resembles in important ways copyright as it was originally elaborated in the early eighteenth century.

Institutions persist in part because they are "grounded in a dynamic of 'increasing returns,'" in which "the costs of switching from one alternative to another will, in certain social contexts, increase markedly over time."[38] As a result of these increasing costs, "political alternatives that were once quite plausible may become irretrievably lost."[39] Actors faced with incentives not to abandon an institution will be more likely to undertake incremental institutional change, even in the face of "considerable political change."[40]

Scholars have proposed many different path-dependence mechanisms, of which utility is only one. Institutions may be seen as being costly to change: they are difficult to create, involving the investment of time, material and ideational resources, to say nothing of the political difficulties of overcoming collective action problems. The greater the cost of creating an institution, the less likely actors will be to abandon it, especially when "powerful interests have grown up around" the institutions.[41] Institutions may also be sustained by the difficulty of definitively claiming institutional failure, given the complexity of politics and principal-agent problems.[42] They can also be subject to network effects, in which "buy-in" from an increasing number of actors makes an institution a de facto standard that then becomes difficult to change. Adaptive expectations may also play a role: actors may wish to back a winner because of future potential negative consequences if they were to back a losing institutional proposal.[43]

Institutional persistence can also result from limited institutional competition.[44] This places potential competitors at a disadvantage, as any potential net positive benefits arising from the implementation of a new institution must be measured against the existing institution. Institutions can also persist because they provide rules of thumb that actors then adopt. In doing so, they become part of actors' social, political, and cognitive landscapes. Actors become used to institutions, and their rules become the accepted, legitimate way of addressing issues.[45]

Power also plays a role. Institutions "are not neutral coordinating mechanisms but in fact reflect, and also reproduce and magnify, particular patterns of power distribution in politics."[46] They create winners and losers, insiders and outsiders. Insider "powerful interests" that benefit from a particular institutional configuration have an incentive to defend their privilege against interlopers. Power-holders in an institution can replicate the institution through their ability to select and socialize their successors.[47]

Effects of Path Dependence The mechanisms discussed in the previous section tend to restrict change, making some logically plausible alternatives (such as the elimination of copyright)[48] highly improbable in practice. That institutions are the result of partisan political battles, often among groups with asymmetrical resources, means that institutional rules will tend not towards some societal optimum, but will favour some individuals, groups, and outcomes over others. Victory depends on skills and resources, and technical expertise deployed in public and private debates.[49] "Inefficient" institutions will not necessarily go gently into that good night.[50] Institutional persistence, therefore, is not an argument for either social utility or effectiveness.[51] The constrained rationality of actors is as (or more) likely to result in institutional regimes characterized by internal and inter-institutional logic and rule "gaps" that can be exploited by disgruntled actors to effect change, as they are to result in institutions that reflect a stable, unchanging equilibrium.

Institutional and policy-path dependence cannot simply be assumed. They must be investigated and the specific mechanisms supporting institutional reproduction identified: "who is invested in what particular arrangements, how is it sustained over time, how other groups not invested in the institution are kept out," and what might impair this form of reproduction and lead to change.[52] A dynamic analysis of these mechanisms over a period of time allows one to ascertain "how and under what conditions historical events do – or do not – shape contemporary and future political choices and outcomes,"[53] domestically and regionally. The likelihood of institutional change is a function of the degree to which "individuals' basic self-definitions are determined by a given institutional structure": the greater the identification, the less likely the change. "Such an institution may collapse because it fails to adapt to changed environmental circumstances, but it will not be undermined by its own members."[54] The ability of opponents of the status quo to influence successfully the development of an institution (or "particular institutional configurations") will depend on "the particular mechanisms of reproduction that sustain them."[55] For example, if a new group becomes interested in an issue, perhaps because of an exogenous shock or because the "insider" group tried to push its existing advantage beyond the pale, institutional change is possible. "The distribution of intensities of preferences" – the extent to which particular groups care about an issue – is a major source of political institutional stability.[56] When this distribution changes, for instance, when the public begins to pay attention to an issue it previously took for granted, we can expect instability, and possibly changes to the institutional framework – the rules – governing the issue in question.

Identifying the mechanisms of reproduction and the specific rules governing institutional configurations, and tracking their changes over time is thus a key part of understanding North American copyright policy convergence and divergence, as will be seen in the coming chapters.

ACCOUNTING FOR CHANGE

One of the main points of contention among HI scholars is how to account for periods of radical change. One influential school of thought[57] holds that institutional histories can be divided into periods of stability and change, divided by "critical junctures" when, for various reasons (such as an external economic shock), institutions and policies can be knocked onto a new "path." This view has been criticized for being logically inconsistent, that is, "institutions explain everything until they explain nothing."[58] In contrast to the "critical junctures" approach, the "unstable institutions" view sees institutions as constantly being made and remade by actors when they follow or deviate from the rules embodied by institutions. The unstable institutions approach argues that there is almost always a degree of continuity between periods.[59] While Mahoney argues that "in a path-dependent sequence early historical events are contingent occurrences that cannot be explained on the basis of prior events or 'initial conditions,'"[60] in practice this rarely occurs. An emphasis on critical junctures tends to understate the continuity even between supposedly dramatic changes in institutional setups.[61] It may also miss the effects of longer-term processes, such as demographic change[62] or the importance of slow-changing, enduring "deep structures."

Continuity between two seemingly disparate institutional periods becomes more obvious if one sees institutions as historically contingent and temporary responses to "enduring problems."[63] Copyright may date to eighteenth-century England, but it was shaped (and continues to be shaped) by the book publishers' monopoly that it replaced.[64] Even technologies that have little in common with physical book publishing continue to be treated as if copyright, a regulatory regime developed for physical books, is appropriate to their regulation. This is not an argument that sudden, dramatic change never occurs, but rather that even dramatic change often has its roots in earlier institutions, which suggests that findings of revolutionary change or dramatic breaks are more likely when researchers examine institutional change over short periods. The researcher's choice of what time period to study can thus affect whether one finds change or relative stability.

In the "unstable institutions" version of HI, institutional change comes from the same place as institutional stability: the mechanisms of institutional reproduction, examined dynamically. It is based on three insights. First, institutions are reproduced or modified by actors' actions. Second, taking seriously the HI insight that institutions' roots are historically contingent requires considering the possibility that institutions are shaped by the previously existing historical and institutional context. In other words, in most cases, the researcher's choice of a beginning date for an institution will involve a certain degree of discretion, as institutions are almost always preceded by proto-institutions.[65] In a sense, institutional history really is "turtles all the way down." Third, institutions are never wholly coherent or accepted: "The basic assumptions on which an institution is constituted and its prescribed behavioural rules are never fully accepted by the entire society. Institutions may recede into oblivion because trust is eroded and rules are not obeyed."[66]

Sources of Change: Exogenous and Endogenous Shocks Change in the unstable-institutions version of HI can result from two sources: exogenous shocks or endogenous pressures. Exogenous political or economic shocks involve an external break with the status quo, while endogenous shocks involve the manipulation of existing institutions within a (relatively) unchanging external environment. This language, however, tends to gloss over the reality that while institutions may look solid in a static analysis, a dynamic analysis reveals that they are always being made and remade by the actions of purposeful actors, even in the absence of exogenous shocks. Just as endogenous change and exogenous shocks can lead to revolutionary changes, exogenous shocks can also lead to evolutionary changes.

Exogenous shocks are equivalent to the introduction of a new resource that can either help or hinder existing and newly created actors. Thelen and Steinmo identify four distinct, though often empirically intertwined, sources of institutional dynamisms, "situations in which we can observe variability in the impact of institutions over time but within countries."[67] Exogenous political or socio-economic changes can work in several ways. They can cause "previously latent institutions" to "suddenly become salient, with implications for political outcomes," and bring new actors, with new objectives, to the fore, reorienting existing institutions towards "different ends," as the result of "changes in the socioeconomic context or political balance of power." They can also cause existing actors to adopt new strategies within the context of existing institutions or to change the institutions themselves, leading actors to "adjust their strategies." As will be discussed in the following chapter, the history of copyright law is often told in terms of exogenous shocks, specifically the way that technological change creates new interests and changes the relative position of existing ones. Each new technological innovation was accompanied by a degree of social upheaval and political conflict, and, eventually, new copyright laws that legitimized a new balance of power.

Change can also emerge endogenously. While an institution viewed statically may seem like a solid structure, it may well contain resources that actors desiring "change" can use to undermine rivals within that institution without necessarily "changing" the institution beyond all recognition. Endogenous change is a consequence of the fact that few institutions, born as they are out of political struggle and compromises among actors with imperfect information, are likely to be completely consistent internally or consistent with the domestic and international regimes in which they are embedded.[68] Actors do not simply wait around for the chance to change an institution. Rather, they exploit conflicting institutional or systemic logics.[69] They can undermine unfavourable rules while seeking to exploit institutional resources: "working around elements they cannot change while attempting to harness and utilize others in novel ways."[70] Similarly, institutions do not exist in a vacuum: different institutions often compete for dominance in a particular subject area. Actors can challenge institutional precepts by appealing to some external authority or authoritative idea.[71]

Institutions may also contain rules to routinize change, through processes such as "the institutionalization of critical reflection and debate, legitimate opposition, and the rights for citizens to speak, publish and organize, including civil disobedience."[72] They may also contain contradictory rules, the tensions among which can also be exploited by actors seeking change. As a result, institutional rules can encourage their own transformation.[73] As this book's three case studies will demonstrate, North American copyright changes have been driven not only by exogenous technological shocks, but also by actors exploiting conflicts within and among institutions to enact far-ranging changes.

HOW CHANGE CAN HAPPEN: BRICOLAGE

Ultimately, however, change depends on the actions of actors. As the outcome of political disputes among actors with imperfect information, institutions will rarely completely satisfy either winners or losers (who are rarely eliminated completely). Beyond the initial decision to establish an institution, "further choice points exist"[74] for actors to press for change. Consequently, there will almost always be agents present who want to effect institutional change. Scholars have elaborated numerous strategies for effecting change, such as "layering" ("grafting of new institutions onto old ones"), "conversion" ("changes in function" of the institution), and "drift" (change through a "loss of relevance" of the current institution).[75] It also depends on the relative strength of institutional rules (including the extent to which actors follow these rules and what outcomes result from following the rules).[76]

This book emphasizes two strategies in particular: bricolage and diffusion. Both address how actors use and are constrained by the various types of ideas underlying their institutional contexts. Campbell defines bricolage as the act of recombining "locally available institutional principles and practices in ways that yield change." Bricolage can be either (or a combination of) "substantive" ("the recombination of already existing institutional principles and practices to address [substantive] problems [following] a logic of instrumentality") or "symbolic" (involving "the recombination of symbolic principles and practices"). Both types of bricolage refer to the recombination of already existing elements, not the introduction of new elements.[77]

For example, an issue like copyright can be defined in different ways, with consequences for how it is treated. It can, for instance, be treated as a professional issue (in which case experts prevail), a political issue (politicians prevail), a legal issue (lawyers), a cultural issue (creators), a market issue (let the market decide), or as a matter to be governed by bureaucratic standards (bureaucrats). Actors have the choice of how to define an issue within an institutional set-up. They can also decide on the specific policy venue, which, as always, advantages some at the cost of others.[78]

Diffusion, meanwhile, refers to "the process whereby imported principles and practices are implemented locally," where these foreign ideas are combined with "locally available principles and practices."[79] As with all types of institutionally based change, the form that bricolage and diffusion take, and whether they are successful, will depend on the material, ideational, and institutional resources and constraints under which they operate. Even this type of change, however, is dependent on the willingness and ability of actors to work to effect change. When actors emphasize a particular combination of copyright's protection and dissemination roles, they are engaging in a form of bricolage.

The common conception of IP (and copyright) as a trade issue emerged from a process of bricolage. There is nothing inherent in IP that requires it to be defined as a trade issue rather than, for example, a purely domestic regulatory policy. As Drahos and Braithwaithe document, the link between trade and IP was the result of lobbying in the 1970s and 1980s by US IP leaders, who argued that maximizing international IP protection would maintain US global economic dominance at a time when this hegemony was being threatened by the rising star of Japan, among others.[80] There was nothing "natural" or inevitable about this linkage, but once made, it exerted, and continues to exert, a powerful hold on our conceptions of how to address copyright and IP issues.

As with all types of institutionally based change, the form that bricolage takes, and whether it is successful, will depend on the material, ideational, and institutional resources available to actors, both domestic and international, and the constraints under which they operate. Even this type of change, however, is dependent on the willingness and ability of actors to work to effect change.

Conclusion

This book's approach to historical institutionalism can be summarized as follows:

1 Institutions – broadly defined as semi-persistent "constraints or rules that induce stability in human interaction"[81] – structure individuals' and groups' interactions with each other and with broader social forces, by providing incentives and disincentives for various actions, and by influencing actors' perceptions of their own self-interests.
2 Actors pursue their objectives within institutional material and ideational constraints, which influence and construct actors' perceptions of their own self-interests.
3 Institutions are historically contingent, the result of political competition among actors in a specific pre-existing socio-political-economic context. Consequently, similar situations (such as economic pressures from globalizations) can lead to different results under different institutional set-ups.
4 The timing and sequencing of institutional creation and change matter. Changes in one period influence later institutional and policy development.

5 Where institutions confront actors as constraints, they can be modified via political action.
6 Institutions rarely demonstrate either complete internal or inter-
  institutional (i.e., at a societal level) logical consistency. Differences
  between periods of revolutionary change (known as "critical junctures") and periods of stability are differences of degree, not of kind,
  and are partly the result of a researcher's methodological choices.
  This lack of logical coherence, combined with the fact that political questions are rarely (if ever) settled definitively, provides actors
  with the ability to drive change in HI theory.
7 Exogenous shocks, the main driver of change in most HI accounts,
  can both create new interest groups and serve as a resource to em-
  power existing groups to either uphold or subvert the status quo.
8 Change can also occur in the absence of external shocks, as actors
  recombine existing institutional/ideational elements.
9 A full analysis of policy or institutional change – such as the implementation of an international treaty – must include the relevant
  institutions, ideas, and interests at all "levels."

An HI-based analysis of copyright reform must do four things. First,
it must identify the relevant institutions and their rules, including inconsistencies within and among institutions, how they constitute actors
and structure their activities. Second, it must identify the actors involved in a policy debate, as well as their interests, resources, and strategies, no matter on which "level" they are located. Third, it must
account for the ideational factors influencing the debate, particularly in
terms of how they are deployed to set limits on the debate, as well as
potential shocks that may disrupt an institution or policy. Finally, an HI
approach must account for the causes of policy change and continuity.

The rest of this book applies this approach to North American copyright politics. It argues, among other things, that copyright reform in
Canada, Mexico, and the United States has been driven by purposeful
actors exploiting external shocks and already existing institutional
rules and ideational tensions within overlapping domestic, regional,
and international institutions. The results are copyright policies that are
constantly being made and remade in an ongoing, never-ending, ever-
shifting debate. Furthermore, each country's policy outcome reflects
the particular nature of its domestic politics and their particular interaction with regional and global institutions and actors.

Domestic path dependence and regional constraints do not mean that copyright policies in North America are immune to change or convergence, particularly in the context of trade negotiations like the Trans-Pacific Partnership, where the United States is able to barter IP reform for other policy changes. Rather, change – as Campbell notes above – will continue to be the result of purposeful actors exploiting copyright's paradoxical objectives of increasing protection and dissemination and linking their desired changes to exogenous shocks and conflicting objectives of the institutions that govern copyright policy.

As already noted, historical institutionalism is in many ways a modest theory. In the case of North America, as developed here, it focuses our attention on a few specific variables – institutional structure, actors and their resources, the mechanisms underlying institutions – without offering any grand predictions. It does, however, suggest that policy outcomes will depend on

- the institutional set-up (the "rules of the game");
- the relative resources of actors, including their position within and in relation to the institutions in question;
- the strength and viability of the mechanisms supporting institutions, wherever they may be; and
- the ability of actors to recognize and exploit exogenous shocks and institutional inconsistencies.

These observations are of a general nature. It will be the task of the next chapter to apply them to a particular dimension of North America: copyright policymaking as seen through the lens of the implementation of the WIPO Internet treaties.

3 The Political Economy of Copyright

Only one thing is impossible for God: to find any sense in any copyright law on the planet. Whenever a copyright law is to be made or altered, then the idiots assemble.

Mark Twain[1]

Although it has only recently emerged into the mainstream of political debate, copyright has long been a controversial subject. The law tends to depoliticize issues so that they seem technical and settled, even as they remain contested.[2] However, underneath the seemingly solid surface of settled law lies an ongoing battle among various business and social groups to expand copyright in some cases and in the service of some interests, and to restrict it in others. In this battle, the United States and its content industries are the primary actors behind the global expansion of copyright since the mid-1980s, as well as the current push for stronger digital-copyright policies worldwide, including in Canada and Mexico.

A historical-institutionalist analysis emphasizes that actors deploy material and ideational resources in order to influence the making of copyright law. Ideationally, they do so by exploiting the tensions inherent in copyright between protection and dissemination, and between competing institutions in pursuit of their perceived interests. Materially, they make use of money, political access, and other resources in order to influence the decision-makers who actually write the treaties and laws that make up copyright law.

Efforts to influence copyright policies occur within specific and interlocking domestic, regional, and international institutional contexts that privilege certain ideas and actors over others, and that can be reshaped by actors' actions, intentional and otherwise. Most countries are members of the main copyright treaties (notably the 1886 Berne Convention for the Protection of Literary and Artistic Work [Berne Convention], the 1961 Rome Convention for the Protection of Performers, Producers of Phonograms and Broadcasting Organizations [Rome Convention], and the 1995 Agreement on Trade-Related Aspects of Intellectual Property Rights at the World Trade Organization). Some eighty-nine are members of the WIPO Copyright Treaty and Performances and Phonograms Treaty, the Internet treaties. Outside the WIPO and WTO systems, in October 2010 eleven countries[3] concluded the Anti-Counterfeiting Trade Agreement, discussed briefly in the book's introduction and covered in greater detail in chapters 6 and 8. Since the 1980s and 1990s, copyright and intellectual property have become standard parts of bilateral and plurilateral trade agreements. As of December 2013, several Asia-Pacific countries, including the United States, Mexico, and Canada, have been negotiating a Trans-Pacific Strategic Economic Partnership, which includes a copyright/IP component. In North America, the North American Free Trade Agreement placed Canada, Mexico, and the United States on the same copyright "path," while the failed Security and Prosperity Partnership (SPP) of North America offers an interesting example of an institutional attempt to move forward a shared North American vision of copyright. This failure holds lessons about the limits to convergence in North American copyright governance.

Despite the existence of this long-standing thicket of international copyright treaties and agreements, each country possesses its own distinctive copyright laws, constrained by these international agreements but also shaped by domestic institutions and actors. This chapter uses the historical-institutionalist approach developed in the previous chapter to understand better the historical, global, and regional context of digital-copyright reform in North America. In keeping with this approach's focus on ideas, institutions, and interests, it surveys these three factors and how they influence the current debate. The first part of the chapter focuses on the development of copyright. The second part outlines the various types of interests involved in the copyright debate, as well as how their interests are being affected by digitization. The third part addresses the international-institutional context of copyright. Given the United States's central role in copyright policymaking, its main internationally focused institutions are covered here. It also discusses the structure and effects of North American regional copyright institutions, specifically NAFTA and the SPP. The fourth part discusses briefly the process of change in copyright from a historical-institutionalist perspective. Together, these sections provide the context for understanding the Canadian, US, and Mexican implementation of the Internet treaties. The chapter concludes with some final comments that set the stage for the book's case studies.

Part 1: Ideas – Constraints on and Resources for Change

Copyright offers an ideal example of a path-dependent institution. It was a response to an enduring problem – how to regulate the market in creative works – that emerged and was shaped by historically contingent events related to the loss of the Stationers Guild's publishing monopoly at the beginning of the Enlightenment. Rooted in this past, this response has since shaped the development of future laws. While the scope and duration of copyright has expanded significantly since the debut in 1709 of the original modern copyright law, the British *Statute of Anne*, the bare bones of this original law can be found in all subsequent copyright laws in the Anglo-American tradition. These include the limited duration of rights, assignable (i.e., alienable) rights provided to authors, as well as the concept that some things are not copyrightable (e.g., ideas, as opposed to the fixation of ideas) and the notion that copyright has a public-interest aspect, namely, the "Encouragement of Learning," in the words of the Statute of Anne's title.[4] All debates over copyright involve actors attempting to emphasize either the need for greater protection or the promotion of dissemination, the two fundamentally irreconcilable objectives of copyright law.[5]

Copyright, more so than tangible property, depends for its existence and legitimacy on ideological justifications "because intellectual property (by design) changes the characteristics of knowledge and/or information by *constructing* a scarcity in its use" (emphasis added).[6] Where tangible goods depend on a mixture of social convention and their materiality to construct the boundaries of property in goods – all property norms derive from law or social conventions – informational goods depend exclusively on the law and social conventions to determine their boundaries.

The paradigms and social conventions underlying copyright can limit actors' perceptions of the range of possibilities available to regulate the market in creative works. As a result, what is actually only one possible, human-created way of regulating the market for creative works is often taken to be *the* means to this specific end. Modern debates tend to focus on copyright (a means) rather than the maximization of creative works (an end). Consequently, copyright can seem "natural," settled, and inevitable.

Copyright touches on two concepts in particular – individuality and private property – that are the foundational concepts underlying Enlightenment society. The concept of originality, like the Romantic notion of the individual author, may be a "conceit"[7] that ignores the messy reality that all works are created through the direct and indirect use of already existing works, but it is nonetheless a powerful "construct that is deeply connected with notions of originality and uniqueness that are Western in origin and relatively recent."[8]

Similarly, the idea of copyright as a property right appeals to "the central norm underpinning the market system," that of private property. "Intellectual property rights ... are a subset of one particularly important component of late-twentieth-, early-twenty-first-century capitalism and are embedded in the deep structure of global capitalism."[9] The concept of "property" is very powerful and thus politically contested.[10] It is "rooted in the fundamental morality of a given society."[11] In the copyright debate, this tension expresses itself in the discursive use of "piracy" as a way to influence conceptions of what should be considered as property, and to determine what an owner's rights of exclusion will be. Often, claims of property precede legal determinations of property. This rhetorical move is usually linked to accusations of "piracy" on behalf of copyright owners against what they feel are unfair (though not necessarily illegal) appropriation of their property. In practice, however, property rights are neither absolute nor natural.[12]

The strength of copyright path dependence can be seen in the fact that it is so tightly linked to fundamental notions of private property and the individual that Rose and May, forceful critics of the concept of intellectual property, argue that copyright is unlikely to be abolished.[13] Few of the critical sources consulted and none of the people interviewed for this book argued for its abolition.[14] This state of affairs is all the more remarkable when one considers that there is a lack of strong evidence that copyright actually promotes the production of creative works. Indeed, the very question of copyright's empirical, as opposed to theoretical, effect on the production of creative works has gone largely unexamined.[15] There is also a lack of evidence for how "successful copyright has been in creating incentives for production, reducing transaction costs and keeping deadweight costs low."[16] Instead, as William Patry, the leading expert on US copyright law, remarks, the copyright debate has been driven much more by rhetoric than evidence.[17]

The existing theoretical and empirical literature on economics and copyright demonstrates that copyright's effects on the production and dissemination of creative works are, at best, indeterminate, dependent on the structure of the specific market in question.[18] Where works are created for reasons other than remuneration (such as to complete a PhD or to fulfil the innate human desire to create), copyright protection can be unnecessary and inefficient.[19]

To a large extent, the debate over intellectual-property rights, including copyright, "is ultimately a narrative [battle] where the struggle is to define meaning and control the discourse."[20] In this debate, actors pursue specific interpretations of how copyright should be defined, and they do so within institutional frameworks that favour certain interpretations over others. Actors can choose to emphasize one part of copyright over another in the pursuit of change, or in order to maintain the status quo. They can engage in "symbolic bricolage," linking copyright protection to a larger narrative about the importance of property rights that must be maintained. Alternatively, they can link it to a narrative that emphasizes copyright's monopolistic character (monopolies generally being seen as something to be avoided) that should be reduced or eliminated.

One can evaluate both the strength and likelihood of significant change by evaluating the way in which copyright's foundational concepts of "property" and "individuality" are either supported or challenged in response to endogenous or exogenous shocks such as lobbying and technological change, respectively. In times of relative stability, relatively little effort will be expended to defend them, as they will be accepted as being "just the way things are." In times of upheaval, however, these concepts will have to be defended vigorously against both alternative concepts and counter-interpretations of what they mean, and questions as to whether they are the most appropriate way to frame the issue.

One of the reasons, as the following chapters demonstrate, that the copyright debate has become so contentious and widely politicized is that digital technologies challenge the necessity of the business models and justifications that have grown up around copyright. The digital revolution has led to a situation in which "the realm of intellectual property has become widely contested and problematic," and where traditional narratives, while perhaps not "completely without merit ...

are of less widespread applicability than hard-line supporters of the extension of the protection of IPRs may suppose or hope."[21] The result has been the start of a tough political fight whose outcome is not predetermined.

Copyright as Instrumentalist Policy

There exist various philosophical justifications for copyright: namely, that a creator deserves to receive "just deserts" for her work; that she deserves property rights because creative works are a manifestation of the creator's personality; and that copyright should maximize some social utility.[22] Interested rational actors deploy these justifications to legitimize specific policy positions and visions of copyright. However, in practice, drawing up rights in intellectual "works" involves making trade-offs among various interests, not least of which is society at large. As a result, actual copyright laws by their nature are instrumental, the result of pragmatic choices by officials that take into consideration many competing interests and philosophies.

Property, intellectual and otherwise, is not a one-dimensional expression of control by an owner over something. Even owners of material assets "are not always free to set the terms and conditions under which others are allowed to use [them]."[23] Rather, "Property rights entail relations between two people *and* between a person and an object"; in this case, abstract objects, which "take the form of a convenient legal fiction."[24] This "commodity fiction," to use Karl Polanyi's term, is a fundamental requirement of capitalism: "The rendering of things not originally produced for sale as commodities required a story to be told about these resources that was not linked to their previous existence, or production, as exchangeable goods or social resources; a story needed to be told about the normality of organizing their production and distribution through markets."[25]

Property ownership, a relational concept, is never absolute. Ownership of even physical objects never involves complete control. Laws govern the situations under which a firearm can be used; state authorities can enter your house under certain circumstances. All property, including copyrighted works, involves politically determined limits on an "owner's" control of that property. Debates over copyright, and all property, are always over where to draw these lines, and these lines are all about conferring power. Property itself can be used as a power base from which such property rights can be further extended, usually in favour of those already possessing property and against social relations that depend on the non-commodification of information.[26] Where these lines are drawn matters.

Property as a social relation accords with the instrumentalist view of copyright (and property in general). Instrumentalism denies that there are any natural rights of property (i.e., that property is a good in and of itself), is "sceptical about any theory of property that is based on the idea that property is a subjective right," and evaluates the justness of any particular property regime on the basis of its effects on society as a whole, often in economic terms, but also in relation to broader standards, such as its effect on privacy or freedom of speech.[27] An instrumentalist approach to copyright (and property) explicitly considers copyright not only in terms of societal costs and benefits, but also, as a corollary, in terms of winners and losers. In other words, it considers the needs not only of the owner, but also of the copier[28] and of society.

Instrumentalism represents both a justification for copyright (i.e., that the needs of all actors, not just those of authors, should be considered) and a description of how copyright policy is actually made. As a justification for copyright, instrumentalism's explicit focus is on copyright as a means to achieve an end – not as an end in itself – with the end being some sort of social utility: "Copyright is not there to 'protect' authors (or other owners of copyright), but rather to maximize the creation, production and dissemination of knowledge and access thereto. In other words, protection is not an end but a means to achieving that purpose, which implies that the level of protection must be properly calibrated."[29]

As a description of copyright policymaking, instrumentalism captures the historical-institutionalist view that policies such as copyright are the outcome of political conflict among actors who promote different justifications for copyright in pursuit of their objectives. The origins of copyright are relentlessly pragmatic, which itself accords with instrumentalism. Copyright's eighteenth-century British originators focused on an author's labour as the thing to which rights should be attached because it was "a quantifiable source for a literary property right."[30] In 1842, the British copyright term was extended to the length of the author's life plus seven years, or forty-two years from the date of publication, to address the practical problem of how to provide for authors' families after the author's death in a period with no social security.[31] Copyright, in other words, has always been shaped by a healthy dose of pragmatism and instrumentalism, the only question being where the boundaries of copyright would be drawn, and to whose benefit.

Part 2: Interests – Actors Promoting and Critiquing Copyright

The dominance of the concepts of individuality and property only explains partly why copyright continues to frame our conceptions about how to regulate the marketplace in creative works. Specific ideas and concepts about copyright must be defended and promoted by interested groups and individuals. As Drahos and Braithwaite argue, "The intellectual property standards we have today are largely the product of the global strategies of a relatively small number of companies and business organizations that realized the value of intellectual property sooner than anyone else."[32] Copyright is supported by powerful interests as well as by foundational ideas that have come to set the limits of allowable debate on and shaped actors' conceptions about how to regulate the market in creative works.[33] Like any path-dependent policy, copyright is sustained in part by the fact that possible alternatives are untested and unlikely themselves to be without costs, whose magnitude cannot be foreseen with perfect accuracy.[34] That copyright provides the underlying structure for a multi-billion-dollar global business has led even critics of copyright like US Supreme Court Justice Stephen Breyer to argue that, rather than reduce copyright, the law should be changed incrementally, that a "heavy burden of persuasion should be placed upon those who would extend such protection and that we might look favourably upon proposals to reduce it."[35]

Copyright actors differ according to the resources (time, money, personnel, and economic and political influence) they can bring to bear on the issue, as well as the extent to which they are recognized and hold influence within the institutional contexts where copyright policy is considered. Their relative power and influence also varies by country and international forum.

Distinctions among publishers and distributors (i.e., the content industries), creators, and the "users" of copyrighted works are somewhat misleading because all "creators" create by using existing works; similarly, a creator or user can also be a distributor.[36] What follows, then, is a rough typology of existing groups based on what interests they are pursuing actively, not on what interests they should be pursuing from some objective perspective.

The Content Industries

Historically, technological and material factors have allowed publishers and distributors to play the dominant role in copyright. Most creators lacked the means to mass produce and distribute their works. As a result, they needed to depend on corporate publishers to reach their audience. This power asymmetry gave publishers and distributors the upper hand in negotiations with creators and provided these intermediaries with a crucial and positive social role in promoting the distribution of creative works.

Superficially, the current situation is not much different. Materially, publishers and distributors dominate the market for copyrighted works and own the vast majority of commercially important copyrights. Four corporations dominate the global music industry.[37] In the United States, "six [firms] account for 90% of film revenues, two dominate radio, five (and shrinking) own the cable TV market, four dominate cell phone services ... Many of these separate markets are dominated by the same vertically and horizontally integrated giants – especially Sony, Viacom, Bertelsmann, News Corp, and General Electric."[38] The main drivers behind international efforts for stronger copyright laws, publishers and distributors act according to a profit-maximization logic, often deploying natural-rights, pro-author rationales in pursuit of this economic objective.[39]

These firms have a disproportionate influence in copyright policy around the world. Of these industries, the most important from a policy-making perspective are the worldwide recording and motion picture industries, although software makers (represented by the Business Software Alliance [BSA]) and traditional publishers are also important. More recently, video-game manufacturers, represented in the United States by the Entertainment Software Association and in Canada by its sister organization, the Entertainment Software Association of Canada, have also become important since 2000. These industries advocate for policy reform in countries of interest as individual companies as well as through a network of domestic advocacy groups. In the motion picture industry, for example, the most powerful player is the Motion Picture Association of America (MPAA), which has branches in countries and regions around the world. In Mexico, the MPAA coordinates its anti-piracy efforts with the main music-industry association, the Asociación Mexicana de Productores de Fonogramas (Mexican Association of Phonogram Producers, AMPROFON), through the Asociación Protectora de Cine y Música México (Association for the Protection of Cinema and Music Mexico, APCM).[40] In the United States, "probably, in matters of intellectual property, trade and culture, the MPA[A] becomes 'the [U.S.] State Department' ... US political parties have been models of bipartisan cooperation when it comes to working with the MPA[A]. It has been one of the key actors in the global demonization of piracy and the resulting process of criminalization of copyright infringement."[41] In Canada, MPAA members are represented by the Canadian Motion Picture Distributors Association (CMPDA).

In the music industry, the major record companies are represented in the United States by the Recording Industry Association of America (RIAA), whose members are represented in Mexico by AMPROFON (which also includes Reader's Digest and Azteca Music; AMPROFON members represent more than 70 per cent of the Mexican music market).[42] In Canada, the Canadian Recording Industry Association (now called Music Canada) has, since 2006, represented primarily the Big Four labels and has been called "the Canadian branch of the RIAA."[43] Internationally, these companies are also part of the International Federation of the Phonographic Industry (IFPI).

The International Intellectual Property Alliance (IIPA) represents another important lobby group for the content industries. Formed in 1984 – the year in which "trade and intellectual property began to merge," according to former United States Trade Representative official and current counsellor to the BSA Emery Simon – the IIPA represents over 1500 corporations, "whose annual output exceeds five per cent of the US Gross Domestic Product." It continues to be the main international advocacy group for the content industry. The IIPA "coordinates policy positions based on shared concerns of its members, tracks copyright policies abroad, provides detailed information on foreign copyright practices and infractions, testifies before Congress, and publishes influential reports that it delivers to Congress and the USTR" (United States Trade Representative).[44] In addition to these copyright-focused associations, the content industries also work through domestic and international business organizations like the Chamber of Commerce (US), the Canadian Chamber of Commerce, and the US-Mexico Chamber of Commerce.

While these sectors are dominated by firms from the United States, Japan, and the European Union, other countries' firms also sometimes play a significant role. In Mexico, for example, Televisa is the world's largest Spanish-speaking media company,[45] producing *telenovelas* and other works for domestic and foreign consumption, including in the United States. Its interest in stronger copyright would parallel that of its competitors in other countries.

The content industries are characterized by both their ability and desire to focus intently on copyright policy. This single-minded focus has been an advantage in their quest to convince government to change copyright laws in their interests.[46] As Scherer remarks in an article defending intellectual property, "There is reason to believe that the enforcement of intellectual property rights is biased in favour of large, well-established organizations" – organizations that are least likely to be motivated to create by the prospects of a windfall from copyright.[47]

This interest in strong copyright stems from the fact that most publishers and distributors, including the large (transnational) publishing houses, record companies, and movie and television studios, base their business model on the control of copies: they thus have a vested interest in protecting this business model. These companies "own" a stable of copyrighted assets, which they can deploy to maximize revenues through licensing, new formats, reissues, and so forth. Unsurprisingly, they are the group that stands to gain the most from stronger copyright protection.[48]

Path dependence in copyright policy is driven in part by these entrenched firms' ability to block or redirect pressures for change in their own interests. As beneficiaries and defenders of the existing system, they have been in a position to shape the evolution of copyright in the face of technological change and the entry of new actors. As a result, new businesses and industries find it harder to get established and innovation is often stifled.

For example, in Canada, before 1911, "a large business in mechanical reproduction had been built up by gramophone companies and manufacturers of perforated music rolls and the like, on the assumption that authors and composers had no right to restrain the reproduction of their works by these means. Those who prefer such language might say that the trade coolly pirated musical works."[49] Publishers used the Copyright Act of 1911 to bring this burgeoning industry to heel.[50]

Hollywood itself was born when New York–based independent film companies moved west to escape demands for royalty payments from the major producers of film and movie equipment.[51] More recently, Rutgers law professor Michael Carrier has provided evidence that the recording industry has used its position and vast financial resources to stifle competition by new-technology upstarts, even in situations where these new firms did their best to comply with existing law and to address the legacy firms' economic challenges. He argues that the record labels were so focused on "the short term and preservation of existing business models" that they saw the digital marketplace and smaller companies as a threat to be put down, rather than as a potential opportunity.[52]

CONTENT INDUSTRIES AND DIGITIZATION

Digitization threatens traditional content industries' scarcity-based business model to a much greater extent than previous technological advances. Technological change has always influenced copyright law, but digital technology differs from previous technological advances in that it alters the very nature of the marketplace. Previous technological advances such as the invention of recorded music and television were advances in degree, not in kind, over existing technologies. Commercial copying – the only kind of real interest to the content industries – remained very expensive. New technologies may have brought new players to the copyright-negotiation table, but they were players that were generally similar to the incumbents. While technologies like the cassette and the photocopier allowed consumers to make copies of protected works, the copies were almost always inferior to the original due to technological limitations. Furthermore, many of these uses (dubbing a cassette for a friend on your home tape deck) would have been technically difficult to prohibit in any case. Except when performed on a large, commercial scale, copying in this era was not an existential threat to existing players.

No so digital technologies. Because of the economies of scale related to commercial reproduction and distribution, the content industries fulfilled the important social and economic function of making works accessible to the general public. But with a technology (computers) and a distribution system (the Internet) that renders copying and distribution trivially easy, the content industries are in danger of losing their raison d'être. Unlike the hierarchical nature of the previous market, a digital, networked economy involves "decentralized peer production"[53] and has less need of large corporate structures to coordinate creative production and distribution, particularly when one considers the degree to which digitization reduces the cost of copying and even shifts it almost completely to the consumer, as when someone prints a document.[54] Digitization also challenges the rationale of copyright as an incentive: since it now costs much less to create, reproduce, and distribute works, "publishers should therefore need fewer, not more, property rights to protect their investment."[55] Regardless, the distribution of digital works "undermines the ability of creators and rights owners to derive profits from their own work, which may in some circumstances lead to the stifling of creativity as the rewards and incentives for producing works disappear."[56]

Digital technology is a double-edged sword for the content industries as they exist today. Alongside the existential threat it poses, digitization also provides copyright owners with the potential to exert an unprecedented control over creative works once the works have been sold, far beyond what is possible in the analogue world.[57] These include price discrimination based on region, "previous purchases, internet service provider, or membership in studio-specific 'frequent buyer clubs,'" and personal information that is "tracked, aggregated, analysed, catered to, and used to set prices based on the best guess of what that user could and would pay."[58]

From this perspective, "the answer to the machine [i.e., unauthorized copying] is in the machine [i.e., digital controls on content]."[59] Whether owners exercise (or are allowed to exercise) greater control over copyrighted works is, in the end, a political discussion as much as a technical one.[60] The WIPO Internet treaties represent an attempt to change copyright law to enable this type of digital control.

CREATORS AND DIGITIZATION

Copyright neophytes may be surprised by the extent to which copyright debates can ignore actual creators – the very people whom copyright is supposed to help. The story of how international copyright law has been strengthened dramatically is often discussed as a battle between industrial behemoths, with creators relegated to a supporting role. While there exist creators' and performers' groups such as unions and collection societies with varying degrees of influence (in Mexico, creators' collection societies, or *sociedades de gestión colectivas*, are particularly important), they tended to be overshadowed by industry interests in the debates, described below, that led to the TRIPS, NAFTA, and the Internet treaties. As recently as the late 1990s, intermediaries were able to argue successfully, and with the support of creators, that their interests were the same as creators' interests. Typically, creators' groups tend to favour a maximalist approach to copyright, though emphasizing different issues than their industry counterparts.

More important, this equivalence of industry and creator interests historically was accepted with little question by policymakers even though it has long been recognized that publishers/distributors and creators face different incentives, motives, and interests.[61] When economies of scale made it difficult for individual creators to create and distribute their works without relying on large publishers and distributors, one could argue that there was a rough alignment between creators' and intermediaries' interests, even though the resulting business models overwhelmingly favour the publisher/distributor over the creator. Only a few ultra-successful creators make significant money from copyright royalties.[62] In general, it cannot be taken for granted that creators benefit from copyright to the same degree as publishers.

Digital technologies have been both blessing and curse for creators. As unfair as it may have been to musicians, writers, and the like, the previous business model at least provided certainty for those wanting to publish, create, or produce other creative works. Publishers and record labels also provided services, including distribution and publicity, that are difficult for individual creators to manage on their own.[63] At the same time, however, digitization has made it less expensive for creators to produce and distribute their works. As a result, an increasing number of artists have taken advantage of this freedom to bypass traditional gatekeepers and deal directly with their fans, who now function as financiers as well as customers. To take only a few well-known examples, American musician Amanda Palmer shocked even herself when she was able to raise over $US 1 million online via the Kickstarter "crowd-funding" website.[64] Also using Kickstarter, Toronto author Ryan North raised over $500,000 to produce a choose-your-own-adventure version of Shakespeare's *Hamlet*.[65] Canadian rock superstars Metric play stadiums across Canada, but their last two albums have been distributed and promoted by the band without them being on a record label.[66] Meanwhile, New York–based singer-songwriter Jonathan Coulton writes of his career: "I honestly don't believe I could have made this thing happen under the old system. So to me, the internet is everything – it changed my life, it saved me, it continues to sustain me today."[67]

This disintermediation has led to a growing realization among creators that their copyright interests are different from those of the content industries. For example, chapter 7 describes the creation of an artists' group, the Canadian Music Creators Coalition, which has articulated a separate position from the recording industry, calling for the recognition of user rights and a truly artist-centred policy; similarly, in the United States, the Future of Music Coalition (futureofmusic.org) is articulating artist-centric policy views, including on copyright. As the digital economy advances, such groups have risen in significance.

While creators' groups are directly affected by much in the Internet treaties (the WPPT was designed explicitly to extend rights to performers and phonogram producers, for example), they are less directly affected by the most controversial part of the treaties, dealing with TPMs. Neither were they much involved in the debate over ISP liability. Copyright is still very much commercial law and therefore the purview of industry interests. This was the case with respect to TPMs and ISP liability, which primarily involved the content industries and ISPs, and other large institutional interests.

"User" Groups

Against those individuals and groups that create and distribute creative works are all those who make use of these works. This is a tricky and somewhat misleading category, as even creators and publishers (e.g., movie studios) rely on existing works in order to create new works, though they differ in their ability to (re-)use these works.[68] "User interests" is a label that encompasses many different types of individuals and groups, with potentially different objectives and priorities. That said, they tend to favour broader access to copyrighted works, in contrast to the absolute control sought by the content industries and some creators groups.

Two of the most obvious "user" groups are individual consumers and non-commercial creators. For consumers, copyright can restrict their access and use of creative works. To the extent that copyright acts as an incentive to create (a questionable assumption as we have already seen), consumers benefit from the products whose creation copyright incentivizes. As well, copyright can interfere with individuals' ability to exercise free-speech rights, to the extent that copyright regulates consumers' behaviour (via its prohibition on unauthorized production and distribution of copies).[69]

Users' claims on creative works can also be discussed in terms of access to culture. In Mexico, copyright is seen as a way to promote and protect the national culture, as an author's human right. Alongside this authorial right, however – less-emphasized, but still there – is a citizen's right to be able to access this culture. In other words, Mexican citizens, in theory at least, have the right to access their culture. When strong copyright threatens this access, this right can be used to counter claims for stronger copyright protection made by authors or intermediaries.

Despite the stake consumers (and citizens) have in copyright, citizens and consumers have been historically excluded from the formulation of copyright policy, largely because they had not shown any interest in the issue. Until the late 1990s, copyright law reflected a balance between large corporate and institutional interests. Even "fair use"-type provisions that seem to reflect a general public interest in the ability to access works have been supported in large part by industry groups such as the consumer-electronics industry,[70] whose interests did not coincide with the control-maximization objectives of the content industries. Until the WIPO Internet treaties, and especially thereafter, this group was not represented directly in the copyright debate.

With respect to developing countries, the early 2000s witnessed a growing awareness within civil society of the importance of copyright policy. Academics such as Alan Story, for example, argue that the current international copyright regimes, centred on the Berne Convention, have disadvantaged citizens in the developing world. In an influential 2003 article, Story argues that "copyright definitely creates a further barrier to access … and the global inequality in the private property rights of copyright further reinforces and, indeed, is one source of global inequality and unequal opportunity more generally." As a result, he concludes, "the *Berne Convention* should be repealed as it does not and, in fact, cannot serve the interests of more than three-quarters of the world's population."[71] The "Access to Knowledge" (A2K) movement emerged at about the same time.[72] This transnational movement "takes concerns with copyright law and other regulations that affect knowledge and places them within an understandable social need and policy platform: access to knowledge goods." The movement is linked in part with longer-standing campaigns to provide affordable drugs to people in developing countries (a patent-related issue).[73] The movement's main objectives, according to a 2005 A2K draft treaty created by a coalition of non-governmental organizations, academics, and activists, and spearheaded by the movement's flagship group, the US-based Knowledge Ecology International, "are to protect and enhance [expand] access to knowledge, and to facilitate the transfer of technology to developing countries."[74] As well, 2004 saw the establishment of the Copysouth Research Group, "a loosely-affiliated group of researchers" based in a number of countries across the South and the North who were interested in conducting research to expose the inner workings of the international copyright system and its largely negative effects on the global South. The work of A2K, Copysouth, and scholars like Story form the backdrop for the latter part of the larger Mexican copyright debate as it relates to rising interest in copyright's effect on economic development and user rights.

INDIVIDUALS AND DIGITIZATION: CUSTOMERS AS COMPETITORS
One of the themes of this book is the way that digital technologies have given individuals both a greater stake in the copyright debate as well

as the means to become involved to a greater degree. The threat posed to the creative industries by digital technologies comes not just from what these technologies can do – easy reproduction and redistribution of anything that can be digitized – but also from *who* is using these technologies. Individuals now have a stake in copyright issues for two reasons. First, digitization has made it relatively simple for individuals to create new works out of existing copyrighted works.[75] These can run from the mundane – a YouTube video of a birthday party in which a Prince song plays in the background – to the sublime – the music of Girl Talk, a New Jersey musician who combines identifiable bits of popular (and copyrighted) songs to create something completely new. Digital technologies have lowered the bar to creation, bringing more and more people into contact with copyright law, which regulates creative production.

Even more important, anyone with a computer and access to the Internet can now be a publisher and distributor. This is the revolutionary fact that lies at the heart of the content industries' crisis. For the first time in history, publishers and distributors are facing competition from their *customers*. Much of this competition is non-commercial – individual uploaders do not make money by making digital works available on peer-to-peer networks – but even this non-commercial sharing affects existing business models.

As a result, what was originally a commercial law designed by lawyers for lawyers now directly affects individuals in ways that would have been inconceivable even twenty years ago because computers, which are now ubiquitous in society, work by making copies. Copyright law was meant to settle commercial disputes, not to target end-users.[76] When copyright suits were targeted mainly against businesses and institutions, the fact that copyright laws are arcane, complex, and internally inconsistent was not that great a problem.[77] It becomes a problem when the law is used to sue individuals, who must then defend themselves against deep-pocketed businesses and industry groups.

As the three North American examples illustrate, individuals reacting to these lawsuits and technologically based attempts to limit existing rights under copyright law through industry's expansive use of TPMs has led more and more people to become interested and involved in copyright policymaking. The Recording Industry Association of America's (RIAA) aggressive pursuit of file sharers in court has largely been a public-relations disaster, most famously, their pyrrhic victory over "the single mother of two who makes $36,000 a year [who] was ordered by a jury ... to pay the ... RIAA $220,000."[78] It also does not seem to have worked out financially: CD sales continue to slide, and even the settlements the RIAA has been awarded by the courts have been dwarfed by their legal costs.[79]

The public's negative perception of TPMs, meanwhile, can likely be traced to the 2005 "Sony Rootkit" debacle, discussed in the introduction. Alongside the negative publicity the music industry received for its strategy of suing customers for hundreds of thousands of dollars for unauthorized uploads of copyrighted songs,[80] this event was one of the first instances of widespread public attention to digital-copyright issues, foreshadowing the larger political battles to come.

This direct involvement of the public fundamentally changes the dynamics of copyright negotiations. It is relatively straightforward to sit a dozen industry representatives at a table and hammer out a copyright law. How do you involve millions of individuals in this process? As they are now directly affected by copyright law, both through lawsuits brought against individuals for infringing activity and because copyright law limits their ability to create and distribute digital works, the "broader public" has begun to demand to be heard in a debate traditionally dominated by authors, publishers, and other institutional interests.[81] With individual consumers in the picture, more points of view must be accommodated, at the cost (for politicians) of potential electoral defeat. On the upside, this rising consumer interest has the potential to inject into copyright negotiations a greater recognition of the general societal effects of copyright. Copyright has always affected society at large, but concern for it tended to be neglected when copyright was viewed primarily as a commercial law.

Greater public interest in copyright also requires greater attention to the issue of copyright's limitations and exceptions. In short: are users equal partners with copyright owners, or are policies such as fair use merely exceptions carved out of a creator's (or, rather, copyright owner's) property right? The main copyright treaties take the former view, enshrining various limitations and exceptions and thus acknowledging their legitimacy. From this perspective,

> uncontrolled, non-commercial use had obvious social utility and gradually developed justifying political rationales. Tolerance for these secondary forms of distribution and use, especially in educational contexts, found a home within traditions of republican political thought that viewed the circulation of information and ideas as a positive social good – indeed, as a prerequisite of democratic culture.[82]

Proponents of stronger copyright – including the content industries and some creator groups – argue that these private rights and exceptions were previously seen as existing in an unregulatable area "where copyright law abdicated its authority by nature."[83] However, now that perfect enforcement is potentially possible, proponents of strong copyright argue that this balance should be eliminated.[84]

In sum, how one feels about digital technology's simplification of the process of creation, copying, and distribution tends to depend on one's particular interests. For the large corporate interests that control most copyrights and whose business models are built on a copy-distribution model, this is unequivocally bad news (absent any decision to pursue a new business model): "These developments look more like the disintegration of culture – their culture – than like cultural democratization."[85] It also hurts top-selling artists – the only ones who make significant amounts from royalties. For other artists, as for the public at large, the digital picture is much brighter.

INTERNET SERVICE PROVIDERS AND OTHER LARGE "USER" GROUPS
Traditionally, the user/dissemination side of the copyright debate has been represented by large institutional interests, such as research libraries, broadcasters, consumer-electronics manufacturers, and, since the popularization of the Internet, telecommunications companies, information-technology (IT) firms, and companies such as Google that make their money by providing access to information, including copyrighted works. In contrast to the content industries, the IT sector, most notably personal computer manufacturers and ISPs, emphasize speed and storage capacity, and have "privileged relatively open technical architectures that, over time, facilitated the transformation of the architectures themselves."[86] The sector's general interest is in maximizing their freedom to create products and services to sell to consumers; in other words, they wish to minimize rights in copyright that would require them to undertake measures that would limit interoperability or the functionality of their products.

Unlike relatively resource-poor user groups such as research libraries, user interests such as broadcasters, manufacturers, and telecommunications companies are often significant copyright actors, domestically and internationally. These large commercial user groups differ from their content-industry counterparts in two ways. First, unlike content-industry firms, which have been dealing with copyright law for decades, many of these commercial-user firms, such as the telecommunications companies and Internet businesses, are relatively new to copyright issues and have faced a learning curve on this issue. These newcomers must also deal with the entrenched positions of the content industries. Second, while the content industries have the luxury of focusing almost exclusively on copyright issues, for many commercial users copyright is only one among a series of policy issues that affect their bottom line. Furthermore, vertical integration has also complicated the position of many corporations: Sony, for example, sells content as well as the consumer electronics that play this content. As a result, such companies may be divided against themselves on specific issues.

The digital age has brought telecommunications and Internet-based companies into direct contact with copyright law. ISPs and online hosting companies allow users to transmit or store copyrighted materials on their networks. When a file is sent over the Internet from one user to another, servers make copies of the file in the process of transmitting it to the end user. ISPs also host materials on behalf of their users (e.g., hosting a website). In both cases, copies are being made as a function of how the Internet works. Under copyright law, these intermediaries potentially face a legal problem regarding "the extent to which firms might be liable for their customers' behaviour and what obligations if any they have in respect of infringing content hosted on or transmitted through their networks."[87] Against this policing problem is the question of how to reconcile the conflicts between copyright law and a socially beneficial system that exists by creating copies in a manner consistent with copyright law, as well as other concerns, such as the privacy rights of individuals.

The main question facing ISPs and Internet companies like Google concerns their liability: how should the companies that provide the "tubes" of the Internet be treated? On the first point – copies made as a consequence of the regular functioning of the Internet – ISPs could be made liable for each copy, or they could receive some sort of dispensation. On the second – how to treat the hosting of unauthorized works by someone else over an ISP or on a website like YouTube – there exist several options, from full liability to no liability, or liability conditional on the company meeting various conditions. This point raises the issue of the extent to which they are, or should be, responsible for the use made of their systems by their clients. To use an analogue analogy, should a telephone company like AT&T be held liable for two people using their telephone system to plan a murder? In the end, this is a political question.

State Interests

The state plays a crucial role in mediating among the various interests affected by copyright. A state's rules and institutions influence the shape of its copyright policy and the interpretation of its international obligations. From a regional and global perspective, the state is acted upon by various interests, as well as being an actor in its own right. As actors, state representatives conclude treaties with representatives of other states; they can also insert themselves into other states' domestic debates. A state's copyright regime is socially constructed by actors working within a domestic, regional, and international set of institutions, treaties, and norms. Some states are more powerful than others; for example, institutional and ideational changes in the United States are more consequential globally than changes in other states because of its place at the heart of the international political economy.[88]

Whether a state favours "strong" or "weak" copyright (and IP generally) depends on several factors. Fink and Maskus argue that a state's position on copyright and IP is a function of its economic structure and IP/copyright export position. The domestic corollary to this argument is that the more important the content industry is to the domestic economy, the louder the voices will be for strong copyright protection.[89] Much as free trade historically has been promoted by developed countries and resisted by developing countries,[90] strong copyright laws benefit disproportionately copyright owners, who happen to live mainly in developed countries, which themselves benefited from weak IP laws when they were developing. Now-"developed" countries like the United States may have industrialized through the free appropriation of other countries' "intellectual property,"[91] but TRIPS makes it impossible for today's developing countries to take the same path.[92] Drahos and Braithwaite call copyright "the invisible but effective servant of Western colonial power," allowing publishers, for example, to keep the price of books – including textbooks – high for newly liberated colonies.[93] Those with a vibrant copyright sector – typically the most developed countries – will experience a net inflow of royalties from stronger international copyright laws, while net copyright importers – typically, developing and some developed countries, like Canada and Mexico – will experience an outflow of royalties.

Specifically, Maskus argues that there are four types of countries, each with conflicting interests in IP rules:

First, IP exporters are net producers and sellers of intellectual property, with a consequent interest in strong international rights. Second, high-income IP importers are net purchasers of intellectual property but their industries require access to sophisticated technological inputs and their consumers prefer high-quality, differentiated products. Thus, they generally favour strong protection but are more amenable to limits on that protection. Third, IP followers are industrializing economies that need access to modern technology but prefer that such access be inexpensive. Such countries have mixed interests between protection standards to encourage incoming investment and technology flows and weak standards to promote imitation and learning. Finally, low-income IP importers produce little IP domestically and rely on foreign suppliers for new products and technologies. Their interests lie in having weak IPRs.[94]

This characterization accords with economist Deepak Lall's finding of an inverted-U-shaped relationship between the strength of intellectual-property rights and income levels.[95] IPR intensity falls with rising income, and then rises with a country's increased "innovation effort." The inflection point, at $7750 per capita in 1985 prices, however, is quite high. Lall's finding that poorer countries actually benefit from lax copyright laws is further supported by the historical evidence that "many of today's economic leader countries were themselves 'knowledge pirates' in the past, and benefited from being so."[96] While this finding does not allow one to conclude that stronger IP protection *causes* economic growth, it does show that countries act *as if* it does.[97]

While this taxonomy is intuitively appealing, it neglects the extent to which state policy preferences represent not only a state's material situation, but also the outcome of domestic policy debates among decision-makers and interest groups, as well as state representatives' perception of these factors. A state's intellectual-property policy is not determined solely by its level of development, but also by "domestic priorities and the relative strengths of domestic players in the copyright system."[98] Governmental institutions provide a non-neutral context within which policy is made. Their structure (the decision-making process, institutions' perceived clients, and the ability of decision-makers within these institutions to make policy) affects which groups get listened to, how policy is made, and in what way these policies are biased.

As the next chapter elaborates, the United States is certainly a net exporter of IP and copyrighted works and has shown an active interest in promoting strong copyright laws internationally. However, its current strong-copyright advocacy is the outcome of historically specific policy battles. The framing of copyright and IP as a way to help the United States maintain its global economic supremacy was as important to the transformation of the United States into a pro-strong-copyright country as the material situation of its content industries. For example, while important, the US IP industry is dwarfed by the information-technology sector.[99] In other words, US policy on intellectual property cannot be derived simply by looking at a ranking of the economic importance of its domestic industrial sectors.

A similar point can be made about Mexico, a country characterized as a relatively low-income, industrializing economy that, as either the world's first or second most-important producer of Spanish-language works, possesses both a vibrant cultural sector and the perception of itself as a cultural superpower. That almost one-half Mexico's citizens are below the official poverty line and cannot therefore afford full-priced cultural products gives the Mexican government an incentive either to pursue lax copyright laws or allow lax enforcement of the same, since stronger copyright policies raise the price of copyrighted works. However, Mexico's status as a cultural superpower and important exporter of Spanish-language cultural products would lead it to support stronger copyright laws. As chapter 8 discusses, the Mexican government squares this circle by pursuing ever-stronger copyright laws that it then chooses not to enforce consistently.

Canada, finally, is a high-income IP/copyright importer whose copyright policies, detailed in chapter 7, fit the profile of a state that desires "strong protection but with limits." Again, however, this preference outcome is the result of a specific configuration of domestic institutional and interest groups.

Part 3: International Copyright Institutions – Sustaining Copyright, Constraining Change

Domestic copyright laws reflect trade-offs between competing ideas (e.g., economic efficiency and fairness) mediated "through a complex set of national and international agencies and institutions, which are in turn pressured by business interests, the IP professions, varied users of IP, and national governments."[100]

The two main international copyright institutions are WIPO, which is responsible for the Berne Convention, the Internet treaties, and other related treaties, and the WTO, specifically TRIPS. In North America, copyright is covered by NAFTA Chapter 17, which deals with intellectual-property issues. It and TRIPS were created "to establish a (near) uniform legislative arena within which rights holders can enforce their rights." This approach treats cultural products as commodities and is thus more concerned with the rights of manufacturers than of creators.[101] Such treaties "are not technical solutions to emergent problems but are rather manifestations of structural power within the global political economy."[102] As discussed below, the negotiation of TRIPS within the context of the Uruguay Round of the General Agreement on Tariffs and Trade (GATT) talks that led to the creation of the WTO was primarily the result of US pressure on behalf of its content and IP industries.[103]

To these institutions one can add the Office of the United States Trade Representative. Although technically a domestic US institution, the USTR has had an outsized effect on international copyright law. In its trade-treaty making and use of US trade law (notably the Special 301 process) to chastise and sanction countries with poor IP laws and enforcement (from a US perspective), it has forced many countries to change their IP laws to conform to US interests.

The World Intellectual Property Organization (WIPO)[104]

The history of international copyright since the mid-1980s can be understood in part as a political conflict between WIPO and member states (particularly the United States) that believed WIPO was not moving aggressively enough on copyright issues of interest to them, and, since the 1990s, between WIPO and the WTO, with which it competes for influence.

WIPO, headquartered in Geneva, Switzerland, was created in 1967 and came into force in 1970 to "promote the protection of IP throughout the world through cooperation among states and in collaboration with other international organizations."[105] It became a specialized agency of the United Nations in 1974. Its core tasks include the development of international IP laws and standards; the maintenance of fee-based services, including registration of trademarks, designs, and appellations of origins, international patent applications, and various classification systems; promotion of IP for economic development; and promotion of a better understanding of IP.[106] It is also "one of the key forums for discussions and policy development to extend the global governance of intellectual property beyond the minimum standards set by the TRIPS agreement."[107]

THE BERNE AND ROME CONVENTIONS

WIPO, which has over 151 members, is responsible for administering the Berne Convention, along with 23 other treaties. These include the Internet treaties, which are considered to be "special agreements" that fall under the two main international copyright treaties, the Berne and Rome Conventions. The 1886 Berne Convention, which has been revised six times (most recently in 1971), mainly to keep up with technological changes,[108] was designed to eliminate the "increasingly strained patchwork of national legislation" that then governed copyright.[109] Its original membership comprised nine countries; it now includes over 130. It was promoted initially by those popular authors, including Victor Hugo, who stood to benefit the most from international recognition of copyright. With respect to states, Britain and France had the most to gain from an international copyright convention in the late nineteenth century because of the vast output of their artists and the large-scale copying of their works in other countries, compounded by the existing reluctance for countries to give coverage to foreign authors.[110]

The Berne Convention requires that all members have minimum levels of protection with no registration requirements and extend protection to authors from other member countries (national treatment).[111] It also requires that members provide authors with moral rights. The Berne Convention was ratified by Canada in 1928 and Mexico in 1967. The United States only joined the convention in 1989. Its reluctance to join was due in part to a reluctance to acknowledge authors' moral rights and because US law required (in deference to its domestic publishing industry) that books be produced in the United States in order to qualify for copyright. It was also concerned with how Berne would affect the US movie industry. Before 1989, it and other countries, including Mexico, were members of the Universal Copyright Convention under UNESCO, which had fewer requirements than Berne.[112]

The 1961 Rome Convention for the Protection of Performers, Producers of Phonograms and Broadcasting Organizations requires that signatories provide "neighbouring rights" to performers, phonogram producers, and broadcasters, alongside approved limitations and exceptions to these rights. The two treaties attempt to balance creators' rights with overall social needs, recognizing "the need to provide for the rights of users to access copyright works in the form of allowable limitations and exceptions and [allow] latitude on the part of domestic policy-makers to enact copyright laws to suit their particular national interests."[113] Canada joined the Rome Convention in 1998, Mexico in 1964; the United States is not a member.

SOURCE OF POWER AND POLITICAL ISSUES

WIPO is unusual among UN agencies in that it does not depend much on state funding, primarily as a result of the fees it receives for administering the Patent Cooperation Treaty,[114] which grants it a degree of independence. Until recently, WIPO was viewed, and characterized itself, as "a technical organization" concerned primarily with "the refinement of the relevant international treaties and establishment of better cross-border enforcement of rights."[115] However, starting with the 1996 Internet treaties and continuing today, it is increasingly seen as "a highly politicized organization" that promotes a particular view of knowledge and intellectual-property rights.[116] "The notion that the WIPO is an organization centrally concerned with socialization is not merely an analysis made by critics, but rather was seen by its long-serving Director General (Arpad Bogsch) as a key element in the organization's mission and activities."[117]

Much of WIPO's political clout comes from its employees' experience and expertise, which have allowed it to maintain its standing as the pre-eminent IP and copyright international organization.[118] Nonetheless, in the 1980s and 1990s it faced a challenge from key members, particularly the United States but also the European Union, which were frustrated by its perceived "inability to change IP policy in the global economy, especially regarding copyright enforcement issues in developing countries."[119] This frustration led the United States in particular to engage in "forum shopping," moving IP issues into the GATT talks that led to the 1995 signing of the TRIPS agreement.

Since the signing of the TRIPS, WIPO has "fought to maintain its position during a period of forum proliferation."[120] The WIPO Internet treaties were a direct result of this battle for relevance, as the next chapter outlines in detail. Concerns about WIPO's relevance remain: the negotiations for an Anti-Counterfeiting Trade Agreement, which covers copyright as well as trademark and patent issues, was concluded in December 2010 by a plurilateral group of states, led by the United States, outside the WIPO *and* the WTO.[121]

The United States Trade Representative and Special 301

Given the importance of domestic US institutions in shaping international copyright law, US institutions can be considered as at least quasi-international.[122] The main agency responsible for international copyright issues is the Office of the USTR. This cabinet-level position (since 1974) is responsible for negotiating trade agreements and coordinating the Special 301 process (discussed below), a congressionally mandated annual review in which American trading partners' intellectual property legislation and enforcement are assessed and those countries whose legislation, policies, and enforcement processes are not up to American standards are placed on various watch lists, each with different consequences. The State Department also represents to other countries American concerns about their IP regimes and places the United States' international IP strategy within the broader context of US interests. Congress, for its part, plays somewhat of an international role, through inter-parliamentary delegations, which sometimes raise IP issues of concern to United States in their meetings with parliamentarians from other countries. It also uses caucuses like the Congressional Anti-Piracy Caucus, to express concern about other countries' protection (or lack thereof) of American intellectual property.

THE CONSTRUCTION OF THE US COPYRIGHT POSITION[123]

Historical institutionalism, as developed in chapter 2, argues that policy and institutional change can occur through the exploitation by interested actors of internal policy or institutional contradictions, or through exogenous shocks that actors can harness to their own needs. The history of US copyright bears this out. Although the current US position on international copyright is "without a doubt"[124] characterized by support for strong copyright protection, this position emerged only relatively recently. Until about 1982, US domestic enforcement of intellectual property was relatively lax.[125] The dramatic turnabout in US policy resulted in the TRIPS, a maximalist interpretation of the WIPO Internet treaties, and the US 1998 Digital Millennium Copyright Act. This change was the result of the increased economic importance of the copyright and so-called knowledge industries,[126] as well as a concerted effort by a group of these industries to link IP and US trade policy and place strong IP protection at the heart of US trade policy.

The success of these companies in placing their particular view at the heart of the US view on copyright involved movement on two fronts. In the one instance, it required promoting internal, incremental change that exploited copyright's protection/dissemination tension. It also involved successfully harnessing exogenous shocks and engaging in bricolage, rebalancing the protection/dissemination dichotomy and linking trade and IP policy, driven by a general malaise about the declining global dominance of the US economy. There is nothing inherent in IP itself that makes it a trade issue: many issues that affect trade are not covered by the WTO, notably labour and environmental standards. Rather, the trade-copyright (and IP) linkage was politically constructed over the course of a decade through intense lobbying by IP industries. Drahos and Braithwaite date the linkage of trade and IP in the United States to US Trade Act of 1974, which included an amendment linking trade to intellectual property.[127] The United States, spurred by its trademark industries, also unsuccessfully tried to introduce a code on trade in counterfeit goods during the GATT's Tokyo Round (1973–9).[128]

The IP industries were more successful in the early 1980s, when the copyright, patent, and semiconductor industries successfully linked their concerns about the international lack of IP enforcement and adequate IP law to concerns that American economic hegemony was being threatened by upstart countries, in particular by those in Asia. The content and IP industries successfully linked American concerns about the potential loss of American economic predominance to a push for stronger IP protection by arguing that protection of American intellectual property abroad (IP sectors being one of the only ones to post consistent current-account surpluses) would support a key sector of American global competitiveness. To do so, they relied on a discursive strategy that blamed US trade problems on the actions of outsiders, specifically "foreign 'pirates,'" instead of on domestic firms' bad choices, framed intellectual property as consisting of "property rights," instead of "grants of privilege" or of consisting of a balance between users' and creators' rights, and presented their preference for stronger IP protection as the solution.[129] In this view, "the relative (and sometimes absolute) lack of effective intellectual property protection in overseas markets" became "a trade-related issue *and* a problem for the U.S. economy that the government ought to respond to."[130]

This view was first popularly articulated in a 9 July 1982 op-ed article by Barry MacTaggart, chair and president of Pfizer International, in the *New York Times*. In his article, "Stealing from the Mind," he alleged that countries like Brazil, Canada, Mexico, India, Taiwan, South Korea, Italy, and Spain had laws that allowed "U.S. inventions to be 'legally' taken."[131]

The content and IP industries also worked to influence the main US trade policy institutions. Working through the Advisory Committee on Trade Negotiations, "a pipeline for U.S. business to the U.S. Executive on trade issues,"[132] these industries worked in the run-up to the GATT Uruguay Round to ensure that the US negotiating position would be "No IP, no trade round." Key to this process, which would culminate in the TRIPS and, indirectly, NAFTA, was the twelve-member ad hoc Intellectual Property Committee, representing the pharmaceutical, entertainment, and software industries, as the central player in this change and the creation of the TRIPS.[133] Corroborating this view, Drahos and Braithwaite cite "a senior U.S. trade negotiator," who told them that probably fewer than fifty people were responsible for TRIPS.[134]

ECONOMIC BASIS FOR US IP POLICY

To be sure, their success was not based merely on words. While politics played a role in linking copyright and trade, US support for stronger global copyright rules is based on economic fact. The United States does have a competitive advantage in IP products. During an era in which the United States has run persistent current-account deficits, it enjoyed a US$84 billion surplus in "royalties and licence fees" (which includes both copyright and patent royalties) in 2011. This surplus is second only to "other private services," which includes items such as business, professional, and technical services, insurance services, and financial services (see table 3.1). In 2009, according to World Bank data, the United States accounted for over 40 per cent of all global royalties and licence fees, compared with 3 per cent for Canada, and 0.6 per cent for Mexico (see table 3.2). It is also interesting to note that the top ten royalties-receiving countries account for 97 per cent of all royalties revenues, and all but one – Mexico – were developed countries.

The US IP advantage becomes even more obvious if one considers global production in terms of "value chains," rather than in terms of cross-border trade. As Drahos points out, intellectual-property rights allow most of an information-technology product's value to be captured not by the low-cost manufacturing country, but by the company (usually Western, often in the United States) that owns the IP rights. Drahos notes: "The true benefits to the US of having, at least for the time being, multinationals located within its borders with high levels of ownership of patents and other intellectual property rights, especially trademarks, are very likely to be greater than suggested by trade data that is confined to payments for technology goods by one country to another."[135]

In the simplest accounts, the US bias towards protection is a direct result of the economic strength of its content industries.[136] Certainly, royalties and licensing have become an increasingly important source

Table 3.1. Service exports, United States, seasonally adjusted, 2011

Sector	Exports	Imports ($ million)	Balance	Share of service exports (%)
Travel	116,115	78,651	37,464	19.2
Passenger fares	36,631	31,109	5,522	6.0
Other transportation	43,064	54,711	−11,647	7.1
Royalties and licence fees	120,836	36,620	84,216	19.9
Other private services	270,193	191,973	78,220	44.6
Transfers under US military sales contracts	17,946	29,510	−11,564	3.0
US government misc. services	1,176	4,854	−3,678	0.2
Total	605,961	427,428	178,533	100.0

Source: US Census Bureau, FT-900, *US International Trade in Goods and Services –* Annual revision for 2008, 10 June 2008. http://www.census.gov/foreign-trade/ Press-Release/2008pr/final_revisions/.

Table 3.2. Royalties and licence fees, top 15 exporting countries, 2009

Rank	Exporters	Value ($ billion)	Share in 15 economies (%)	Global share (%)
1	**United States**	**90**	**41.9**	**40.9**
2	European Union (27)	77	35.9	35.0
	Extra-EU (27) exports	37	17.3	16.8
3	Japan	22	10.1	10.0
4	Switzerland	16	7.3	7.3
5	**Canada**	**3**	**1.6**	**1.4**
6	Korea, Republic of	3	1.5	1.4
7	Singapore	1	0.6	0.5
8	Israel	0.8	0.4	0.4
9	Australia	0.7	0.3	0.3
10	**Mexico**	**0.6**	**0.3**	**0.3**
	Top 10	214	100.0	97.3
	Remainder	6		3.9
	Total, world	**220**		**100.0**

Source: World Trade Organization, International Trade Statistics 2011, http://www.wto.org/ english/res_e/statis_e/its2011_e/its11_trade_category_e.htm, table 3.31 and author's calculations.

Table 3.3. Trade balance, United States, 2011 ($ million)

	Exports	Imports	Balance
Goods	1,497,406	2,235,819	−738,413
Services	605,961	427,428	178,533
Total	2,103,367	2,663,247	−559,880

Source: US Census Bureau, Historical trade statistics, Balance of payments basis; http://www.census.gov/foreign-trade/statistics/historical/gands.pdf.

of export growth over the past decade. With overall exports totalling $US2.1 trillion in 2011 (see table 3.3), royalties and licensing, at $121 billion, represented a significant 19.9 per cent of total US service exports and 5.7 per cent of total US exports. Royalties and licensing rose a remarkable 45 per cent since 2006. However, their dominance of the US trade agenda cannot be explained solely in reference to its economic importance. In the period covered by this book, other export categories have been just as important as royalties. In 2006, exports of telecommunications equipment, computers, and computer accessories, taken together, totalled $US74.8 billion,[137] $US4 billion more than patent and copyright royalties combined in that year. Absent political lobbying – the crucial factor determining US government support for stronger copyright – the content industries' contribution to the US bottom line may not be enough to justify the one-sided pursuit of an agenda (stronger copyright) that disadvantages other American companies and interests – some of which, like Google, may have more upside potential than legacy media companies like Disney.[138]

SECTION 301 AND SPECIAL 301

This framing of stronger international copyright and intellectual-property protection as a fundamental US trade concern culminated in amendments in 1984 and 1988 that allowed the US government and IP industries to publicize and punish countries with IP laws that they felt were unfair. In 1984, the Trade and Tariff Act, which amended the Trade Act, amended the US General System of Preferences (GSP), which provided preferential access to goods and services from developing countries. The amendment required that the president factor in the potential GSP recipient country's IP laws when deciding on its eligibility for GSP benefits.[139] In 1987, the United States denied Mexico GSP benefits for its failure to offer protection to pharmaceutical products. Mexico refused to comply with US pressure, as it "had long held that the availability of affordable pharmaceuticals was a matter of the public interest."[140] This refusal to comply with US wishes offers an interesting contrast to the Mexican willingness to rewrite its copyright laws in order to conclude NAFTA. Mexico's actions on pharmaceuticals demonstrate that domestic contexts matter and that raw economic power does not always carry the day.

Congress also amended section 301 of the Trade Act in 1984. Section 301 allows the president to withdraw trade benefits or impose tariffs on goods from countries deemed to have unfair trade laws. The 1984 changes extended the areas examined for unfair trading practices to partners' IP laws. Investigations could be initiated by industry or be "self-initiated" by the USTR.[141] These reforms were strongly influenced by the content industries. Drahos and Braithwaite report that a Washington lobbyist told them: "It was the Motion Picture Association that introduced an amendment to the Bill." The first IP use of section 301, which had been based on language in a 1982 trade agreement with the Caribbean Basin, was to force Japan to protect software with copyright rather than a sui generis form of protection.[142]

Today, the most visible means by which the United States attempts to influence foreign copyright laws, including those of Canada and Mexico, comes from an amendment to section 301 that created the "Special 301 process." Passed in 1988 as part of the Omnibus Trade and Competitiveness Act, Special 301 requires that the USTR annually "identify each year those foreign countries that deny adequate and effective protection for IP rights or that deny fair and equitable market access to persons who rely on protection of IP"[143] – that is, whether their laws meet US approval, not whether they conform to international standards. In practice, each year, the USTR asks for and receives submissions from industry groups and other interested parties regarding their experiences with other countries' IP laws.

Based on these submissions and their own analyses, those countries that the USTR determines to have IP laws and policies that are not favourable to US companies and products or are not working in good faith to improve their IP policies are placed either on a "Watch List" or the more serious "Priority Watch List." The latter is reserved for those "most onerous or egregious acts, policies, or practices and whose acts, policies, or practices have the greatest adverse impact (actual or potential) on the relevant U.S. products."[144]

Though focused outward, the annual Special 301 exercise is as much about forcing the US government to articulate a coherent IP policy and to keep IP protection at the forefront of US trade policy. Internationally, it is a way of reminding countries and their governments about US IP and copyright views. The weight given by other countries to the Special 301 process varies, from those that use it as an excuse to push through domestically unpopular IP reforms to those that ignore it completely. This process generally no longer serves as it did before the WTO as a prelude to sanctions against targeted countries, as all actions arising out of the Section 301 process now result in a complaint being filed at the WTO. Exceptions include issues that do not fall within the WTO's mandate, or when the United States is dealing with a non-member of the WTO or one that prefers bilateral negotiations.[145] For North American cases, the United States could use NAFTA's Chapter 20 dispute-resolution process, though no copyright cases have yet been brought under this chapter. As Nafziger remarks, this process is intergovernmental (requiring that an aggrieved party convince their government to file a challenge) and, thus, highly political.[146]

Neither the Special 301 process nor the agency that administers it, the USTR, is neutral. The resources needed to file complaints tilt the field towards the content and IP industries. Drahos and Braithwaite document the tight links between the USTR and the IIPA. A relatively small office, "the USTR came to rely heavily on the figures on piracy provided to it by U.S. companies and business organizations like the IIPA."[147] Given the size of the process, which involves grading more than seventy countries annually, Special 301 "is only really possible because corporate America picks up the tab. It provides the global surveillance network, the numbers for the estimates on piracy and much of the evaluation and analysis. The U.S. state, in return, provides the legitimacy, the bureaucracy that negotiates, threatens and if necessary carries out enforcement actions."[148] It also benefits from the heft given to its recommendations by its association with these powerful corporations. Trade negotiators could look forward to jobs working for corporations that need trade/IP experience.[149] Nonetheless, according to the Assistant USTR for Intellectual Property and Innovation in a 2008 interview, the USTR currently has sufficient resources to make its own independent conclusions.[150]

With such tight linkages and data being supplied by companies facing "no real downside to overestimating the size of the problem,"[151] the

Special 301 process reflects the content industries' view of copyright. This is likely at least partly the result of the composition of groups that have traditionally taken part in the Special 301 consultations. Dominated by content industry groups like the IIPA, those with a different perspective on copyright, such as Google, and the various US-based public-interest groups concerned with copyright and access issues, have only recently become involved in the process.

For example, in 2010 the Computer & Communications Industry Association (CCIA) participated for the first time, filing a brief that recommended a step away from maximalist copyright: "'stronger' is not necessarily better or more effective."[152] As well, US public-interest groups like Public Knowledge unsurprisingly are more concerned with domestic issues (their resource constraints are likely also tighter than those faced by the content industries, though they have started to participate in the Special 301 process).[153] Thus, aside from foreign governments (who are invited to participate in the process), consumer/public interests have tended not to be strongly involved in the Special 301 process.

The result has been a process that is remarkably indiscriminate in identifying countries that do not meet US standards. In 2010, 11 countries, including Canada, were placed by the USTR on the Priority Watch List;[154] these were joined by 29 other countries on the Watch List, including Mexico.[155] Overall, in 2010 over half of the 77 countries that the USTR examined had IP laws with which the US was dissatisfied.

The Agreement on Trade-Related Aspects of Intellectual Property Rights (TRIPS)

The TRIPS agreement, which came into being through the Uruguay Round of trade talks (1986–94) as part of the package that begat the World Trade Organization, represents the global "floor" in intellectual-property rights. Since adherence to TRIPS is required of all WTO members, it established a global common baseline for IPR protection, and thus constitutes the background conditions under which the WIPO Internet treaties were negotiated and are being implemented.

The negotiation of what became the TRIPS was part of a coordinated push for stronger international IP protection by the United States and several US IP industries, as detailed above. TRIPS was the price demanded by the United States for the creation of World Trade Organization and a deal on agriculture desired by developing countries.[156] The TRIPS agreement represented the culmination of an American business and state strategy linking effective copyright/IP enforcement by other countries to American trade preferences (through section 301 and Special 301 of the US Trade Act) and the successful completion of the Uruguay round of GATT talks that culminated with the creation of the WTO:

> The insertion of "trade-related" intellectual property rights into the Uruguay Round agenda and the subsequent adoption of an agreed text for an intellectual property agreement could not have been achieved without the effective lobbying activities in the USA of legal and policy activists and corporations, and a government and political establishment that, during the 1980s, was especially receptive to the diagnoses and prescriptions propounded by these individuals, firms and business associations.[157]

TRIPS was a US-led agreement: "It is widely accepted that the US made virtually no concessions in the Uruguay Round negotiations of GATT and imposed upon the world not only the economic interests of its own IP-based industries ... but a degree of protectionism that is economically and culturally destructive to developing countries."[158] Despite the United States' strong position, some countries, such as Brazil and India, opposed greater intellectual property protection on the grounds that it would restrict the flow of advanced technology needed to address social issues.[159]

Drahos and Braithwaite argue that the agreement passed because, for the most part, other countries did not yet understand the central role that IP was beginning to play in the global economy: countries "did not have a clear understanding of their own interests and were not in the room when the important technical details were settled." Technical information and expertise was concentrated in the United States. Even a developed country like Australia negotiated counter to its objective interests: the more-concentrated Australian IP industries out-lobbied their more diffuse opponents, such as consumers and public health agencies, who "generally did not even recognize their interests until after the horse had bolted."[160]

TRIPS "constitutes the most significant strengthening ever of global norms in the intellectual property area. Enforcement of TRIPS obligations amounts to a marked movement toward international harmonization of standards and a definite solidification of the international regime."[161] For the content industries, it represented "a U.S.-led [with support from the European Union] attempt to globalize intellectual property protection through the formation of a common IP regime" that moved copyright and IP to the centre of the global political economy.[162] TRIPS extended property rights and required high levels of protection, effectively narrowing states' and firms' IP options; it was "a significant victory for U.S. private sector activists from knowledge-based industries."[163]

Unlike WIPO agreements and treaties, TRIPS is backed by the WTO's dispute-settlement body, which "makes it possible for net copyright exporters (such as the UK and U.S.) to impose cross-sectional trade sanctions on those countries which fail to enforce copyright protection (over the last 10 years various countries – such as Ukraine, India and China – have been threatened with such action)."[164] TRIPS also has reach: accession to the WTO – which currently stands at 153 members and 30 observers[165] – requires accession to TRIPS as a "single undertaking." Given its reach, scope, and strength, TRIPS has become the main treaty governing copyright and intellectual property generally.

TRIPS delivered stronger global rights to copyright owners, including a minimum fifty-year term of protection, the protection of computer programs and databases as literary works, requirements for rental rights for computer programs, audio recordings, and, "to a limited extent, cinematographic films," as well as neighbouring-rights protection for phonogram producers and performers. It also requires "civil, criminal measures and border enforcement."[166] Crucially, it does not cover moral rights, at the request of the United States and its motion-picture industry.[167]

While TRIPS continues to support the concept of limitations in the rights enjoyed by copyright owners, it also limits significantly the conditions under which countries can limit copyright owners' rights. TRIPS Article 13 expands the Berne Convention's "three-step test" by limiting exceptions to copyright owners' rights "to certain special cases which do not conflict with a normal exploitation of the work and do not unreasonably prejudice the legitimate interests of the right holder." Although the interpretation of Article 13 is evolving, "the three-step test does not undermine the discretion enjoyed by national legislatures to enact limitations and exceptions so long as they remain consistent with the *Berne Convention* and conform to the objectives the test was formulated to achieve";[168] consequently, it continues to recognize the view of copyright as a balance among competing policy objectives.

From a governance perspective, TRIPS suffers from a significant flaw: it contains no mechanisms for implementing future changes short of opening up the whole agreement. Since copyright law historically has not dealt well with the regular exogenous shocks to which it has been subjected, the significance of this flaw is obvious. TRIPS may be institutionally strong in the sense of defending the status quo embodied in the agreement, but, dynamically speaking, it is quite weak: it is very hard to reform TRIPS directly, in any direction. The collapse of the 1999 WTO talks in Seattle and the subsequent failure of the Doha Development Round are a testament to this fact. As a result, it is not a useful forum for actors wishing to promote future international copyright treaties.

North American Copyright Governance:
The North American Free Trade Agreement

In addition to these international treaties and organizations, copyright is a key component in modern trade and economic agreements. Canada, Mexico, and the United States, on their own, have negotiated bilateral and plurilateral trade agreements with several other countries. Each of these treaties imposes obligations and privileges on their signatories. Of these, the most significant, in terms of effect on the three countries' domestic copyright policies, is the 1994 North American Free Trade Agreement.

The effect of NAFTA on copyright policymaking in the three countries offers a good example of how trade agreements interact with domestic policy regimes. While NAFTA provides the formal regional institutionalization of the North American economy, including copyright, its significance to North American copyright governance is only partly related to its actual copyright provisions. Although the United States had been actively linking intellectual property to trade since the 1980s, NAFTA was "the first regional trade agreement to expressly entrench intellectual property (IP) standards."[169] The United States saw NAFTA as a way to push forward talks on what would become the TRIPS agreement, and as a "fallback position – albeit with respect to Canada and Mexico" – should its other initiatives fail,[170] its copyright-related articles largely parallel the TRIPS.

As discussed in chapter 2, change can occur when purposeful actors link issues and subjects. Chapter 17, NAFTA's copyright (and IP) chapter, is no exception to this observation, especially as it relates to Mexico. The United States has been most successful in convincing other countries to reform their copyright laws when it offers increased access to its market or threatens to remove preferential market access. In this case, the NAFTA negotiations offered the United States an opening to pursue copyright reform in its neighbours, particularly Mexico. As with TRIPS, the United States used the promise of market access during the NAFTA negotiations to exact concessions on copyright, primarily from Mexico. Before NAFTA and the subsequent 1997 overhaul of Mexico's Ley Federal del Derecho de Autor, Mexican copyright had been rooted in the Continental moral-rights tradition, which was mainly concerned with authors' rights, and primarily with their moral rights.[171] Unlike the US and (for the most part) Canadian regimes, Mexico did not focus primarily on copyright as a tradable property right. The US view of Mexico as a potentially lucrative market and a source of "pirated" works drove the negotiations.[172] The United States largely triumphed, as can be seen by the fact that NAFTA "does not impose any obligations on the United States to give effect to [the Berne Convention's] article 6bis[173] on moral rights, pursuant to NAFTA Annex 1701.3," even as it requires that the three countries adhere to the Berne Convention.[174]

This was a "major victory for the United States, because it allows authors to transfer their rights to companies and employees without later disrupting the exploitation of their works to the disadvantage of the holder of the economic rights." NAFTA also included several new contractual and related rights, including "the free transfer of economic rights by contract for purposes of their exploitation and enjoyment by the transferee," and recognition of the "work-for-hire concept for works and sound recordings" that form the basis of the American entertainment industries. These changes were "a major achievement for the United States. It reverse[d] the trend in other countries – namely in Europe – where regulations often restrict the transferability of copyright and related rights."[175]

Like TRIPS, NAFTA's Chapter 17 establishes a (TRIPS-plus) floor of copyright rules that are, in practice, largely harmonized around the American example. For Mexico, it does so directly in the way it required Mexico to adapt its domestic copyright laws. In the case of Canada, which already had copyright rules similar to those in the United States, the effect was more indirect. NAFTA Annex 2106 continues the Canada-US Free Trade Agreement's (CUSFTA) "cultural exemption" (found in CUSFTA Article 2005). This annex effectively exempts Canada's cultural (i.e., content) industries from NAFTA's copyright provisions, among others. As it relates to copyright, however, the actual effect of this exemption is minimized by the reality that Canadian law already shared the same general economic orientation of US law, and accorded with most of NAFTA's specific provisions.[176] Furthermore, the 1993 North American Free Trade Agreement Implementation Act "contained a significant number of largely trade-mandated changes to the *Copyright Act*" that followed the NAFTA model.[177]

NAFTA, like TRIPS, represents the continued privileging of copyright owners, undertaken in order to "establish a (near-)uniform legislative arena within which rights holders can enforce their rights." The rules "are intended to remove restrictions on the flow of commodities across borders." This approach treats cultural products as commodities and is thus more concerned with the rights of manufacturers than of creators.[178] NAFTA "homogenized the copyright environment and adopted rules that enhance the making of contracts in the context of ... new technologies."[179]

NAFTA'S EFFECT ON NORTH AMERICAN COPYRIGHT GOVERNANCE

While NAFTA reoriented Mexican copyright law and seemed to put the continent on track to a harmonized copyright regime, the structure of NAFTA itself actually inhibits future efforts at copyright harmonization, for two reasons related to NAFTA's institutionalized rules.

First, the United States, which is driving global and regional copyright reform processes, must work within the context of NAFTA, and NAFTA sets de facto limits on member states' ability to influence their neighbours' copyright policies. US governments have depended mainly on trade agreements to convince other countries to adopt US-style copyright and IP regimes, specifically, offering market access (or threatening economic sanctions) in exchange for stronger IP protection. However, because NAFTA effectively guarantees Canadian and Mexican access to the US market, it is much more difficult (but not impossible) to link its demands on copyright to greater market access without reopening NAFTA.

Second, NAFTA's very structure makes it difficult to promote region-wide changes in copyright policy. Institutions, the creations of purposeful actors, can be changed. Just as some institutions can have the potential for change built into their rules (e.g., voting mechanisms), others can be designed to discourage change. Institutions that do not contain easy-to-use rules for managing change are likely to be more resistant to actors' attempts to change them. NAFTA was designed explicitly to minimize infringements on members' autonomy: "The refusal of the NAFTA members to include any form of supranationalism in the integration process made it necessary to devise an agreement which was both extremely precise in its wording and comprehensive in terms of subject matter."[180] As a result, NAFTA acts like the "external constitution" of North America, imposing obligations and constraints on the three countries and the various agents within them.[181] Rather than fostering policy harmonization, NAFTA functions as a de facto mechanism for maintaining difference, which would, after all, be in keeping with its negotiators' stated desires to maintain each state's sovereignty.

North American Copyright Governance: The SPP and the Difficulty of Regional Change

The ill-fated 2005 Security and Prosperity Partnership of North America was an attempt, driven primarily by North American business interests, to push deeper integration forward and to avoid a "thickening" of the US-Canada and US-Mexico borders that could disrupt the continental economy. Following much business-group lobbying, the SPP was announced by the leaders of Canada, Mexico, and the United States in March 2005 in Waco, Texas.

Though originally remarkably wide-ranging in scope, covering a laundry list of regulatory changes that would not require legislative oversight,[182] the SPP eventually was narrowed considerably, to the point where, while coordination continues among the three countries, the SPP itself no longer exists in the form it was initially envisioned. The SPP's copyright section, for example, was devoted primarily to promoting education and information sharing among stakeholders. Implementation of the WIPO Internet treaties, which would have required legislative changes, was expressly not included. According to Canadian documents obtained through the Access to Information Act, a preliminary SPP draft included as one of its objectives implementation of the Internet treaties by the three countries; however, this goal was absent from the final document.[183] Consequently, the SPP's copyright-related objectives focused on best practices, public outreach to business communities, and "measuring piracy and counterfeiting," according to the SPP's Intellectual Property Rights Action Strategy.[184]

While it is unclear which country demanded that mention of the Internet treaties' implementation be removed, it likely was not the United States, which had already implemented the treaties by then and was the strongest proponent for their implementation by its neighbours. Mexico also seems to be an unlikely source of pressure for their removal, as it had already committed to implementing the treaties. The process of elimination, combined with the fact that the Canadian government, in 2005, had begun to recognize that copyright was becoming a sensitive issue, suggests strongly that the Canadian government demanded that the Internet treaties be removed from the list of SPP deliverables.

Because the SPP brought together the North American leaders to discuss a wide variety of issues of common concern, it created a forum in which linkage among issues could be created – and such linkage appears to have played a role in the Canadian debate over WIPO implementation.[185] The potential for formal systematic region-wide linkage, however, disappeared with the SPP. Consequently, changes to North American copyright policy must come through domestic institutions and processes, or via extra-regional arrangements, such as the Anti-Counterfeiting Trade Agreement or the Trans-Pacific Partnership, that include all three countries.

Part 4: Copyright and Change

Change in copyright is always the result of the actions of purposeful actors deploying ideas, exploiting the protection/dissemination contradiction inherent in copyright itself (i.e., the process of bricolage), and linking issues in support of their preferred style of copyright protection. As Campbell notes, the degree of change depends on institutional compatibility, actors' resources, the number and type of allies, and the ability to deploy resources to ease institutional constraints.[186]

Change can emerge endogenously, as actors exploit existing tensions among and within institutions and policies. Change can also emerge from actors' responses to external shocks such as technological change (exogenous change). Each has its own logic. Exogenous shocks – technological change or the foreign imposition of changes to domestic copyright law – can create new copyright interests, challenge the viability of existing interests, and provide new opportunities for groups to pursue change to their advantage. However, these shocks only create the *potential* for change. Changes in copyright law are driven not just by technological change, but by actors' perceptions of their interests expressed in political contexts.[187] The rules governing these activities are the outcome of political debate. Incumbent players, threatened by changes, can attempt to preserve their business models by working to shape the law in a way that blunts the effects of these new technologies.

In doing so, they will be countered by groups with conflicting interests and ideas about how this market should be structured.

As important as technological innovations like the printing press and the Internet are for disrupting copyright law, these innovations cannot be separated from their social and historical contexts. Technologies are not politically neutral: they can make it easier for some groups to organize than others, and can create new interests where there were none before. They are "socially constructed ... They are built and deployed inside of social and political contexts that shape what gets designed, by whom, and to what ends."[188]

While the potential for revolutionary change from exogenous shocks is obvious, and while such shocks (particularly technological ones) are usually thought to drive copyright reform, endogenous change has the potential to be just as revolutionary. Endogenous change involves actors exploiting inconsistencies and contradictions within the existing institution of copyright, or between copyright and other institutions. Endogenous change does not create new actors, or change the underlying material logic of production; however, it can allow actors to redraw the boundaries of copyright to favour one interest or policy objective over another. In this way, it can be just as revolutionary as the types of exogenous technological changes that are usually thought to drive copyright reform.

The period under investigation demonstrates evidence of both endogenous and exogenous shocks. The WIPO Internet treaties clearly were a response to technological change. However, the changes pursued in these treaties, as well as in TRIPS and NAFTA, predate the late-1980s popularization of digital technologies. Instead, they, and the Internet treaties, can be seen as an ongoing battle by copyright interest groups to manipulate existing copyright ideas and institutions to their benefit.

Part 5: Conclusion

As a historical-institutionalist approach would suggest, copyright is a historically rooted, politically contested institution that has developed along a path-dependent track. Like any other human-made set of rules, copyright creates winners and losers, privileging certain groups (existing publishers and distributors, bestselling authors, developed countries) over others (emerging creators, users, future distributors and creators, developing countries) within a non-neutral institutional setting. At the same time, however, change in copyright policies and laws can occur in two ways. Actors can exploit the contradictions inherent in copyright, in particular the user/owner balance. They can also attempt to link desired changes to external shocks (e.g., technological changes) or external events, as with US policymakers' worries about declining economic competitiveness.

As this chapter has discussed, various groups, led by the content industries and working primarily with and through the US government, have worked successfully to implement the TRIPS and NAFTA, which have required countries, including Mexico and Canada, to reform their copyright laws to bring them into line with the US view of copyright as a tradable, economic right that primarily benefits industry groups, rather than creators or "users" (who themselves may be future creators).

One of the most interesting aspects of copyright's global political economy is the way that copyright-related institutions can alternately enable and inhibit copyright reform. The United States has been very successful in promoting copyright reform via trade agreements like TRIPS and NAFTA, linking copyright reform to market access. The US record outside of such negotiations, however, is more mixed. That NAFTA and TRIPS lack any mechanism to modify these agreements easily has effectively set their copyright provisions in amber. These treaties cannot be adapted easily whenever a technological advance renders their rules obsolete. It also seems that US ability to effect global copyright change is more hampered when it cannot credibly link copyright to wider trade issues. In North America, NAFTA's guarantee of access to the US market for Canada and Mexico effectively removes from the United States its most potent carrot to convince these two countries to change their laws. As a result, even though NAFTA Chapter 17 brought the three countries' copyright laws closer together, the overall agreement may not necessarily promote further copyright harmonization. The experience of the SPP suggests that while harmonization may be possible, it will not necessarily occur uniformly across the whole continent, even in the presence of a common international trade or IP treaty.

While technological change (i.e., digitization) has threatened the central role of publishers and distributors in the marketplace for creative works, as well as the underlying justification for copyright, copyright persists because it is defended by institutions and interests that draw their power and influence from copyright law. Their political and economic power has at least as much of an impact as technological change in shaping future copyright rules.

Materially, copyright depends for its existence on the groups, namely, the content industries, concentrated in the US and, to a lesser extent, the European Union, that own the vast majority of copyrights and that benefit from copyright. They work to preserve, extend, and strengthen it in their favour. Since copyright, even more than other types of property, depends on the law for its existence, state governments and international institutions play a crucial role in shaping the outcome of copyright policy debates. Ideationally, copyright's appeal to Enlightenment notions of individuality and property make it difficult to change, even as digitization challenges what is meant by these two concepts when it comes to creativity.

The effect of the popularization of the personal computer and the Internet is only superficially similar to the effect of previous technological innovations in that they have altered the balance of power among copyright stakeholders and introduced new groups. At the same time, they have also allowed individuals to perform easily tasks that previously could only be undertaken by large companies – copying and disseminating creative works. The technological empowerment of the individual represents a fundamental challenge to copyright. The reaction of the various interests involved in this debate – distributors and publishers, creators, users, as well as the governments of Canada, Mexico, and especially the United States – to the challenges posed by the arrival of the digital age, specifically the negotiation and implementation of the WIPO Internet treaties, will be examined in the rest of this study.

4 The United States, the Internet Treaties, and the Setting of the Digital-Copyright Agenda

The United States – its government and agencies, its industries and other interested groups – is the key player in global copyright reform, occupying a unique niche in the copyright policymaking world. Its outsized effect on global copyright policies and trends makes understanding how US copyright policy is developed a key task for any copyright scholar. An analysis of its copyright policymaking process as it relates to the WIPO Internet treaties reveals a country whose own policies are almost completely a function of domestic ideas, institutions, and interests, rather than of regional or international institutions. While the configuration of US copyright ideas, institutions, and interests matter for the United States and the rest of the world, this effect is largely one-way.

The WIPO Internet treaties are particularly fascinating for the picture they paint of how the dominant state actor – the United States – was able to shape, but not determine completely, the negotiations' outcome. As will be seen in the discussion of the Internet treaties in the following chapter, the United States and its industries were able to use their economic and political influence to affect international treaties in a way unavailable to smaller countries.[1] Yet, even a superpower remains somewhat beholden to the institutional context within which negotiations take place, and not all of WIPO's rules were conducive to US desires to impose its version of the Internet treaties on its negotiating partners. The negotiation process also reveals the extent to which both the negotiations and their eventual outcome reflected the tensions of the domestic US debate, which pre-dated the international negotiations, with key parts of the treaties being arranged in advance by some of the main US actors almost as an extension of the domestic US legislative process.

The United States has been driving the global push for ever-stronger copyright protection for so long – since the mid-1980s, at least – that it is sometimes easy to overlook the extent to which its domestic copyright laws and its international position remain contested. The analysis in this chapter suggests that while the dominant content industries and institutions remain devoted to the pursuit of stronger property rights in creative works at the expense of users and other interests, the diffuse nature of power in the American political system, and copyright's fundamental protection/dissemination conflict, make the current state of affairs much more open to change than is generally appreciated. The 18 January 2012 "Internet blackout" – discussed in the book's final chapter – provides a dramatic example of how the dominant copyright paradigm might be shifted towards a greater emphasis on the needs of the users of creative works, an event foreshadowed in the work of copyright critics during the 1993–8 US debate over the Internet treaties. Since the current copyright debate is taking place within the same institutional setup that gave birth to the Digital Millennium Copyright Act (DMCA), understanding how that law came to be offers a way to understand how domestic US and international copyright policy will be shaped in the future.

The following three chapters examine the intertwined US digital-copyright debate and the WIPO negotiations. This chapter outlines the relevant ideas, institutions, and interests that have shaped US copyright policy, and provides a historical overview of US copyright law. Chapter 5 begins the account of the US digital-copyright-reform process that encompassed the negotiation and conclusion of the Internet treaties and led to the passage of the 1998 DMCA. It focuses on the period from 1993 to 1996 and includes an account of the negotiations and outcomes of the 1996 WIPO Internet treaties negotiations. Chapter 6 returns to the United States for the conclusion of the DMCA debate. It concludes with an analysis of the effect of the DMCA on the United States and considers what the DMCA debate tells us about the place of the United States within the North American and global copyright policy community. It also details US attempts, with mixed results, to expand the Internet treaties via the Anti-Counterfeiting Trade Agreement.

Copyright in the United States[2]

Ideas: Copyright, Property, and the Public Interest

The purpose of, and tensions inherent in, the US concept of copyright can be seen in article 1, section 8, clause 8 of the US Constitution. This "copyright clause," which covers copyright as well as intellectual property generally, gives Congress the power "to promote the Progress of Science and useful Arts, by securing for limited Times to Authors and Inventors the exclusive Right to their respective Writings [copyright] and Discoveries [patents]."[3] In other words, the property right embodied in copyright is justified in public-benefit terms: "The philosophical core of U.S. copyright law is that the individual's right of ownership is lashed to a societal aspiration."[4] This framing of copyright as a balance between the need to remunerate authors and the desire to encourage the public good of the dissemination of works shows the influence of the original British 1709 Statute of Anne, itself "an Act for the Encouragement of Learning, by vesting the Copies of Printed Books in the Authors or purchasers of such Copies, during the Times therein mentioned." Similarly, the first US federal copyright statute, 1790 Copyright Act, was named "An Act for the Encouragement of Learning."

Change in US copyright policy has both exogenous and endogenous roots. As was discussed in chapter 2, actors can effect change not only by responding to external events, but also by exploiting tensions inherent within institutions and policies (i.e., substantive and symbolic bricolage) while remaining on a particular "path."[5] US debates over copyright – both with respect to the 1998 DMCA and historically – largely take place within the ideational confines of the copyright clause. Content industries, user groups, and other domestic actors exploit the tension between authors' (in practice, copyright owners') exclusive rights, which are seen as necessary to encouraging production, and the public's interest in limiting these rights in order to encourage dissemination.

A (VERY) BRIEF HISTORY OF US COPYRIGHT LAW

Since the mid-1970s, successive US administrations have supported strong copyright domestically and internationally, a position that enjoys strong bipartisan support in Congress. However, as Knopf points out, it is probably more accurate to say that the United States is in favour of its particular version of strong copyright, which reflects a uniquely American balance of interests.[6] Canadian and Mexican copyright laws are sometimes "stronger" than American copyright law. For example, Mexican moral rights go beyond what is available in the United States, while Canadian copyright law, unlike US copyright law, contains provisions for payments for performances in small business establishments. The United States itself is a relatively recent convert to the cause of strong intellectual property.[7] Like many countries in the years before the 1886 Berne Convention, which applied the principle of national treatment to member countries' authors, the United States initially offered copyright protection only to US citizens. This protection annoyed British authors and led to the proliferation of (legal) reprints of foreign works and inexpensive magazines and newspapers.[8]

Copyright law in the United States, as in other countries, has followed a path-dependent development, increasing in strength and scope over the past 200-plus years in response to lobbying and technological change. US copyright terms have expanded from fourteen years with a possible fourteen-year renewal under the original 1790 Copyright Act, to life of the author plus seventy years in 1998. As has happened elsewhere, US copyright expanded to cover new forms of expression and now protects works by US citizens and non-citizens alike. US copyright law offsets these protections in two ways. First, the Copyright Act includes specific limitations on owners' rights usually negotiated by groups with a commercial or social interest in limiting these rights. Second, section 107 of the current Copyright Act also contains a general "fair use" right, permitting copying without permission "for purposes such as criticism, comment, news reporting, teaching (including multiple copies for classroom use), scholarship, or research." While this right has been interpreted fairly liberally, the strength and status of this doctrine in the aftermath of the DMCA is a controversial subject.

Institutions: Copyright in a Pluralist Arena

Understanding copyright policy outcomes in the United States requires an appreciation of two aspects of its policymaking process. First, copyright negotiations occur in a largely pluralist setting consisting of inter-industry negotiations that reflect the relative political and economic influence of involved groups. Pluralism describes a system in which "government policy reflects the vector of forces created by different pressure groups."[9] Pluralism as a political theory, in its most basic form, is individualist and ahistorical in orientation, with institutions treated merely as "necessary scaffolding for interest group activities and for 'game forms.'"[10] The pluralist US copyright regime is far from ahistorical or "natural." Rather, it was consciously designed.

This regime dates from the beginning of the twentieth century. As University of Michigan law professor and copyright expert Jessica Litman documents extensively in her account of US copyright policymaking and the DMCA, copyright-law reform has, since the early

1900s, involved inter-industry negotiations overseen by a state that acts as an arbiter, ratifying the consensus reached by the players at the table.[11] This process, which Litman dates to the negotiation of the 1909 Copyright Act, emerged in response to "the dilemma of updating and simplifying a body of law that seemed too complicated and arcane for legislative revision." The result was "a scheme for statutory drafting that featured meetings and negotiations among representatives of industries with interest in copyright." Congress encouraged "representatives of the industries affected by copyright to hash out among themselves what changes needed to be made and then present Congress with the text of appropriate legislation."[12] In short, Congress's primary role has been to ensure that all affected industries are represented in negotiations. This scenario has been repeated regularly up to the present day: only the specific participants and the technology have changed.

Second, and related to the first point, until the mid-1990s copyright was seen in the United States as a technocratic (albeit high-stakes) issue, of interest only to those content industries, creators, and copyright lawyers directly affected by copyright law. While general interest in copyright began to rise during the debate over the DMCA, copyright did not emerge fully onto the public political agenda until after the DMCA had already been passed. It would take until 2012 for public opinion to become intense enough for it to become a significant factor shaping US copyright policymaking.

In the United States, domestic responsibility for copyright is shared among several institutions.[13] Congress passes legislation, which is either signed or vetoed by the president. Administratively, the lion's share of the domestic responsibility for copyright is shared between the US Copyright Office and the United States Patent and Trademark Office (PTO). While the PTO is an executive agency, the Copyright Office is actually located in the Library of Congress and is therefore formally a creature of the legislature. As the previous chapter outlined, the Office of the United States Trade Representative (USTR), which is located in the executive branch, is the United States's lead international agency on copyright. The following section focuses exclusively on the domestic US copyright institutions.

THE COPYRIGHT OFFICE AND THE PATENT AND TRADEMARK OFFICE

The Copyright Office, housed in the legislative not the executive branch, administers US copyright law. Although registration is not mandatory, the Copyright Office also houses a registry for those wishing to register their copyright. Furthermore, it "administers the mandatory deposit provisions of the copyright law and the various compulsory licensing provisions of the law, which include collecting royalties."[14]

The Copyright Office also provides expertise to Congress and the executive, analysing and drafting legislation and reports. Alongside the Department of State, the USTR, and the Department of Commerce, it provides expertise in multilateral trade negotiations and "provides technical assistance to other countries in developing their own copyright laws."[15] Formally, the PTO focuses on IP generally, advising the president, the secretary of commerce, and US government agencies on IP "policy, protection, and enforcement; and promotes the stronger and more effective IP protection around the world."[16] However, Bruce Lehman,[17] a particularly effective PTO commissioner, pushed the PTO to the centre of the story of the DMCA and the Internet treaties, temporarily surpassing the Copyright Office as the primary US governmental organization focused on copyright.

Observers agree that the US institutional position on copyright is relatively consistent across agencies. While those interviewed for this project agreed that the Copyright Office and the PTO generally treated their industries fairly, they also agreed that the two offices generally share what copyright lawyer Seth Greenstein, whose background includes involvement in the negotiations of the WIPO treaties on behalf of the consumer-electronics industry, calls a "pro-proprietor" approach to copyright. This approach is itself the result of the shared view that "copyright is better promoted by ensuring proper economic incentives" for copyright owners, and a privileging of content-industry issues over "the opportunities for personal use that are opened by digital technology."[18] In the congressional hearings for the DMCA, both Bruce Lehman and Marybeth Peters, register of copyrights and head of the Copyright Office from 1994 to 2010, were very supportive of the bill that eventually became the DMCA, with the Copyright Office urging "prompt ratification of these treaties."[19]

COPYRIGHT AND CONGRESS

Copyright is that rare issue, not so much bipartisan as nonpartisan. Congressional divisions on copyright tend to reflect subnational regional and industrial divisions, not partisan ones. The most powerful supporters of stronger copyright come from areas like Nashville and Hollywood, where the content industries are the most prominent.[20] For example,

House Resolution 2281, whose content formed the basis for the eventual DMCA, was introduced in the House of Representatives in July 1997 by two Democrats (John Conyers and Barney Frank) and two Republicans (Howard Coble and Henry Hyde). The House of Representatives is home to one of the most powerful advocates of the motion picture industry and strong copyright, Democrat Howard Berman of California, and, until the 2010 midterm elections, the most effective supporter of the myriad groups advocating for a more "balanced" approach, such as the consumer-electronics industry, Rick Boucher of Virginia.[21] Copyright lawyer Jonathan Band, who was involved in the drafting of the DMCA and whose clients include Internet companies, remarks that in the Senate the support of Utah Republican Senator Orrin Hatch (chair of Senate Committee on the Judiciary during the DMCA hearings) for a reverse-engineering limitation in the DMCA arose from his familiarity with the Utah-based Novell Corporation.[22]

Although US copyright negotiations are long, complex, and contentious processes, the underlying rules are relatively straightforward. US copyright policymaking is a pragmatist's game, involving trade-offs among various interest groups that have a seat at the table.[23] As already noted, copyright negotiations take place in a pluralist setting among identified copyright interests and are overseen by Congress. This is not to say that Congress has been completely absent or wholly neutral in this process. According to Greenstein, up until the mid-1980s, Congress played the role of a "genuine arbitrator" between the various interests, and "would take various proposals, analyze them, and synthesize their own [view] of what they thought proper policy would be." Since then, and especially since the 1992 Audio Home Recording Act, "more often than not, what you will hear from legislators is: 'When you [interest groups] agree, come back with the language.'"[24]

Though this process requires competing interests to negotiate among themselves to achieve a sort of balance, Congress itself has been relatively more disposed to favour the interests of the content industries rather than copyright users like libraries, universities, and consumer-electronics groups. This bias towards stronger copyright can be seen in the one-way tendency to strengthen and extend copyright law to cover ever more creative works. For example, in 1998, the Sonny Bono Copyright Term Extension Act (named after the former Cher partner and then–recently deceased Representative) retroactively extended the term of protection for copyrighted works from life of the author plus fifty years to life plus seventy years. As Boldrin and Levine note, there is no possible economic or philosophical justification for retroactive term extensions other than as a grant of a rent-seeking windfall to owners of copyrighted works, such as Disney (which led the lobbying for the extension),[25] leading them to conclude that Congress has been "bought and paid for" by the content industries.[26] It was not lost on critics that this law was enacted just as the copyright term of Disney's prize asset, Mickey Mouse, was about to expire, and the law has become widely known as the Mickey Mouse Protection Act. Events subsequent to the period covered by this book also suggest a copyright-owner bias. In 2008, when fair-dealing proponent Boucher was slated to take over the Judiciary Committee's Intellectual Property Subcommittee from the pro-IP Berman (who had moved on to chair the more prestigious House Foreign Affairs Committee), Congress eliminated the committee (the Judiciary Committee was chaired by John Conyers, himself a big supporter of the content industries). Following Boucher's defeat in the 2010 midterm elections, the committee was reinstated.[27]

Effects of Inter-Industry Negotiations The ultra-cool shininess of the Internet and gadgets like the iPhone make it easy to think that there is something new happening in copyright, with upstart "pirates" taking on stodgy old Hollywood and the dinosauric record companies, but below the flashy surface we see the same story that has played out in American copyright law since its inception. The defining characteristic of the US copyright policymaking regime since at least the early twentieth century has been structured inter- and intra-industry negotiations over the content and direction of copyright law within an institutional setting that ratifies the resulting compromise. The matter is then settled, for better or worse, until the next new technology comes along, and then, *Groundhog Day*–style, the process repeats.[28]

For example, in 1905 existing copyright interests, namely, composers and music publishers, worked to exclude the "then-youthful phonogram industry" and the motion picture industry from negotiations and to put that industry at a disadvantage. While initial legislative proposals would have ignored their interests, in 1908, all interested parties sat down together and were assured that if every industry could agree on a bill Congress would pass it. The result was the 1909 Copyright Act and a legislative process that endures to this day.[29]

Generally, any given actor's ability to influence policy outcomes depends on its access to resources, including personnel, money, and officials, and on the actor's political and economic importance.[30] US copyright law reflects the interests and relative strength (economic and political) of those who have been invited to the table. Already established groups tend to have an advantage over upstarts, specific interests (i.e., industries) generally outclass the overall "public interest," and every invited guest does better than the wallflowers.

This style of copyright negotiations historically has been successful in incorporating traditional and new interests, from the sound recording industry to photocopier producers and (as will be seen with the DMCA negotiations) telecommunications companies. However, the process, almost by definition, excludes what can be defined loosely as the public, or societal interest, leading to narrow exceptions that are traded off against one another.[31] Similarly, the interests of those groups that have yet to be created by future technological change, such as the motion picture industry in 1909 and VCR makers in 1976, are also poorly represented. The end result is a process in which negotiators take pains to protect their existing business models against potential future challengers, using terminology (i.e., narrow exceptions) that could be undermined easily by evolving technology.[32] This process also provides existing interests with the ability to block unsatisfactory legislation and with incentives to trade rights for exceptions, until a consensus that leaves no existing party worse off than before is reached. This "potential surplus ... most often comes at the expense of outsiders."[33]

This type of zero-sum negotiation among groups with specific interests at stake has resulted in a brittle law that has required renegotiation with every new technological advance that creates a new interest group upsetting the status quo. Every technological change, be it the invention of motion pictures, the photocopier, or the computer, has increased the complexity of copyright negotiations by increasing the number of stakeholders wanting to be heard, making it harder to come to an agreement.[34] Unsurprisingly, the end result of this institutionalized pluralist style of negotiations is legislation that is littered with narrow exceptions required to get all involved to agree to the final draft.

Interests: All Animals Are Equal, but Some Are More Equal than Others

US copyright policy, then, is made within an institutional process based on inter-industry negotiations. The debate over what copyright should look like is framed by Congress, based on the copyright clause, in which "the individual's right of ownership" coexists uneasily with copyright's "societal aspiration" related to the promotion of education.[35] As in other countries, US copyright law involves a balance between copyright's "protection" and "dissemination" functions, to use Doern and Sharaput's terminology.[36]

Within these parameters, various interests compete to promote their view of what US copyright (and, by extension, the US foreign-policy position on copyright) should look like and where the balance will fall. In the United States, as elsewhere, one can divide copyright interests into two main groups: those that favour stronger protection and those that favour the dissemination function of copyright. These categories are analytical in nature, as groups in both camps may have objective or conflicting interests in "protection" and "dissemination." While the protection side tends to dominate for reasons of political and economic clout, groups on both sides of the debate must be accounted for.

Four main groups were most prominent in the debate that led to the 1998 DMCA's provisions on technological protection measures and ISP liability. First, on the protection side, were the content industries. On the dissemination or user side, the three main interests groups were: businesses such as telecommunications companies, consumer-electronics industries, and large-scale ISPs; large non-business institutional interests like research libraries; and civil-society groups, including academics and some lawyers.

INTERESTS PROMOTING PROTECTION
The Content Industries Of these groups, the content industries were the most important in the DMCA debate. In the United States, copyright policy is driven largely by the content industries. These include the lobbies representing primarily the motion-picture industry (the Motion Picture Association of America [MPAA], generally seen as the main proponent of stronger copyright rules), the music industry (the Recording Industry Association of America [RIAA]), and the computer software industry (the Business Software Alliance [BSA]), as well as the video game industry (the Entertainment Software Association [ESA])[37] and the publishing industry (the Association of American Publishers [AAP]). Generally, they have favoured stronger copyright protection, maximalist legal protection of TPMs, and strong rules regarding ISP liability.

In his indispensable *Agendas, Alternatives, and Public Policies*, US political scientist John Kingdon remarks that an interest group's success is at least partly dependent on its resources, which include the ability to affect electoral outcomes, economic importance, and the ability to be heard (in the words of one of Kingdon's interviewees, "The louder they squawk, the higher it gets").[38] The success of the content-industry lobby in the copyright debate can be explained by several factors, only one of which (and not even the most important) is its actual financial importance to the US economy. While their numbers have been criticized for being the result of methodologically suspect analyses relying on biased sources (the affected industries themselves), the International Intellectual Property Alliance (IIPA), which represents US content industries, claims that in 2010, the "core"[39] content industries accounted for 6.4 per cent, or $931.8 billion of overall US gross domestic product (GDP), while "total" content industries – a very permissive definition that includes computer manufacturing, administrative services, and wood and paper products, accounted for 11.1 per cent, or $1.6 trillion, of US GDP.[40]

In addition to their perceived and actual economic importance, content-industry lobbies like the MPAA and the RIAA have the luxury of focusing their well-funded lobbies on one issue that can be summed up in a few words: piracy is bad; we need stronger copyright protection. In 1998, the year the DMCA was passed, the MPAA spent $1.2 million on lobbying and employed 35 lobbyists; the RIAA, meanwhile, spent $820,000 and employed 30 lobbyists. In 2011 the MPAA spent $2.1 million and employed 28 lobbyists, the RIAA $5.7 million and employed 41 lobbyists.[41]

In contrast, "user" groups face financing and messaging hurdles. On financing, public-interest groups simply cannot compete with the content industries' lobbying budgets. Although telecommunications companies have large lobbying budgets, they must divide these, as well as their time, over various issues, whereas content industries have the luxury of focusing on a single issue of overwhelming importance to them: copyright. In terms of messaging, user groups have a more difficult pitch to make: they have to frame their arguments in terms of "balance," in which ownership rights must be balanced against rights of use. Where content industries can argue that more protection is always better, user groups must be more nuanced in their policy prescriptions.

Because the content industries are well-established, well-funded lobbies that can put forward a relatively simple, coherent message in a way that other industries or public-interest groups cannot, they receive "a lot of deference," according to Jennifer Schneider, legislative counsel to then Representative Rick Boucher, a leading supporter of fair-use legislation in Congress until his defeat in the 2010 midterm elections.[42] The content industries, and the motion picture industry in particular,

can also draw on support from groups representing labour and capital
– those who work on film sets and the companies that fund them, for
example.[43] They can also draw on cultural resources that dwarf their
actual economic contribution to the US economy. Says Greenstein:

> If you want to look at the actual dollars contributed to the United States
> economy, far greater dollars are generated by the technology industries
> than by copyright industries. But when you also look at it from a cultural
> point of view, the culture of the United States is far more defined by its art
> than by its technology in some ways … [Motion pictures are] more quint-
> essentially American and technology is much more international.[44]

Recognizing that debates over copyright and intellectual property
are "ultimately … narrative [battles] where the struggle is to define
meaning and control the discourse"[45] and thus are subject to symbolic
bricolage, the content industries have worked valiantly, and with no
small success, to rhetorically define copyrights as equivalent to real,
physical property.[46] The common reference to unauthorized individual
downloading as "piracy," a term that conflates commercial-scale law-
breaking and high-seas nastiness with non-commercial activities, is a
result of the rhetorical efforts of individuals such as the late Jack Valenti,
former chair of the MPAA, pre-eminent copyright lobbyist, and undis-
puted master of copyright scaremongering. Valenti played a key role in
promoting the idea that copyrights are equivalent to rights in physical
goods. It is hard to understate Valenti's penchant for hyperbole, some
of it remarkably offensive. In 1982, when the MPAA was concerned that
the VCR would drive Hollywood out of business (rather than act as its
saviour, which is what actually happened), Valenti claimed, before
Congress "that the VCR is to the American film producer and the
American public as the Boston Strangler is to the woman home alone."[47]
Valenti's evocation of murdered women in defence of his industry's
bottom line makes the "pirate" slur levelled against individual computer users who have never hijacked a boat or taken anyone hostage
seem benign and enlightened in comparison.

Overall, this combination of cultural capital, economic and political
influence, and the successful linkage of the welfare of the copyright/IP
industries to perceptions of US international economic competitiveness
have allowed the content industries to position themselves so they
could drive (although not dictate) the US copyright agenda, as well as
copyright perceptions.[48]

INTERESTS PROMOTING DISSEMINATION

Against the content industries, one finds a variety of interest groups whose interests run towards greater protection of users' rights. These include the consumer electronics (CE) industry, research libraries, electronics wholesalers, the telecommunications industry (notably ISPs, but also including telephone companies, and television and radio broadcasters) and public-interest groups. While several of these groups had previously been involved in the negotiations, the DMCA debate that began around 1993 and ended with the bill's passage in 1998 was the first time ISPs and public-interest groups took a strong interest in copyright reform.

These groups lack the single-message and single-issue focus of the content industries. The latter can focus on promoting stronger copyright, which provided the foundation for their entire scarcity-based business model. However, the primary business concerns of the CE industry, for example, extend beyond copyright and intellectual property to include such issues as competition policy and product standards. Even their interest in copyright is not necessarily completely focused on minimizing its burden: that their products are covered by patents, another form of IP, provides them with mixed incentives regarding whether IP should be strengthened or weakened.

The Telecommunications and Industry and Internet Businesses Of the groups joining the copyright debate at the time of the Internet treaties, the telecommunications industry and ISP providers by far had the most significant impact on the process. With revenues of US$190 billion in 1995,[49] at the beginning of the copyright debate that led to the DMCA, the telecommunications sector represented (and continues to represent) a significant part of the US economy, much larger than the motion picture and sound-recording industries.[50] In 2007 the motion picture and sound recording industries posted US$95 billion in revenues, against US$491 billion for the telecommunications industry.[51] While they were new to the issue and faced a copyright learning curve, as large companies (including such stalwarts as AT&T and Bell Atlantic [now Verizon]) they had significant resources to spend to lobby for their positions and were well represented during the DMCA hearings before the Commerce and Judiciary Committees, with five out of the thirty-seven witnesses appearing, not counting allies in other industries.[52]

As the firms over whose networks Internet traffic flowed, their main interest was in avoiding liability and responsibility for their customers' actions. The telecommunications industry unquestionably had a significant effect on the DMCA and the WIPO Internet treaties. Despite their inability to focus only on one issue, the telecoms are not insignificant players in Washington: in the DMCA debate, the telecommunications industry was seen as being more important than other user groups.[53] The eventual DMCA hinged on a compromise between the content industries and the ISPs, trading strong TPM protection for an ISP-liability regime favourable to the telecommunications industries.

Some groups' interests are not necessarily easy to deduce. Gillespie notes the potential for change in the consumer-electronics' industry's views on copyright. While the consumer-electronics industry's interest in being able to create devices that allow consumers to watch and copy copyrighted works is similar to the social good promoted by the concept of fair use/fair dealing, vertical integration of Internet and consumer-electronics companies may realign the industry's interests.[54] As Band notes, the relative importance of fair use in vertically integrated companies "depends on the company." While Google (which didn't yet exist in the 1990s), Verizon, and Yahoo! have been relatively consistent in their approach to fair use, for "Microsoft it depends on the part of the company" to which one is talking.[55]

The Public Interest Comparing the efforts of the telecommunications industry with those of "public interest" groups demonstrates the validity of Olson's classic observation that smaller, richer, more-focused groups have an organizational advantage over larger but poorly coordinated groups, such as consumers.[56] Various industry groups' interests may coincide with the public interest, but this alignment is coincidental and contingent. Congress, which should represent the public interest, had agreed as far back as 1909 to rubber stamp legislation agreed to in inter-industry talks.[57] However, were "the public" (however one wants to define the term) to take an interest, it would still be at a disadvantage compared with more-focused, better-funded lobby groups. It is difficult, if not impossible, to identify *all* affected groups, especially as changes in copyright technology increase the number of affected groups. Although some groups claimed to represent the public interest in certain narrow areas, during the 1976 overhaul of the Copyright Act, "the citizenry's interest in copyright and copyrighted works was too varied and complex to be amenable to interest-group championship"; it was "not somehow approximated by the push and shove among opposing industry representatives."[58]

The DMCA debate marked the first time that groups and individuals were involved who represented something other than the narrow concerns of interested industry and institutional groups such as libraries. Consumer interests had been present in previous debates, but not in the same way. Just as the content industries often use friendly artists to claim that they are acting in the best interests of creators, the consumer-electronics industry has also used consumers to make similar arguments. For example, in the early 1990s the Home Recording Rights Coalition, an "advocacy arm" of the electronic industries association, was created "to intervene in these sorts of copyright battles on behalf of consumer rights interests and the interests of consumer electronics manufacturers."[59] New public-interest groups that arose in opposition to the DMCA were more autonomous from existing interests than they had been in this previous debate.

The debate over the DMCA and the Internet treaties also broke open the technocratic, inter-industry negotiations to involve consumers and groups representing what could be thought of as a public interest, that is, an interest that could not easily be reduced to the defence of a particular industry. In particular, a group of concerned lawyers helped to coordinate a coalition of library groups, online service providers, consumer organizations, writers' organizations, computer hardware manufacturers, Internet civil liberties groups, telephone companies, educators, and consumer electronics manufacturers under what was called the Digital Future Coalition (DFC). However, their influence on the final legislation was limited.

Summary: Historical Institutionalism and US Copyright Policymaking

Historically, then, US content industries have tended to support the protection side of copyright, within the parameters set by the copyright clause of the US Constitution. They have done so by exploiting the protection-dissemination contradiction inherent in copyright, as well as the technological shocks that occasionally upset the copyright status quo. On the dissemination side, traditional user groups such as libraries cannot match these resources, while other groups, such as the consumer-electronics industry, do not have the singular focus on copyright of the content industries. Among the dissemination/user groups, the telecommunications industry, a new but politically and economically significant industry, stands out as a particularly powerful interest.

Crucially, the institutionalized policymaking process within which the US copyright debate takes place tends to favour established actors and those with specific interests over less influential actors and groups (such as those representing what could be thought of as the overall societal interest in copyright). The content industries have tended to drive the debate, although other groups must be accommodated. In the case of the Internet treaties, the telecommunications industry in particular is an important, economically powerful newcomer to the debate.

As might be inferred from their absence from the above discussion, with some small exceptions, regional and international institutions do not have much influence on US policy debates. North American Free Trade Agreement copyright provisions, which entered into force in 1994, reflected existing US laws and preferences. As the following two chapters argue, not even audacious attempts to use WIPO to influence what was happening in the United States could significantly alter this long-standing copyright policymaking process, although creative attempts to launder US legislation through WIPO by one man – Bruce Lehman – would shape the copyright debate in the United States and beyond for years to come.

5 1993–1996: US Copyright Reform and the WIPO Internet Treaties

As the preceding chapter discussed, the central rule in US copyright policymaking since 1909 has been inter-industry consensus. There may be a bias towards the content industries in the resulting legislation, but each industry's interests have to be represented. No consensus, no legislation. Based purely on precedent, we would expect that digital-copyright reform in the area of TPMs and ISP liability would primarily address the concerns of the content industries and other large players, with exceptions for other groups depending on their political and economic clout. True to form, and despite an eventful detour to Geneva for the Internet treaties, this is what happened. Eventually.

Before the Digital Millennium Copyright Act could be negotiated, however, the US administration would attempt to stack the deck in favour of the content industries, instigating a public outcry that would be familiar to the Canadians involved with the Fair Copyright for Canada Facebook group a decade later. Before the checks and balances of the US legislative process would have their day, the Clinton administration would earn the ire of the Senate by attempting to launder a pro-content-owner agenda through WIPO in the form of the Internet treaties.[1] This strategy was only partly successful, frustrated both by a domestic US political system that tended towards a rough balance among politically and economically powerful constituencies, and by WIPO's own institutional rules. Consequently, while the United States was able to influence the treaties' direction and subject matter, their actual language fell short of what it was looking for, even as the treaties – by design – kept the global copyright debate alive. All told, the policymaking process that led to the DMCA demonstrates that while long-standing institutions cannot be altered easily, creative, resourceful actors can influence results by switching fora and exploiting the rules.

The US policymaking process, shaped by the country's particular conceptions of copyright, its specific institutional context, and its unique constellation of actors, matters to Canada and Mexico, as well as to the rest of the world. Decisions reached within this process shape the US position on copyright internationally, and therefore the copyright policies of countries throughout the world. The DMCA "has acted as a template for other states, particularly through its impact on ensuing U.S. free-trade agreements."[2] Proponents explicitly acknowledged the role it would play in setting copyright policies around the world.[3]

The first part of this chapter covers the initial US attempts to implement a digital-copyright law. The second part moves from Washington, DC, to Geneva, for the negotiation of the Internet treaties. It offers a historical-institutionalist analysis of the ideas, institutions, and interests that shaped the outcomes of the Internet treaties' TPM and ISP-liability provisions.

Part 1: 1993–1996 – US Copyright Reform and the Importance of Being Lehman[4]

What eventually became known as the Internet treaties and the Digital Millennium Copyright Act were shaped in large measure by the efforts of one person who was in the right place at the right time to have an outsized effect on US and global digital-copyright policy. In 1993, the new administration of Bill Clinton had struck an Information Infrastructure Task Force (IITF) to consider how government should regulate the "Information Superhighway." The IITF included a working group on intellectual property, one of whose priorities was to formulate US copyright policy for the Internet age.

The working group was chaired by Bruce Lehman, undersecretary of commerce for intellectual property, director of the Patent and Trademark Office, and a former representative of the computer software industry on copyright issues.[5] He was also the main US representative to WIPO. A forceful personality described by one technology-company lobbyist interviewed by the author as a "petty tyrant," he also "knew more copyright law than anyone else in the government ... He had information, he had knowledge and he was also willing to use his very sharp elbows, so people, he really ran over people, and people stayed out of his way." Lehman made copyright a primary concern of the PTO, building up its staff of copyright lawyers. Keith Kupferschmid, senior vice-president for intellectual property policy and enforcement at the Software and Information

Industry Association, who worked with Lehman at the PTO and helped negotiate the WIPO Internet treaties, attributes Lehman's desire to run American copyright policy out of the PTO to his copyright background and his view that the PTO, as an executive agency, rather than the Copyright Office, a congressional agency, should set American IP policy. "The Administration's views may be very different than Congress' views on [copyright], so Bruce Lehman believed that the Patent and Trademark Office is really the Intellectual Property Office of the United States and should make intellectual property policy ... So he was much, much more proactive in terms of copyright issues as a result."[6]

Lehman's position at the centre of US and international copyright reform allowed him to influence strongly domestic and international copyright policy. His work on the IITF allowed him to see "the need for legislation in the United States, and also the need for international protection, because the Internet as a global network is only as strong as its weakest link."[7]

Lehman's vision of what had to be done to address digital-copyright issues and the Internet was, by all accounts, heavily biased towards the content industries. As chair of the IITF's IP working group, he produced the September 1995 "white paper" titled *Intellectual Property and the National Information Infrastructure: The Report of the Working Group on Intellectual Property Rights.*[8] This paper represented the policy position of the Clinton administration on what US intellectual property should look like in the digital age and was the foundation for the US position during the negotiations over the Internet treaties. It was also overwhelmingly focused on copyright: although it was supposed to address all forms of intellectual property,[9] 135 pages of the report were devoted to copyright-related issues; patents, trademarks, and trade secrets combined got only 19 pages.

Lehman's working group was extensively criticized for being too favourable to the content industries. His senior staff, which included former copyright lobbyists for the computer and music and recording industries, controlled the process, maintaining extensive informal communication with private-sector copyright lobbyists.[10] The working group's membership, which came from across the government and the-executive branch, complained that they were effectively shut out of the process: "All decisions were made and all documents were drafted by the commissioner and his senior staff without any consultation."[11] The 1995 white paper reflected these biases. Despite some conciliatory language, it betrays an overwhelming emphasis on protecting the rights of copyright owners and reflected a vision of creative "works" as tradable products. Users' rights were treated as a residual.[12] It proposed that copyright owners be "given control over every use of copyrighted works in digital form by interpreting existing law as being violated whenever users make even temporary reproductions of works in the random access memories of their computers," and that online service providers become "copyright police," enforcing copyright law. On TPMs, it proposed attaching "copyright management information to digital copies of a work ensuring that publishers can track every use made of digital copies and trace where each copy resides on the network and what is being done with it at any time," as well as to "protect every work technologically ... and make illegal any attempt to circumvent that protection."[13] This legal protection for TPMs would have represented a completely new right, signalling an even further reorientation of the US copyright regime away from a protection-dissemination balance towards the protection of owners' rights at the expense of users'.

An Unsurprising Stalemate

The white paper's recommendations represented a departure from the traditional process of inter-industry negotiations that had characterized previous copyright reforms. However, as one would expect from the previous chapter's discussion, once an actual bill reached Congress, it ran into immediate difficulty with those groups that previously had been sidelined, as well as with their representatives.

Despite bipartisan support for the ensuing white paper legislation, the NII Copyright Protection Act of 1995, introduced as HR 2441 in December 1995, those who had been excluded from the process, such as "library groups, online service providers, consumer organizations, writers' organizations, computer hardware manufacturers, Internet civil liberties groups, telephone companies, educators, consumer electronics manufacturers, and law professors," mounted a fierce opposition to the bill. As a result, it was stalled at the House Judiciary Committee.[14]

This opposition occurred under the umbrella of the Digital Future Coalition (DFC), which represents the first major foray of "public-interest" groups into the US copyright debate.[15] The brainchild of Peter Jazi, a law professor at American University in Washington, DC, the DFC initially brought concerned lawyers and library organizations and, later, members of the technical community who actually understood what the Internet was, to oppose the bill. Initially, its main effect was to raise the temperature on the issue. Foreshadowing online anti-copyright protests in Canada a decade later (see chapter 7) and the events around the January 2012 Internet blackout (see chapter 9), the DFC used the Internet to communicate and coordinate their activities, and to publicize the issue. The resulting uproar led to more traditional negotiations among the content industries, the telecommunications industry, computer and consumer electronics manufacturers, and libraries. However, while the DFC successfully linked these groups and worked behind the scenes to coordinate positions, it was not represented "at the copyright negotiating table. Supporters of the legislation essentially ignored them."[16]

This opposition came as a surprise to Lehman, who said, six years later, "None of these companies have been shut down over this. None of them have experienced one iota of discomfort. And, I'm still figuring out what's wrong with them having some responsibility – when they control the pipe through which the signals go – to help out a little bit in the enforcement process."[17] Faced with this vocal opposition, and in keeping with the traditional approach to copyright reform, the PTO, Copyright Office, and key senators and representatives encouraged the various groups to negotiate among themselves, cementing a dynamic that would eventually produce the 1996 WIPO Internet treaties and the 1998 DMCA.

The initial result, however, was a stalemate.[18] This outcome was very much in keeping with the pluralist mode of negotiations that typically has characterized US copyright policymaking when the sides could not reach a compromise. In an inter-industry negotiation setting, it is relatively easy to block legislation. What happened next, an attempt to use an international treaty (in this case, two treaties) to influence domestic policymaking, was a novel, if only partially successful, manoeuvre.

Part 2: 1996 – Negotiating the WIPO Internet Treaties

Originally, Bruce Lehman had planned to build bipartisan support for his white paper to get legislation introduced in the House and Senate by the end of September 1995, with the bill to be passed in time for the WIPO Committee of Experts' meeting on the proposed treaties in February or May 1996. US legislation would form the American position. At WIPO, Lehman and the United States, so the original plan went, would work to instigate, marshal support for, and conclude treaties supporting the white-paper agenda, including the treatment of

temporary digital copies in computer memory like any other reproduction, and the banning of devices that could circumvent TPMs.[19] The
treaties could then be used to shape other countries' digital-copyright
reforms. However, faced with a domestic stalemate, Lehman decided to
tackle his problem in reverse. As head also of the US delegation to the
WIPO Committee of Experts charged with creating the draft treaties, he
did not shift the US negotiating position on the WIPO treaties. "Bruce
Lehman went to Geneva and got [his digital agenda] included in the
treaty there and then he came back and said, 'Oh, we need to implement the treaty.'"[20]

According to Greenstein, who attended the WIPO negotiations as a
representative of the consumer-electronics industry: "I think there was
also some feeling of kind of a triangulation occurring here, where the
best way for the content owners to achieve their goals in the United States
was to be compelled to increase protections domestically through an international treaty instrument." Asked if the intention was to use the treaties to create the need to change the laws at home, Greenstein replied, "I
would say that that is consistent with my personal experience."[21]

While this may have been Lehman's intention, accomplishing this
objective required transplanting the US debate over copyright from a
domestic legislative arena to a well-established international treaty-
making organization. As an international organization that has existed
since 1970 and that administers (among other treaties) the Berne
Convention, originally negotiated in 1886, WIPO has its particular institutional history and relevant actors, all of which contributed to the
outcome of the Internet treaties. As the following pages discuss through
an analysis of negotiation process and the final text of the Internet treaties, WIPO's rules, particularly those that required consensus among
members, and a membership that included countries whose interests
would not necessarily align with those of the United States or Bruce
Lehman, would thwart the creation of a "maximalist" copyright treaty.
This outcome demonstrates the limits to the influence of power of even
the dominant copyright power, in certain circumstances at least.

WIPO's Institutions, Ideas, and Interests

Every institution and political order has its specific configuration of institutions, actors, and sustaining ideas – its own politics – and the World
Intellectual Property Organization is no different. From a historical-
institutionalist perspective, the following three issues must be accounted

for: WIPO's decision to address digital-copyright issues; its adoption of the US white paper's positions into the draft treaties; and the final treaties, which (against initial US wishes and WIPO draft treaties' language) conform to obligations expressed in the existing Berne Conventions and TRIPS. These outcomes can best be understood through an examination of WIPO as an institution, and of the actors working within it.

INSTITUTIONS: WIPO'S BID TO STAY RELEVANT

WIPO's decision to negotiate digital-copyright treaties was rooted in the intersection of international-institutional politics and domestic US priorities. As discussed in chapter 3, while WIPO had long been the pre-eminent international organization devoted to copyright and IP issues, in the early 1990s it was running the risk of being eclipsed by the upcoming TRIPS agreement, hosted at the WTO. Since then, WIPO had been relegated to providing technical support to the WTO and serving as a forum to build upon the minimum standards of the TRIPS.

From the perspective of WIPO officials, the 1996 Internet treaties were part of a "sustained campaign ... to return the organization to the centre of global intellectual property policy making" and an attempt to remain relevant in the WTO era.[22] Convening a conference that ended with the signing of the WIPO Internet treaties was a "proactive" move by the WIPO to incorporate the "digital agenda" into its protocol revision process.[23] This WIPO-WTO rivalry was also partly personal. In the colourful words of former USTR official and current BSA counsellor Emery Simon, WIPO officials resented the intrusion on their turf by "these filthy trade people ... soiling this fantastic pure universe that they had lived in ... The WTO's a trade turf. The WIPO is a pure intellectual property turf, and that [WIPO] community really needed to re-establish its personhood."[24]

WIPO's quest for continued relevance was helped by the fact that the recently concluded TRIPS agreement did not address Internet-related issues. While it had settled issues such as the protections of computer programs and databases, the right of rental, and the term of protection of the rights in performances and phonograms, at the time that TRIPS came into force the Internet was not yet the cultural phenomenon it would eventually become and policymakers were only beginning to come to terms with the implications of the communications revolution. Not surprisingly, TRIPS was seen as having already been overtaken by the explosion in digital media and the emergence of the information superhighway.[25]

What became the WIPO Internet treaties began life around 1989 as an exercise to modernize the Berne Convention. The European Commission thought – and the United States agreed – that it would be a good idea to have a "safety net" so that "if TRIPS fails, we can still do something positive on copyright."[26] Internet-related issues were added to the agenda relatively late in the process, as late as 1993 or 1994.[27] After TRIPS passed, WIPO had to decide how their treaties would be different from TRIPS, "and that's when we started including some of these internet-related issues in the treaty," says Simon. During the drafting of possible provisions related to traditional copyright concerns, negotiators began to pay attention to TPMs.[28] The WIPO Performances and Phonograms Treaty arose from the desire to bring neighbouring rights (in this case, performers' and phonogram producers' rights) in line with authors' rights without modifying the Rome Convention, which covers neighbouring rights and of which the United States is not a member.[29] Bruce Lehman, who wanted to use the treaties to push a white-paper-based copyright reform in the United States, was instrumental in convincing WIPO to focus on digital copyright: his influence can be seen in the similarities between the white paper and the draft treaties that served as the starting point for the final negotiations in December 1996.

Lehman worked to build consensus among like-minded industrialized countries, specifically the European Union, the United States, Japan, Canada, and some other developed countries (all indications are that the United States, Japan, and the EU were the main actors; Canada played a minimal role). These countries referred to themselves as "Group B," and were also known as the "Stockholm Group," after their initial meeting place. While the countries had different positions on the issues under discussion, their work kick-started WIPO's digital-copyright work and originated what eventually became the Internet treaties.[30]

INTERESTS AND IDEAS

Because WTO-based negotiations involve all member countries, the possibility that dissident members would stymie talks was significant. Furthermore, developing countries were unwilling to reopen TRIPS negotiations lest the result be even more extensive IP protection.[31] Moving copyright negotiations to WIPO offered the possibility of being able to "conduct negotiations, and establish treaties among non-comprehensive groupings [of countries], and thus sideline those likely to object to a further expansion of the realm of governance for intellectual property."[32]

For the United States and its allies – primarily the European Union and Japan – negotiations over digital-copyright treaties at WIPO were also preferable to negotiations at the WTO.

Despite these advantages, concluding treaties at WIPO nonetheless required negotiation with countries (eventually eighty-nine signed or acceded to the Copyright and the Performances and Phonograms treaties), many of which had interests that did not necessarily coincide with those of the United States, in a context in which cross-sector trade-offs of the type that characterize trade negotiations are more difficult. Furthermore, they had to be concluded within the context of the Berne Convention. Just as the TPM provisions in the white paper would represent a significant change in the balance of US copyright law, so would similar provisions involve a shift the balance of international copyright law, whose principles had been established and reinforced over the course of more than a century.[33]

The Internet Treaties: Moving Copyright into the Digital Age

Several things stand out about the WCT and WPPT diplomatic conferences, held in Geneva from 2–20 December 2006. At the time, the conferences were the largest ever for copyright and related-rights issues, attended by representatives from 127 countries, including the United States (whose delegation numbered almost 30 representatives), Canada (7) and Mexico (5), and a record number of NGOs and observers. They were also completed in three weeks, an instant in international-treaty-making time.[34] This speed was especially impressive considering that the first week was consumed by procedural issues.[35]

The treaties also marked the first time that a copyright treaty was negotiated *before* member states had passed laws on the subject under discussion. As well, for the first time, the language of "balance" became explicit in a copyright treaty, most strikingly in the language of the treaties' preambles about "*recognizing* the need to maintain a balance between the rights of authors and the larger public interest, particularly education, research and access to information." [36] This language represented a departure not only from the WTO/TRIPS,[37] but also from the initial US-influenced draft treaties' "trade-based approach to copyright policy."[38]

In their final form, the WCT consists of twelve substantive and thirteen administrative articles and applies to authors while the WPPT consists of nineteen substantive and fourteen administrative articles and applies to performers and phonograms producers' "neighbouring rights" in copyrighted works (i.e., rights exercised by non-authors). Audio-visual works (i.e., movies) were excluded from the WPPT, the result mainly of pressure from the United States (representing the interests of the Hollywood film studios), supported by India; both have film industries based on a contractual system largely incompatible with moral rights in audio-visual works.[39] The WCT builds upon earlier treaties, notably the Berne Convention, while the WPPT "is a free-standing treaty that does not seek, like the WCT or the TRIPS Agreement, to build upon what has gone before in earlier treaties such as *Berne*."[40] Both work on the principle of national treatment and set minimum, not maximum, standards. As well, despite the fact that the United States came to Geneva with a clear "maximalist" opinion, the final treaties do not reflect this preferred view. Although the subjects of the treaties, notably the legal protection of TPMs, reflect US concerns, they allow all countries a significant degree of flexibility in choosing how they implement their treaty obligations.

The following analysis is based on a comparison of the draft and final treaties, supplemented by primary-source interviews. It also relies on the extensive account of the treaties' negotiation by Mihály Ficsor, the secretary general to the conference and WIPO assistant director general in charge of the copyright sector (and current IIPA consultant), Sam Ricketson and Jane Ginsburg's magisterial commentary on the Berne Convention and related treaties, as well as Jessica Litman's and Pamela Samuelson's accounts of the treaty negotiations. Additionally, it notes the Canadian contribution to the debate, primarily around TPMs. Mexico's individual contribution was not obvious from the record and written accounts.[41]

At the beginning of the conference, the draft treaties and the US position largely reflected the views put forward in the white paper. Greenstein confirms that the official US position was closer to that of the content industry than that of, for example, the consumer-electronics industry. The official US position was also reflected in the draft treaties that served as the basis for negotiations.[42] In his analysis, Brown concurs, arguing that the white paper was the "most significant input into the process that resulted in the WIPO Internet treaties."[43]

LEGAL PROTECTION OF TPMS: DRAFT PROVISIONS
Draft WCT article 13, "Obligations concerning Technological Measure," was taken almost straight from the US white paper:

(1) Contracting Parties shall make unlawful the importation, manufacture or distribution of protection-defeating devices, or the offer or performance of any service having the same effect, by any person knowing or having reasonable grounds to know that the device or service will be used for, or in the course of, the exercise of rights provided under this Treaty that is not authorized by the rightholder or the law.

(2) Contracting Parties shall provide for appropriate and effective remedies against the unlawful acts referred to in paragraph (1).

(3) As used in this Article, "protection-defeating device" means any device, product or component incorporated into a device or product, the primary purpose or primary effect of which is to circumvent any process, treatment, mechanism or system that prevents or inhibits any of the acts covered by the rights under this Treaty.

This article introduced something new to international copyright laws and treaties: "While the other provisions of the Treaty consist more or less of interpretations and certain adaptations of the existing international copyright norms at the Berne-*plus*-TRIPS level, Article 11, along with Article 12 [on rights management information], includes wholly new provisions."[44] These provisions, "for the first time, provide protection for copyright owners outside the usual framework of a law of authors' rights with its traditional classifications of conditions for protection, protected subject matter, exclusive rights, and allowable limitations and exceptions."[45] The draft article 13, which became article 11 in the final WCT, was "closely modeled on the U.S. proposal."[46]

In the draft treaties, "protection-defeating device" was defined in a "maximal" manner.[47] As in the eventual article 11, contracting parties would have been required to provide "appropriate and effective remedies against" the offences covered in the article. This language was very much in the spirit of the US white paper, and was the model for the DMCA.

Legal Protection of TPMs: Final Provisions Negotiations over Draft WCT article 13 were so controversial that "it was an accomplishment to get any provision in the final treaty on this issue."[48] Supporters were unable to overcome sceptical delegates' concerns about draft article 13, as "even a knowledge-based standard for regulating technologies having infringing uses represented a dramatic change in policy."[49] This ban is linked in the second part of clause (1) to "the exercise of rights provided under this Treaty." In the end, these provisions fell victim to worries that these prohibitions were "overbroad and would lead to abuses by copyright holders, particularly if the prohibition could be applied to prevent non-infringing uses of protected works."[50]

As a result of effective opposition (discussed in further detail below), including from the Canadian delegation,[51] WCT article 11[52] (mirrored in WPPT article 18) is much more permissive than Draft WCT article 13:

WCT Article 11: Obligations concerning Technological Measures

Contracting Parties shall provide adequate legal protection and effective legal remedies against the circumvention of effective technological measures that are used by authors in connection with the exercise of their rights under this Treaty or the Berne Convention and that restrict acts, in respect of their works, which are not authorized by the authors concerned or permitted by law.

The final article 11 is targeted much, much more narrowly than was the draft TPM article, which would have made it illegal to import, manufacture, or distribute "protection-defeating devices," or to offer services with the same effect, by people who would know (or have "reasonable grounds to know") that they would be used to "exercise ... rights provided under this Treaty that is not authorized by the rightsholder or the law." This is not directly required by the final treaty language. At the same time, it "is drafted in broad terms and leaves a great deal to the discretion of member states."[53]

While it does not seem to prescribe any particular measures, the language of article 11 created a great deal of controversy and confusion. The problem lies with the phrase "adequate legal protection and effective legal measures," which are nowhere defined in the treaties. This absence gives the treaty its flexibility, while providing little guidance as to its proper implementation.

There are two schools of thought on the subject. The first argues that "adequate legal protection" and "effective legal remedies" require the prohibition of circumvention devices. Anything less than a wholesale ban of circumvention devices (à la Draft article 13) would not prove "adequate" or "effective" protection against the circumvention of TPMs. This view is shared by Ricketson and Ginsburg, Ficsor, and representatives from the motion picture, video game, and music industries interviewed for this project.[54]

On the other side of the issue, Canadian copyright experts Michael Geist and Myra Tawfik, and representatives of public-interest groups and the consumer-electronics industry contend that the treaty requires only that circumventions linked to copyright infringement be prohibited.[55] They argue that banning circumvention devices effectively allows copyright owners to control access to works even when other individuals have a legal right to use the work, to expand control over works that may be in the public domain, or to protect locks on works in order to lock individuals into specific platforms. Similarly, copyright lawyer Jonathan Band argues that the "very minimalist" requirement of adequate legal protections and effective legal remedies can be covered with secondary liability laws that already exist in countries like Canada and the United States.[56]

As mentioned in the introduction, a 2003 WIPO survey of how thirty-nine countries (including the United States and Mexico) had implemented these provisions found wide variations in both the laws' language and coverage.[57] This same survey also noted that the line between protection of rights (i.e., copyright) and access (which has nothing to do with copyright) has become blurred. An earlier report on implementation issues noted that "protection of systems monitoring access seems, in fact, to go beyond the scope of the measures in the WIPO treaties."[58] That laws regulating circumvention devices will be used to control access to works not protected by copyright remains a main criticism of such laws.

Though the debate continues, a review of the conference record and the record of implementation provides support for the minimalist interpretation of article 11. Conference participants, who rejected the more concrete language of Draft WCT article 13, are on record as being concerned about an unbalanced TPM right for copyright owners. Ficsor remarks that during the deliberations the Canadian delegation spoke up against a too-broad rule regarding the prohibition of anti-circumvention devices.[59] While the United States and the European Union both stressed "the importance of the proposed provisions without which owners of rights could not make their works and recordings available on the global network, ... they also expressed their readiness to consider some changes in order to achieve an appropriate balance between the various interests involved."[60] A maximalist interpretation of article 11 implies that the rights of the person controlling the lock are supreme, while even Ficsor's account suggests that other groups' rights and interests must be considered as well, offering at least partial support for the minimalist camp's interpretation.

ISP LIABILITY: DRAFT AND FINAL PROVISIONS

WCT and WPPT proposals around ISP liability were also modelled on the US white paper, notably its assertion that that temporary copies stored in a computer's random access memory (RAM) have "been found to be sufficient fixation."[61] This language was reproduced in WCT Draft article 7, "Scope of the Right of Reproduction." This article would have extended copyright to cover "direct and indirect reproductions of [authors'] works, whether permanent or temporary, in any manner or form" (article 7(1)). Meanwhile, Draft WCT article 7(2) would have tied any limitations on this right to reproductions for purposes authorized by the copyright holder or permitted by law, subject to the three-step test.

Both the white paper and the draft treaties' explanatory notes argue that such protection is justified on the basis that "a work that is stored for a very short time may be reproduced or communicated further, or it may be made perceptible by an appropriate device."[62] However, this article "would have given copyright owners control over all temporary copies, even those never fixed in tangible form and those that under United States law would be deemed legal fair use."[63] In the final treaties, the issue of ISP liability was addressed tangentially, in two agreed statements. This final result masks both the energy that negotiators and industry lobbyists put into the issue and the importance of the statements for the development of US and other laws. According to Kupferschmid, the issue was discussed extensively by the US delegation, which "had more discussions on ISP liability than any other topic and ultimately could not agree. We had huge meetings on that topic."[64]

In the face of strong opposition from other countries and the telecommunications industry, Draft article 7 was dropped from the final text. In its place was a controversial agreed statement attached to article 1(4): "The reproduction right, as set out in Article 9 of the Berne Convention, and the exceptions permitted thereunder, fully apply in the digital environment, in particular to the use of works in digital form. It is understood that the storage of a protected work in digital form in an electronic medium constitutes a reproduction within the meaning of Article 9 of the Berne Convention."

The meaning of this statement is highly contested. One view holds that it means that temporary RAM reproductions are covered by copyright,[65] while the other argues that it does no such thing.[66] The situation is further complicated by the fact that, unlike all the other WCT agreed statements, and the agreed statements attached to articles 7, 11, and 15 of the WPPT, it was not adopted by consensus.[67] As does the "adequate" and "effective" language in article 11, this agreed system allows interest groups to continue arguing the issue on domestic stages around the world. That copyright experts disagree about the meaning of the agreed statements suggests that, politically (and probably legally), member countries possess a significant amount of leeway in being able to decide how they wish to implement this part of the treaty.

The big reward for telecommunications companies was a broadly written agreed statement attached to WCT article 8 – "It is understood that the mere provision of physical facilities for enabling or making a communication does not in itself amount to communication within the meaning of this Treaty or the *Berne Convention*" – that limited ISPs' liability in cases of infringement by their customers. That agreed statement "essentially laid the groundwork for section 512 of the DMCA, the notice-and-takedown-type provisions, as opposed to imposition of secondary liability on passive carriers or on websites or other ISPs that store information."[68]

ACCOUNTING FOR THE FINAL TREATIES

The final Internet treaties reflect the balance between users' and owners' rights that has traditionally characterized international copyright treaties, including the Berne Convention. Given the opportunity to tilt the playing field to owners' advantage, which was Lehman's original plan, delegates refused. Instead, he would have to return to the United States with treaties that addressed many of his issues but without going as far as the original US position. Instead, member countries endorsed the language of balance and were careful not to create new rights. Even the articles regarding TPMs required that prohibitions of circumvention devices be linked to an underlying copyright.

Negotiating countries were divided on the issue of the protection of temporary copies. The United States argued that RAM copies should be treated as copies under the Berne Convention, the European Union called for clarification, and Japan argued against RAM copies as copying (Canada did not put forward any amendments on the issue; neither, apparently, did Mexico).[69] The treaty drafters attempted to argue in their explanatory notes that this was not a new right: "The result of reproduction may be a tangible, permanent copy like a book, a recording or a CD-ROM. It may as well be a copy of the work on the hard disk of a PC or in the working memory of a computer. A work that is stored for a very short time may be reproduced or communicated further, or it may be made perceptible by an appropriate device."[70] Against this interpretation, more moderate language emerged as the result of push-back against the US and draft treaty positions by industry groups and interested NGOs, as well as by the WIPO member states whose votes were required to pass the treaties. ISPs were particularly active in this debate. According to Kupferschmid, "other copyright owners, as well as other copyright users like librarians and museums, generally stuck to trying to convince the U.S. government that this is what the position should be. They really didn't lobby foreign governments that much. The ISPs just got in front of everybody that would listen to them."[71]

Delegates objected that these changes would have resulted in an excessive level of protection, leaving ISPs open to infringement claims;[72] more fundamentally, they argued that such a proposal would make it difficult to run the Internet and computers. Because the negotiations were occurring simultaneously with the debate in the United States, domestic US interests and Congress also challenged the official US position and the draft treaties. Developing countries, most prominently African countries,[73] were reticent about increasing copyright protection, and some US allies also harboured reservations;[74] a majority of countries voted down the treaties' most controversial parts.[75] As a result, the United States and the European Union, as the two copyright "superpowers," had to compromise on issues like the treatment of digital transmissions.[76] As this episode demonstrates, institutions, properly designed, can constrain large powers and, conversely, enable developing countries and smaller powers to exert influence, if only to block unfavourable policies, in fora like WIPO that run on consensus or majority voting in which they have a formal vote.

Path Dependence and the Internet Treaties The final Internet treaties stand as an excellent example of path dependence, in which institutional rules and ideas, and the particular mix of interests active in the negotiations combined to maintain international copyright on a familiar path. However, the path-dependent nature of the Internet treaties can also be seen in what was not covered in the treaties. Chapter 3 discussed at length the revolutionary nature of digital technology in terms of the possibilities it allows for creation and dissemination. Coming as they did relatively early in the digital age, the Internet treaties represented a perfect opportunity to rethink the foundations of copyright law, embrace these new technologies and promote laws that would leverage the possibilities inherent in these new technologies. Instead, member states chose to defend the status quo, not to create a new regime. In all cases, they erred in favour of not creating new rights and reaffirming existing rights. Nowhere in the treaties does one find language that attempts to rethink the very idea of copyright, and whether it is an appropriate tool for the regulation of cultural production in a digital environment. At the same time, the language of the treaty seems to go out of its way to link any new provisions with existing treaty obligations, as with article 11's linkage of legal protection of TPMs to "the exercise of their rights under this Treaty or the Berne Convention."

The ideas of property in intangible works or the Romantic notion of the author were not seriously challenged, as all the major players in the negotiation process were constrained by these ideas or by their material interests. The institutional actors at WIPO had no reason to question copyright, since their job involves administering copyright treaties, not increasing creative production and dissemination. The draft copyright treaties, which were set largely by the US delegation in response to its domestic debate, set the overall parameters for what would be considered as "copyright reform." Once set, these parameters made it very difficult for any radical ideas to become associated with a digital-copyright-reform agenda.

The Internet Treaties and the Domestic US Policy Debate The extent to which the Internet treaties can be seen as an extension of the domestic US debate is fascinating. Important members of Congress, such as Republican senator and chair of the Senate Judiciary Committee Orrin Hatch, expressed their displeasure at Lehman's attempt to sidestep them.[77] Opponents' lobbying in the United States weakened the position of the main demandeur of strong copyright reform. Invitations for public comment on the draft treaties and a review of the American position a month before the conference resulted in "substantial opposition to the draft treaties insofar as they would implement the U.S. White Paper's digital agenda"; this reaction tied Lehman's hands "at least in part"[78] and represented a watershed in public involvement in copyright law, even if the public at large had yet to engage with copyright on the scale seen in Canada in 2007 or as would be seen in the United States in 2012. Domestic opponents of the white paper also successfully lobbied to limit the application of the draft limitations and exceptions article in order to preserve fair-use-like privileges in national laws.[79] A proposed Database Treaty was also scuttled in part due to stiff domestic opposition from, among others, the National Institute of Medicine, and President Bill Clinton's science adviser, who were concerned that it would negatively affect access to research data.[80]

Role of Industry Groups These international treaty negotiations obscure somewhat the crucial role that inter-industry negotiations played in finalizing the treaties. Industry groups helped bridge differences among US interests by lobbying from all perspectives, effectively giving the US delegation

> several arms ... to get its position on the digital agenda across to the various delegations. So, for example, you had groups like the Business Software Alliance who were there and were lobbying in favour of very strict regulation, and you had representatives from the computer industry and from the consumer electronics industry and the library communities, and the telecom companies, who were lobbying for various exceptions or for more ambiguous provisions or for no provisions in some cases.[81]

The negotiation of the Internet treaties also provides a glimpse into the way that the Internet would challenge the transparency of treaty and other negotiations. As a representative of the electronics industry, Seth Greenstein posted nightly reports to a mailing list called Cyberia, "which is mostly [for] lawyers and professionals who are interested in this sort of thing, and legal practitioners as well." "I basically reported ... what people were saying," he says. The result was "a kind of real time history of what was happening" at the WIPO meetings. In the age of live-blogging and Twitter, Greenstein's actions seem routine, almost banal. In the mid-1990s, however, they were nearly unheard of. "There were certain points," he remarks, "where the public sessions were kind of put on hold while all the private meetings occurred. And so all of the delegates would kind of sit around in the hall, known lovingly as the Bunker because it was windowless" – he laughs – "mostly unpleasant. We would basically sit around and wait until these sessions broke and then you would kind of split off and everybody would take their delegates and try to find out what was going on, and you would reconvene and piece it together and try to come up with a strategy to address it." His postings were greatly appreciated, he says. "I was actually getting emails from people ... thanking me because they had no idea what was going on. Their representatives were not keeping them nearly as well informed as I was!"[82]

The final language of WCT article 11, the treaties' centrepiece, was shaped directly by bargaining industry interests. The deadlock over TPMs was broken by finessing the issue – requiring "adequate legal measures and effective legal remedies" rather than the wholesale banning of circumvention devices. Formally, the compromise was offered by the South African delegation;[83] however, Vinje and Band report that what eventually became WCT article 11 "was based on language that had been agreed by certain interested parties in advance of the Diplomatic Conference."[84]

In an interview with the author, the BSA's Simon confirmed that the agreement was actually reached between the consumer-electronics and content industries. "The language that ended up in the WIPO treaty ... was worked out between the consumer electronics industry and the content industries before all of us actually went to Geneva for the diplomatic conference ... The outcome was pretty much a foregone conclusion." During the diplomatic conference, "the consumer electronics guys found the South African delegate, who was kind of an interesting guy and a curious guy, [and who] took their issues on board."[85]

For the consumer-electronics industry, this debate harkened back the Supreme Court's "Betamax" decision in 1984, which found that VCRs were not illegal simply because they could make copies. The CE industry "was quite adamant to prevent that kind of liability from being part of the treaty."[86] The content owners wanted the question to be absolutely clear as to whether a device could be viewed as circumventing and whether circumvention itself should be the act proscribed by law. The manufacturers of equipment, and consumer and library interests wanted to ensure that circumvention for purposes that would otherwise constitute an infringement would lead to liability, but that circumvention that would be considered for fair-use purposes would still be permissible.[87] The resulting article on TPMs "was vague enough to allow either result to emerge, although it probably tilted in the direction of there being some responsibility, some disciplines. But it was deliberately done as a way to avoid that level of confrontation."[88]

Formal negotiations that largely reflect a dominant-power agreement are not unusual. However, that inter-industry negotiations shaped the rules on TPMs is significant given the fact that Bruce Lehman went to Geneva in an attempt to *avoid* making just these types of compromises, or, at the very least, to return to the United States with an agreement that would have strengthened the hand of content owners in their legislative negotiations. In the end, however, the Internet treaties merely allowed the US debate to continue.

Analysis: Delaying the Inevitable

The final treaties were much less ambitious and more vague as the result of domestic US interests lobbying the Clinton administration "to moderate or abandon parts of its digital agenda at WIPO,"[89] as well as the objections of other states. From another perspective, however, the treaties were wildly successful. Despite the opposition that thwarted the explicit banning of circumvention devices and the treatment of temporary copies, among other things, the final treaties did not take these issues off the table, thus ensuring they could be part of future copyright debates.

This moving to a higher level of abstraction in the treaties' language allowed the domestic US debate to continue without restricting any options. It would, for example, allow for the banning of circumvention devices under the 1998 DMCA. The TPM article "was written in such a way that it would give the United States the flexibility to impose a regime under the DMCA that would be consistent with it but on the other hand it would allow other countries that wanted to link circumvention, only proscribe circumvention that also infringed copyright from enacting legislation of that nature."[90]

Its role in forming the draft treaties allowed the United States to set the parameters for international digital-copyright reform. The treaties' flexibility essentially tabled countries' decisions on what was actually required to implement the treaties at the same time that it defined digital-copyright reform to include TPMs and ISP liability. The final treaties should be seen as the first, not the final, word in the debate over copyright in the digital age, a first step along a "path" that rejected any revolutionary changes to copyright while maintaining the possibility that future laws could be tilted in favour of copyright owners. In this, the treaties have played an important role in setting the digital agenda in a way that may not have happened simply from the emergence of a new technology. While the nature of computers suggests that eventually all countries would have had to think about how to treat interactive digital works (as transmissions or as communications to the public), the Internet treaties require that countries also address circumvention devices, even though circumvention devices have nothing to do with copyright, in and of themselves.[91] The final treaties also continued to cast doubt on how temporary copies should be treated. In all of this, the United States, led by its content industries, was central in setting this agenda.

While the maximalist, US-based version of the treaties was stymied, there is nothing in the final treaties to *prevent* a country from implementing a maximalist digital-copyright agenda, or from lobbying in good faith for another country to implement a maximalist policy. Member countries explicitly removed provisions requiring countries to ban circumvention devices; however, one can still plausibly argue that such a ban is required in order to ensure "adequate … and effective" protection of copyrighted works. Similarly, while Draft article 7 was removed completely, the agreed statement to article 1(4) keeps the door open to treating works stored temporarily in RAM as copies; this approach has actually been followed in several countries,[92] including Mexico.

Nonetheless, the treaties also leave countries free to disagree with this interpretation or to ignore the treaties completely: signing a treaty does not require its ratification or implementation. The treaties also contain no mechanism to compel members' adherence. The WIPO Internet treaties should be regarded as norms that frame a debate rather than rules that must be implemented. Unlike a European Union directive, for example, there ultimately is no force standing behind them. Mainly, the treaties allow the digital-copyright debate to continue in other fora and ensure that this debate will focus on issues of concern to the United States and its content industries. Furthermore, in other fora, such as bilateral trade negotiations, the United States could trade stronger copyright protection against other issues.

In the final analysis, though he was able to shape the subject matter of the draft treaties, domestically Lehman's "end run" around Congress only ended up delaying the inevitable inter-industry showdown that had been a feature of US copyright policymaking for almost a century. With the Internet treaties finalized, the confrontation between the copyright industries and user groups, particularly the telecoms industry, would finally come to a head with the Digital Millennium Copyright Act.

6 1997–1998: The Digital Millennium Copyright Act

The conclusion of the Internet treaties marked the beginning, not the end, of the battle over digital copyright in the United States, as in Canada, Mexico, and the rest of the world. The Internet treaties, highly influenced by the United States, set the parameters for global digital-copyright reform, but decisions on whether and how to implement the treaties were left to the discretion of member countries. In the case of the United States, this meant that the ongoing copyright negotiations could continue in the same vein that they had since the early 1900s. While this phase of the domestic US debate would conclude in 1998 with the passage of the Digital Millennium Copyright Act, the United States would continue its international push for copyright reform in various arenas. In these subsequent efforts, US actions suggested it had learned from its WIPO adventure and would pursue copyright reform via more friendly international venues.

The first part of this chapter concludes the previous chapter's account of the negotiation and passage of the DMCA, focusing on the TPM protection and ISP liability measures that constituted the grand bargain at the heart of the bill. It also assesses the overall effect of the bill, not only in terms of who won and lost, but also regarding its impact on society at large. The second part covers the negotiation of the Anti-Counterfeiting Trade Agreement. It argues that not only was ACTA a US-driven attempt to move beyond the Internet treaties, but also that its final form suggested limits to the United States' ability to shape international copyright agreements outside of wider trade negotiations. The chapter concludes by situating the US experience within the global copyright regime.

Part 1: Implementing the Internet Treaties –
The DMCA Negotiations[1]

Following the conclusion of the Internet treaties, the US digital-copyright debate that had begun with the National Information Infrastructure 1995 white paper returned to Washington for a final round. The debate stood much as it had before: both the "protection" and "dissemination" sides had to be satisfied for any bill to pass. The language of the bill, furthermore, had been designed to be vague enough to allow any likely US law to fulfil US treaty obligations.

Politically, the Clinton White House wanted to satisfy Hollywood and Silicon Valley, but did not want to spend "significant political capital to do so."[2] In Congress, the House Commerce Committee (specifically, Democratic Rep. Rick Boucher), which had jurisdiction over Internet and electronic-commerce issues (including the manufacture and sale of anti-circumvention devices) and the House Judiciary Committee, which traditionally covered copyright, each wanted control of the issue. The Commerce Committee was seen as sympathetic to the consumer-electronics and user lobbies, while Mitch Glazier, the Judiciary Committee's chief counsel, was close to the content industries.[3] Each produced their preferred version of what would eventually become the DMCA: "At stake was not only the character and shape of digital copyright law, but also the disposition of enormous sums of lobbying and campaign contribution money expended by the major copyright-affected industries."[4]

The resulting House bill, shepherded by Glazier, gave the House Commerce Committee oversight while also gutting "many of the safeguards that the library and education communities had bargained to make part of that procedure."[5] The bill satisfied the Commerce Committee and the content industries, but not libraries, universities, or consumer groups. It "passed the House essentially without debate."[6] The Senate and House leadership were similarly at odds, with the Senate objecting to the involvement of the Department of Commerce. However, with the 1998 election break looming and both sides wanting a resolution, a deal was eventually struck. The resulting legislation was a "hodgepodge, incorporating bits and pieces of both versions," with several last-minute additions and subtractions. "In final form, the Digital Millennium Copyright Act runs to nearly 30,000 words and more than 50 pages."[7]

The final bill provides compelling evidence of the persistence of the US copyright policymaking institutions and their effect in shaping the eventual DMCA. Despite Bruce Lehman's Geneva detour, the DMCA reflects the long-standing, path-dependent, multi-stakeholder process that had produced so many other American copyright laws: "long, detailed, counterintuitive, kind to the status quo, ... hostile to potential new competitors, [and] overwhelmingly likely to appropriate value for the benefit of major stakeholders at the expense of the public at large."[8]

The DMCA: WIPO-plus and Unholy Alliances

The WIPO Internet treaties imposed few, if any, new obligations on the United States. As an industrialized country with a well-developed copyright regime, it, for example, arguably already had a "making available" right, while the obligation to provide "adequate legal protection and effective legal remedies" for TPMs could have been met by existing secondary liability provisions.[9] Initially, US negotiators had thought that changes to US law would not be necessary.[10] Less than a month after the conference, Lehman himself suggested that US law was already in compliance with the treaties and that no new provisions would be needed.[11]

The DMCA was made possible by a compromise between the content industries and the telecommunications industry, the most powerful groups at the copyright table. Before the DMCA, reforms to limit ISP liability and to protect TPMs had been advancing on separate tracks. ISP liability was covered in HR 2180, the Online Copyright Liability Limitation Act, while HR 2281, the WIPO Copyright Treaties Implementation Act, addressed WIPO implementation issues, including legal protection of TPMs. However, the two issues "were in essence getting nowhere."[12] The content industries argued that the only way the IP committee would get agreement for the WIPO implementation was to agree to ISP safe harbours: once that agreement was made, everything fell into place.[13] The DMCA's passage reflected both the process's compromise/negotiation-based nature and that the process is weighted in favour of those actors with the greatest economic and political resources.

TECHNOLOGICAL PROTECTION MEASURES[14]
Similarly, the TPM provisions reflected the relative power of involved groups, with content industries receiving much of what they wanted

and others receiving narrow exceptions. As the content industries wanted, DMCA section 1201 effectively bans – with narrow exceptions – the circumvention of digital locks and trafficking in the tools that can break these locks. This section is descended directly from the white paper and the WIPO draft treaty language on TPMs. It deals with two types of TPMs, those that regulate access to a work and those that control use. With respect to access, the basic provision forbids the circumvention of "a technological measure that effectively controls access to a [copyrighted] work" (DMCA 1201(a)(1)(A)). This provision bans circumvention that "effectively controls access to a work subject to copyright, regardless of whether or not such access would itself amount to an infringement."[15] Republican Representative Thomas Bliley, chair of the House Commerce Committee at the time, argued that these were sweeping new changes: "The 'anti-circumvention' provisions of the Administration's bill create entirely new rights for content providers that are wholly divorced from copyright law."[16]

With respect to the TPMs that control use, section 1201(b)(2)(B), protects a TPM if it "in the ordinary course of its operation, prevents, restricts, or otherwise limits the exercise of a right of a copyright owner"; that is, TPMs that restrict fair use or protect non-copyrighted materials would not be protected.[17] While the DMCA distinguishes between acts of circumvention (access, use), it does not distinguish among purposes of circumvention.[18] The DMCA also forbids people to "manufacture, import, offer to the public, provide, or otherwise traffic in any technology, product, service, device, component, or part thereof" that would allow individuals to circumvent TPMs designed to control access or limit copying of a work, if the device is primarily designed for circumvention, is marketed as being such a device, or has only limited commercial significance otherwise (ss. 1201(a)(2) and 1201(a)(3)(b)). Despite section 1201(b)(2)(B), this blanket ban reduces legal access to circumvention devices for non-infringing purposes that have nothing to do with copyright or for fair-use purposes.

User groups received specific exemptions to section 1201. The DMCA does not formally override fair use and other rights (DMCA 1201(b)(2) (c)), although individuals must break the locks on their own. It also clarifies that manufacturers of consumer electronics, telecommunications, or computing equipment are not required to design their equipment to respond to any particular technological measure (section 1201(c)(3)), except for analogue VCRs (1201(k)). Other exceptions for access and copying were provided for law enforcement, intelligence, and other government activities (1201(e)), and for ongoing rulemaking related to TPMs (s. 1201(a)(1)(B–E); see below), in addition to a number of exceptions that are allowed for access.[19] Kerr, Maurushat, and Tacit argue that "a number of these exceptions are written so narrowly that they are not useful as a matter of practice. For example, [several] exemptions neglect to indicate whether tool making is permitted as a privileged circumvention. This raises serious doubt as to the true availability of these exemptions since many of them simply cannot be exercised without the use of circumvention tools."[20]

For user groups, the most significant part of this section is a requirement[21] that the Librarian of Congress, in consultation with the Copyright Office and the Commerce Department, review the legislation every three years to determine whether further exemptions should be added to this list.[22]

The Negotiation of Section 1201 When the DMCA was being negotiated, many groups with an objective interest in digital-copyright issues had not yet awoken to the importance of copyright law. In the mid-to-late 1990s relatively few individuals and groups had a strong understanding of the myriad ways that a copyright bill, and particularly one introducing novel concepts such as widespread legal protection for TPMs, could affect their lives. (It would not be until the very public battles over Napster in 1999, a year after the passage of the DMCA, that the general public would begin to wake up to the importance of copyright law.) It also explains why the initial public-interest alarms were sounded by copyright lawyers and computer technologists such as the ones in and affiliated with the Digital Future Coalition.

As a result, these interests were either not represented or were addressed in an ad hoc manner. In some cases, groups that should have been at the table chose not to be. Band recounts the efforts made by him on behalf of the American Committee for Interoperable Systems to "broaden our coalition" in order to constrain TPM protection. However, despite identifying issues like TPMs' potential effects on encryption research, security testing, and privacy ("We basically came up with the parade of horribles"), they had difficulty getting groups interested: "There was no one asking for those exceptions. We basically made them up. And then tried to find people who cared with varying degrees of success, and when we went around from office to office, we said, oh, look at all the problems, you have problems with the VCRs and Macrovision and you have problems with reverse engineering and then all those other problems too."[23]

Consequently, Band and other industry representatives negotiated the exemptions on encryption research (working with the CCIA and the BSA) and privacy. Lacking experience on this issue, they reached out to the encryption research community but were unable to find anyone interested in the issue: "They had no clue what was going on." Similarly, they were unable to find groups interested in addressing other issues, such as TPMs and the protection of minors (which would allow the overriding of digital locks in order to allow parents to protect their children). The resulting sections "were just completely something that I made up."[24]

ISP Liability Section 512 of the DMCA, which establishes the mechanism for exempting ISP and online service providers from liability, was the price demanded by the telecommunications industry for the DMCA. Its inclusion in the final bill is a testament to the political and economic clout of the telecommunications industry. It sets out the terms under which both online service providers and "information location tools" (such as search engines, online directories, and hyperlinks) are liable, or exempt from liability, in cases when users of their services are accused of infringing copyrights on sites hosted on their system. The actual wording focuses on actions, such as hosting and linking, because the PTO was unable to draft a definition of ISPs that was narrow enough to satisfy all stakeholders.[25] These provisions were the first of their kind, internationally, to address the issue of ISP liability.[26] As for the legislation itself, paragraphs 512(a) and (b) implement US obligations under the WIPO Internet treaties by ensuring, respectively, no liability for routine transitory communications (i.e., routing) or for system caching (intermediate or temporary storage). Non-profit educational institutions are also, in some cases, eligible for access to limitation of liability (paragraph 512(e)).

Paragraph 512(c), the centrepiece of this section (paragraph 512(d) is the equivalent for search engines), implements a "notice-and-takedown" regime. Under notice and takedown, an ISP, search engine, or other Internet site that hosts content is not liable for copyright infringement if, upon receiving a proper notification of claimed infringement, it takes down or blocks access to the material (it must notify the user that this action has been taken). The service provider must not have actual knowledge of infringement or benefit financially from the infringement. Subscribers alleged to have infringed copyrights have the opportunity to respond to the notice-and-takedown action by filing a counter notification.[27]

This system satisfied both content owners and ISPs. For ISPs, it provided a degree of certainty and exemption from liability, although

Litman characterizes the reporting requirements and steps involved in avoiding liability as "a long, complicated series of hoops."[28] Content owners, meanwhile, received the ability to sue copyright infringers without having to prove liability in court: a good deal for ISPs and copyright owners, if not for users.

Effect of the DMCA

In keeping with US copyright policymaking's pluralist set-up, the DMCA was basically a "draw" between large user groups and content industries, as a consumer-electronics lawyer put it in an interview with the author. The content industries realized their main objective: a ban on the trafficking of circumvention devices. This ban, however, was subject to certain narrow exemptions obtained by other parties at the table. For example, the consumer-electronics industry's main concern was that their products would not have to respond to two different or contradictory technology measures. They were able to negotiate paragraph 1201(c)(3), the "no mandate clause," which ensures that their products need not respond to any particular TPM.

TPMS

Observers agree that the DMCA has operated as intended. Early cases, including one involving garage-door openers, led to fears that the DMCA would have a chilling effect on research, even in areas that had nothing to do with copyright.[29] However, the courts generally have interpreted the DMCA to require a "nexus" between copyright infringement and circumvention.[30] Court decisions have "given good guidance to practitioners, they've given good guidance to litigants as to the situations they would be successful in and those in which they likely would not, and there haven't been any catastrophes," says Stevan Mitchell of the Entertainment Software Association, an industry group representing computer and video-game publishers and one of the groups most affected by TPMs.[31]

Concerns remain. A review of the academic literature and case law associated with the DMCA finds that it has been criticized for impairing fair use and freedom of speech, inadequate privacy protections, inviting nuisance lawsuits, and skewing the balance between "private rights and the public interest."[32] There is also the question of whether legal protection of TPMs will actually stop infringements, given the fact that "the pirates figure out a way to hack things," and whether it will inhibit legitimate research or actions, only some of which may be exempted under the triennial rulemaking exercise.[33] Rather than stopping infringement and protecting publishers, there is growing evidence that digital locks have transferred market power from publishers to companies like Apple and Amazon. By locking consumers to these companies' platforms, these digital locks reduce the potential for competition from smaller book distributors.[34]

Specific cases also raise the spectre that the DMCA has resulted in a chill on research and innovation.[35] Michael Petricone, Consumer Electronics Association senior vice-president of government affairs, remarks that the combination of a litigious American society and high statutory damages for digital infringement make it difficult for consumer-electronics manufacturers to innovate.[36] For example, the CSS encryption program, agreed to by the movie and consumer-electronics industries, ensures that only authorized machines can play DVDs. This authorization not only limits copying, but also "allows the movie studios to dictate the terms for what the technologies allow or prohibit."[37]

The "rulemaking" provisions of the DMCA continue to be hotly debated. As has already been noted, TPMs can potentially give copyright owners the ability to set unilaterally the terms of access to and use of a work, ignoring others' rights to use a work without seeking permission. The eight exemptions that have been granted in the three "rulemakings" between 1998 and 2007 were narrow, the outcome of an expensive process in which each proposed exemption can be challenged but that is not well suited to the involvement of either individuals or resource-constrained groups.

In contrast, the 2010 rulemaking was quite consequential. On 26 July 2010, the Librarian of Congress, as mandated by the DMCA, concluded the fourth triennial rulemaking proceeding to determine if any new TPM-related exceptions should be added to the law, based on whether affected persons "are, or are likely to be ... adversely affected by the prohibition ... in their ability to make non-infringing uses ... of a particular class of copyrighted works" (DMCA s. 1201(a)(C)). This round of rulemaking continued a judicial trend to link TPM circumvention to copyright,[38] and more generally accepts the principle that TPMs should not inhibit a user's fair-use rights, including in situations where a user has a good-faith belief that an act of circumvention is "in aid of an actual fair use."[39] Nonetheless, the formal prohibition of trafficking in the tools that can actually circumvent TPMs remains in place.

On a side note, changes in US copyright law as a result of this rule-making have led to a sharp divide between de facto US law and the US government's international position on digital copyright, which continues to advocate a blanket prohibition on TPM circumvention mirroring the original Lehman white paper and draft Internet treaties. This divide suggests that even US copyright policy is experiencing a moment of transition. How long this split can continue is a matter for future research. It is possible that, eventually, US domestic and international copyright politics will realign, particularly if domestic political pressure for greater user rights increases. Chapter 9 revisits this issue.

Generally, content owners have been satisfied with the rulemaking process, while users claim that the process is tilted towards those with the resources to navigate a lengthy, expensive process that often (and, to date, usually) results in very narrow exceptions.[40] In response to such complaints, a US Copyright Office official said in an interview that the rulemaking process and the DMCA have been successful in achieving their goals, arguing that there has not been the predicted assault on copyright. The official further argues that the narrowness and low number of exemptions (two in the first triennial rulemaking, four in the second, six in the third) suggest that fair use has not been negatively affected by DMCA section 1201.[41] While this is one possible conclusion, it is more likely that, given the resources needed to participate in this process and its resulting bias towards well-funded interests, the small number of triennial exemptions likely understates the DMCA's effect on fair use in the United States.

ISPS / NOTICE-AND-TAKEDOWN

Content owners and ISPs are relatively satisfied with the notice-and-takedown regime. ISPs are responsive to owners' notices: refusing to take down allegedly infringing content opens ISPs to liability, which they can avoid if they comply with the takedown request. Says Kupfer-schmid, whose firm represents content and software owners: "In the United States, because of the DMCA, we get near 100% compliance with our notice and takedown because it's the law." At the same time, he adds, accused infringers have the opportunity to file a counter-notice.[42]

Band argues that section 512 represented a win for the ISPs and a disaster for the content industries because it assumed that content hosted on ISPs' networks, not peer-to-peer file sharing (which has since become the dominant form of unauthorized copying), would be the greatest threat to the content industries' monopoly over distribution. ISPs' blanket exemption if they act only as a conduit means that the content industries now "have no way of pressuring, or it's very difficult for them to pressure, the Verizons of the world to do anything to help them."[43]

While section 512 sets the legal parameters for ISP liability and remains the most important framework in this area, it has not been the final word on how ISPs have addressed copyright infringement on their networks. Since February 2013, several of the largest US ISPs, such as AT&T, Verizon, and Time Warner, implemented a voluntary "six strikes" Copyright Alert System in conjunction with the content industries. After being caught six times downloading copyrighted works illegally via peer-to-peer systems (for example, using the torrents downloaded from a site like The Pirate Bay), ISPs have committed to taking action against the user. The Center for Copyright Information, which runs the Copyright Alert System, has explicitly stated that users will not lose their Internet access, but would rather face penalties such as reductions in the speed of their Internet connection.[44] However, according to a Copyright Alert sent out under this system and obtained by the website TorrentFreak, which covers BitTorrent-related news and has paid particular attention to this issue, AT&T is threatening its users with "mitigation measures including limitation of Internet access and even suspension or termination."[45]

While this may sound severe, the alert system would apply only to peer-to-peer file sharing through systems such as BitTorrent, not those who access infringing materials via systems such as Usenet and file-hosting services. Whether this will be an effective tool remains unclear. TorrentFreak contended before the launch that "since ISPs have little incentive to apply such stringent measures we expect that the punishments will be rather mild."[46] As of October 2013, it appears that no American subscriber has yet been kicked off the Internet for downloading copyrighted material.

OVERALL EFFECT

The DMCA, which became law on 28 October 1998, continues to attract criticism. "At best, it could be said that the DMCA balances the rights of one industry with the rights of another."[47] The RIAA, one of the main beneficiaries of the DMCA, argues that, viewed from the perspective of 1998, the DMCA was a rational and thoughtful response to pressing policy issues: Congress recognized that US society had a large interest in ensuring continued production of creative goods. From this perspective, the DMCA represented, on the whole, "a very forward looking perspective" on how to continue to fuel creativity.[48]

Even on its own terms, its record is mixed. Congress passed the DMCA to "facilitate the robust development and world-wide expansion of electronic commerce, communications, research, development, and education in the digital age" and to "make available via the Internet the movies, music, software, and literary works that are the fruit of American creative genius."[49] Discussing the DMCA's effect on unauthorized uses of copyrighted works, the BSA's Emery Simon says that the DMCA's impact has been "substantial but not dramatic." While it has not solved the "piracy" problem, it has offered some legal certainty without preventing the evolution of the Internet, "which is what people alleged at the time it would do. It has provided some points of leverage and some tools for people to attack particular piracy problems.[50] Neil Turkewitz, RIAA executive vice-president, expressed relative satisfaction with the way the DMCA has allowed the RIAA to defend its copyrights while noting that it fails to provide sufficient discipline with respect to technological developments that have taken place since its adoption.[51]

According to a Copyright Office official, the DMCA was one of the factors that encouraged companies to put their works online.[52] Former Future of Music Coalition executive director Ann Chaitovitz agrees that it helped create a "legitimate digital marketplace." Before the DMCA, "all we had was an illegitimate marketplace. I think what it did was lay the groundwork that persuaded the big content owners to agree to take the risk. And that then enabled a legitimate music market to develop."[53]

In evaluating these opinions, it is perhaps useful to make a distinction between content owned by the large media conglomerates and that produced by others, and to recall that the pre-DMCA Internet was already full of content, some distributed by corporate entities, some by individuals. As a result, it is difficult not to conclude that the DMCA was not necessary to encourage creative production online – the ostensible purpose of copyright – but rather to create the conditions under which the large content companies would put their works online. It is even difficult to argue that the DMCA has reduced unauthorized uses of copyrighted works; authorized digital sales are still "dwarfed" by unauthorized downloads, as Chaitovitz notes. Neither has it halted the decline of the recorded-music industry, which has been hardest hit (to date) by file-sharing technologies.

A further irony: while the legal protection of TPMs was championed by the content industries, particularly the music industry, TPMs have failed commercially in the digital-music market: most music sold online is sold without TPM protection. However, predictions of the demise of TPMs are exaggerated. The content industries continue to patent TPMs regularly, and digital books, films, videos, television shows, computer programs, and video games continue to depend on TPMs. Even in music, TPMs may yet prove to be resilient. Subscription-based services, such as Spotify, allow consumers to pay a monthly fee for access to a library of music that becomes inaccessible to them should they not renew their subscriptions. Such a model is akin to the licensing of a computer program, in which song ownership remains with the copyright owner and does not transfer to the consumer, as happens when one purchases a CD.

Whatever the benefits and drawbacks of such services, given the strength of the view that copyright is an absolute property right that allows owners to set conditions of access, TPMs will continue to be important for content owners, as much for what they imply about the proper protection-dissemination balance in copyright as for the success of any particular business model. The acceptance of the legal protection of TPMs and the legitimization of the position that copyright owners have the right to control access to the use of copyright works has the potential to be an "evolutionary" change in copyright that moves it closer towards being exclusively a right that recognizes only the interests of copyright owners.

Part 2: The Anti-Counterfeiting Trade Agreement

Ten years after the conclusion of the Internet treaties, US officials began discussing the possibility of a new plurilateral agreement on counterfeiting. Unlike the Internet treaties at WIPO or TRIPS at the World Trade Organization, it would be negotiated among like-minded countries outside of established international organizations. Unencumbered by having to deal with consensus votes among dozens of developing countries, negotiations began in July 2008 among the United States, Canada, Mexico, the EU, and Japan, among others. Talks concluded in early December 2010.[54] Despite its name, ACTA was mainly concerned with digital-copyright issues; content industries received privileged access to the negotiations, while telecoms were generally shut out.

ACTA represented a classic example of forum shifting; it was essentially an attempt to avoid having to make the compromises that characterized the Internet treaties by moving talks to a more flexible and easily controlled venue; any result could then be exported to non-signatory countries. With respect to its copyright provisions (it also covered issues such as counterfeiting and medicine patents), ACTA was an obvious attempt by the United States to continue pushing and expanding the Internet treaties, which were then about a decade old. The ACTA negotiations are instructive for those interested in digital-copyright policy-making and treaty negotiations generally. While the Internet treaties had required consensus among dozens of developed and developing countries, ACTA was designed only to include like-minded countries, with Mexico in particular joining as a fig leaf to counter criticisms that ACTA was merely an attempt by rich countries to set global copyright standards in their own interest.[55]

The treaties were negotiated largely in secret, with US content industries receiving privileged access and favourable treatment in the process: the initial US position effectively echoed its advocacy for the same maximalist approach to copyright (for example, calling for a ban on circumvention devices) that had informed its initial position at WIPO. However, even with these advantages, the ACTA outcome was similar in many respects to that of the Internet treaties. In both cases, the United States and its content industries faced real limits on their ability to influence international copyright laws. It seems that in the absence of a direct linkage between trade and IP, the United States' resources, including the size of its market and the reach of its content industries, do not give it as high a degree of influence as it enjoyed in the TRIPS negotiations. The experience with ACTA and the Internet treaties suggests real limits to the US ability to influence international copyright laws. Future research on international copyright and the US influence on domestic laws will have to consider how copyright treaties and laws will develop in a world in which the United States cannot credibly link IP reform to market access.

On TPMs, for example, the United States backed down in July 2010 from its original position in the face of opposition from the EU (the most important player other than the United States), Japan, Mexico, Singapore, Morocco, and Australia, all of which preferred language closer to that of the Internet treaties.[56] As was the case with the Internet treaties, the US position, advanced on behalf of its content industries, proposed a maximalist copyright treaty, only to be rebuffed, resulting in a more balanced treaty that continues to allow countries leeway in interpreting their treaty obligations.

The US government and content industries' efforts can be seen in ACTA article 27. Unlike the Internet treaties, article 27, paragraph 6 explicitly defines "adequate legal protection and effective legal remedies," as they apply to the circumvention of TPMs. Like the DMCA, it prohibits the sale, manufacture, and importation of circumvention devices. However, it is immediately undercut by article 8, which explicitly allows that members "may adopt or maintain appropriate limitations or exceptions" to prohibitions on circumvention devices, and that related obligations "are without prejudice to the rights, limitations, exceptions, or defences to copyright or related rights infringement under a Party's law." This paragraph is important because it not only grandfathers current exceptions in copyright laws, but also allows for the adoption of new exceptions. As a result, the language of ACTA's TPM provisions largely mirrors that of the Internet treaties.

Similarly, for ISP liability, article 27 requires the implementation of a process to allow for "effective action against an act of infringement of intellectual property rights which takes place in the digital environment, including expeditious remedies to prevent infringement and remedies which constitute a deterrent to further infringements." While it also discusses notification regimes (such as notice-and-notice and notice-and-takedown), it says only that a party *may* set up a specific regime to require ISPs to provide rights holders with information that identifies accused infringers. Nothing more stringent is required.

Article 27 also requires that any measures not create "barriers to legislative activity, including electronic commerce, and, consistent with that Party's law, preserves fundamental principles such as freedom of expression, fair process, and privacy." Canada's notice-and-notice approach to limiting ISP liability would fit comfortably within this framework. Ironically, the US notice-and-takedown approach may be in violation of the requirement that ISP liability not interfere with the principles of fair process and freedom of expression, as notice-and-takedown requires that allegedly infringing materials be taken down *before* an accused can plead his or her case.

Concluding the treaty, however, was the easy part. As this book has argued, that stage merely signals the start of the political battle, not its end. Getting every country to actually sign the agreement has proved to be more difficult than anyone had suspected. The treaty was signed in October 2011 by all negotiating countries except the European Union, Switzerland, and Mexico (the latter of which signed, amid much controversy, in July 2012). The EU had been expected to sign without much controversy until tens of thousands of Europeans protested in the streets in February 2012. In Mexico, as noted in the introduction, the Senate effectively rejected the treaty in 2011. Both events came as a surprise to copyright observers worldwide. As chapter 8 will explain, the 2012 European and Mexican conflicts over whether to sign ACTA signalled in many ways the culmination of the first phase of the digital-copyright debate that began with the Internet treaties. Domestic politics holds the key to understanding these outcomes.

Part 3: Analysis – First among Equals

Returning to the United States and the Internet treaties, the US response to the Internet treaties – the DMCA – emerged from the conflict and negotiations among domestic interests acting both within the US policymaking process and on the international stage at the WIPO. From an historical-institutionalist perspective, the story of the DMCA is largely a domestic one, marked by institutional consistency and path dependency, with outcomes driven by the biases of the US political process.

United States: Master of Its Domain at Home, First among Equals Abroad

Due to their political and economic resources, the US content industries, through their contacts within the US government, were able to influence the direction of the WIPO Internet treaties to ensure the treaties would be useful as normative tools to continue the push for American domestic copyright reform in their interests. The final DMCA, however, was the result of many small compromises (as is typical in American copyright history) and a grand compromise between the content industries and the telecommunications industry. The WIPO Internet treaties functioned more as a normative justification for the DMCA rather than dictating what the United States could and could not do.

INSTITUTIONAL PERSISTENCE

The DMCA was the result of a historically contingent pluralist-style negotiation process that privileged certain interests over others. From a governance perspective, one of the most interesting things about the legislative battle that led to the DMCA was the extent to which its development was divorced from global – to say nothing of regional –

politics. Despite Bruce Lehman's dramatic attempted end-run around the domestic policy process, the DMCA followed the same well-trodden path as all the copyright bills of the previous century. In the US quasi-pluralist, interest-based copyright regime, in which affected interests are expected to negotiate among themselves, and in which powerful interests (such as the telecommunications industry) can make themselves heard in Congress, it is hard to imagine a political scenario that ends in something other than a limited-liability regime for ISPs and strong protection for TPMs with limited exceptions. No matter the outcome at WIPO, any legislation affecting ISP liability would have had to be approved by a Congress in which the telecommunications industry was not lacking in influence. The eventual deal – notice-and-takedown in exchange for the legal protection of TPMs – emerged wholly out of the unique dynamics of US copyright policymaking. The same conclusion can be reached for the (relatively less powerful) interests that opposed TPM protection. In the end, from a purely domestic US perspective, the WIPO negotiations were little more than a sideshow.

The persistence of a pluralist-style domestic US copyright negotiating process can be explained in part by the fact that while technological change over the years required periodic adjustments to the law, copyright itself remained a technical and still largely apolitical issue. While public interest started to rise before and during the DMCA negotiations, it was only with the 1999 invention and subsequent shutdown of Napster that ordinary Americans began to pay close attention to copyright. This politicization has the potential to complicate further the difficult process of making and passing copyright laws in the United States. It also suggests that the days of apolitical inter-industry bargaining to create copyright laws are numbered if not over.

INTERESTS TREATED DIFFERENTLY

With respect to the various actors involved in the debate, some groups' views were clearly seen as being more important than others. Most important were the motion picture industry, the music recording industry, and software publishers on the content side, and the online and ISP industry, the telecommunications industry, television and radio broadcasters, computer and consumer-electronics manufacturers, and libraries on the dissemination side.

Digital technology acted as an external shock that led to the involvement of ISPs and "the public," in large part through the Digital Future Coalition. The telecommunications industry had a significant effect on the DMCA and the WIPO Internet treaties, wresting significant concessions that have led several observers to argue that they were the big winners under the DMCA. The effectiveness of public-interest groups was subtler. In the debate that led to the Internet treaties and the DMCA, public-interest organizations, copyright lawyers such as Peter Jazi, and Internet civil-liberties groups – groups that had previously been involved peripherally or were absent in copyright reform discussions (excepting copyright lawyers) – weighed in on the subject. Jazi's strategy with the DFC was to link the interests of less-powerful groups like university lawyers with those of lobbies to whom Congress would listen, such as the consumer-electronics industry;[57] what influence they had on the debate came by finding like-minded allies to whom Congress would listen. However, they did not have a full "seat at the table." At WIPO, while NGOs were present in Geneva during the negotiations, their "expressions of concern [finding] a receptive audience among many national delegations,"[58] accounts such as Ricketson and Ginsburg's and Ficsor's seem to accord them a relatively small effect on the actual outcome; member states and major industry were still the primary drivers of the treaties.

At the time of the DMCA, copyright was just starting to emerge as a political issue. Groups like Public Knowledge, which focus on copyright and similar issues from an access perspective, did not yet exist. "The public interest" was represented mainly by academics and experts who were sounding alarm bells for a public not yet fully aware of how their direct interests could be affected by copyright policy. As Greenstein's early blogging on the Internet treaties negotiations suggests, the Internet had only just arrived as a means to help disparate interests coordinate in a way that would allow individuals to coordinate and organize effectively to counter more traditionally organized lobbies.

In 1996 and 1998, US copyright policy had not yet been fully mass politicized. That would come later, a result of the 1999 arrival of Napster and enactment of the DMCA itself. Ten years of experience with the DMCA and the sue-everyone response of the US music industry would create widespread protest groups in Canada, the United States, and (to a lesser extent) Mexico. Absent these concrete examples of the negative effects of copyright law on individuals' lives, the lack of strong public interest in the DMCA negotiations was unsurprising, even as the contours of the DMCA fight presaged what was to come.

IDEAS AND CHANGE: SOWING THE SEEDS OF CHANGE

The US debate over copyright reform occurred within the protection/ dissemination parameters set by the Constitution's copyright clause.

Since the 1980s, purposeful actors, namely, the content industries, have engaged in substantive bricolage (linking calls for stronger copyright to US trade law) and symbolic bricolage (emphasizing copyright's protection function over that of dissemination). While opponents attempted to re-emphasize copyright's dissemination function with some success, the DMCA's TPM rules demonstrate that, for the moment, the protection forces have the upper hand and have pushed US copyright closer to being primarily a copyright owner's right, rather than a policy to balance different interests. Whether this represents an "evolutionary" change that demonstrates the path-dependent nature of copyright or a "revolutionary" change that puts copyright on a new "path" is, ultimately, in the eye of the beholder. What matters is that the concept of institutional persistence suggests that established policies securely embedded in a solid institutional structure are harder to change than new policies in weak institutional structures. Given the enduring persistence of US copyright institutions, DMCA rules on TPMs (and ISP liability, for that matter) would be very hard to reverse. Their presence will likely prove a solid base for the content industries' arguments for greater protection in the next round of copyright reforms, whenever that may be.

There is, however, nothing in this account to suggest that protection interests will always have the upper hand. Even in 1996 we can see the emergence of new copyright interests – the telecommunications industry, an activist legal community – promoting their interests and view of the common good. By engaging in symbolic bricolage, emphasizing copyright's dissemination role over its protection role, they effectively weakened the protection narrative that underlies the content industries' vision of ever-stronger copyright protection. And, as will be seen in the conclusion's account of the 2012 Internet blackout, which dealt the pro-stronger-copyright forces their first major legislative setback in decades, the arrival of a new and organized (more or less) interest group – individual voters – has the potential to change US copyright policy by exercising its influence within a porous US political system.

REGIONAL AND INTERNATIONAL POLITICS: A US TEMPLATE FOR IMPLEMENTATION

Just as it had shaped the draft treaties, the United States, and its content industries, would try to influence how countries implemented the treaties. With the sideshow (from the US domestic perspective) of the WIPO Internet treaties concluded, the domestic American debate over digital-copyright reform could continue. Its stakes would be much higher than simply defining the copyright regime of a single nation. The negotiations that led to the DMCA also set the US position on what it would consider acceptable for other countries' attempts to implement the Internet treaties. Given its relative economic and political importance, the United States' choices matter for all WIPO members, including Canada and Mexico.

The WIPO Internet treaties played different roles in the three North American countries. The United States was able to shape the treaties to allow it to fulfil its domestic and global objectives. The WIPO Internet treaties increased the US capacity to influence other countries without sacrificing its domestic autonomy to implement its own digital-copyright regime.[59] While Mexico and Canada were present at the negotiations, their influence on its outcome was obviously much less than that of the United States.[60] Although they were smaller players, the treaties did not necessarily affect their autonomy. For these two countries (as well as for most other countries), the effect of the WIPO Internet treaties would depend upon the interaction of the fairly loose requirements of the treaties with domestic institutions and interests, and the context within which they interact with the United States. In the case of Canada and Mexico, as will be seen in the next two chapters, this context is defined by their bilateral relationships with the United States and, regionally, by NAFTA.

7 Canada and the Internet Treaties: Aborted Implementations

The twenty-ninth of June, 2012, marked the end of one of the stranger legislative journeys in Canadian history. When Bill C-11, the Copyright Modernization Act, received royal assent two days before Canada's 145th birthday celebrations,[1] it capped a decade of debate that witnessed three failed attempts to pass a copyright-reform bill, the mass, grassroots politicization of copyright via the first-ever successful Canadian political use of social media (and one of the first in the world), and a rare retreat by a never-retreat, never-apologize Conservative government on an issue of great interest to the US administration.[2] While copyright is an increasingly mainstream issue around the world, Canada's drawn-out copyright debate provides us with an unusually vivid opportunity to evaluate how domestic contexts have interacted with regional and international economic, political, institutional, and cultural factors to shape distinctively the implementation of the Internet treaties, while also allowing for a more subtle understanding of how Canadian copyright policy is made.

Choice is a key theme of this chapter. Canada's long march towards treaty implementation offers a telling illustration of the potential for and limits to national autonomy when it comes to setting domestic copyright laws that respond to domestic concerns. Far from being a pawns of their larger neighbour to the south, Canadian politicians demonstrated the potential to diverge from the United States on key issues, when they chose to do so. An in-depth examination of Canadian copyright reform strongly suggests that global copyright-harmonization pressures face very real limits when they are interpreted through domestic political, social, and economic imperatives.

This chapter is presented in three parts. The first part elaborates on the historical-institutional framework – the ideas, institutions, and interests – that shaped Canadian copyright policymaking as it relates to efforts to implement the Internet treaties. The second part examines how these factors interacted to produce the 2005 and 2007–8 copyright-reform bills, neither of which made it beyond first reading in the House of Commons, and the two, largely identical 2010 and 2012 bills. The third part offers some reflections on what this debate can tell us about domestic and regional copyright governance.

Part 1: The Canadian Copyright Landscape

Ideas: Canada's Copyright Ambivalence

Historically, copyright in Canada, as elsewhere, was not considered to be a high-priority issue. In Canada, as in the United States and Mexico, copyright is officially a federal responsibility. Section 91(23) of the Constitution Act, 1867, places copyright exclusively under federal jurisdiction, although provinces can pass laws that indirectly affect copyright, in areas such as publication, distribution, licensing, and sales of literature.[3] More recently, law regulating technological protection measures, or "paracopyright" measures, may also fall under provincial jurisdiction, as TPMs touch on issues such as "contractual obligations, consumer protection, e-commerce, and the regulation of classic property" in ways that go beyond the regulation of copying that is the purpose of copyright law.[4]

Although the Constitution provides the federal government with responsibility for copyright, it lacks the explicit guiding principles in legislation or the constitution of the type found in the US "copyright clause" or article 18 in the Mexican Constitution of 1917.[5] Instead, the orientation of Canadian copyright law must be teased from the legislative process, government reports, the legislation itself, practice, and jurisprudence. Historically, Canada's copyright regime and discourse are firmly rooted in the utilitarian tradition of the United Kingdom and the United States: a pragmatic, technocratic, economics-focused law that balances the interests of copyright owners and the users of copyrighted works.

This utilitarian approach has been acknowledged by the Supreme Court of Canada, which contends that "the economic purpose of copyright law is instrumentalist in nature, namely, to ensure the orderly production and distribution of, and access to, works of art and intellect."[6] In other words, its main objective is the balancing of competing interests (not rights) in pursuit of an overall societal optimum, and not the maximization of copyright owners' rights. This view is reflected in past touchstone studies of Canadian copyright, in particular the Economic Council of Canada's 1971 report into Canadian copyright reform and the 1957 Ilsley commission report, whose work from 1954 to 1960 occurred under the Liberal government of Louis St Laurent and the Progressive Conservative government of John Diefenbaker. More recently, it is echoed in the mission statement of Industry Canada, which has formal legislative responsibility for copyright.[7]

This history is acknowledged in the Copyright Act's preamble, added to the act by the 2012 Copyright Modernization Act, Bill C-11, which asserts, "The *Copyright Act* is an important marketplace framework law and cultural policy instrument that ... supports creativity and innovation and affects many sectors of the knowledge economy." It also recognizes both rights holders' rights to "recognition, remuneration and the ability to assert their rights," with limitations existing "to further enhance users' access to copyright works or other subject-matter."

While Canadian copyright falls primarily within the Anglo-American tradition, in some areas the Copyright Act draws on the Continental (i.e., French) view of copyright as an author's inalienable moral right. However, while Canadian copyright law shows traces of the Continental moral-rights approach, this approach is overshadowed by economic rights in copyright.[8] In 1931, the Copyright Act recognized moral rights for the first time, as a condition of signing the Berne Convention; however, they were not made enforceable until the passage of a 1987 bill, which also enacted a public lending right that compensates Canadian authors when their books are lent to the public by libraries.[9] However, even though such "moral rights" are enforceable, they are not inalienable under Canadian law.

CANADIAN CULTURAL INDUSTRY STATISTICS

Canadian domestic cultural production, which includes the production of books, music, motion pictures, and software, while not insignificant, is a relatively minor part of the economy. Canada was, and remains, a net importer of copyrighted works. This state of affairs helps to explain at least partly why stronger copyright traditionally had not been high on the Canadian policy agenda.

According to the Cultural Human Resources Council, cultural employees accounted for 3.1 per cent ($39 billion in 2002 dollars) of Canada's

Gross Domestic Product (GDP) and about 3 per cent of the total labour force in 2009.[10] This accords with figures produced earlier in the decade by Statistics Canada, which found that the "cultural sector"[11] of the Canadian economy accounted for an average of 3.8 per cent ($33.7 billion in current dollars) of GDP, and an average of 3.9 per cent of overall employment between 1996 and 2001.[12] In contrast, Canada's financial sector accounted for 20.9 per cent of Canadian GDP in 2010, while manufacturing accounted for 12.8 per cent.[13] With respect to employment, the most significant categories in 2008 were trade (15.7 per cent of the labour force), health care and social services (11.9%), and manufacturing (10.2%).[14]

The cultural-sector-specific statistics do not include software, which is also covered by copyright. A study on Canadian copyright-related industries, commissioned by the Department of Canadian Heritage and including the software industries, found that, including the software industries,[15] Canadian content industries accounted for 4.5 per cent of Canadian GDP between 1997 and 2004. Employment in the "core" content industries was just over 655,000 in 2004, accounting for 4.1 per cent of total Canadian employment; together with non-core employment (219,000 jobs), the content sector accounted for 5.6 per cent of total Canadian employment. Growth in the copyright industries was led by the software and database industries and tended overall to outperform the rest of the economy.[16]

Over sixty years passed between the introduction of Canada's first proper Copyright Act in 1924 and the next major revision in 1987. The small size of the domestic sector and copyright's low profile as a vote-getting issue, combined with a net deficit position in copyrighted works and the fact that stronger copyright would worsen this deficit position, has tended to temper governmental interest in reforming copyright. In 2004, Canada posted a $3.2 billion deficit in royalties, primarily with the United States (software royalty payments and advertising mitigated this deficit somewhat with surpluses of $317 million and $242.4 million, respectively).[17]

CHANGING THE BALANCE IN CANADIAN LAW

The period from 1924 to 1987 was characterized by minor revisions in the Copyright Act and by occasional reports calling for a modernization of an increasingly outdated act. From a policy perspective, this period was also marked by the low profile of IP generally. Doern and Sharaput refer to the "leisurely low-priority nature of IP during this period."[18] The three major studies of Canadian copyright over this period – the 1957 Ilsley commission report, the Economic Council of Canada's 1971 report, and the 1977 Keyes and Brunet report – all demonstrated a consistent approach to the idea of copyright as a policy that should balance the protection of copyright owners and the promotion of the dissemination of creative works. They also see the two objectives as being in tension with each other: strengthen protection too much and dissemination and users of copyrighted works will suffer. The reports also took a sceptical view of copyright. The Keyes and Brunet report, prepared for the Department of Consumer and Corporate Affairs,[19] argued that stronger protection for copyright owners was not necessarily in Canada's interest as a developing country.[20]

This approach began to change in the mid-1980s, first with the publication of Consumer and Corporate Affairs Canada's joint 1984 white paper with the Department of Communications, *From Gutenberg to Telidon: A While Paper on Copyright. Proposals for the Revision of the Canadian Copyright Act*.[21] The key change of perspective found in this report, as Bannerman notes, is from scepticism about the benefits of stronger copyright to arguing for "the importance of stronger copyright protection to stimulate economic growth."[22] The white paper viewed copyright as a way "to provide new opportunities for growth in Canadian cultural, entertainment and information industries."[23] Before the paper could be acted upon, the reigning Liberal government was defeated in 1984 and replaced with the relatively more pro-American Progressive Conservative government of Brian Mulroney. Under Mulroney, in 1985, the House of Commons Standing Committee on Communications and Culture tabled the report *A Charter of Rights for Creators*.[24] Where *From Gutenberg to Telidon* framed its advocacy for stronger copyright protection with the desire to strike "an appropriate balance amongst the various interest groups involved to ensure that creators are properly compensated while the efficient dissemination of information and ideas is assured," *A Charter of Rights for Creators* eschewed the language of creator-user balance in favour of an exclusive focus on maximizing the rights of copyright owners (or, in the language of the report, "creators").[25] This shift can be explained in terms of changes in actors and ideas, not material conditions. Canada was still a net importer of copyrighted works. Stronger copyright protection would almost certainly not reverse this situation, especially given the small size of the country and English Canada's penchant for consuming US cultural products.

What had changed were prevailing opinions about how copyright *should* be viewed. *From Gutenberg to Telidon* and especially *A Charter of Rights for Creators* are notable for their lack of consideration of the balance-of-payments effects of stronger copyright (i.e., that stronger protection would lead to increased net outflows of royalty payments), which had been central to previous analyses.[26] Key to this change was the linkage (substantive bricolage) between IP and international trade agreements that had been made initially in the United States and now had migrated to Canada. Handa argues that the post-1987 period has been characterized by linkages between IP reform and international trade agreements "entered into by Canada that reflect largely U.S. motives, especially where new works are concerned."[27] The 1988 Canada-US Free Trade Agreement (CUSFTA), for example, required that Canada begin paying US broadcasters to retransmit their television signals as part of a larger agreement to ensure access to the US market. However, the reorientation of Canadian thought on copyright seen in *A Charter of Rights for Creators* predates these agreements. The timing suggests that this new tendency to see copyright in terms of maximizing a country's competitive position has its basis in ideological and personnel changes in government. On the ideological side, this new approach is likely an example of Campbell's concept of diffusion, related to the influence of similar arguments emanating from the United States at the same time.[28] It also reflects the general championing of market forces that accompanied the crisis in the Keynesian welfare state and gave rise to Canadian pressures for free trade with the United States.[29] This view was solidified by the replacement of the Trudeau Liberal government with Progressive Conservative Mulroney's pro-business, pro–United States, and (eventually) pro-free-trade government.

Following this period, Canadian copyright reforms in 1988 and 1997 tended to privilege copyright owners over other groups. Flora MacDonald, the Progressive Conservative minister of communications and sponsor of the 1988 Bill C-60, An Act to Amend the Copyright Act, described the bill as "pro-creator."[30] The bill, the first major copyright legislation in over sixty years, also marked the emergence of the content industries as the "primary stakeholders" in the copyright debate.[31]

Despite promises that "user" rights would be addressed in a second phase to follow immediately after the 1988 bill, user groups had to wait almost a decade for the sequel. Bill C-32, An Act to Amend the Copyright Act, was passed in 1997, this time by a Liberal government.[32] While this second bill was marketed to user groups as a complement to pro-owner

1988 legislation, the 1997 reforms resulted "in more rights under the Act for producers and copyright owners and fewer exceptions for users and consumers."[33] In particular, for the first time in Canadian law Bill C-32 recognized neighbouring rights – rights in works that are not directly related to creation – for recording artists and the makers of sound recordings. This change allowed Canada to adhere to the 1961 International Convention for the Protection of Performers, Producers of Phonograms and Broadcasting Organizations (the Rome Convention).[34] The WIPO Performances and Phonograms Treaty – one of the two Internet treaties – would also address these neighbouring rights from a digital perspective. Although Bill C-32 was passed soon after the conclusion of the 1996 Internet treaties negotiations, the bill did not address the substance of the treaties.

Between 1988 and 1996, governments passed five other bills amending the Copyright Act, "largely because of the impetus of successive trade agreements," particularly NAFTA and WTO.[35] The NAFTA changes, for example, introduced a commercial "rental right" for computer programs and sound recordings, which requires the "effective protection and enforcement of intellectual property rights, while ensuring that measures to enforce intellectual property rights do not themselves become barriers to legitimate trade."[36] After the 1997 changes, the government passed minor amendments to the Copyright Act, in 2002, 2003, and 2007. Of particular interest to this study are the 2007 changes, which, at the behest of the Canadian Motion Picture Distributors Association (the Canadian counterpart to the Motion Picture Association of America) and Hollywood-based interests,[37] introduced provisions to deal with the (already-illegal) camcording of movies in theatres.[38]

Though the protection approach favouring copyright-owner interests has tended to drive and dominate Canadian copyright debates since the mid-1980s, recent court rulings suggest that the dissemination aspect of copyright remains important. A 2002 ruling by the Supreme Court of Canada[39] argued that a creator's right to a "just reward" is limited and must be balanced against other public-policy objectives, although the court does not tell Parliament how to balance these objectives.[40] More recently, five Supreme Court decisions handed down on 12 July 2012 strongly supported the principle that user rights are a central part of Canadian copyright law.[41] However, as the Canadian debate over the Internet treaties suggests, this perspective remains contentious.

This brief survey of the Canadian copyright scene from the mid-1980s to the late 2000s reveals that the underlying justifications for

Canadian copyright have changed significantly since the 1924 Copyright Act. Before the mid-1980s, copyright's objective was generally agreed to be to provide a balance between protection for copyright owners and dissemination interests, supported by the understanding that stronger copyright was not necessarily in Canada's interest. In the mid-1980s, this rhetoric was displaced largely by an emphasis on copyright as a way to increase the competitiveness of the cultural industry, the result of the diffusion of ideas from the United States, and the linkage of trade to IP. More recently, however, the 2002 and 2012 Supreme Court rulings reaffirming limitations on creators' and owners' rights in copyright have complicated, though not reversed, the tendency to view copyright as primarily an owner's right.

The Canadian IP debate since the mid-1980s provides ample evidence that ideas about copyright are not static. Furthermore, as Canada's experience with the Internet treaties demonstrates, these ideational changes can be driven not just by large corporate interests, but also by individuals, consumers, and public-interest groups, many of whom challenged successfully this dominant protection perspective.

Institutions: Balance, with a Twist

INTERNATIONAL INSTITUTIONS

Canadian copyright policy is embedded in a series of international and regional institutions that limit Canadian policy autonomy, often in exchange for other objectives, such as improved market access and protection of Canadian copyright owners abroad. Internationally, in addition to being party to the WIPO Internet treaties, Canada is a full member of the Berne (copyright) and Rome Conventions (neighbouring rights), as well as TRIPS. Canada is also a member of the 1952 Universal Copyright Convention, although not a particularly enthusiastic one. This sentiment is a reflection of the fact that the national treatment principle that underlies the Berne Convention and TRIPS – which stipulates that Canada must accord the same level of copyright protection to other countries' citizens as it does to its own nationals – does not provide net economic benefits to small-producer countries that are net importers of copyrighted works. Even during the NAFTA talks, the Canadian government fought successfully the US insistence that cultural issues, including copyright, be included in the agreement through the inclusion of CUSFTA's "cultural exemption." Canada tried unsuccessfully to convince the Mexican government to support the Canadian anti-copyright-inclusion stance, but Mexico refused, as its language protected it from the cultural assimilation that formed the basis for the Canadian objection to including copyright in the deal.[42] As noted earlier, while Canada's cultural industries are formally exempted from NAFTA's copyright provisions, Canada did implement several NAFTA-related copyright changes in its 1993 NAFTA enabling legislation. As well, Canada's long delay in implementing the Internet treaties suggests that the long-standing official Canadian ambivalence about international copyright is alive and well in the twenty-first century.[43]

As noted in chapter 3, the NAFTA (and WTO) dispute-resolution mechanisms have limited US ability to retaliate against countries with what it perceives to be unfair copyright laws. Consequently, NAFTA's copyright rules were less important to Canadian policymaking than the way NAFTA limited the United States' ability to link increased market access to Canadian copyright reform.

DOMESTIC INSTITUTIONS

Within these international contours, Canadian copyright policy is shaped significantly by Canada's distinctive copyright institutional framework.[44] While this study generally accepts Doern and Sharaput's path-breaking institutional analysis of Canadian intellectual property, it departs from their institutional taxonomy in two areas. First, it accords lesser importance to Foreign Affairs and International Trade Canada (DFAIT; now Foreign Affairs, Trade and Development Canada) in the setting of Canadian copyright policy. Doern and Sharaput argue that DFAIT has supplanted the Department of Canadian Heritage and Industry Canada as the primary copyright policymaking department due to "the growing trade policy aspects of copyright and IP."[45] They correctly note that only after copyright and IP were linked to trade issues did copyright become a key governmental priority.[46] However, it would be more correct to say that DFAIT only has a central copyright role during trade negotiations, particularly with a major trading partner with a strong interest in IP (i.e., the United States, the European Union, and Japan). In such situations, IP becomes one sector among many to be traded off against other objectives. In the absence of trade negotiations, Industry Canada and Canadian Heritage remain the main agencies; DFAIT plays a coordinating role, relaying information to and from Canada's foreign partners and making recommendations based on its perception of Canada's interests. In the negotiations that led to the WIPO Internet treaties, for example, Industry Canada and Canadian Heritage led the Canadian delegation, while DFAIT played a coordinating role.[47] In the case of the implementation of the Internet treaties, DFAIT has played a secondary role, primarily as one of the conduits for making Canada aware of the US position and informing the United States of Canadian actions on copyright. Because DFAIT has played a relatively minor role in the negotiation and implementation of the Internet treaties, the following analysis does not focus on its role, except in passing.

In fact, and this is the second departure, Doern and Sharaput's emphasis on DFAIT somewhat obscures the significant role of the Prime Minister's Office (PMO) and his secretariat, the Privy Council Office (PCO) in the copyright policymaking process. The PMO/PCO not only has the final say on the inevitable departmental conflicts, but the decision to initiate trade negotiations is a political one that cannot be made only by DFAIT. Outside trade negotiations, the PMO/PCO also plays a pivotal political role, acquiescing to or resisting foreign political pressure and placing political pressure on the departments to behave in a certain way. In an era of "court government,"[48] the role of the PMO/PCO in influencing and making public policy cannot be excluded from any institutional analysis of Canadian federal policymaking. Parliament itself, particularly in periods of minority parliaments, can also have a decisive effect on the progress of copyright legislation.

Central Institutions: Heritage and Industry In the United States, the debate between owners and users takes place within Congress, which requires that all recognized interested parties reach a consensus that Congress will then approve. In Canada, the rough equivalent of that process primarily occurs not in Parliament but within the bureaucracy. The specific nature of this arena has significant effects on the outcomes of policy debates. Canada is unusual in that the responsibility for copyright is divided between two departments.[49] The Copyright Act gives formal responsibility for copyright to the minister of industry. In practice, however, Industry Canada and Canadian Heritage share the copyright file.[50] While Industry Canada is involved by statute, Canadian Heritage owes its involvement to its responsibility for the Canadian Radio-television and Telecommunications Commission (CRTC), and aspects of the broadcasting industry, as well as its "broad heritage and cultural policy mandate that includes citizenship and Canadian identity, cultural development and heritage, and national politics."[51]

Although Canadian Heritage's responsibility is not enshrined in the Copyright Act, copyright has assumed a greater relative importance for Canadian Heritage than Industry Canada. Where Industry Canada is also responsible for patent-related issues (which are generally seen as more economically important than copyright issues), Canadian Heritage can focus solely on copyright on behalf of industries and groups such as the music and movie industries, for which stronger copyright is their main priority. Doern and Sharaput speculate that the 1993 re-assignment of the Department of Communications' responsibility for the technical aspects of telecommunications to Industry Canada "may have had the effect of requiring the heritage minister to search for her remaining areas of influence in the cultural sector. This included more prominence on the creators of copyrighted property."[52] That copyright offered policy-makers the opportunity to recast a seemingly market-based policy as cultural policy in an age of market liberalism made it even more attractive.[53] Canadian Heritage's search for influence has yielded some results. A study of the rhetorical battle over copyright found that Canadian Heritage's articulation of its view of copyright "as a tool to protect Canada's creators and cultural industries from digital technologies has been much more insistently articulated in Ottawa than Industry's perspective of copyright as a part of the government's declared 'innovation strategy.'"[54]

The departments' opposing mandates institutionalize copyright's user-creator, or protection-dissemination, dichotomy and complicate any efforts to pass copyright legislation. As Michele Austin, chief of staff to Maxime Bernier while he was the Conservative industry minister, from February 2006 to August 2007, told the author, were copyright policy to be made the purview of only one department, "life would be a thousand times easier."[55] Industry Canada's mandated focus on innovation is biased towards dissemination, ensuring that copyright law does not hinder access to knowledge and information. Canadian Heritage's goal, meanwhile, is to maximize protection for creators for cultural reasons, although in practice this means maximizing copyright protection for copyright owners; that is, record companies and movie studios, which are usually not Canadian.[56] Interest groups tend to gravitate towards one department or the other. Groups representing performers, writers, creators, and the content industries coalesce around Canadian Heritage, while Industry Canada is seen as the representative of ISPs, consumers, businesses, investors, and "user industries, such as the broadcasting sector."[57]

This dichotomy is not ironclad. Canadian Heritage officials, at least in 2005, expressed concern about DMCA-like protection of TPMs[58] even though their main clients, the Canadian Recording Industry Association and the Canadian Motion Picture Distributors Association were strongly in favour of them. As well, Industry Canada's general interest in balance may be tempered by the view of strong copyright as a means to strengthen innovation for certain industries, such as the computer and video-game industries.

The vigour with which each bureaucracy defends its mandate often interferes with the timely pursuit of reform, even when the respective ministers are in agreement about what should be done.[59] These institutional divisions were key contributors to the long delays in implementing Canada's obligations under the WIPO Internet treaties.[60] That these divisions delayed Canadian implementation of the Internet treaties in the face of an ever-rising US desire for their implementation further suggests the extent to which Canada still retains political autonomy on the copyright file.

The debate has also offered ample evidence of the importance of individual ministers in shaping their department's actions and resulting legislation. While Industry Canada has traditionally held the lead on the copyright file, Liberal heritage minister Sheila Copps emerged as the central figure in Canadian copyright reform from the late 1990s to the mid-2000s, working (unsuccessfully, in the end) for the implementation of the WIPO Internet treaties along the lines of the US DMCA.[61] Similarly, industry minister Bernier's libertarian views were one of the reasons why he resisted strong protection for TPMs.[62]

The Prime Minister's Office and the Privy Council Office The role of the Prime Minister's Office and his secretariat in Canadian policymaking should never be ignored, particularly at a time when political power has been centralized more than ever in the hands of the prime minister and his aides.[63] In the Canadian political system, the PMO/PCO can and does arbitrate and facilitate inter-departmental disputes. This role is particularly important in a case like that of copyright, where two departments share responsibility. In the 1997 debates over Bill C-32, the PMO of Liberal prime minister Jean Chrétien had to arbitrate between Industry Canada and Canadian Heritage, whose polarization reflected that of their main constituents. According to then-Canadian heritage minister Sheila Copps, the two departments were at such loggerheads that Prime Minister Chrétien had to set part of the balance in the bill, eventually deciding that, "because Canadian universities had recently received substantial funding, they could make do with a limited copying exception."[64]

The PMO/PCO, however, can also serve as an originator of policy, which it then can task the responsible departments with carrying out. Its position can reflect an overall judgment on how a decision might affect electoral chances, whether a policy may favour one group too much over another, or it may reflect purely ideological considerations that have nothing to do with the policy itself and everything to do with political perceptions.

Parliament and Copyright The direct relevance of Parliament, the legislative body that actually passes legislation, is primarily limited to minority-government situations. In majority parliaments, Parliament's role is usually limited to non-existent, since no matter which committee is assigned responsibility for the copyright file, the government controls the parliamentary committees. While majority governments face very little risk that any legislation it introduces might not pass, a minority government must convince one or more opposition parties to support its legislative agenda, and the survival of any bill depends on the government not being defeated in a confidence vote. Consequently, politicians in a minority parliament must pay close attention to how copyright is playing politically.

Throughout most of the twentieth century, Canadians did not express much interest in copyright. In the relatively tranquil period from the first Copyright Act in 1924 to the flurry of copyright-related activity in the mid-1980s, the Ilsley commission was able to conduct its work under Liberal and Progressive Conservative governments in the 1950s, keeping a low profile in the process. Even as copyright and intellectual property has moved to the centre of the global political economy, since the mid-1980s there has been little to distinguish between the two major parties on this file. Both the 1988 Progressive Conservative and 1997 Liberal copyright reform bills, described above, focused more on copyright owners and creators than on users and consumers. Since the beginning of the 2000s, however, copyright has become an increasingly contentious issue in Canada. This increased public interest, combined with a series of minority parliaments between 2005 and 2011, made it more difficult to pass any copyright bill.

Of the four major political parties, only the left-leaning New Democratic Party (NDP) is now consistently critical of a strong copyright policy, largely as the result of the efforts of NDP MP Charlie Angus, a musician and author.[65] The separatist Bloc Québécois, which prior to 2011 was still a force in Canadian politics, approached copyright in much the same way as does Mexico, as a cultural support for Québécois artists and as a creator's moral right.[66] It is largely in favour of stronger copyright and is thus (ironically) aligned with the foreign entertainment industries that dominate the Canadian entertainment landscape. Neither the Liberal nor the Conservative parties currently have a discernibly coherent, principled view on copyright. Each has proposed legislation to implement the Internet treaties, with the Liberals favouring an incremental approach to copyright reform and the Conservatives favouring the US position on TPMs.

Governments can signal how they feel about copyright legislation in their choice of the reviewing committee. The House of Commons Standing Committee on Canadian Heritage is generally more favourable to the creative community and the content industries; the House Standing Committee on Industry is more favourable to user groups; and special joint committees fall somewhere in between.

Interests: A Changing Balance

As recently as the 1997 debate over Bill C-32, copyright lobby groups could be classified relatively easily. On the one side were those favouring increased protection for copyright owners and creators: the content industries, creators' copyright collectives, artists' groups, and the US government. Of these groups, the US government and the music recording and motion-picture industries have led the call for stronger copyright protection, with the Canadian Recording Industry Association (CRIA) as the most vocal and public advocate for the Canadian adoption of US-style implementation of the Internet treaties.[67] While Canadian creator groups are also interested in stronger copyright reform, their focus is more on issues like increased performers' rights, with issues like ISP liability and the legal protection of TPMs as secondary issues. On the other side were those groups that emphasize the dissemination part of copyright law, namely, large institutional groups like universities, libraries, and television broadcasters.

The popularization of digital technology and the Internet in the 2000s, however, has upended the Canadian copyright debate to a greater extent than that in the United States over the 1998 DMCA. At the time of the DMCA, the Internet and activities like file sharing and downloading were not yet as ubiquitous as they are today. The US DMCA debate witnessed the birth of groups not directly aligned with any of these large interests, but with a "public interest." Over the past ten years in Canada, groups and individuals affected directly by the digital technologies and media covered by the Internet treaties have emerged as a potent political force. While the US-based content industries continue to be the main proponents for stronger copyright protection, as they were in 1988 and 1997, these new "public interest" groups have challenged traditional approaches to copyright and complicated the passage of any Canadian copyright bill. As in the United States, the Canadian telecommunications industry has also become increasingly involved in copyright politics, primarily with respect to the issue of ISP liability.

THE UNITED STATES

Before Confederation, Canada was ruled by a succession of imperial copyright acts, placing it squarely in the Anglo-American tradition. These acts were, unsurprisingly, insensitive to the needs of a developing country with a minuscule publishing industry.[68] After Confederation, the United Kingdom continued to keep a tight leash on Canadian copyright laws. Early attempts to implement made-in-Canada legislation, in 1872 and 1890, were thwarted by the UK through its 1865 Colonial Laws Validity Act because the acts were deemed to be inconsistent with UK legislation.[69] The 1890 bill would have replicated the US manufacturing clause, providing copyright only to those books printed in Canada. It was stopped with "British power ... bluntly applied," as were subsequent attempts to enact the bill in 1890, 1891, and 1895.[70]

Internationally, Canada became a member of the 1886 Berne Convention after the United Kingdom decided that its nominally independent colony would join the convention. Canada attempted unsuccessfully to renounce the treaty in 1889. Canadian copyright scholar Sara Bannerman notes: "Canada would have been the first country to withdraw from the Berne Union, and fears that such an action would destroy the nascent copyright union led the British government to use its Imperial control to prevent Canada's withdrawal."[71] That Canada's first wholly indigenous copyright legislation, the 1921 Copyright Act (passed in 1924) was designed to fulfil its obligations under the Berne Convention – a treaty it had tried to renounce – and was essentially the same as the UK Imperial Act of 1911,[72] demonstrates the direct influence that the United Kingdom had over Canadian legislation.

Early Canadian copyright debates were couched largely in regional, not global, terms. Canadian law of the time reflected "the grip of British law and the weight of U.S. market forces on a cluster of small colonies,"[73] the United States being a source of cheap books that benefited readers while posing a threat to the nascent Canadian publishing industry and to British publishers. As an example of this push-and-pull one can look to the 1842 Imperial Copyright Act, which prohibited the importation of reprints into the United Kingdom and its colonies and which was partly overturned with the 1847 Foreign Reprints Act, which permitted imports subject to a 12.5 per cent duty "that was in practice seldom collected."[74] Early copyright actors acknowledged this US influence. In 1895, the Copyright Association of Canada remarked that "the geographical position of Canada, side by side with the United States ought not to be overlooked. This fact makes Canada's position very different indeed from that of any other British colony."[75]

Half a century later, in 1957, in its review of Canadian intellectual property laws, the Ilsley commission acknowledged the continuing economic importance of the US market for Canadian publishers in its recommendation that Canada ratify the 1952 Universal Copyright Convention (UCC), negotiated under the auspices of the United Nations Educational, Scientific and Cultural Organization. The UCC had been negotiated at the United Nations in part to deal with the US refusal to join the Berne Convention, primarily because of its resistance to eliminating its manufacturing clause. In a report that was otherwise concerned about how international agreements such as the Berne Convention limited Canadian sovereignty, the Ilsley commission recognized the economic interest of ratifying a treaty that would provide protection in the lucrative US market to Canadian authors who first publish in a place other than the United States.[76]

Today, the United States and its content industries loom large in Canadian copyright (and intellectual property) policymaking as the main drivers for change: stronger copyright protection, a downplaying of copyright's dissemination role in general,[77] and DMCA-style implementation of the Internet treaties (strong legal protection for TPMs and a notice-and-takedown ISP-liability regime) in particular.

The US government relies on a variety of other diplomatic tools in its attempt to influence the Canadian government, as NAFTA's copyright provisions can be modified only with great difficulty and because NAFTA effectively limits the ability of the three countries to link issues by taking the carrot of increased market access off the table. For example, the United States used meetings under the Security and Prosperity Partnership of North America (SPP) to inquire about Canada's lack of

WIPO implementation.[78] Despite its limited scope, the SPP was significant for the discussion of regional copyright because it was a forum in
which copyright reform (a US interest) could be linked credibly to
movement on trade and border issues.[79]

Then-US ambassador to Canada David Wilkins also met with
Canadian officials on several occasions during his tenure from 2005 to
2009 and was not shy about expressing the American pro-content-industry position. At an April 2008 Public Policy Forum conference on
intellectual property, Wilkins remarked: "The USTR continues to have
concern about Canada's failure to ratify and implement two WIPO
Internet treaties."[80] Michael Shapiro, attorney-adviser from the Office of
Intellectual Property Policy and Enforcement of the US Patent and
Trademark Office, elaborated on the US position, arguing for Canadian
DMCA-type legislation. He posited that the difficult nature of copyright policy "should not be a reason for further delay in ratifying and
fully implementing the WIPO Internet treaties."[81] The United States
has also exerted pressure on other copyright-related issues. In 2007,
California governor and action movie superstar Arnold Schwarzenegger
directly and successfully lobbied Conservative prime minister Stephen
Harper for a bill to outlaw the camcording of films in movie theatres.[82]

The United States has also placed Canada on its Special 301 Watch
List every year since 1988 save one (1993). In 2009, it "upgraded"
Canada to the Priority Watch list, where Canada remained until 2013,
when it was downgraded back to the Watch List.[83] Since 2004, Canada's
lack of movement on the Internet treaties figured prominently in its
placement on these lists. While such placement can be a prelude to
sanctions, in practice the United States would have to pursue any resulting sanctions through the dispute-settlement mechanisms of the
WTO or NAFTA, which it has yet to do. Officially, Canada rejects the
Special 301 process as being "deeply flawed and inappropriate ... It's
reflective of industry views," says Yannick Mondy, first secretary at the
Canadian embassy in Washington.[84] Statements in a 2007 parliamentary committee hearing by Nancy Segal, deputy director of DFAIT's
Intellectual Property, Information and Technology Trade Policy
Division, further support this view: "Canada does not recognize the
301 Watch List process. It basically lacks reliable and objective analysis.
It's driven entirely by U.S. industry. If you aren't on the Watch List in
some way, shape, or form, you may not be of importance."[85]

The US Congress, for its part, has also made declarations highlighting
Canada as a "pirate" nation, through its Congressional Anti-Piracy Caucus

and has raised the issue during inter-parliamentary meetings. More recently, the United States has attempted to influence Canadian law via the negotiation of other agreements, notably the Anti-Counterfeiting Trade Agreement and the Trans-Pacific Partnership.

In a historical-institutionalist analysis, institutions can also be actors. The previous three chapters treated the US government as a collection of institutions that shaped and maintained a specific copyright policy. In Canada and Mexico, the United States is an actor whose position on copyright, as well as its persistence in promoting internationally this position, is the outcome of the confluence of ideas, institutions, and interests described in chapter 3. It has several resources at its command, notably Canadian (and Mexican) asymmetrical dependence on the US market and its ability to work in tandem with its content industries, which have a strong presence in the Canadian and Mexican markets. Consequently, Canadian governments have demonstrated sensitivity to US views on copyright (e.g., the 2007 anti-camcording bill). However, there is a difference between agreeing with how the United States frames an issue – that, for example, digital-copyright reform requires regulating digital locks – and accepting its preferred policies. The US ability to link copyright reform to an issue that Canada cares about, such as access to the US market, is one way in which the United States has been able to effect changes in Canadian laws. In other situations, making such a linkage is more difficult. The United States is an important actor in the Canadian copyright-policymaking process, but it must work through existing domestic institutional set-ups just like other actors, since existing regional institutions, such as they are, cannot be used easily to modify Canadian (or US or Mexican) copyright laws.

PROTECTION GROUPS

The Content Industries The content industries have always played an important role in the Canadian copyright debate: "Throughout history the Canadian government increased the strength of its copyright laws in close consultation with the content industries."[86] Dominated by multinational businesses with strong links to US-based lobby groups and well resourced, the content industries enjoy relatively easy access to decision-makers and civil servants. They also are aligned with, or are part of, industry groups, such as the Canadian Chamber of Commerce, that have also lobbied for stronger copyright laws. Overall, these businesses tend to support a DMCA-like approach to TPMs and a notice-and-takedown regime for ISPs. As with their counterparts in the United

States, copyright law is the foundation of their business models, and they spend significant resources on lobbying to influence government copyright decisions. Doyle reports that the 2005 Bill C-60, Canada's first attempt to implement the Internet treaties, was the most heavily lobbied bill in Canadian history.[87]

The Canadian Recording Industry Association has been the most visible, vocal, and important proponent of stronger Canadian copyright reform.[88] One of Canada's foremost digital-copyright experts, University of Ottawa law professor and Canada Research Chair in Internet and E-commerce Law Michael Geist, says that copyright is "their number one issue, by far."[89] CRIA's views largely parallel those of the other main industry associations, the Canadian Motion Picture Distributors Association (CMPDA), the Canadian Publishers' Association, and the Entertainment Software Association of Canada (ESAC).

Like the CMPDA, CRIA represents foreign, primarily US-based, companies (the four major international record companies), which share about 95 per cent of the Canadian music market.[90] CRIA also has close ties to its US sister organization, the Recording Industry Association of America (RIAA), including an overlapping client roster. CRIA was founded in 1964 as the Canadian Record Manufacturer's Association, "to represent the interests of Canadian companies that create, manufacture and market sound recordings,"[91] although its main clients have always been the dominant multinational recording labels.[92] While these are primarily foreign-based interests that do not create works themselves, they traditionally have framed their policy interventions with reference to their role in promoting Canadian culture and Canadian artists. In the motion-picture industry, the CMPDA represents the US motion-picture studios that dominate the Canadian market (Canadian films accounted for only 3.1 per cent of total box-office receipts in 2010/11).[93] As with CRIA and the RIAA, the CMPDA's membership is the same as the MPAA, and each group's members are represented in the International Intellectual Property Alliance, the main umbrella US intellectual-property lobby group.

On the video-game front, ESAC has emerged as a new voice in Canadian copyright with the potential to have a significant effect on the development of Canadian copyright law. ESAC was formed in 2003–4 from the Canadian branch of what was then the US Interactive Digital Software Association (now the Entertainment Software Association [ESA]) and became significantly active in the run-up to 2008's Bill C-61.[94] Although ESAC's views differ from the ESA on some issues, they both support a complete prohibition on the trafficking of devices that can circumvent TPMs, arguing that it would damage their business model. Most interesting, however, is the extent to which ESAC, unlike the CMPDA and CRIA, couches its defence of copyright in economic terms. Notes ESAC's director of policy and legal affairs Jason Kee: "We employ over 10,000 people in all provinces, and are basically responsible for quite a lot of job creation and contributions to the knowledge economy, which basically makes our industry increasingly of interest to policymakers."[95]

Creators' Groups Traditionally, actual creators have served two roles in the copyright debate. On the one hand, creators were used to legitimate industry demands for greater copyright protection to copyright owners, even though this protection does not necessarily translate into more revenues for artists. On the other hand, creator groups have actively lobbied for greater rights in their own work. Industry and creator groups have in the past formed temporary coalitions,[96] such as the Copyright Coalition of Creators and Producers in the run-up to the 2005 copyright bill.[97] In Canada, creator groups tend to divide along linguistic and provincial lines, with Quebec-based creators and performers forming their own associations. Both traditional English- and French-Canadian creator groups, however, generally support WIPO implementation, particularly provisions extending protection to performers, but not necessarily those related to TPMs or ISP liability. While primarily domestically focused, creator groups also maintain loose affiliations with foreign and international groups.[98] Overall, they are best characterized as "national" (in the sense of "Canadian"), not North American or international, with a subsection of French-language, Quebec-focused groups.

Since the early 2000s, however, Canadian artists have taken advantage of the reduced production and distribution costs afforded by digital technologies to loosen their dependence on traditional production and distribution channels. Some artists have also articulated a view on copyright separate from the maximalist approach expressed by traditional content industries and creator groups. Through the early part of the digital-copyright debate, the Canadian Music Creators Coalition (CMCC) was the most prominent example of a creators' view of copyright distinct from an industry view. The CMCC was formed in April 2006 by several prominent Canadian artists (whose ranks now count Sarah McLachlan, Avril Lavigne, and the Barenaked Ladies) "and some lawyers in Ottawa who want to remain anonymous."[99] It was created in large part in response to the fear that record labels would start suing Canadian file sharers as has been done in the United States, a move these artists saw as being bad for business. The CMCC has also come out against DMCA-like TPM protection and advocates for a copyright policy that recognizes the need to satisfy consumers/users/individuals and their own need to be remunerated for their work. Although a small, ad hoc organization, the CMCC has changed the way copyright is discussed in Canada, forcing industry groups increasingly to frame their advocacy more in terms of copyright's effect on investment and jobs than on culture.

DISSEMINATION GROUPS
Traditional User Groups As in the United States, large institutional users, such as the Association of Universities and Colleges of Canada (AUCC), the Canadian Library Association, the Canadian Association of University Teachers, and the Council of Ministers of Education, Canada, have tended to represent "users" in the Canadian copyright debate.[100] They, like industry groups, continue to be important in the copyright policymaking process. Generally, they are against strong protection of TPMs, as TPMs can interfere with the ease of use, lending of, and access to books and other materials for educators.[101] Like industry groups, they have relatively good access to decision-makers, although their interests, like those of user groups in the United States, are more defensive. They are not as well resourced as their industry counterparts. They also confront the same issues in advocating for "balance" that similar groups do in the United States: it is easier to call for stronger copyright than it is to describe how it should be balanced among various competing interests.

Internet Service Providers[102] The Canadian ISP industry is dominated by three large "legacy" providers, including Bell Canada (phone), TELUS Corp. (phone), and Rogers Communications Inc. (cable). They are joined in turn by a number of much smaller ISPs who serve largely rural and niche markets that accounted for about 4 per cent of the Canadian ISP market in 2010.[103] Until 2006, all ISPs were represented by the Canadian Association of Internet Providers (CAIP, founded in 1996); cable companies were further represented by the Canadian Cable Television Association (CCTA). The CCTA has since been disbanded, with the large telecommunications companies undertaking their lobbying directly.

CAIP continues to represent smaller ISPs, although according to CAIP chair Tom Copeland, CAIP works with the larger companies on issues of mutual interest.[104] These groups work to influence government individually and through coalitions, namely, the Balanced Copyright Coalition in the run-up to 2005's Bill C-60, and the Business Coalition on Balanced Copyright (BCBC), a group started in February 2008 that counts the CAIP, Rogers, Bell, TELUS, the Retail Council of Canada, the Canadian Association of Bankers, and other politically and economically important business groups among its members. ISPs enjoy a long-standing, active relationship with governmental officials through Industry Canada, whose responsibility for issues like e-commerce and innovation makes it their natural representative in government.[105]

ISPs are primarily concerned with limiting their liability for infringing actions committed by their subscribers and minimizing the cost of maintaining any regime that requires them to police the actions of their users. They have consistently advocated for a notice-and-notice regime. Unlike many other groups on the user side of the copyright debate, ISPs are financially and politically powerful, consisting as they do of some of Canada's most economically successful companies. Though focused "almost exclusively on the issue of ISP liability," the wider user lobby has been able to benefit from their economic strength via the attention they bring to general user issues.[106]

The Public Interest Since the passage of Bill C-32 in 1997, public interest in copyright has risen, primarily as a reaction to the way that copyright law increasingly directly affects individuals and their control over what they consider to be their own property. While these individual/consumer/public-interest groups lack the resources and access to governmental officials needed to be on an equal footing with the content industries, they have changed the way copyright policy is made, as well as the tone and, to a lesser extent, the direction of the debate.

In the early part of the 2000s, individuals' interest in copyright was highly influenced by organizations and events in the United States, with citizens receiving most of their copyright information from US sources like the libertarian electronic-rights group Electronic Frontier Foundation (EFF) and slashdot.org, a computer-tech website. As a result, their submissions to initial public consultations on copyright reform in 2001–2 (discussed below) referred often to the DMCA and used US terms like "fair use" instead of Canadian concepts like "fair dealing." Many who participated in these consultations did so via form letters provided by Electronic Frontier Canada, a Canadian branch of the EFF.[107]

The Canadian online community has now matured to the point where Canadian experts and groups can satisfy individuals' demand for information on copyright. To a large extent, this maturation is the result of the efforts over the previous decade by a number of bloggers, notably Ottawa copyright lawyer Howard Knopf, independent software developer Russell McOrmond, and, in particular, University of Ottawa law professor Michael Geist. In 2003, Geist started the Canadian Internet Policy and Public Interest Clinic (CIPPIC) with a grant from the US-based Amazon.com's Cy Press fund (it continues to receive support from US and Canadian sources).[108] CIPPIC has been instrumental in helping smaller organizations become involved in the copyright debate. Geist has focused on digital-copyright issues with a combination of education and advocacy for user rights through his blog and weekly column in the *Toronto Star* newspaper. A perceptive political actor with extensive contacts within government and internationally, and a sharp understanding of digital media, Geist used Facebook to spur grassroots opposition to the Conservative government's 2007 legislation (discussed below), the first effective political use of social-networking media in Canada, and one of the first in the world.

Distinctive Canadian Ideas, Institutions, and Interests

This historical-institutionalist picture of the ideas, institutions, and interests that shape the Canadian copyright debate suggests the potential for either convergence with or divergence from the US model of implementation of the Internet treaties. The past ten years have been a time of upheaval. The United States and its allied content industries continue to have significant resources at their disposal when arguing for copyright reform. The ability of the United States to get a hearing on copyright issues (along with the US motion picture industry, which dominates the Canadian market) was evidenced by the passage of the 2007 anti-camcording bill, despite the presence of relevant existing legislation and no strong evidence that any new legislation was needed. The exogenous technological shock of the arrival of the digital age helped to bring new groups and voices to the fore, such as the telecommunications industry and ISPs, individual creators, individuals, and public-interest groups. While the telecommunications industry possesses the largest resources (in terms of economic and political clout), individual creators and users have also deployed their own resources. Their attempts to engage in symbolic bricolage, emphasizing copyright's supposed role in promoting creation and dissemination, had the potential to reframe the entire copyright debate. As the account below suggests, in this they largely succeeded.

Overall, enough uncertainty existed at the beginning of the treaty-implementation process that it was unclear how the treaties would be implemented. Based on past example and the divided institutional responsibility for copyright, one would expect a tendency to balance as in 1997, when the PMO arbitrated a law that attempted to reach a balance between user and owner interests. Two factors, however, had the potential to upset this rough balance: the emergence of a new force in the copyright debate – individuals and public-interest groups – and the existence of a PMO with very few checks on its powers.

Part 2: Implementation of the Internet Treaties – Users Find Their Voice

In the debates over the Internet treaties, the ideas, institutions, and interests described in the previous part combined to produce one of the more surprisingly contentious issues in Canadian political history, transforming Canadian copyright from a sleepy backwater to being an issue that has captured the attention of the Canadian political class. The Canadian debate over implementation of the treaties reveals a process influenced by the regional hegemon, whose domestic constellation of institutions and interests retains the potential for policy outcomes different from those in the United States.

2001–2002: Government Consultations

A FRAMEWORK FOR COPYRIGHT REFORM

Given the rate of technological change, the drafters of Bill C-32 in 1997 included a provision requiring that the government review its copyright legislation within five years. In 2001, the government launched its "section 92" review, which consisted of a series of public consultations and three papers. *A Framework for Copyright Reform*[109] provided a high-level overview of the issue and set out possible options with respect to copyright reform; a *Consultation Paper on Digital Copyright Issues*;[110] and a *Consultation Paper on the Application of the* Copyright Act's *Compulsory Retransmission Licence to the Internet.*[111] The latter two were designed "to launch the online portion of ... public consultations." More traditional consultations were held in Halifax, Vancouver, Montreal, Toronto, Ottawa, and Edmonton, and attended by over three hundred Canadians.[112]

At the WIPO negotiations, Canadian delegates favoured a "minimalist" approach to the legal protection of TPMs, making it a crime to break a digital lock only if it were done for the purposes of violating an underlying copyright; their views on ISP liability were unclear from the conference proceedings and documents. However, the government's discussion documents themselves did not commit it to any one position in any area, including legal protection for TPMs and ISP liability. Instead, they expressed generic core principles: the framework rules must promote Canadian values; the framework rules should be clear and allow easy, transparent access and use; the proposals should promote a vibrant and competitive electronic commerce in Canada; the framework should be cast in a global context and be as technologically neutral as possible.[113] Futhermore, the government's decision to undertake two years of consultation suggests an interest in delaying implementation of the Internet treaties.[114] The documents suggest that the government was not committed to one particular interpretation of the treaties.

Government Position on TPMs and ISP Liability These papers' perspective on TPMs was consistent with the Canadian government's position at the WIPO negotiations (discussed in chapter 5), namely, a reluctance to create new rights that would go too far beyond existing ones. They explicitly noted that restricting the trade in circumvention devices could impair existing rights under the law while also expressing concern about issues such as privacy.[115] They concluded that more consultations were necessary.

The government's ISP-liability approach presented an interesting contrast to its non-position on TPMs. While the papers gently critiqued the US approach to TPMs, they proposed a notice-and-takedown regime for ISPs in line with the US approach. The papers also noted that, in addition to the United States, the European Union, Japan, and Australia all use variations of notice and takedown. This position, as will be seen, did not last long.

SUPPORTING CULTURE AND INNOVATION

In October 2002, the departments tabled their section 92 report, whose title mirrored their differing priorities: *Supporting Culture and Innovation: Report on the Provisions and Operation of the* Copyright Act.[116] The report proposed addressing digital issues and implementation of the WIPO treaties within one to two years (i.e., by 2004), with other issues to be dealt with in the medium (two to four years) and long (four-plus years) term.[117]

These papers set out a government vision of a digital agenda that accepted the Internet treaties as the legitimate frame for engaging in digital-copyright reform. Indeed, digital-copyright reform in Canadian debates is largely synonymous with the Internet treaties. Gervais argues that this prioritization of WIPO implementation and digital copyright reflected political priorities.[118] However, although the section 92 report committed the government to addressing those "digital issues for which consultations and preliminary policy analysis have taken place" (i.e., ISP liability, legal protection of TPMs and Rights Management Information, and a "making available right"), it did little more than canvass possible alternatives.[119]

PUBLIC CONSULTATIONS

To officials' surprise and consternation,[120] Canadians expressed a strong direct interest in copyright reform during the 2002 consultations. The government paper attracted comments from more than seven hundred individuals and organizations when it was posted on a government website.[121] Articles in the mainstream press on the potential implications for Canada of the implementation of the WIPO treaties complemented the work of a small but active number of Canadian copyright bloggers, including Knopf, McOrmond, University of Western Ontario law professor Samuel Trosow, and Queen's University English professor Laura Murray. Most notable of these new voices was Michael Geist, who was emerging as one of the most vocal proponent of users' rights. The consultations also gave activists, some of whom were becoming involved on copyright issues for the first time, the opportunity to begin networking.[122] These activists were relatively resource- and contact-poor compared with traditional content-industry lobby and institutional-user groups. The advocacy by these new activists and the traditional user-rights lobbies was complemented by the economic strength of the ISPs, including Bell Canada, TELUS, and Rogers, although these companies focused "almost exclusively on the issue of ISP liability."[123] For their part, the ISPs formed the Balanced Copyright Coalition with the Public Interest Advocacy Centre (PIAC), the Retail Council of Canada, the Canadian Advanced Technology Alliance, and several professors,[124] to counter calls for notice-and-takedown and strong legal protection for TPMs.

STATUS REPORT: GOVERNMENT SETTLES ON NOTICE-AND-NOTICE

On 25 March 2004, the government submitted its "Status Report on Copyright Reform" to the House Standing Committee on Canadian

Heritage. The report committed the government to addressing the legal protection of TPMs, again without making specific recommendations.[125] It also revealed an evolution of the government's position on ISP liability. In contrast to the government's initial position in favour of notice-and-takedown, the status report announced that the government was considering two variations on notice-and-notice. The document did not mention notice-and-takedown at all.

While various groups, including the US government, continued to advocate for notice-and-takedown, it seems that the issue was settled in favour of notice-and-notice by the courts and then by an informal agreement among ISPs and the content industries soon after the publication of the government's original 2001 consultation papers. In 2004, the Supreme Court upheld the ruling in *SOCAN v. CAIP* that ISPs could not be held liable for copyright infringements committed by their subscribers since they only provided the means of communication.[126] Earlier, the Copyright Board of Canada had ruled in the "Tariff 22" case that ISPs were not required to collect tariffs for digital works shared by subscribers on their system. These findings, which limit ISPs' liability for subscribers' infringement, essentially took notice-and-takedown off the table, and led to the creation of an informal notice-and-notice regime among the members of CRIA, CAIP, and the CCTA with which all concerned seem to be satisfied.[127]

While the government could have overruled this informal arrangement via legislation, its 2004 status update explicitly cast its support for a version of notice-and-notice. This update was followed by attempts to formalize notice-and-notice in the Liberal government's 2005 Bill C-60 and the Conservative government's Bills C-61 (2008), C-32 (2010), and C-11 (2012). The existence of an informal consensus between ISPs and rights holders in favour of notice-and-notice, combined with the political and economic power of ISPs,[128] heavily favoured notice-and-notice, despite the fact that it rejects the international consensus in favour of variations of notice-and-takedown.

This outcome is significant for our understanding of Canadian copyright policymaking for three reasons. First, the telecom industry's ability to obtain a low-impact limited-liability regime, even given later content-industry attempts to reverse it, demonstrates that industry's relative strength in the Canadian copyright debate. Second, it further demonstrates that, under certain conditions, Canada possesses significant autonomy in forming copyright policy. In particular, it is more difficult to change an established, path-dependent process (and one that had been legitimized by the courts) than it is to create something new. In contrast, legal protection of TPMs is a new right and thus is more open to influence. Third, the timing of the court decision that affirmed the user-friendly notice-and-notice regime suggests that the Canadian judicial system's openness to the concept of copyright as something that must balance owner and user interests was not the result of the strong outpouring of individual-user interests that would occur nearer to the end of the decade. Rather, it was based in existing Canadian copyright traditions.

2004–2005: The Politics of Bill C-60

The time from 2004 to the introduction of Bill C-60 by a minority Liberal government in June 2005 was marked by lobbying and bureaucratic and parliamentary positioning, but also suggested the extent to which the Canadian copyright bureaucracy tended towards the status quo. In this period, the bureaucracy seems to have come to a consensus on the treatment of TPMs. Despite the traditional rivalries between Industry Canada and Canadian Heritage and between their client bases, in the run-up to Bill C-60 departmental officials supported a "balanced approach … responding to copyright's role in the new digital environment" – that is, a minimalist approach to TPM protection and a notice-and-notice ISP liability regime.[129] Even Canadian Heritage "did not view the protection of TPMs and the outlaw of circumvention devices as the best solution to the problem," claiming that a maximalist approach was "not smart public policy." A 2005 internal and informal policy review favoured a "minimal approach" to treaty implementation[130] of the kind promoted by Canadian delegates to the WIPO negotiations and reflected in a plain-language reading of the Internet treaties.

The US example served as a cautionary tale about what not to do (a form of reverse emulation). The departments observed the DMCA and its aftermath, and came to resist "for public policy reasons … the maximalist proposals of the content lobby and to empathize with many of the basic concerns of the user lobby."[131] For policy and political reasons (most public-consultation participants were opposed to the DMCA), a "maximalist interpretation of the treaties … did not appeal to some Canadian policy makers, who viewed digital-copyright reform with far more caution than haste."[132]

In the period before the introduction of Bill C-60, the content industries enjoyed a significant advantage in access to departmental officials.

In 2004 only two of seventy-five meetings between the Copyright Policy Branch at Canadian Heritage and stakeholders included groups representing the public: "one with the Electronic Frontier Foundation ... and one joint meeting with ... CIPPIC and the Public Interest Advocacy Centre."[133] Rights holders, led by CRIA but supported by other industry and creators' groups, disagreed with the (eventual) departmental view. As part of the Copyright Coalition of Creators and Producers, a temporary formal coalition of industry groups and the major copyright collectives, photographers, and artists' organizations,[134] they proposed in 2002 a detailed, DMCA-like approach to circumvention. CRIA also expressed its support for notice-and-takedown.[135]

CRIA, other industry groups, and creators' groups found a useful ally in Heritage Minister Sheila Copps, who supported fully their position.[136] In 2002, Copps "cleverly shifted the pressure from herself to the bureaucracy, especially Industry Canada." This pressure forced Industry Canada (and its minister, David Emerson) "to compromise on the departments' plans for a short-term, incomplete WIPO package."[137] CRIA, representing the rights lobby, bypassed the bureaucratic policy process and appealed directly to the minister, realizing "some of its key aims in the form of a bill by working from the top down." Throughout the process, CRIA's relationship with Copps, which dated to 1997, was its single most powerful lever.[138] The relationship was mutually beneficial: Copps "earned political capital and positive publicity" while supporting, as she saw it, Canada's "cultural community," and the content industry could count on an influential ally.[139]

CRIA's strategy of emphasizing the political level to bypass the bureaucracy's policy concerns in the run-up to the introduction of Bill C-60 met with mixed success, best exemplified by the events surrounding what became known as the "Bulte report." In May 2004, the House Canadian Heritage Committee, chaired by Liberal MP Sarmite Bulte and heavily influenced by the rights-holder lobby and comprising MPs who little understood the topic,[140] released its *Interim Report on Copyright Reform*.[141] This report quickly became infamous among users groups. Bulte had extensive links to the content industries. Her committee's report read much like the 1985 *A Charter of Rights for Creators*.[142] It took an "extreme copyright-holder slant," arguing for maximalist legal protection for TPMs and a notice-and-takedown regime for ISP liability.[143] These recommendations were based in part on the false argument that without changes to the law, Canada would be "vulnerable to sanctions under international trade rules" and that exceptions and limitations to copyright were somehow illegitimate, rather than being an essential part of copyright.[144]

The report had a counterproductive effect. Its extreme position created "a whipping-boy for public interest advocacy."[145] Within government, Bulte's committee irritated "some public servants" and came to be seen as a rogue committee because its recommendations and analysis were so transparently biased towards one group. Bulte herself, whose very close relationship with the content industries was harshly criticized, in particular a $250-a-plate fundraising dinner hosted by these industries to raise money for her re-election,[146] would go down to defeat in the January 2006 federal election.

As a result, the government agreed that a joint Industry-Heritage Committee would study the resulting legislation, not the Heritage Committee, as had happened in 1997.[147] Given the relative friendliness of the Heritage Committee to copyright owners, this rebuke was a setback to their cause.

BILL C-60 (JUNE 2005)

These studies and analyses culminated in the June 2005 tabling of Bill C-60, An Act to Amend the Copyright Act,[148] by the minority Liberal government of Paul Martin. Bill C-60 did not follow the DMCA lead on either the legal protection of TPMs or ISP liability. It addressed the legal protection of TPMs in one paragraph. Clause 27 would have made it illegal to break a TPM protecting any material form of a work for the purpose of infringing the underlying copyright or moral right. Rights holders would also have the right to sue someone who "knows or ought to know that the measure has been removed or rendered ineffective and, without the owner's or holder's consent." Unlike the preferred US approach, which prohibits the manufacture and sale of anti-TPM devices, it avoids creating any new right related exclusively to the presence of a TPM by linking TPM infringement to infringement of the underlying copyright.

On ISP liability, Bill C-60 proposed a notice-and-notice regime, which would have formalized the system that had been operating for several years. ISPs would not have been liable for copyright infringement if they were only providing the network the alleged infringer had used (clause 20). This clause was not wholly uncontroversial. Geist,[149] for example, argues that under Bill C-60 search engines would effectively have been subject to a "notice-and-takedown" regime. However, this part of the bill did not attract much criticism.

TRIUMPH OF THE BUREAUCRACY?

Although it could have been reformed at the committee stage had the government not fallen in September 2005, Bill C-60 represented a victory for the user lobby and the bureaucracy on TPMs, while the notice-and-notice regime represented a victory for ISPs. On these two issues, the Liberal government decided to ignore US pressure to implement stronger protection for TPMs and a notice-and-takedown regime. The content industries did not lose completely: most notably, they received a making-available right for which they and the US government had lobbied hard. Doyle concludes: "Perhaps what is most interesting about the political pressures surrounding copyright and the recording industry is not how the government responded with a making available right, but that, even in the face of such pressures, the government came forward with a minimalist bill."[150]

Doyle argues that Bill C-60 was a triumph of the bureaucracy. Convinced by public opinion and the observed effects of the DMCA that a minimalist approach was best for Canada, and struggling to deal with unforeseen high levels of public interest, "the bureaucracy adopted a slow, staged and deliberative copyright reform process."[151] Meanwhile, the formalization of the notice-and-notice regime was also due in part to the economic and political clout of the Canadian telecommunications industry.[152] Both outcomes demonstrated Canada's ability to implement policies different from those in (and favoured by) the United States.

However, Doyle seems to have overestimated the power of the bureaucracy to resist political pressure, as well as failed to account for the ever-present (if sometimes only latent) power of the prime minister. He concludes that one cannot win a policy battle based on resources and access alone; if something, for example the DMCA, is seen by policy experts within the bureaucracy to be bad policy, civil servants will resist the implementation of these policies.[153]

2007–2008: Bill C-61 and the Triumph of the US Lobby

Events have unfortunately disproved Doyle's prediction and his faith in the ability of good policy to trump bad policy.[154] Only three years after Bill C-60, a minority Conservative government, led by Stephen Harper – with the same bureaucracy in the face of even greater public opposition than before – introduced a *maximalist* bill that mirrored the DMCA on TPMs – prohibiting the trafficking of tools that can break digital locks as well as the breaking of digital locks under most circumstances – even as it kept C-60's notice-and-notice ISP regime.

The overlooked element in Doyle's analysis is the always-present potential for the Prime Minister's Office to overrule the departments. Before 2006, the influence of the PMO/PCO would have been easy to miss because the Liberal prime ministers of the day, Jean Chrétien and (in 2005) Paul Martin, seem to have given the lead on this issue to their departments (although Chrétien intervened to settle a specific inter-departmental dispute in 1997). However, as Savoie argues persuasively, the increasing centralization of federal political power in the PMO and away from the departments makes it imperative that one always consider the effect of the PMO in federal policymaking, if only to note that the PMO has decided to let individual departments work without interference.[155]

Two developments shaped the emergence of the Conservative government's Bill C-61 in June 2008. The first was the PMO/PCO's decision to place itself at the centre of the copyright policymaking process. In Stephen Harper, Canada had a prime minister with a very hands-on approach to governing. The second, and certainly the most dramatic, was the full emergence of copyright as an issue capable of engaging thousands of ordinary Canadians, an emergence spurred by the innovative use of Facebook by a politically savvy law professor.

INTER-DEPARTMENTAL POLITICS AND THE ROLE OF THE PMO/PCO
The historical-institutionalist approach posits that change can emerge from the manipulation of contradictory institutional logics. In Canada, Industry Canada and Canadian Heritage had opposing mandates, while the PMO could decide to rule in favour of either department. Following the election of a minority Conservative government in January 2006, copyright lobbying continued. During this period, the large copyright lobbies kept a low public profile but continued to lobby behind the scenes and be consulted by the two departments. The larger copyright-user lobbies also seem to have been consulted during this period. However, according to CIPPIC director David Fewer, neither he nor any other public-interest groups met with government officials specifically about copyright reform,[156] although Conservative industry minister Maxime Bernier's chief of staff, Michele Austin, says she met with Geist repeatedly, and Bernier met with the Retail Council of Canada (a "user" group).[157] User-rights groups called for a new round of public consultations, citing the rapid pace of technological changes, new stakeholders, and greater awareness of the significance of

copyright on everyday life.[158] However, government officials and industry representatives, in interviews with the author in the first half of
2008, argued against further consultations, claiming that all interested
parties had already been canvassed.

The government proceeded slowly on what Heritage Minister Bev
Oda and Industry Minister Bernier appreciated was a complex file complicated by the lack of a unified governmental approach. Each minister
was working under opposing "mandate letters," the letters from the
PMO that set out a department's objectives for the government's term.[159]
According to Austin, the four main issues on copyright when Bernier
came to Industry in 2006 were: WIPO implementation, ISP liability,
TPMs, and fair dealing. Of these issues, TPMs provided the only large
source of disagreement between the two departments. Industry Canada
favoured a more permissive approach to breaking digital locks while
respecting any underlying copyright and Canadian Heritage argued for
much stronger protection. TPMs were also a difficult ideological issue
for the libertarian Bernier: he supported the rights of individuals to
break digital locks that impeded their rights, but as a Quebec-based
politician he was sensitive to the fact that Quebeckers favour strong
copyright protection.[160]

By May 2007, Bernier and Industry Canada had prepared a presentation to the PCO to outline Industry Canada's views on copyright – dealing mainly with TPMs, education, and private copying – and to receive
permission to write a bill. Austin describes discussions with the PCO
and PMO as "intense." While Heritage's initial reaction to the Industry
package was less than positive, by July 2007, Bernier and Oda reached
an agreement, entitled "Moving Forward on Copyright Reform," on all
WIPO-related issues except for TPMs, ISP liability, and the treatment of
publicly accessible material. However, the two bureaucracies were unable to come to an agreement on these issues.[161]

Faced with a fundamental inter-departmental disagreement, they unsuccessfully sought the intervention of the PCO to help negotiate a compromise. However, the PMO and PCO were unwilling to overrule
"either department." The PMO itself had specific, if vague, views on
what should be done: "satisfy the United States."[162] Says Austin: "The
Prime Minister's Office's position was: move quickly, satisfy the United
States. And both of our positions were, politically speaking, 'Listen,
there have been mistakes made in the DMCA, there are a list of exceptions that have been created by court, can we not have DMCA lite?' And
they said, 'We don't care what you do, as long as the U.S. is satisfied.'"

During the 2005–6 election, Stephen Harper had distinguished his Conservatives from the Liberal party by promising to improve relations with the United States that had been strained by Canada's refusal to join the United States in the Iraq war or to sign on to the US Ballistic Missile Defence program, and by the long-standing trade dispute over Canadian softwood-lumber exports to the United States. Upon coming to power, the Harper government quickly settled the softwood-lumber dispute on terms that were exceedingly favourable to the United States.[163]

Part of the problem, according to Austin, was Bernier's assessment that a US-style implementation of the Internet treaties would be unwise for political and policy reasons. In addition to the policy reasons described above, Bernier and Austin argued that the bill would hurt the Conservatives with potential Conservative voters, such as young men who understood computers and mothers whose children could end up being sued.

Prime Minister Harper seems to have viewed the issue in terms of Canada-US relations, rather than as a strictly Canadian issue:

> It's not often that the Prime Minister is exposed to issues like that [copyright] in bilaterals [with the United States]. Usually, he will be in a room where he's in charge of the agenda, he's in charge of the discussion. But when you go and you see the Americans, when you're in a bilateral situation or an international situation, they say, "Where's copyright [as an issue]?" And he would [say]: "Yeah, that's a good question. Where's copyright?" [H]e would say, "Well, we just want to make the Americans happy." "Well do you understand what that means, politically?" "Just do it." "No, I positively won't just do it until you understand what this means."[164]

Faced with a PMO that did not understand the issue and a PCO that refused to broker a deal, Bernier and Oda "proposed a fairly large package not exclusive to copyright," including "counterfeiting, … time shifting, levies, fair use, ephemeral recordings." Austin characterizes the proposal as "a consumer-based package" and as "DMCA-lite."

US pressure on Canada was evident at the August 2007 SPP summit in Montebello, Quebec. Unlike the calcified NAFTA, the SPP provided a forum in which the three countries could discuss a wide range of issues. In a bilateral/trilateral relationship typically characterized by an absence of cross-issue linkage,[165] the SPP provided the United States with a novel opportunity to link Canadian copyright reform to an issue of great importance to Canada: the border and trade. Under the SPP process, the US secretary of commerce could (and did) ask about Canadian WIPO implementation. Often, a "we're working on it" was all that was required. However, according to government documents obtained through Access to Information by Geist, in the run-up to the August 2007 SPP summit at Montebello, the United States linked American movement on border issues to Canadian movement on copyright.[166]

It is unclear how significant this attempted linkage was for a PMO/PCO already interested in satisfying the United States on copyright (and which continued to pursue DMCA-style policies long after the end of the summit). Bernier, partly because of his continued insistence that Canada could not follow the US approach to copyright reform,[167] was shuffled to Foreign Affairs in August 2007 and replaced by then minister of Indian affairs and northern development Jim Prentice.

FACEBOOK ACTIVISM COMES TO CANADA[168]

Historical-institutionalist analyses hold that change is the result of actors' purposeful actions. In practice, this means that it is not enough for conditions to be ripe for change, but that individuals or groups have to recognize this potential for change. Power resources may be lying around on the ground, ready for someone to pick them up, but someone still has to look down *and* come up with an idea of how to use what they're looking at to achieve their goals. This is the essence of symbolic and substantive bricolage, and provides a good illustration of what historical institutionalism means by the concept of agency.

Copyright history is replete with examples of such agency. In the 1970s and 1980s industry leaders realized they could link their IP concerns with American fears over losing their economic hegemony. And in 2007, a Canadian university professor did something similar: he harnessed the then largely unrecognized power of social-networking media to create a powerful constituency of individual users that would change the direction of Canadian copyright law.

Following his arrival at Industry Canada, Industry Minister Jim Prentice attempted to introduce a DMCA-style copyright bill and ended up fomenting widespread public protests that panicked the government, confounded cabinet colleagues, and led to a six-month delay in the bill's introduction that rendered it collateral damage when the September 2008 election was called. This uprising vindicated Austin and Bernier's intuition about the political dangers of copyright reform.

In the end, the Conservative's Bill C-61, like the Liberals' Bill C-60, never got beyond first reading.

In the 16 October 2007 Speech from the Throne, the Conservative government pledged to "improve the protection of cultural and intellectual property rights in Canada, including copyright reform."[169] When the government placed An Act to Amend the Copyright Act on the Order Paper on 10 December 2007, observers of Canadian copyright expected that this new bill would be much closer to the DMCA than the Liberals' C-60 had been.[170]

Despite years of signs that copyright was on the verge of becoming a mainstream issue, what happened next caught everyone in Ottawa off guard. On Saturday, 1 December 2007, University of Ottawa professor Michael Geist set up a Facebook page, Fair Copyright for Canada (FCFC), "to help ensure that the government hears from concerned Canadians. It features news about the bill, tips on making the public voice heard and updates on local events. With regular postings and links to other content, it also provides a central spot for people to learn more about Canadian copyright reform."[171]

As this quote suggests, the basic initial demands were for the government to engage in consultations with Canadians and that user rights be addressed – that copyright law not be strengthened in a way that impedes Canadians' access to knowledge, culture, and information. Geist and others critiqued the upcoming bill by referring to it as the "Canadian DMCA." This approach not only focused on a bad policy (i.e., DMCA-like law would be bad for Canada), but linked the issue to the always-latent sentiment of Canadian anti-Americanism. This symbolic bricolage was made more potent given the fact that the United States, and US-based industries, were the main groups lobbying for this bill. It was such a powerful linkage that it necessitated a direct rebuttal from the government, which insisted that the bill was indeed "Made in Canada" and that their opponents were practising base anti-Americanism.

The Fair Copyright for Canada Facebook group ended up doing much more than informing Canadians about a potentially bad new law. It dramatically demonstrated the power of social-networking media to educate people and to help people organize themselves in a very politically effective manner. As Geist noted in a post on his blog a week later, the group exceeded his expectations:

As many readers of this blog will know, last Saturday night I started a Facebook group called Fair Copyright in Canada. I sent an invitation to

100 or so "Facebook friends" in the hope that some would join and that we could create a useful resource for discussion on the upcoming Canadian DMCA. One week later (almost to the hour), the Fair Copyright in Canada group passed the 10,000-member mark. The group, which will hit 11,000 members a few hours after I post this, has led to hundreds of letters and phone calls to [Industry] Minister Prentice, Prime Minister Harper and MPs from every political party. It has fostered a robust conversation among many Canadians about balanced copyright ... It has been a very good week.[172]

With Geist's Facebook page, the public interest in copyright that had been building for almost a decade, and which Geist and other bloggers had been fomenting for as long, exploded into full view. After only a month (in January 2008), the page had almost 40,000 members; as of June 2010 it had just under 88,000 members. The FCFC movement was a textbook example of "online organizing" the creation of a movement that would have been very unlikely to occur in the absence of these new technologies.[173] It was a remarkably decentralized movement. Geist's original webpage set the tone and direction of the popular critiques of the Conservative government's bill, focusing on user rights such as the potential for the legal protection of digital locks applied to creative works (such as those that prevent you from reading Amazon eBooks on anything but a Kindle or via a Kindle app). However, he had very little to do with the actual organization of direct protests. Once created, FCFC took on a life of its own, with individuals setting up their own "Fair Copyright For Canada" chapters across the country, many of which engaged in direct lobbying.

While countless Canadians did take that step to contact their MPs through traditional means – letters, in-person visits to constituency offices, and so on – probably the most innovative direct action was undertaken by Kempton Lam, a Calgary-based blogger and documentary filmmaker. A complete newcomer to copyright politics, Lam used the FCFC Calgary chapter Facebook page to organize an impromptu demonstration/attempted meeting with the industry minister during his Saturday, 8 December 2007 Christmas Open House at his Calgary North riding office. The objective, according to Lam's Facebook meeting invite, was to "**respectfully** share with the minister what we think about a Canadian DMCA politely, clearly and firmly."[174]

The Facebook announcement convinced between forty and sixty people to show up at Prentice's riding office to talk with the minister.[175]

They were able to, briefly, although according to media reports – Lam worked to get maximum publicity by alerting the mainstream media – Prentice was noncommittal about the bill, which had not yet been introduced. (Lam says he got the idea for this "remarkable meeting" from reading Geist's blog; Geist says he had spoken to Lam "a number of times" before the Calgary protest and helped publicize the event, "but it was his initiative and he brought the people together.")

Over the next several months, newly minted copyright activists kept calling and visiting MPs' offices to make their concerns known. The unexpected protests and particularly the face-to-face meetings with government MPs, many of whom had never heard of copyright and who now had to deal with irate constituents on an unfamiliar issue.[176] It unnerved the government, which at the time did not control a majority in parliament and technically could face an election at any moment.

FCFC proponents argued these numbers represented frustration with the "resistance on the part of our policymakers to grapple with what's really going on and to produce solutions that are right for us," in the words of Toronto-based technology lawyer and FCFC member Rob Hyndman.[177] In contrast, the government saw the protests as representing only a passionate minority causing "a lot of miscommunication, a lot of misinformation," according to Jean-Sébastien Rioux, chief of staff to then industry minister Jim Prentice.[178]

Bad Timing for the Government This unexpected public outcry was effective primarily because it occurred during a minority parliament, in which individual members' electoral fates could mean the difference between a party achieving a majority or a minority government. Moreover, it came at a time of unusually high vulnerability for the Conservative government. In December 2007, the government was anticipating a contentious early 2008 vote on Canada's participation in the Afghanistan war, and it was not yet clear how badly the Liberal party wanted to avoid an election. Even though the government could have passed any copyright bill with only the support of the Bloc Québécois, this unexpected crisis was too much for the government to handle, and the bill was not tabled for several months. This delay was a vindication for critics like Fewer, who attributes the government's clumsiness on the issue to a lack of consultation.[179]

The delay meant that the Conservatives' first bill, discussed below, would become a victim of the September 2008 election call. In the winter and spring of 2008, however, the ultimate fate of the legislation was unknown. With the bill on hold, government and interest groups remained active. The United States kept Canada on its Special 301 Watch List in 2008 and US ambassador to Canada David Wilkins continued to pressure Canada publicly to implement the Internet treaties. The US State Department arranged a meeting between the Parliamentary IP Caucus (an all-party group of MPs and senators interested in IP issues) and the Entertainment Software Association, which was also attended by its Canadian cousin, the ESAC; the State Department also arranged for a brief cross-country tour for the ESA and ESAC to talk with interested groups.[180]

Industry groups, meanwhile, built alliances in an attempt to bring more resources to bear on the issue. In May, the Canadian Chamber of Commerce launched the Canadian Intellectual Property Council, "a co-alition of Canadian businesses from a wide range of industry sectors," which called for a review of Canada's intellectual property regime, with an emphasis on protecting and enforcing IP rights. Its first step was to fund a Conference Board report "regarding the lack of appropriate intellectual property protection in Canada," and its initial press release specifically mentions WIPO implementation.[181]

On the user side, a number of companies, spurred by Ottawa lawyer Jay Kerr-Wilson, formed the Business Coalition for Balanced Copyright, with representatives from CAIP, Bell Canada, Google, Rogers, TELUS, and the Retail Council of Canada, among others. The BCBC released an agreed-upon set of principles, including support for notice-and-notice and C-60-like TPM rules.[182] Each member would decide how much weight to give each issue.[183] Within government, the main lesson the Conservative government took away from the Facebook uprising was that the problems with the bill were not substantive, but with how the bill was communicated to Canadians and to the Conservative caucus.[184] As a result, the government focused on messaging, not substance.

BILL C-61 (JUNE 2008)

On 12 June 2008, Industry Minister Prentice and Heritage Minister Josée Verner finally introduced Bill C-61, An Act to Amend the Copyright Act, which had languished on the Order Paper for six months. According to Rioux, the legislation was "90–95 per cent the same bill from December to June."[185] After its introduction, opponents quickly argued that the bill was "born in the USA" by pointing to its treatment of TPMs. The government, meanwhile, claimed that Bill C-61 was a "made in Canada" response to domestic conditions that fulfilled Canada's international obligations."[186] In defence of the government's position, Rioux argues that the bill was a good policy that also smoothed a rift with the United States: "Did the US have this high up on their radar screen? Yes ... We have a bad rep internationally ... We signed a treaty in 1997 [the WIPO Internet treaties] that we are not even close to being compliant with. You add all this stuff up and we have to update copyright law. And has the added benefit [of] doing something to turn the temperature down with the US – why not?"[187]

While subsequent Conservative bills would differ from Bill C-61 in small but important ways, Bill C-61's position on ISP liability and the legal protection of TPMs would remain essentially unchanged. On the issue of ISP liability, Bill C-61 largely followed the Liberals' Bill C-60, rejecting the US notice-and-takedown approach in favour of Canada's already existing (informal) notice-and-notice regime.

On TPMs, however, it rejected the Liberals' 2005 approach in favour of the maximalist DMCA approach, making it a crime to break digital locks except under certain circumstances[188] and outlawing circumvention devices. At fifty pages, the bill was almost twice the length of Bill C-60 (32 pages), mainly because of its much more complex treatment of TPMs.

Bill C-61 was even stricter than the US DMCA with respect to the system for determining future TPM exceptions. Instead of a US-style process of mandated triennial adjustments to account for new exceptions,[189] Bill C-61 called for a more opaque process: changes would be made via regulation, with no regular review process.

Under Bill C-60 it would not have been a crime to circumvent a TPM if the underlying work were in the public domain, if one were entitled under fair dealing to copy the underlying work, or if the work were not otherwise protected by copyright. Not so Bill C-61 and subsequent copyright bills. Bill C-61 "basically says that technology trumps whatever rights consumers or competitors might have otherwise had. So the law no longer matters. People only have whatever rights content owners choose for them."[190] Rather than the minimal changes of Bill C-60, Bill C-61 proposed a significant reorientation of Canadian copyright law towards the US-desired position that the presence of digital locks should effectively trump user rights, adding a new layer to copyright that could potentially eliminate any user-owner balance in the law decidedly in favour of the owner.

REACTION TO BILL C-61

Industry associations and their lobbyists and lawyers, copyright owners and creators' associations (with the significant exception of the Canadian Music Creators Coalition) generally supported the bill. Opponents of the bill included the CMCC, the BCBC (though this group, which counts ISPs among its members, was satisfied with Bill C-61's notice-and-notice regime), CIPPIC, the Canadian Library Association, Canadian privacy commissioners, the Canadian Software Innovation Alliance (which represents Canadian open-source software developers), the Canadian Association of University Teachers, the Canadian Federation of Students, the Songwriters Association of Canada, and campus bookstores, as well as the Film Studies Association of Canada, the Canadian Newspaper Association, and the Hamilton Chamber of Commerce. Other groups expressed mixed opinions, including the Writers' Guild of Canada (screenwriters)[191] and the Canadian Artists' Representation/Le Front des artistes canadiens Ontario (representing visual artists).[192]

2008–2012: The Brief Life and Quick Death of C-61, and the End of a Long-Running Saga

The period following the introduction of Bill C-61 in June 2008 was eventful for copyright lobbyists and observers. While copyright remained a lively political subject, little, if anything, had changed in terms of the tendencies and biases witnessed in the earlier copyright debate on the key issues of ISP liability and TPM protection. Like the Liberal's Bill C-60, introduced three years earlier, Bill C-61 was a victim of an election call (on 7 September 2008) and never made it beyond first reading in the House of Commons. Although it was sidelined by political circumstances unrelated to copyright, the bill's inauspicious death represented a clear victory of the individual and user interests that had congregated around Geist's Facebook activism. Had Bill C-61 been introduced as planned in December 2007, it would have had a much greater chance of making it through the legislative process before the September 2008 election call, although its passage in any form would not have been assured. As it is, public criticism managed to delay the bill long enough to ensure that it would not pass in the current parliament. Since inaction itself is a policy outcome, a few more months without being subject to a bad law can be seen as a clear victory for critics of strong legal protection of TPMs and as evidence that Facebook and other social media can be used to influence the political process.

BILLS C-32 (OCTOBER 2010) AND C-11 (SEPTEMBER 2011): CONSERVATIVE COPYRIGHT REFORM REDUX

If the death of Bill C-61 confirmed the importance of individuals and public-interest groups in the Canadian copyright debate, events following the re-election of Stephen Harper's minority Conservative government in the fall of 2008 emphasized both the potential for and limits to the newfound power of Facebook activism. Following the 2008 election, Harper replaced Industry Minister Jim Prentice with Tony Clement, and Minister of Canadian Heritage Josée Verner (who replaced Bev Oda in the same August 2007 shuffle that claimed Minister of Industry Maxime Bernier) with James Moore.[193]

On the movement's main demand, for public hearings, the protests were an unqualified success. Although government officials on both sides of the copyright divide had argued that the 2001–2 hearings had been sufficient, the Conservative government held widespread public copyright consultations from 20 July to 13 September 2009.[194] Canadians responded enthusiastically, attending ten roundtables across the country. The government received over 2800 separate submissions from individuals and groups, in addition to about 5500 form letters, the vast majority of which originated from a balanced copyright (as opposed to pro-content-industry) website.[195] This remarkable level of participation demonstrated Canadians' continued and rising interest in copyright: in 2001 officials had been amazed by hundreds of submissions; now, submissions numbered in the thousands.

Participants were overwhelmingly in favour of stronger user rights. According to a tabulation of the 8300 submissions by Geist, 6138 were against "another Bill C-61," while only 54 expressed support.[196] As well, 6641 submissions expressed an opinion "against anti-circumvention [rules] or in favour of limiting of DRM/Digital locks,"[197] and 6027 expressed satisfaction with a notice-and-notice system of ISP liability. Of all the issues raised in the consultations, the legal protection of TPMs attracted the most attention.

On the actual content of the Conservative bills, particularly with respect to TPMs, the FCFC's record was more mixed. Following the Harper Conservatives' re-election (with another minority government) in October 2008, the government introduced Bill C-32, The Copyright Modernization Act, in June 2010. That bill made it to the House committee stage before being scuttled by the May 2011 election that would finally nab Harper his long-coveted majority government. Bill C-11, which was essentially identical to C-32, was tabled in September 2011. With a majority government (finally) behind it, Bill C-11 received royal assent on 29 June 2012, seven years and nine days after the Liberal government first introduced their Bill C-60.

All three bills maintained largely the same ISP-liability and TPM-protection rules in that the presence of a digital lock could effectively trump new and existing fair-dealing rights. Because so much of the FCFC movement had concentrated on TPMs, this has to count as a loss. At the same time, there is strong evidence that the movement was able to realize other significant substantive and ideational goals. On the substantive side, all three bills included a series of new user rights, notably an expansion of fair dealing to include education, parody, and satire, a new right to format- and time-shift (e.g., to rip CDs to a hard drive or to record a TV show to watch later), and to make backup copies, an exception to allow for the generation of non-commercial user-generated content from copyrighted works, and a cap on statutory damages for non-commercial infringement. As Geist notes, none of these were present in the original, non-tabled bill, and several of these provisions were strengthened between C-61 in 2008 and C-11 in 2012.[198] As already noted, however, the presence of a digital lock on a work effectively overrides many of these new user rights.

While it is impossible to know for sure, it seems likely that the ultimate outcome largely reflects the government's original view, that the problem with the bill circa December 2007 was with the communication strategy, not the actual policy – hence the lack of movement on digital locks. At the same time, the Conservative government introduced user rights that initially it had not planned on including. The mere inclusion of *any* user rights in the bill, while they could have been stronger and less qualified, represents a victory for the FCFC movement. The government's sensitivity to public opinion can also be seen in the fact that the bill was referred to a special joint legislative committee, rather than to the Heritage or Industry committees.

As Geist, who jump-started the Canadian user-rights debate, remarked as the bill was concluding its journey through Parliament, "Bill C-11 remains a 'flawed but fixable' bill that the government refused to fix, but that it is a significantly better bill than seemed possible a few years ago owes much to the hundreds of thousands of Canadians that spoke out on copyright."[199] In other words, it could have been worse.

Explaining Outcomes

The different outcomes for TPMs and ISP liability illustrate nicely how distinct Canadian institutions and interests can lead to outcomes different from those in (and desired by) the United States. For TPMs, the decisive factor, in both 2005 and 2008, was the institutional power of the PMO, although it was most evident in 2008. In 2005, the PMO (passively) allowed the industry and heritage departments to maintain the status quo by not providing legal protection to TPMs in cases in which TPMs were not applied to copyrighted content. This position was abetted by the fact that both bureaucracies were critical of the DMCA. In 2008, however, in the face of this bureaucratic consensus and available information on the problems with the US approach to TPMs, the Prime Minister's Office overruled the departments in order to "make the Americans happy," in Austin's phrase. That the TPM reversal was the result of interference from the PMO is further suggested by government documents unearthed via Access to Information in June 2012 by Michael Geist. In them, the Department of Justice argues that the Conservative government's decision not to link TPM protection to actual copyright infringement (which the Liberals had done in 2005) was potentially unconstitutional, "especially with respect to the freedom of expression entailing the right to access information."[200] The PMO decided to accord the US government's views on TPMs more importance than those of user groups and individual Canadians who had spoken out insistently against stronger legal protection on TPMs.

This outcome reveals two things about the relative influence of interest groups in Canada. First, despite their dramatic large-scale entry into the copyright debate in December 2007 and some important victories, the ability of civil-society groups to influence the course of the debate was constrained by the institutional context within which Canadian copyright policy is made. The disproportionate effect of the Fair Copyright For Canada Facebook group was itself the result of a very unusual confluence of events. It occurred

- during a minority Parliament;
- at a time when the government was unsure of the strength of the opposition;
- a couple of months before a highly contentious vote on Canada's continued involvement in the war in Afghanistan;
- in response to an issue that the Conservatives did not think would be politically contentious; and
- via a new communications technology that politicians did not know how to interpret.

Following the Afghanistan vote, the Liberals were revealed to be little more than paper tigers, headed by historically inept leaders who then led their party to catastrophic electoral defeats in 2008 and 2011. With an election less of a concern, with the Afghanistan issue disposed of, and with the separatist Bloc Québécois in favour of stronger copyright legislation and likely to support the Conservatives in the end, the opposition inside and outside of Parliament had little political ammunition to use against the government. In a majority situation, the government – the prime minister – could do largely as he wished. And he did, particularly in C-61. Given the governmental position that the Conservatives' copyright bill suffered from bad communication, not bad policy, the introduction of user rights that can be overridden by digital locks was largely a tactical, though still important – these are new rights, after all – concession to a potentially troublesome new interest group.

The ultimate Conservative government position on TPMs favoured the United States and the traditional content industries. Second, and more important, the fact that a Liberal government had decided against the views of the United States and content industries in 2005 suggests that the Canadian government retains significant autonomy when making copyright law, and that the decision to follow the US lead on TPM protection was almost completely contingent on the presence of Stephen Harper in the PMO. Another prime minister could have made (and did make) a different decision.

That Liberal and Conservative governments adopted the same ISP-liability policy reinforces the conclusion that effective control over Canadian copyright policy remains firmly rooted in domestic contexts, institutions, and processes. Liberal and Conservative governments consistently supported the pre-existing voluntary notice-and-notice regime for ISP liability, which operated without any significant controversy since the beginning of the decade and has withstood opposition from rights holders and the US government.

The difference between Canadian consistency on ISP liability and the changing position on TPMs is the result of two factors related to institutions and actors. First, US actors had prioritized TPM protection over ISP liability. Second, Canadian courts early on forced the content industry and ISPs to reach an agreement, with which all concerned were reasonably satisfied. In contrast, there remains no such legal position – formal or informal – on TPMs. The difference in the way TPMs and ISP liability were treated also reflects the relative influence and resources of the interest groups involved. Given the economic importance of ISPs, there was no reason for the government to upset a proven, workable balance and annoy politically and economically powerful actors like

Bell and Rogers. Faced with a pre-existing, truly made-in-Canada standard, it was easier for the government to ratify the status quo than adopt
a controversial new regime whose benefits were open to debate. This
conclusion accords with the findings of Banting, Hoberg, and Simeon
that "one expects greater convergence between Canada and the United
States in the newer areas of public policy."[201]

Even though they are rising in importance, Canadian user groups and
creator groups like the CMCC are at a distinct resource disadvantage
compared with copyright-industry groups and the large ISPs. The full
effect of individual-user groups, however, will likely be felt in the longer
run. The inclusion of any new user rights in Bill C-11 suggests that even
a government hostile to this constituency realizes that they are now a
legitimate part of the copyright debate. The Conservative government's
public consultations in 2009 further demonstrate that individual users
are becoming increasingly important in copyright debates.

While user rights are now part of the Canadian copyright debate, they
remain contested, existing in tension with industry concerns about "piracy." Many of the new user rights proposed by Bill C-32 can be overridden by a digital lock. The ongoing debate over this balance can even be
seen in the proposed (as of October 2013) implementation of a formal
notice-and-notice regime. In October 2013 the government launched a
consultation to establish the system's specific rules. The government
states that its goal is a system "that is both balanced and functional; but,
most importantly, it must endeavour to *deter infringement*" (emphasis
added) As Michael Geist uncovered via an Access to Information request, an earlier draft read "that the system be balanced and functional
for both copyright owners and internet intermediaries."[202] The priority
accorded to TPMs over user rights, and of infringement over balance,
suggests that while the Conservative government has learned the importance of paying lip service to user groups, the traditional protection-
oriented copyright interests continue to hold sway.

Part 3: The Domestic, Regional, and International Context of Canadian Copyright Reform, 2005–2012

Copyright in Canada and the United States

Although global, regional, and domestic groups, institutions, and ideas
influence Canadian copyright policy, Canadian copyright policymaking
– as in the United States – remains a domestic story at heart. While the

same general interests and ideas are at play in both copyright debates – content industries, user groups, consumers, and so on – the composition of these groups, as well as their relative influence, differs between the two countries. However, considering the Canadian case from a regional historical-institutionalist perspective reveals two major differences from the US policy debate. The first difference is that regional institutions and actors have influenced outcomes in the Canadian government's decisions on how to implement the treaties, although not in a direction that promotes regional policy convergence.[203] In particular, NAFTA has constrained the US ability to influence Canadian policy.

Second, where the US debate has been driven primarily by internal domestic concerns, Canadian copyright reform, with minor exceptions, has largely been driven by the United States, partly as a consequence of the close economic relationship between the two countries. To use Campbell's terminology, change in Canadian copyright policy has tended to occur through a form of "diffusion" – "the process whereby imported principles and practices are implemented locally"[204] – of ideas that originate in the United States. At the same time, symbolic and substantive bricolage are also in evidence, particularly in the way that the United States in the SPP talks linked copyright reform to market access, a trade issue (substantive bricolage), and how new creator and user groups have reframed the copyright debate to emphasize its dissemination side.

Ideas

Ideationally, Canadian copyright policies are firmly entrenched within the Anglo-American tradition, largely as the result of the historical and ongoing influence of, first, the United Kingdom and, currently, the United States. This particular path is reinforced by NAFTA and TRIPS. The United States continues to influence Canadian copyright policy through the Internet treaties and the example of the DMCA, particularly with respect to the bundling of the issues of ISP liability and the legal protection of TPMs. The United States, via its influence over the Internet treaties and its domestic process (which linked treaty implementation to ISP liability), largely set the overall agenda on digital-copyright reform for Canada (and the world).

However, the outcome of the Canadian debate over implementation of the Internet treaties was shaped decisively by the regional and domestic institutional context, the specifically Canadian configuration and relative influence of domestic interests, and the traditional Canadian "go slow" approach to copyright reform. Furthermore, the strength and effect of the FCFC movement demonstrated the extent to which copyright's traditional "property"/"protection" pole is being displaced by an emphasis on copyright's dissemination side. This ideational change portends future changes, or at least complications, in the direction of Canadian copyright law. The FCFC movement placed user rights squarely on the Canadian political agenda, to the extent that the government saw it as necessary to at least pay lip service to them in pursuit of their final objective. User rights, previously all but invisible in the Canadian copyright discourse, came to be the dominant frame through which the copyright bills were discussed. Debates never end in politics, and copyright is no exception. With user rights firmly on the Canadian copyright agenda, the next copyright debate will have to take their proponents into account.

Regional and Domestic Institutions

The WIPO treaties' implementation process in Canada reveals several important aspects of the nature of regional governance in copyright. First, as does the US government, the Canadian government enjoys a great deal of leeway in deciding how to implement its international copyright commitments. It put off even trying to implement the treaties for four years with the 2001–2 consultations, which suggests a high degree of control over the timing of the debate. On the issue of ISP liability, the Liberal government (in 2005) and the Conservative governments (in 2008, 2010, and 2012) rejected the US notice-and-takedown approach in favour of a more moderate notice-and-notice regime. On the issue of legal protection for TPMs, the Liberal decision to adopt a minimalist approach was reversed by the Conservatives in its two subsequent bills. These outcomes reflect a situation in which the United States can influence, but not dictate, Canadian copyright laws.

Second, formal regional institutions affected Canadian copyright reform. While NAFTA Chapter 17 reinforces the baseline for Canadian copyright and led to some changes in Canada's copyright laws, NAFTA's more important effect, from a regional governance perspective, is the way that it indirectly forces the US government and its industry allies to seek out other means of influencing Canadian copyright policy that do not require linking copyright to trade issues. These alternative means of influence, outside of international forum shifting in the form of ACTA and the Trans-Pacific Partnership, include policy emulation (e.g., the example of the DMCA as a preferred model for implementing the Internet treaties) and penetration (i.e., lobbying by the US government and the US content industries). Consequently, while the United States has an effect on the Canadian debate, it is much less than one would expect from a regional power that, only a decade earlier, had set rules in NAFTA that were seen by some to be a continuation of the harmonization of regional IP law.

Third, North American regional copyright governance is primarily binational in scope, with the United States at the centre. Mexico does not figure at all in the Canadian copyright debate. Canadian officials pay no attention to Mexican copyright policymaking,[205] and Canadian non-government actors have minimal to no contact with their Mexican counterparts on copyright. Overall, this analysis reconfirms that the North American region is a de facto "hub and spoke" regime: asymmetrical in nature and organized in a double-bilateral manner around a US hegemonic power that itself is not all-powerful.

Rhetorically, the charge that Bill C-61 was "born in the USA" proved damaging enough to require a response from the government that the bill was, indeed, "made in Canada." The most significant "regional" actor in the Canadian copyright debate – as in the Mexican copyright debate – is the US government, which operates more through moral suasion and domestic lobbying than through coercion or (largely non-existent) regional institutions.

Interests

As with institutions, copyright engages both transnational (e.g., the international music industry) and domestic interests. The industry groups that have driven the debate in Canada – particularly CRIA, CMPDA, and, more recently, ESAC – are largely offshoots of their parent US lobby groups. The members of these groups, however, are organized globally, not regionally. ISPs, meanwhile, are primarily domestically based interests, several of which are politically and economically significant. The content industries – the strongest proponents of US-style copyright reform – are largely seen as foreign actors. This perception hinders their ability to influence Canadian copyright law. Creator groups, meanwhile, have contacts with US groups and work with international partners (including in the run-up to the WIPO Internet treaties), but advocacy with respect to Canadian copyright-law reform is largely limited to domestically organized groups.

The greatest change over the past decade has occurred among individual-user groups and new creator groups. Reduced barriers to participating in the copyright debate, thanks to Facebook and other social-networking tools, have given individuals and their advocates a place in the debate. Furthermore, the past decade has witnessed a *reduction* in cross-border activity among such groups as a result of the efforts of particular individuals and groups. By 2008, copyright was being covered as a mainstream news topic and public involvement had become Canadianized, in large part due to the efforts of Michael Geist and individuals involved in the FCFC network. New creator groups also benefited from increased capacity to participate in the copyright debate, in part due to the work of CIPPIC, itself partly funded from US sources. This funding, while important, is as far as these regional ties go, and it represents a change from the early part of the decade, when user-group lobbies were directed largely from the United States. In fact, Canada is becoming an exporter of copyright ideas, namely, through the rising profile of Geist. Since 2007, he has become a high-profile and sought-after commentator in Europe, Australia, Mexico, and the United States, among other places.

Constrained Autonomy

The difference of opinion on TPMs between the Conservative and Liberal governments, combined with the made-in-Canada ISP liability regime, indicate that Canada retains the ability to set its own copyright policy. Where kowtowing to the United States would upset previously existing programs and powerful stakeholders, the benefits of following the US lead with respect to treaty implementation will be diminished. In the absence of any set policies, the Canadian government is more open to influence from all sides. In both cases, domestic factors – the structure of departmental decision making, the relative power and influence of interest groups, and the identity of the prime minister – are paramount: the decision to follow the US or any other country's lead on copyright is politically and domestically determined, and it is not set in stone.

8 Mexico and the Internet Treaties, 1996–2010: International Pressure, Domestic Politics

To get a sense of the extent to which copyright has been politicized since the Internet treaties were signed in December 1996, we should consider the events, oceans apart, of 11 February 2012 and 20 July 2011. The former date witnessed a scene that would have been unthinkable a decade earlier: massive European protests against an *intellectual property treaty*. Throughout Europe, tens of thousands of people – organizers put the number at more than 100,000[1] – took to the streets to protest the Anti-Counterfeiting Trade Agreement (ACTA), the US-led treaty discussed in chapter 6. *The Guardian* newspaper put the number of protestors at 25,000 in Germany alone, including 16,000 in Munich.[2] Although ACTA's provisions on TPM protection and ISP liability had been watered down, protestors and public-interest groups were unhappy with much of the treaty, including the fact that it had been negotiated in secret and seemed to be on the verge of being rammed through the European parliament. Amnesty International, for example, argued that "the pact's content, process, and institutional structure impact in a number of ways on human rights – especially the rights to due process, privacy, freedom of information, freedom of expression, and access to essential medicines." It also expressed concern about "ACTA's broad coverage, vague language, and tendency to value private law enforcement over judicial review."[3]

The protests were hugely successful, putting an exclamation point on activists' and domestic politicians' concerns with the treaty. Public opinion was firmly against the treaty: the German copyright lobby was reduced to offering to pay students 100 euros to attend a two-hour pro-ACTA demonstration.[4] Soon after, several European countries announced that they would either not ratify or sign ACTA, including Germany, Bulgaria, the Czech Republic, Latvia, Lithuania, Slovakia, and Slovenia. As it contains criminal provisions, which are in the purview of member states, ACTA must be approved by the EU and its member states. Consequently, ACTA received what many commentators saw as a death blow on 29 May 2012, when the Dutch parliament "approved three resolutions that oppose ACTA or any future similar agreement."[5] By the beginning of July, ACTA was more or less dead in Europe, having been voted down by the European parliament, 478–39, an unprecedented rejection of an international treaty.[6] Having been rejected by the world's second-ranked economic heavyweight, ACTA itself will likely end up on the scrap heap of history.

The European protests justly received a great deal of attention, but the EU was not the first ACTA negotiating partner to say no to the treaty. That honour belongs to Mexico, one of only two developing countries involved in the negotiations (the other being Morocco). On 12 July 2011, the Mexican Senate unanimously approved a report, the product of months of committee work, calling on the president not to sign the treaty.[7] This resolution, which effectively told the Executive that the Senate would not pass the treaty even if the president signed it, was all the more remarkable for coming from a body that only eight years earlier had extended, with little debate and nearly unanimously, the term of copyright to a world-leading life of the author plus 100 years.[8] The Senate's decision, like the European anti-ACTA protests, were part of a general international opposition to ACTA, as well of domestic anti-ACTA civil-society campaigning that started building from the moment that a secret draft of the agreement was leaked by Wikileaks in May 2008.[9] Making sense of it, however, requires understanding the domestic context within which it occurred.

The Senate's ACTA vote complicates not only Mexican copyright politics, but also the politics of its implementation of the Internet treaties, as ACTA and the Internet treaties cover similar ground. Unlike Canada and the United States, Mexico has yet to implement fully the treaties, particularly with respect to ISP liability and digital-lock protection. While the United States passed its Digital Millennium Copyright Act in 1998 and Canada proposed its first implementation bill in 2005, no similar bill has been, as of this writing, proposed to the Mexican congress, although the government is committed to their implementation.[10] As a result, this chapter seeks to answer two questions. First, given that inaction is as much of a policy choice as action, why has

Mexico taken so long to implement treaties that are quite important to its hegemonic neighbour? Second – and this is where the ACTA vote comes in – what will treaty implementation look like?

Many of the lessons of the Canadian case study apply to Mexico: international and regional institutions affect outcomes in Mexican policy debates. And, as in Canada and the United States, findings of divergence or convergence on a US or North American policy in Mexico can only be understood with reference to domestic ideas, institutions, and interests. This finding agrees with findings by sociologist John C. Cross in his study of street vendors and "piracy" in Mexico. He argues that Mexico's distinctive legal, social, and political structure have hindered Mexican harmonization with "stronger" international "IP norms and enforcement practices."[11]

Mexico's path towards implementation demonstrates even more sharply the conditions under which the United States can and cannot influence Mexican copyright policy. Mexico completely overhauled its copyright law, the Ley Federal del Derecho de Autor (LFDA), in 1997 as a result of US demands during the negotiation of the North American Free Trade Agreement. While these changes brought it more in line with US copyright law overall, they did not address fully its obligations under the Internet treaties. Looking forward, the Senate's rejection of ACTA suggests that domestic politics will complicate the implementation of the Internet treaties and any future copyright-related legislation.

Mexico's case has significance even beyond its contribution to our understanding of North American copyright governance. Much of the literature on developing-country copyright treats these countries as passive policy takers.[12] Mexico's experience with the Internet treaties serves as a partial corrective to this view. In the way that past experiences with and ideas about copyright influence policy outcomes, developing countries' copyright politics are just as complex, and uncertain, as those in the United States or Europe.

This chapter is divided into four parts. The first part presents an overview of the significant changes in Mexican copyright ideas, institutions, and interests in the post-NAFTA period. The stage thus set, the second part examines the interplay of these ideas, institutions, and interests in the context of the Internet treaties. Based on this analysis, the third part looks forward to what Mexican implementation of the treaties might look like in the context of the ongoing (as of December 2013) ACTA debate. The final part places the Mexican copyright debate in its larger regional and international context.

Part 1: Copyright in Mexico

Ideas: The Persistence of History in Mexican Copyright Reform

The modern account of Mexican copyright policymaking begins with the 1994 NAFTA. The trade agreement marked a watershed in Mexican copyright policy, transforming a system primarily focused on the protection and promotion of the national culture and of authors' moral rights in the Continental copyright tradition to a more Anglo-American regime that emphasizes the enforcement of copyright owners' economic rights. It also expanded the scope of copyright to focus on neighbouring rights[13] as much as on authors' rights.[14]

It is tempting to interpret the NAFTA copyright provisions purely as being imposed by the United States on Mexico. The narrative of the developing country sacrificing intellectual property rules for market access is common, and not wholly without justification.[15] Undoubtedly, Mexico and other developing countries are at a disadvantage in trade talks with an IP component and will tend to trade IP rules for concessions they deem to be more valuable, such as rules on agriculture or general market access. Such a narrative, while not inaccurate – the NAFTA copyright provisions were driven by the United States and did target Mexico – ignores the tendency of domestic institutions and ideas to persist and influence newly introduced concepts, ideas, and policies. Taken too far, the view that developing countries are international "policy takers" can obscure developing countries' agency. In the case of Mexico and NAFTA, it can obscure the extent to which many existing Mexican copyright interests welcomed and benefited from NAFTA-related changes.

While NAFTA-related changes laid the groundwork for Mexico's coming Internet treaty-related reforms, the context in which the commercialization of Mexican copyright law continues to be carried out is as influenced by Mexico's past as by the external influences (the United States, the Berne and Rome Conventions, TRIPS, the Internet treaties, and so on). Specifically, the historical interpretation of *derechos de autor* (literally, authors' rights) as a constitutionally mandated means to protect and promote authors' rights (and thereby the national culture) has created a narrative that tends to reinforce calls for a maximalist interpretation of the (commercial) WIPO Internet treaties that has only begun to be challenged by a counter-narrative that emphasizes users' rights.

INTERNATIONAL INFLUENCES ON MEXICAN COPYRIGHT LAW

As with Canada, Mexico's copyright tradition was bequeathed to it, first by its colonial master and then by its most important trading partner. Mexican regulation of literary and intellectual production historically is based in the Continental European tradition, which emphasizes an author's inalienable moral rights related to issues such as attribution, as opposed to an owner's economic rights (i.e., treating the copyright as an alienable right that can be bought and sold). It dates to Spain's Real Orden of 1764.[16] While predecessors to the current law can be observed in the various nineteenth-century constitutions and laws,[17] modern Mexican copyright law dates to, and draws its authority from, article 28 of the 1917 Mexican constitution. Article 28 prohibits monopolies except in certain cases, including "the privileges that, for a limited time, are recognized for authors and artists to produce their works."[18] Fernando Serrano Migallón, Mexico's foremost copyright authority, argues that the granting of these privileges represented the state's recognition of an author's inherent rights, specifically, an author's permanent inalienable moral rights and temporary and alienable economic rights in his/her work.[19]

Mexican *derecho de autor* laws historically have addressed two fundamental objectives: public order and the social interest, with social interest defined as all that benefits Mexico and its development. Specifically, copyright law must address the educational and cultural needs of the society on one side and on the other side must fulfil its international obligations to protect and enforce copyright in Mexico.[20] Mexican copyright policy, a federal responsibility, draws its legitimacy not from a balancing of interests or maximizing the production and dissemination of knowledge and the "useful arts," as in the United States.[21] Rather, it is intimately intertwined with Mexican culture and national identity (the "national spirit," as Serrano Migallón puts it),[22] whose defence is a central preoccupation and responsibility of the Mexican government. The main academic text on Mexican copyright law and history frames copyright as *the* way in which Mexican culture, and culture more generally, is safeguarded.[23] Writing after the 1997 transformation of Mexico's copyright regime, Serrano Migallón remarks:

In the past, as today, *derecho de autor* norms are not just economic or market norms; its end is not solely related to the trade in cultural goods and services. Its ultimate purpose has been always of a much more transcendent nature, its juridical norms destined to preserve the dignity of the labours of creators of these works of ingenuity and the spirit, in a way that allows, regarding respect and remuneration, an apt environment for creation and its enjoyment.[24]

The continued influence of this perspective in the post-NAFTA legislation suggests the historical-institutionalist notion of path dependence. This focus on the production and preservation of Mexican culture is restated in article 1 of the 1997 LFDA, according to which, copyright's objective is "to safeguard and promote the Nation's cultural heritage; to protect the rights of authors, performers, as well as publishers, producers and broadcasters, in connection to their literary or artistic works in all their forms, their publications, their phonograms or video recordings, and their broadcasts, as well as other intellectual-property rights."[25]

While previous LFDAs focused more on authors, their expressed motivating sentiment – the protection of rights in order to preserve and strengthen the national culture – has remained consistent since the 1963 revisions to Mexico's *derecho de autor* law.[26] The (limited) Mexican academic literature on Mexican copyright[27] suggests that Mexican copyright law bases its international legitimacy to a large extent on article 27 of the Universal Declaration of Human Rights.[28]

Mexican copyright officials have always been sensitive to the international context in which Mexican copyright policy is made.[29] For over a century, Mexican officials have paid attention to international copyright. One of the Mexican government's main objectives in introducing its first proto-copyright law, the 1846 Reglamento de la Libertad de Imprenta (Freedom of the Press Regulations), was to insert Mexico into the community of more-advanced nations.[30] Unlike Canada, which until the 1990s had been a reluctant joiner of international copyright treaties, and only joined the 1886 Berne Convention as a consequence of its quasi-colonial relationship with the United Kingdom, Mexico has been an enthusiastic joiner of international copyright treaties. In 1947, Mexico ratified the Interamerican Convention on Copyright and Literary Property; in 1957, the Universal Copyright Convention;[31] in 1964, the Rome Convention; in 1967 the Berne Convention;[32] in 1995 the Agreement on Trade-Related Aspects of Intellectual Property; and in 1996 the Internet treaties. In turn, the conventions ratified in 1947, 1957, and 1964 directly influenced Mexican copyright reforms in 1947, 1956, and 1963, respectively.[33]

More recent changes to the Mexican copyright law, which reoriented Mexican copyright towards an Anglo-American focus, were unquestionably related to US influence and preparations for and the implementation of NAFTA.[34] This includes the 1997 reforms, which implemented

Mexico's NAFTA copyright obligations, as well as relatively minor changes in 1991 that, among other things, extended copyright protection to phonogram producers, a move in which the US-based Recording Industry Association of America was instrumental and which it was estimated would earn record companies around US$75 million per year.[35]

As a smaller country like Canada, Mexico's copyright law has been influenced by the country's international trading partners. Even here, however, one sees how the diffusion of a "foreign" approach to copyright has been interpreted in light of existing domestic approaches. The traditional Mexican idea of *derecho de autor* as a moral right has influenced its treatment of copyright as an economic right that encompasses both users and creators. Copyright lawyer and scholar Cesar Callejas remarks: "In Mexico there is still the myth that industrial property protects commerce and *derecho de autor* protects artistic ideas (moral rights)."[36] This myth holds despite the fact that post-1997 Mexican copyright law is focused primarily on the economic rights of owners. As copyright lawyer Manuel Morante remarks, "Today the *derecho patrimonial* (economic right) takes precedence over moral rights."[37]

The result of the commingling of these two approaches is that the traditional moral-rights goal of maximizing an *author's* moral rights (who would argue against minimizing someone's human rights?) provides support for an economics-focused approach to copyright that favours the maximization of copyright *owners'* rights. Both types of rights are pointed in the same direction: NAFTA represents not only a "critical juncture" in the making of Mexican copyright policy, linking trade-access issues to Mexican copyright reform, but also a larger degree of path dependence than one might otherwise suspect given the large change that NAFTA wrought on Mexican copyright law.

The institutions created for the protection and defence of copyright, according to their functions, ensure compliance with the exclusive rights provided by the law governing the subject.[38] Like all copyright laws, Mexico's contains several exceptions – primarily in articles 147–50 – that allow either for copying or licensing of works without the need to obtain the permission of the copyright owner. Many of these can be found in other copyright laws: exemptions for purposes of criticism, educational, and scientific research purposes. One of the more interesting allows for a one-time, one-copy reproduction of a work for personal, private, non-commercial use (article 148(4)).

These limitations, argues Serrano Migallón, are both inherent in Mexican *derecho de autor*, and are needed to balance the needs of rights holders with those of society and users.[39] They are also consistent with

Mexico's status as a civil-law jurisdiction, in which judges interpret statutes and do not make law through the principle of *stare decisis*.[40] Since they require that a list of specific conditions be met, these exceptions resemble the more close-ended Canadian fair-dealing limitations than they do the open-ended US fair-use exceptions.

The 1997 reforms, discussed below, may have refocused Mexican copyright from (Mexican) creators' moral rights towards copyright as a commercial right available to foreigners as well as Mexicans, distributors, and artists, but they did not fundamentally challenge the idea, inherent in previous laws, that the national interest is best served by maximizing artists' rights in their work. This maximalist approach to copyright protection suggests a fundamental symmetry between the objectives of Mexico's past and present copyright regimes. In short, Mexican copyright law's traditional bias towards copyright owners' rights was refocused, not created, by these NAFTA reforms.

CULTURAL SUPERPOWER AND/OR DEVELOPING COUNTRY
Economically, Mexican copyright policy is drawn in two opposite directions, by its not-unjustified self-image as a global cultural heavyweight and its material status as a developing country. The former tugs the country towards a desire for stronger copyright laws, the latter towards their relaxation. The result is a paradox, common in much of Mexican policy: while Mexican copyright laws are among the strongest in the world (unusual for a developing country), they are also poorly enforced.[41]

As either the most or second-most (after Spain) dynamic producer of Spanish-language cultural products, Mexico has an objective interest – similar to that of the United States – in promoting strong international copyright protection for its artists and copyright owners. The country also has a subjective view that, in the words of Alfredo Tourné, director of protection with Mexico's main copyright agency, the Instituto Nacional del Derecho de Autor (National Copyright Institute, INDAUTOR), "we should be leaders in this topic in Latin America."[42] This self-image of Mexico as a cultural superpower tends to reinforce the idea, promoted most directly internationally by the United States, that copyright protection should be strengthened, and contributes to the path dependence and Mexican institutional bias in favour of copyright owners in the debate over copyright generally and the implementation of the Internet treaties in particular.

Mexico's net international economic benefits from copyright are actually somewhat unclear. By a generous measure of the cultural industries, Mexico has been a consistent net exporter of cultural-industry products – defined very broadly to include industries directly and indirectly involved in copyright – with copyright-related industries accounting for 13.4 per cent of total exports and 8 per cent of total imports in 2000.[43] However, by some measures, Mexico may actually be a net importer of copyrighted works. In 2000, US$1.8 million in Mexican mechanical royalty payments accrued to foreigners, against US$1.5 million to Mexicans.[44] Nonetheless, the content industries are not unimportant to Mexico. For example, Mexico is the world's third most important producer of phonograms, after the United States and the United Kingdom.[45] Overall, the US-based Business Software Alliance's Emery Simon says that Mexicans "perceive themselves much less as net importers and they see themselves as having a more balanced set of interests on copyright-based [material]."[46]

For example, the Mexican company Televisa, the largest media company in the Spanish-speaking world, "has built itself into the world's largest exporter of Spanish-language programs on the strength of its 'domestic opportunity advantage,' its more-or-less 'unique access to the world's largest domestic market' in that language."[47] Televisa was able to build this advantage due to its status as a "virtual monopoly,"[48] the result of decades of collusion with the PRI (Partido Revolucionario Mexicano, or Institutional Revolutionary Party) government, which ruled Mexico until 2000 (and which regained the presidency in 2012). With roots in television stations allied with PRI president Miguel Alemán (1946–52), Televisa received decades of concessions from the PRI in return for acting as the "ruling party cheerleader."[49] It enjoyed a virtual monopoly over broadcasting until the 1990s.[50] Its relationship with President Carlos Salinas (1988–94), who brought NAFTA to Mexico, was particularly tight. While its influence in Mexican politics has diminished somewhat since the Salinas and one-party rule, it remains a key player in Mexican telecommunications. As an example of its influence on copyright policy, Televisa was the only company that was part of the five-member Mexican delegation to WIPO for the negotiation of the Internet treaties.[51]

The importance of strong international and domestic copyright law to Mexican officials was evident during the NAFTA negotiations. In those talks, the Canadian government fought the US insistence that copyright be included in the agreement; instead, it successfully imported the "cultural exemption" from the Canada-US Free Trade Agreement. Canada tried to convince Mexico to support the Canadian anti-copyright-inclusion stance, but Mexico refused. "Protected by an ancient and vigorous cultural identity and a rich language of its own which had survived North American penetration," Mexico did not regard national culture as being on the negotiating table.[52] Rather, Mexico, and particularly Televisa, were interested in the large and increasing Spanish-speaking market in the United States, which would be prime targets for the export of Mexican *telenovelas*, music, and books,[53] as well as in renewing copyright on Mexican films that had reverted to the public domain in the United States.[54]

At the same time, Mexico is also a developing country facing resource constraints, in which just under half of the population lived under the official poverty line in 2008.[55] As a result, the strength of Mexican copyright laws is matched by the lack of enforcement of the same, even as governments pass ever-stronger copyright laws. For example, Jalife Daher calls the 1999 copyright-related changes to the penal code and the Ley de la Propiedad (property law), which includes penalties of up to ten years in prison, "our system's most extreme reaction against piracy."[56]

Cross notes that, according to industry-supplied figures, "in terms of per capita losses [due to copyright infringement], Mexico is generally surpassed only by Russia and Italy."[57] Fears of social unrest because of the informal sector's contribution to GDP and employment, and the involvement, in some cases, of organized crime and corruption, reduces officials' political and economic incentives to enforce copyright laws.[58] As Karaganis remarks:

> The relationships between Mexican street vendor organizations and police are marked by negotiated truces that reflect the integration of these organizations into the political system. Raid-based enforcement [of copyright law] is inherently fragile and subject to a political calculus that weighs external pressure from the USTR and multinational groups against internal pressure from domestic business constituencies.[59]

Copyright lawyer Callejas argues that the government is not interested in enforcement for several reasons, including a lack of clear data on the scope of the problem, since the only data on the losses from *pirateria* (piracy) come from companies that have refused to reveal their methodology and sources.[60]

The production and consumption of bootlegged copyrighted works in Mexico is related to the state of the economy. As *The Economist* notes, 1996 witnessed an explosion in the sale and production of bootlegged CDs and DVDs, a fact it attributed to the severe economic downturn of the previous year as "many normally legitimate firms ... entered the black market.[61] A study on Mexico City's informal economy links its rise, including that of vendors of bootlegged goods, to Mexico's "lost decade" of the 1980s.[62] Such vendors are ubiquitous throughout Mexico, and are particularly visible in Mexico City. One can purchase the latest Hollywood films for the equivalent of $2 or $3 everywhere: outside subway stops, in the park across from the offices of the Secretaria de Relaciones Extranjeros (Foreign Affairs), or outside UNAM, Mexico's largest university, to name only three places. Some vendors even specialize in subgenres, such as art films. In the metro itself, hawkers move from car to car blasting out samples of the hit songs on the CDs they have for sale. For 10 pesos (about 80 cents), a commuter can buy 237 Beatles songs, or the latest hits by Pitbull and the depressingly ubiquitous Black Eyed Peas.

Black markets in copyrighted works in developing countries, as a major 2011 empirical study by New York's Social Science Research Council (SSRC) demonstrates, is driven by the lack of affordable legal material.[63] Official CDs and DVDs cost the same in Mexico as they do in the United States and Canada, even though wages are much lower: the daily minimum wage in the Distrito Federal (Mexico City) in 2012 was 62 pesos (about US$4.66). As a result, Mexicans must pay developed-country prices if they want to buy a CD or DVD legally. The SSRC study points out that, in Mexico, US$14 for Coldplay's 2008 opus *Viva la Vida* CD is equivalent to an American paying $80.50.[64] In contrast, the "pirate price" – what street vendors charge for an unauthorized CD – for *Viva la Vida* is about 1 dollar, equivalent to $5.75. The numbers are even more ridiculous for Christopher Nolan's superhero epic *The Dark Knight*: a legal price of $27 is equivalent to an American paying $154, versus the pirate price of 75 cents, or $4.25.[65] These high prices mean that a large share of Mexico's population is effectively priced out of the market for books, movies, and films. Faced with low wages and a product that can be sold profitably for much less than the list price with minimal fear of arrest or sanction, Mexicans' widespread purchases of bootlegged works is understandable.

NAFTA AND THE REORIENTATION OF MEXICAN COPYRIGHT LAW

The wholesale 1997 revision of the Ley Federal del Derecho de Autor (LFDA) represented the culmination of a reform process that began with changes to Mexico's overall intellectual property laws in 1991 in reaction to US-based pressure and the run-up to NAFTA.[66] The reforms were part of the general Mexican reaction to the economic crises of the

1980s that rejected a more autonomous model of economic development for the outward focus of neoliberalism, and culminated in the implementation of NAFTA in 1994.[67]

With that caveat, the most significant legacy of the 1997 revisions was its shifting of Mexican copyright law from a more "humanist" to an economic approach. The 1997 law expanded what had been "a completely authorial law in the strict sense that it dealt with the author and the protection of the author" to include a greater focus on the protection of neighbouring rights,[68] including those of performers, phonogram producers, audio-visual producers, and editors, both Mexican and foreign.[69] Some did better than others. Composers and musicians received greater protection, but audio-visual workers, especially cinematographers, saw their rights diminished: only films as a whole received a copyright, but with no special rights for the people who actually make them.[70]

NAFTA was the impetus to change a law that, it was generally agreed in Mexico, needed to be modernized.[71] Serrano Migallón argues that the new law was the result of government lobbying by "the intellectual community, artists, authors and all those who participate in the creation of culture goods and services,"[72] and addressed both domestic and international concerns.[73] NAFTA's copyright provisions were included at the insistence of the United States and targeted at reforming Mexican copyright, in particular mandating punishments for commercial violations of copyrights.[74]

Mexico emerged from NAFTA having "lost" more of its demands of the United States than it "won."[75] That the United States may have come out the "winner" in the copyright part of NAFTA is not to say that Mexico simply adopted US policies wholesale. Mexico was able to negotiate fairly broad reservations for its broadcast and film industries, requiring that a majority of time in each day's live broadcast programs feature Mexican nationals, limiting non-national ownership in cable service providers to minority interests, and requiring that 30 per cent of theatre movie screen time be reserved for Mexican films.[76] However, another view holds that the 1997 LFDA, which implemented NAFTA's copyright provisions,

> is a law that, rather than addressing the authentic needs of Mexican society, is a product of the compromises made by Mexico at the international level, especially with respect to NAFTA … Our country had to cede to American pressure to provide "adequate" copyright and neighbouring rights protection, for owners who are nationals and residents of that country, for purely commercial purposes.[77]

This view correctly emphasizes that the reorientation of Mexican copyright policy towards a US-style regime was not a significant concern to the Mexican NAFTA negotiators, although Cameron and Tomlin report that "there was contention over differences in legal frameworks – the Mexican system, for example, gave greater weight to the rights of authors than producers."[78]

Of the changes required by NAFTA, two stand out for the purposes of this study. First was the requirement that NAFTA partners (i.e., Mexico) enforce their domestic copyright laws. While treaties typically do not "constrain the criminal law of other countries," NAFTA requires that partners set prison terms and/or fines "to provide a deterrent 'consistent with the level of penalties applied for crimes of a corresponding gravity.'" Second was the extension of copyright to groups that had previously been ignored (including the music recording and satellite TV industries).[79] Together, these changes provide an idea of the significance of NAFTA Chapter 17 as it relates to copyright, particularly for Mexico.

The 1997 changes were thus important for the future development of copyright policy in Mexico not because they sparked a trend towards stronger copyright protection: this tendency was already inherent in Mexican copyright policymaking. Rather, they rearranged the agenda of Mexican policymakers to emphasize the interest of new groups. Alongside traditional interests like Mexican creators, record producers – foreign and domestic – now had greater rights under NAFTA and the LFDA. While Mexico may have "lost" more than it "won" on copyright in the NAFTA negotiations, it is difficult to conclude that, overall, the domestic groups most involved in the making of copyright policies – "the intellectual community, artists, authors and all those who participate in the creation of culture goods and services" and so on – were either opposed to NAFTA's outcome or have not come to see it in a favourable light. Certainly, there is little evidence of widespread discontent among these groups. Furthermore, copyright was a technical, apolitical commercial policy: both houses of Congress unanimously adopted the 1997 LFDA.[80] This is not to argue that the NAFTA deal was objectively positive from a public-policy perspective or that certain groups did not or do not oppose it, only that it seems that the NAFTA copyright chapter had the broad support of those groups that were *listened* to in the process.

Institutions: Corporatism, (Mostly) Uninterrupted

The structure and focus of institutions affects both what policies get advanced and which actors are listened to in the policymaking process.

In Canada, a divided bureaucracy with departments advancing diametrically opposed views of copyright gives both "protection" and "dissemination" interests an institutional base from which to promote their points of view. This set-up tends towards compromise and stalemate, but can be overridden by political power exercised by the prime minister. In the United States, the bureaucratic institutions with responsibility for copyright tend to favour copyright's "protection" function over its "dissemination" function. The balance between the two, meanwhile, is set via inter-industry bargaining, with the US Congress tacitly agreeing to pass consensus copyright bills, so long as all relevant (in its view) interest groups are represented. The resulting copyright bills have reflected the relative power and influence of the involved groups.

Of its two NAFTA partners, Mexico's institutional copyright regime more closely resembles that of the United States, in which bureaucratic institutions tend to emphasize copyright protection, and in which affected interests are involved in setting policy. However, unlike the United States' institutional structure, Mexico's emerged from a formal corporatist tradition. From 1910 through the 1990s, regulation of society and the economy was corporatist in nature: "The government has sought to act as the ultimate arbiter and to see to it that no one group becomes predominant."[81] Mexican corporatism had been characterized by state-created organizations "requiring those persons meeting the criteria of a special interest to belong to it."[82] However, the election of Vicente Fox in 2000 led to the demise of one-party rule and this corporatist structure suffered a setback. While membership in accredited groups is no longer mandatory for those who wish for standing in copyright discussions and Congress matters much more than it previously did,[83] Mexican copyright policymaking continues to follow a loose corporatist model. Although "Mexico has witnessed a flowering of popular movements since 1989," these are "the result of the action of elite economic and cultural groups."[84] The groups one would expect would be most directly affected by changes in digital-copyright rules have only very recently started to take an interest in copyright policy. As a result, copyright policy, at least before 2010, was largely untouched, likely because it was not politically sensitive.

In Mexico, a not-completely-neutral state coordinates negotiations among accepted groups representing capital (i.e., the copyright industries, both domestic and foreign) and labour (i.e., the *sociedades de gestión colectivas*, the creator-focused collection societies) from an oligopolistic sector.[85] Overall, those institutions directly responsible for

Mexican copyright policy are biased towards copyright protection, comfortable with the new economic emphasis of copyright law, and open to US perspectives on copyright. In terms of the Internet treaties, this bias privileges the passage of DMCA-style TPM and ISP liability rules. However, parts of Congress and the Mexican bureaucracy responsible for the telecommunications industry that were not previously a significant part of the copyright debate have the potential to challenge this view of copyright.

CONGRESS

Over the past decade, and certainly since the election of Vicente Fox in 2000 ended seventy-one years of one-party rule, the Mexican policy-making process has changed dramatically. Where previously Congress was largely a rubber stamp for decisions made by the Executive, the Senate and House of Deputies are increasingly asserting their legislative independence. This is no less true of copyright policy and has led to a situation in which Congress has demonstrated increasing power with respect to policymaking. The 2003 changes to the LFDA (discussed below) emerged from Congress, not the Executive.[86] More routinely, individual members and senators also introduce copyright legislation; as with their US counterparts, few of these bills become law.

Where previously groups wanting changes to Mexican copyright law could only go through the Executive and its departments (*secretarías*), they now also have the choice of lobbying legislators, in a process reminiscent of US congressional lobbying (they also continue to lobby the president as well).[87] Not surprisingly, lobbyists take advantage of this situation and focus their attention on individual legislators as well as those on key committees, the most prominent of which are the culture committees of the two houses of Congress.[88]

Until the ACTA debate, politicians from all parties treated copyright as an apolitical issue. Copyright's reputation as a technical issue, combined with the traditional perception of copyright as a policy to safeguard Mexican culture, did not provide politicians with many reasons to oppose its extension. At the request of the *sociedades de gestión colectivas*, which represent authors, the government in 2003 increased the general term of protection to life of the author plus *one hundred* years, easily the longest term of protection on the planet, longer than Canada's life plus 50 years term, the US term of life plus 75 years, and far beyond copyright's original 14-year term. This change benefited the *sociedades*, which stood to collect royalties on works that were about to fall into the public domain. However, it was so drastic that even INDAUTOR's director of protection, Alfredo Tourné, a proponent of strong copyright protection and copyright owners' rights, says the changes may have gone too far.[89] Nonetheless, this change gave rise to only cursory congressional debate.[90]

Mexican politicians also face important incentives not to engage in strong crackdowns on bootlegged copyrighted works. González, Torres, and Jiménez remark that lax enforcement due to corruption is generally recognized to be one cause for widespread copyright violations in Mexico.[91] Street vendors, who are represented by vendor organizations that "protect over 300,000 street vendors throughout Mexico City," have connections with various parties, with "most of these organizations hav[ing] access to one or more political patrons, to whom they can turn for help should local officials try to remove them." What's more, "the history of conflict and accommodation between street vendors and the state means that leaders have a strong tendency to see any punitive policy as an attack on their hard-won de facto right to sell in the streets."[92]

EXECUTIVE-BRANCH INSTITUTIONS
INDAUTOR and the Instituto Mexicano de la Propiedad Industrial (IMPI)
Despite the rise in power of Congress, the Executive (i.e., the presidency and its agencies) continues to wield significant power. As Camp notes: "Groups in Mexican society who want some part in national policy decisions must make their concerns and interests known to the executive branch at the highest possible level."[93] One interviewee mentioned that lobby groups try to communicate with the presidency to make their concerns known.[94] Similarly to the United States but in contrast to Canada, Mexican copyright policy is the main responsibility of one department, which historically has emphasized the "protection" role of copyright over that of "dissemination." In Mexico, perhaps befitting the traditional view of *derechos de autor* as being about the promotion and protection of Mexican culture, copyright is the formal responsibility of the Secretaría de Educación Pública (Public Education Department, SEP). Within the SEP, copyright policy rests primarily with INDAUTOR, a quasi-independent entity created in 1997 from what had been a SEP Dirección General de Derecho de Autor (General Directorate of Copyrights), with roots going back to Mexico's 1947 copyright law.[95] INDAUTOR's director-general serves at the pleasure of the Executive and can be fired for cause by the secretary of the SEP. INDAUTOR is responsible for protecting *derechos de autor* in Mexico and establishing

derecho de autor-related policies.[96] Specifically, article 209 of the LFDA gives INDAUTOR the responsibility to:

1 protect and promote *derechos de autor*;
2 promote the creation of literary and artistic works;
3 run the Public *Derecho de Autor* Registry (works are not required to be registered, but registration is offered as an option to copyright owners to better help assert their rights);
4 maintain its historical heritage; and
5 promote international cooperation and exchanges with institutions charged with the registration and protection of *derecho de autor* and neighbouring rights. (translation of legislation by the author)

The responsibilities of INDAUTOR under LFDA article 210 include protecting authors' moral rights and setting tariffs.[97] Interestingly, since 2001 the Instituto Mexicano de la Propiedad Industrial (Mexican Institute of Industrial Property, IMPI), a much-better-funded and relatively more independent agency under the Secretaría de Economía, has been responsible for pursuing commercial copyright violations, which happen to be of greatest interest to foreign (and domestic) copyright holders. Nonetheless, INDAUTOR is the lead agency with respect to copyright policy and is the primary governmental contact point for copyright-related individuals and groups wishing to discuss or reform the LFDA. While it is open to all opinions, INDAUTOR sees its main clients as being the *sociedades de gestión colectivas*, which represent authors, artists, and other creators (discussed below) and the groups representing Mexican-based content industries, such as the phonogram and motion picture industries (also discussed below).[98]

INDAUTOR houses Mexico's recognized governmental copyright experts. For example, the Mexican delegation to the 1996 WIPO Internet treaties negotiations was led by Dr Fernando Serrano Migallón, then head of the entity replaced by INDAUTOR (and the author of the most authoritative book on Mexican copyright law).[99] While INDAUTOR's semi-independence has increased its authority on copyright issues, it remains subservient to the SEP and must work within that bureaucracy, which tends to view copyright as a secondary priority, in order to promote and propose changes. It does not make political decisions.[100]

Like the rest of the Mexican copyright apparatus, INDAUTOR's focus has gradually moved towards a greater emphasis on economic concerns.

Under the 1947 law, the Derecho de Autor department was a director-ate of the SEP, which had a strong focus on promoting Mexican culture. For example, the SEP's objectives were (and largely are) to:

- organize, control and maintain the literary and artistic property register;
- stimulate the development of theatre in the country and organize contests for authors, actors, and set designers, and, in general, promote the betterment of these fields;
- organize artistic expositions, fairs, pageants, contests, auditions, theatre festivals, and film exhibitions of cultural interest;
- coordinate the artistic, cultural, recreation and sporting activities of the federal public sector; and
- promote the film, radio, television production and the publishing industry.[101]

INDAUTOR is focused primarily – one is tempted to say almost exclu-sively – on authors' rights, as opposed to user rights. This finding rein-forces Deere-Birkbeck's remark regarding the tendency for developing countries to delegate responsibility for IP to technical institutions, re-sulting in a generation of "deference to technical IP experts with only a narrow policy perspective."[102] Among these stakeholders, all those inter-viewed reported good relations with INDAUTOR. These include US in-dustry officials: even as the US International Intellectual Property Alliance (IIPA) remains highly critical of Mexican copyright enforce-ment and other issues, its submissions to the USTR Special 301 process[103] continually refer to good relations, cooperation, and consultations be-tween its members and Mexican authorities.

Secretaría de Comunicaciones y Transportes (SCT) While INDAUTOR and IMPI have been the primary institutions responsible for copyright law, digital technology has brought the Secretaría de Comunicaciones y Transportes (Communications and Transportation Department, SCT) into the debate. Any reforms that touch on ISP liability and TPM issues will require the acquiescence of the relevant departments, which in this case would mean, at the very least, the SCT, which regulates the tele-communications industry, and the Secretaría de Economía (the Economy Department), which oversees economic policy. Each of these has its own industrial clients, whose membership does not overlap with those of INDAUTOR.

Of the two, the SCT's interest in ISP liability would likely be the largest hurdle for proponents of DMCA-style copyright reform (TPM protection appears to be a secondary issue in Mexico). Currently, Mexico has no "safe harbour" rules for ISPs; while this suggests that ISPs could be potentially liable for infringement carried over their networks, the typical ISP contract with a client shifts all liability onto the consumer.[104] Easy agreement on ISP liability has been elusive, mainly because SCT and its client industries' goals are potentially in conflict with the pursuit of maximalist copyright in general and ISP liability in particular. The telecommunications industry, for example, can be expected to fight any proposal requiring investments that could threaten their profitability.

The Mexican government has made increasing Internet access a key part of its developmental platform. The government's Plan Nacional de Desarrollo 2007–2012 (National Development Plan)[105] set the objective of increasing the number of Mexicans with online access from the 18 million online in 2006 to cover 60 per cent of the population (currently around 111 million people), and improving the quality of services available to them. The Plan Nacional mentions intellectual property only generally (copyright is not mentioned at all) as it relates to the uncertainty of property rights, with no specific objectives attached. Furthermore, the section of the Plan Nacional devoted to culture and art[106] proposes the objective that "all Mexicans have access to participation and enjoyment of Mexico's artistic, historical and cultural heritage as part of their full development as human beings."[107] While the plan does call for support for various forms of culture, including on the Internet, its emphasis on access could be seen as an endorsement of users' rights.

According to Jorge Basurto of the Comisión Federal de Telecomunicaciones (Federal Telecommunications Commission, COFETEL), which regulates ISPs on behalf of SCT, it is unlikely that SCT would agree to anything that went against this objective. Furthermore, the SCT can counter the rhetoric of copyright as a means to protect Mexican culture with rhetoric trumpeting the need for economic development via an open Internet.[108] COFETEL deployed such arguments to great effect during the Senate ACTA debate, as will be seen in the following part.

The current institutional regime, with the exception of the SCT and its related congressional commissions, shapes Mexican copyright policymaking in a specific direction. The administrative institutions – INDAUTOR and IMPI – favour the "protection" role of copyright, as do the *sociedades de gestión colectivas* and the content industries. While not formally closed to actors with strongly differing views, such interests are not easily reflected by these institutions' official mandates.

The corporatist state of affairs, which would normally favour the US position on digital-copyright reform, is thus open to challenge from intra-institutional conflict, notably the SCT and Congress. As the debate over ACTA suggests, rising public interest in digital-copyright issues, related to increasing broadband Internet use, combined with an increasing academic and legal focus on digital-copyright issues, has created increasing pressure for better user and consumer rights.

Interests: Some Challenges to Traditional Actors

SOCIEDADES DE GESTIÓN COLECTIVAS

In Mexican copyright negotiations, the government recognizes the interests of authors as being represented by *sociedades de gestión colectivas*.[109] These groups are non-profit organizations authorized by INDAUTOR and mandated by article 192 of the LFDA to protect authors and neighbouring-rights holders' moral and patrimonial rights, both foreign and domestic.[110] The LFDA gives *sociedades* the power to collect royalties on behalf of its members. It also requires that they be constituted for the purpose of mutual aid among its members, based on the principles of partnership, equality, and equity.[111] While the *sociedades* maintain linkages with collection societies in other countries (though not with a specific North American focus), they are primarily domestic groups.

The main roles of *sociedades de gestión colectivas* include representing their members' interests, exhibiting their members' works, and safeguarding Mexico's intellectual and artistic traditions.[112] As José Cárdeno, general coordinator of legal affairs of the Sociedad de Autores y Compositores de México (Authors and Composers Society of Mexico, SACM), the most important of Mexico's *sociedades*, remarks: "We want to balance of course the rights of the community, but at the same time, we want to balance the rights of the copyright owners that were going into public domain."[113]

Their roots can be traced back to the authors' guilds that were established to protect their member's rights, the earliest being the Sociedad Mexicana de Autores Líricos y Dramáticos (Mexican Lyricists and Dramatic Authors Society), created in 1902.[114] They had a distinctive corporatist role: the 1956 legislation formally designated the Sociedad General Mexicana de Autores (General Society of Mexican Authors), a confederation of *sociedades*, as the formal interlocutor with the government with respect to copyright.[115] Over time, more societies were created; they now number 14.[116]

They also serve as creators' representatives in copyright negotiations, although following the 1997 changes to the LFDA (specifically section 195), creators are no longer limited to mandatory membership in one group, as a way to give individual artists bargaining power when dealing with publishers and distributors.[117] The *sociedades* continue to dominate authorial representation in their dealings with the government; unlike in Canada and the United States, creators have not made their voice heard strongly through alternative organizations, such as the Canadian Music Creators Coalition or the US Future of Music Coalition. Creator groups seem somewhat more important in Mexico than in Canada or the United States due to their long history of involvement in the corporatist copyright-negotiation regime as the authoritative voice of Mexican creators. They were the main force behind the successful 2003 extension of the term of copyright to life of the author plus 100 years,[118] spurred by the fact that the "Catálogo de Oro" (Gold Catalogue) of classic Mexican music was about to pass into the public domain. De la Parra Trujillo argues that the change will not benefit authors or the public, but rather SACM, the main lobbyist for the change, which stands to collect royalties for works that would have otherwise fallen into the public domain.[119] Many of the authors who created these works are either long dead or stand to receive, on average, relatively little from this increased protection.

The *sociedades* have consistently advocated (and stand to benefit from) stronger rights, since they are in the business of collecting royalties, rather than creating. The extent to which these societies look out for interests separate from those of their members is suggested by a 2009 newspaper article on the SACM alleging poor conduct by its executive, citing millionaire heads of SACM, chosen through nepotism, and a system that gives high royalty earners a greater say in SACM's decisions.[120] With respect to the 2003 law, as Obón León suggests above, collection societies, not artists, are the main beneficiaries of extensions of copyright a full century after the creator is dead. Consequently, they can be expected to pursue a copyright regime stronger than might be preferred by individual artists. ISP liability is their primary digital concern; TPM protection is not a priority for these groups.

CONTENT INDUSTRIES

Like the *sociedades*, the various associations representing the content industries – most but not all of which represent foreign-based multinationals (as in Canada) – have de facto standing in the copyright policymaking process, including recognition by INDAUTOR, access to lawmakers and access to the Executive. NAFTA and the resulting 1997 law recognized and strengthened a host of neighbouring rights that have benefited mainly, but not exclusively, foreign businesses. Televisa, the world's largest Spanish-language media company and a crucially important player in Mexican politics generally, is the most obvious exception. Televisa in particular has a strong incentive for Mexican copyright law to accommodate US demands, as it is very interested in the growing US. Spanish-speaking market.[121]

The content industries have a history of cooperating to deal with copyright infringement. For example, the Motion Picture Association (MPA, representing the same clients as the Motion Picture Association of America) and the Asociación Mexicana de Productores de Fonogramas y Videogramas (Mexican Association of Phonogram Producers, AMPROFON), which represents foreign music companies, formed the Asociación Protectora de Cine y Música (Association to Protect Film and Music, APCM) in 2008.[122] As well, the Institute for the Protection of Intellectual Property and Legitimate Commerce (IPIIC), an anti-piracy group, was founded in March 2006 by AMPROFON, the BSA (the Business Software Alliance), CNIV (Cámara Nacional de la Industria del Vestido, The National Chamber of the Garment Industry), and PRONAPHON (the National Producers of Phonograms). According to the IIPA, "this association essentially gave a legal status to the group that was meeting with PGR and other government agencies."[123]

While the interests of these content industries – strong ISP liability, stronger copyright protection, strong legal protection for TPMs, and especially better enforcement of existing copyright laws – are similar to the interests of content industries worldwide, there are three things worth noting about the Mexican-based industries interests. First, they were arguably the main beneficiaries of the 1997 changes to the LFDA. As noted above, the 1997 law had the result of creating or strengthening economic rights in copyright, particularly for industry interests. Mexico was able to protect some of its traditional limitations – for example, neighbouring rights applied only to producers or performers of sound recordings on primary use, not secondary use (in Mexico, performers' secondary-use rights are not protected; they are in the United States).[124] Consequently, García Moreno argues, the 1997 law was more concerned with the rights of intermediaries than of actual creators and, in contrast to previous copyright laws, was more focused on protecting the businesses that profit from authors, not the authors themselves.[125]

Second, while interview subjects from the content industries saw a need to implement fully the Internet treaties, ISP liability – generally supporting a notice-and-takedown, or "three-strikes" legislation[126] – was seen as the most pressing concern. For example, AMPROFON favours TPM protection; however, the association has no official position on how protection should be implemented and does not see it as a priority.[127] Those most interested in TPM protection appear to be videogame producers,[128] who have little production in Mexico and tend to see the country mainly as a market.[129] On the other side of the issue, consumer-electronics producers – the group that in the United States opposed TPM protection – do not have a large production presence in Mexico.[130]

THE UNITED STATES

The United States has exerted a strong influence on Mexican copyright law. In the pre-NAFTA period, the United States was able to threaten Mexico credibly with the removal of its preferential access to the US market under the Generalized System of Preferences in order to coerce changes. The 1997 law can be seen as the last successful use of this threat, since NAFTA more or less guaranteed Mexican access to the US market and took this critical bargaining chip off the table. In addition to the diplomatic tools discussed in the Canadian case study (Special 301 and US trade policy, diplomatic representations of the US position, working with and through industry associations), the United States has also been active in providing training to Mexican judges and other officials with respect to copyright-law enforcement through the IPR (Intellectual Property Rights) Training Coordination Group.[131] This government-industry group, which counts the Patent and Trademark Office, the Copyright Office, and the IIPA among its members, provides "intellectual property training in a variety of different topics primarily that focus on enforcement, patents, trademarks, and copyrights." Participants are "officials of intellectual property offices of their respective governments, or of the agencies of their governments that are responsible for enforcement, patent, trademark, or copyright policies."[132] In April–May 2010, for example, the PTO and US State Department held training sessions for Mexican officials on IP enforcement and the application of IP laws in copyright cases.[133]

INTERNET SERVICE PROVIDERS

ISPs themselves have interests that are potentially at odds with those of copyright owners. As in Canada and the United States, they would be very reluctant to implement any system that requires substantial resource investments on their behalf. They also would resist any requirements that reduced the integrity of their networks, which they promote to consumers based on their ability to download movies and music at rapid rates.[134] SCT's recommendations on ISP liability are likely to be heeded since Telmex, which controls 95% of the ISP market, is owned by Carlos Slim, who has been named the world's richest man by *Forbes* magazine for several years running and whose words carry weight with the Mexican government, particularly given the pro-business slant of recent governments, including the *Partido Acción Nacional* (National Action Party, PAN) governments that held the presidency between 2000 and 2012.

THE PUBLIC, BEFORE ACTA

Widespread Mexican public interest in copyright dates only to about mid-2011. Before this period, it was rare to see any discussion of copyright from the perspective of users, and the public was not perceived as being active in the debate. In an April 2010 interview with the author, Mike Margáin, then of the American Chamber of Commerce, Mexico (and current head of IMPI), which represents US businesses in Mexico, commented that public interest in copyright was limited to a few young "cybernauts."[135]

The general lack of interest in copyright was picked up in opinion polls. Public-opinion polling suggests that overwhelming majorities saw no moral or economic problems with buying unauthorized CDs or DVDs, and that they bought them largely because of their relatively low price. The same surveys demonstrated that Mexicans in 2006 and 2009, the years the surveys were conducted, had yet to experience their "Napster moment of awareness," that is, the moment the importance of digital copyright became clear. In 2006, 50% of computer programs, 84% of video games, 92% of movies, and 93% of CDs were bought on the street.[136]

In Mexico relatively few households have Internet access (22.3% in 2010, compared with 71.1% of Americans in the same year), or broadband Internet access (21.1% in 2010, compared with 68.2% of Americans) (see tables 8.1 and 8.2). However, the lack of civil-society involvement in copyright issues in Mexico is also likely attributable to the newness and weakness of Mexican civil society in a nominally post-corporatist

Table 8.1. Households with broadband access, 2002–2010 (%)

	2000	2001	2002	2003	2004	2005	2006	2007	2008	2009	2010
Mexico	–	0.3	0.4	–	1.8	2.3	4.1	6.1	9.6	13.8	21.1
Canada	–	21.6	29.3	35.5	44.1	50.1	57.9	64.2	66.9	72.2	–
United States	4.4	9.1	–	19.9	–	–	–	50.8	–	63.5	68.2

Notes: (1) For Canada: Statistics for 2001 and every other year thereafter include the territories (Northwest Territories, Yukon Territory, and Nunavut). For the even years, statistics include the 10 provinces only. (2) For Mexico: For 2001 and 2002, households with Internet access via cable. From 2004, households with Internet access via cable, ADSL or fixed wireless. (3) Dash indicates that no data is available.
Source: OECD Broadband portal, http://www.oecd.org/dataoecd/20/59/39574039.xls. See the OECD broadband portal for data on sources and estimations.

Table 8.2. Households with access to the Internet, 2000–2010 (%)

	2000	2001	2002	2003	2004	2005	2006	2007	2008	2009	2010
Mexico	–	6.2	7.5	–	8.7	9.0	10.1	12.0	13.5	18.4	22.3
Canada	42.6	49.9	54.5	56.9	59.8	64.3	68.1	72.7	74.6	77.8	–
United States	41.5	50.3	–	54.6	–	–	–	61.7	–	68.7	71.1

Notes: (1) Internet access is via any device (desktop computer, portable computer, TV, mobile phone, etc.). (2) For Canada: Statistics for 2001 and every other year thereafter include the territories (Northwest Territories, Yukon Territory, and Nunavut). For the even years, statistics include the ten provinces only. (3) Dash indicates that no data is available.
Source: OECD Key ICT indicators http://www.oecd.org/dataoecd/19/45/34083073.xls.

era. Until the mid-1990s, civil society was a "highly restricted space," "tightly controlled from above, creating a political culture characterized by verticalism and hierarchy, as well as the exclusion of large segments of the population not represented in corporatist system."[137] Mexican civil society's relative newness thus presents groups and individuals not already directly involved in copyright policymaking with an additional challenge of gaining a toehold in the debate.

US digital-copyright news is now covered extensively in the Mexican blogosphere on sites like alt1040.com and criticapura.com, and the work of people like US scholar Lawrence Lessig is followed by Mexican copyright scholars and influences Mexican activists' critiques of copyright (as does the libertarian, open-Internet message of the Electronic Frontier Foundation). The United States, however, is not the only direct foreign influence on Mexican civil-society copyright groups. In March 2010, for example, the Centro Cultural de

España México (Cultural Centre of Spain in Mexico), which is affiliated with the Spanish embassy in Mexico, hosted a three-day workshop, "Comunidades, cultura libre y propiedad intellectual" (communities, free culture, and intellectual property) as part of the 2010 Festival de México, an annual arts and culture festival held in Mexico City. The Centro Cultural also co-published the first Mexican academic book on digital copyright and free culture (available as a free download under a Creative Commons licence).[138]

The situation before 2010 was little better in academic circles. As in any civil-law jurisdiction, academics play an important role in Mexican politics; politicians usually seek to form strong links with academics in order to secure their endorsement and legitimacy for their policy proposals. Often, academics are asked to study an issue beforehand in anticipation of a policy reform; while lobbying is important, these academic studies provide moral authority to back political change.[139] Copyright law has attracted few legal scholars and practitioners,[140] though this is changing.[141] Nivón remarks that journals that one might have thought would have taken an interest in the issue – the *Revista Internacional de Filosofía Política* (The International Journal of Political Philosophy) or *Derecho y Cultura* (Law and Culture) – had not published a single article on the subject of copyright and culture as of mid-2009. [142]

Summary

This Mexican combination of ideas, institutions, and interests reflects a copyright policymaking situation considerably more complex than would be suggested by a cursory glance at the relative economic power of the United States and Mexico. While it suggests a strong domestic bias towards implementation of the treaties along US-preferred DMCA lines, this tendency is driven as much by domestic considerations as by US pressure. The new focus on copyright as an owner's economic property right has interacted with a continued perception of copyright as an *author's moral right* to support an approach of the economic view of copyright as an *owner's economic right* that should be maximized. The Mexican approach to the Internet treaties, and to international copyright negotiations in general, is also driven by its self-image, similar to that of the United States, as a cultural superpower that benefits from strong international copyright protection. Unlike the United States, however, Mexico's developing-country status provides an incentive not to enforce these strong laws too enthusiastically.

With respect to institutions, as in the United States, Mexico's formal copyright institutions tend to favour copyright's protection dimension over its dissemination role. Officials at these agencies have enthusiastically embraced the view of copyright protection as something to be maximized, and while exceptions and limitations exist in Mexican copyright law, they tend to be underemphasized. However, the Internet treaties have involved new governmental agencies concerned with telecommunications in the copyright debate, which serve stakeholders outside the copyright industries (i.e., telecommunications companies and ISPs) and which have priorities other than the maximization of copyright protection.

With respect to actors, the Mexican copyright debate has tended to be dominated by nationally focused interests, the primary exceptions being the United States, the multinational content industries, and the lesser involvement of the Spanish embassy. Protection interests – the *sociedades de gestión colectivas*, the content industries, and the United States – enjoyed a relatively favourable position in the Mexican copyright negotiations process. In contrast, before the ACTA debate, groups reflecting the "user" or "dissemination" position – the public and academics critical of Mexican copyright in particular – did not have as strong a standing in the process, nor do their concerns fit well with traditional Mexican copyright narratives. That said, the lack of enforcement of Mexican copyright laws can be seen as a tacit acknowledgment of their interest in affordable creative works. The main exception to the lack of formal involvement of user interests in the making of copyright policy is the telecommunications industry, which has political influence and an institutional base in the SCT. Meanwhile, general-user interests, traditionally neglected in Mexican copyright policymaking, had the potential to intrude on copyright negotiations, much as they have in Canada and the United States, and as they would in the context of the ACTA debate.

Part 2: Mexico and the Internet Treaties – A Work in Progress

The government of Mexico ratified the WIPO Copyright Treaty on 6 March 2002 and the Performances and Phonograms Treaty on 20 May 2002. They are considered to be in force, since under Mexico's civil law, treaties are deemed implemented when they are ratified, and become part of the law. While their implementation does not require incorporation into Mexican copyright law, groups within and without the country have continued to call for full implementation of the treaties via changes in Mexican copyright law.

According to the Mexican government, Mexico is mostly in compliance with its WIPO Internet treaty obligations.[143] The 1997 LFDA, which was being debated at the same time as the Internet treaties, includes several related amendments that were inserted "in anticipation of the final outcome of the WCT and WPPT."[144] These include a "making available" right[145] and a "transmission right"[146] (WCT article 8; WPPT article 15); and a measure protecting TPMs placed on computer programs (WCT article 11).[147]

With respect to TPMs, in language similar to language that would be drafted into the 1998 US DMCA, article 112 of the LFDA prohibits "the importation, manufacture, distribution and use of equipment or the services intended to eliminate the technical protection of computer programs, of transmissions across the spectrum of electromagnetic and telecommunications networks and programs' electronic elements" (author's translation).

Article 424bis of the Código Penal Federal (Federal Criminal Code) imposes criminal sanctions on the importation, sale, lease of any program, or performance of any act that would have as its purpose the deactivation of the protective electronic controls of computer software. Violation of these articles is punishable by imprisonment for three to ten years and a fine of 5000 to 30,000 times the minimum wage. Furthermore, while the LFDA does not define circumvention, a non-paper[148] presented at WIPO by INDAUTOR suggests that it is only an issue when the underlying copyright or author's rights have been infringed.[149] That Mexican copyright law is designed to punish for-profit copying and not the non-commercial copying that constitutes the vast majority of individuals' online file sharing only complicates matters.

While the 1997 reforms expanded the protection of creative works, it is generally argued that the LFDA requires more precision to address Internet-related issues regarding online content.[150] It contains no provisions limiting ISP liability; neither does it address fully the legal protection of TPMs beyond that provided to TPMs applied to computer software. Although the LFDA was amended in 2003, these amendments did not extend to treaty-implementation issues. Although implementing legislation has yet to be tabled (as of October 2013), a full review of and subsequent amendments to the LFDA are likely in the medium term.

Explaining Partial Implementation

The partial implementation of the treaties (to date) is the result of three factors: fluctuating US ability to link copyright with trade issues;

Mexico's low level of digital-infrastructure development; and the continued importance of domestic copyright actors, particularly the *sociedades de gestión colectivas*.

TRADE LINKAGES

At heart, the extension of protection to TPMs protecting computer software can be understood as the overall result of NAFTA-negotiating dynamics. In particular, it was the Mexican response to US pressure at the time of the NAFTA negotiations. For the United States, software protection was a, or rather the, pressing digital-copyright issue at the time.[151] The decision to protect TPMs reflects US involvement in the Mexican copyright process:

> Interaction between the U.S. and Mexican governments is evident during the legislative discussions of the Mexican Copyright Law and the rules on anti-circumvention evidence that fact. In keeping with this, the Federal Penal Code imposes criminal sanctions against manufacturers of devices or systems that deactivate the protective electronic controls of computer software.[152]

US involvement in Mexican copyright policy post-NAFTA can be understood as part of the same process of IP-trade linkage that led to the reorientation of Mexican copyright law. However, in the post-NAFTA era, as has already been noted, the United States has been able to influence (through training) and lobby, but not coerce. After placing Mexico on its Special 301 Priority Watch List in 1989, the United States continued to criticize Mexican copyright laws and enforcement, placing Mexico on its Watch List in 1998 and 1999, and from 2003 to the present. While the United States has seen some improvement in Mexico's enforcement of its copyright laws, the WIPO Internet treaties continue not to be implemented fully in Mexican law.

POWER OF DOMESTIC GROUPS

That copyright reform in Mexico historically has been driven by international treaties does not mean that domestic groups are passive actors. The 2003 changes to the LFDA, more adjustment to the 1997 reforms than wholesale reform, reflected the power of the *sociedades de gestión colectivas*. They, rather than the United States or its content industries, were the driving force behind the bill.[153] Their main demands included extension of the term of copyright to a world-leading life of the author plus 100 years. While the changes were driven by the *sociedades*, IIPA members were able to remove the provisions it deemed most trouble-some, notably a private copying levy, while supporting the copyright term extension.[154] Conspicuously absent from the uncontroversial legis-lation,[155] however, was any mention of the Internet treaties. Their ab-sence, while suggestive of the fact that actors prioritized issues other than digital copyright (discussed in the next section), also suggests that the US and its content industries, the main proponents for the treaties' implementation in Mexico and around the world, do not drive all copy-right changes. Under the reasonable assumption that the United States would prefer the implementation of the treaties to their non-implemen-tation, the 2003 reforms show that the United States lacks the ability to force the issue of copyright reform in Mexico.

In the Mexican copyright policymaking process, the United States can be thought of as one interest among many, and not necessarily pow-erful enough to dictate the copyright agenda post-NAFTA. In the ab-sence of trade negotiations and regional mechanisms through which the United States can have a direct voice in setting Mexican copyright policy, and in the presence of a NAFTA that restrains US ability to link copyright to other economic issues, the United States must work through lobbying and the building of sympathetic epistemic communi-ties (i.e., through training of Mexican copyright officials). To the extent that it is able to move its neighbours' copyright policies closer to its own preferred outcomes (and thus to common "North American" stan-dards), the United States must do so indirectly, through Mexico's (and Canada's) domestic policymaking processes. Even here, the ability of the United States to affect Mexican policy is limited by the Mexican state's resource constraints and domestic political and economic pres-sure not to enforce the law. As a developing country, Mexico regards copyright enforcement as only one among several competing priorities. US aid, through training programs and other direct support of Mexican copyright officials, discussed above, suggests that the United States rec-ognizes this weakness in the Mexican state.

THE ROLE OF TECHNOLOGY

American and Mexican copyright experts interviewed for this study in 2009 and 2010 were unanimous in emphasizing that problems related to enforcement and old-fashioned commercial piracy (bootlegged DVDs, CDs, and books) – specifically, enforcement of existing laws – dwarfed the problem of unauthorized Internet downloading and up-loading. For example, while Special 301 submissions by the US-based

IIPA throughout the 2000s called for the full implementation of the WIPO Internet treaties, the issue of "Internet piracy" in Mexico received its own section only in 2009 and 2010. Low levels of broadband penetration (see table 8.1) are a significant contributor to industry and creators groups' relative lack of interest (until now) in Internet-treaty ratification.

Part 3: ACTA – Mexico's "Napster Moment of Awareness"

As Mexican copyright infringement occurs increasingly online, which is likely as broadband penetration rates continue to rise, the pressure to update Mexican copyright law for the digital age will continue to grow, particularly from the United States. Treaty implementation has been a consistent, if secondary, demand by the US government and industry over the years since their signing and ratification by Mexico in 2003.[156] Since Mexico was placed on the Special 301 Watch List in 2003, for the first time since 1999, enforcement has been the perennial concern. In 2006, for example, the IIPA recommended fourteen enforcement and training-related measures,[157] and only eight related to legislation, including full implementation of the Internet treaties; these numbers were similar in 2007, and the 2008 report contained twenty-six enforcement-related recommendations.[158] In contrast, recent Canadian IIPA and Special 301 reports have focused more consistently on policy objectives, in particular implementation of the Internet treaties.

In 2009 digital copyright took its place alongside enforcement as the United States' primary Mexican-copyright concern, as expressed by its annual Special 301 reports. The IIPA's 2009 Special 301 submission, its first to discuss in-depth their concerns with "Internet piracy," recommended "(1) a notification procedure [i.e., notice-and-notice or notice-and-takedown]; (2) a stepped approach to subscriber termination [i.e., cutting off a person's Internet usage following more than one accused or actual copyright infringement]; and (3) deterrent sanctions against serious or repeat offenders."[159]

Mexican copyright policy is made within a quasi-corporatist framework in which user/individual rights are poorly represented. Ideationally, the traditional concept of *derecho de autor* has effectively been married to the economic concept of copyright, both as something to be maximized for creators/owners. With respect to actors, the United States, on behalf of its industries, has worked, with some success since NAFTA, to reshape the Mexican copyright landscape.

Such a framework would seem to suggest a relatively high probability that Mexico would follow the US model on digital locks and possibly on ISP liability. With respect to actors and institutions, collection societies, the content industries, the US government, the US Chamber of Commerce in Mexico, INDAUTOR, and IMPI all favour stronger copyright protection. The public and other dissenting voices have, until very recently, been underrepresented in the copyright debate. If one were only looking backward, the 2003 reforms would suggest that Congress is not against the idea of further strengthening copyright. With respect to ideas, current official views on copyright reflect a complementary mix of the traditional Mexican view of copyright as an author's right that should be maximized and the US view of copyright as an economic right that should be maximized for copyright *owners*. However, while these traditional biases in the Mexican copyright policymaking regime would tend to favour a maximalist approach to copyright reform, events since 2011 suggest that the current situation is much less stable and predictable than it was previously, thanks to the arrival of Mexico's "Napster moment of awareness," courtesy of the Anti-Counterfeiting Trade Agreement.

Forces for Harmonization

On the side favouring a US-style maximalist approach, collection societies, the content industries, INDAUTOR, and IMPI all favour stronger copyright protection. Already predisposed towards strong support for authors' rights, INDAUTOR's disposition towards copyright as an economic right has become more pronounced. In 2007, Manuel Guerra Zamarro,[160] a widely respected copyright lawyer[161] and a former Mexican representative at WIPO, was appointed by PAN President Felipe Calderón (elected in 2006) as INDAUTOR's director general, a post that had never before been held by an industry lawyer.

While the precise reasons for his appointment are unclear – those interviewed on the subject alternately emphasized its continuity with and break from the past – Guerra's appointment can be seen as a turning point in Mexican copyright, for several reasons. He is widely credited for bringing a renewed energy, order, and focus to INDAUTOR, including pushing the agency to adopt the idea that Mexico should implement fully the Internet treaties.[162] He has also staffed INDAUTOR with younger people from the private sector who are seen as being more interested in the copyright sectors for which they are responsible,[163] and as being sympathetic to the idea of copyright as an economic right rather than simply a moral one. Perhaps tellingly, Guerra's appointment was received favourably by US officials.[164]

These moves represent a generational shift in Mexican copyright policy and suggest a greater sympathy with the idea of implementing international treaties, a subject that Tourné says was not a high priority for INDAUTOR's previous leadership, although he expected the government would undertake a comprehensive reform of Mexican copyright policy eventually. He argued that it was important for the government to implement fully the WIPO Internet treaties before Internet penetration rates rose too high.[165]

With respect to actors, creator groups and the content industries have been working to promote their case. In late 2009, thirty-seven copyright-related groups representing both creators and the content industries formed the Coalición por el Acceso Legal a la Cultura (Coalition for the Legal Access to Culture).[166] This novel coalition of interests – industry and creators – that traditionally worked separately, had the blessing of INDAUTOR and IMPI (which have observer status in the coalition), and allows them to present a united front to the government when proposing recommendations. That this coalition would give members a united front when dealing with ISPs on the thorny issue of ISP liability was an implicit objective behind the coalition's formation.[167] While TPM protection was not mentioned, those in the industry say it remains an objective. Its absence, however, suggests its relatively low level of importance.[168] The creation of this coalition suggested that these groups – the traditional players in Mexican copyright – were preparing for a showdown with ISPs over the future of digital copyright and Internet access in Mexico. With the corporatist nature of Mexican copyright policymaking, the existence of the coalition also suggests the difficulty users and citizen groups would face in arguing their position.

Forces for Divergence

Against these stronger-copyright proponents are the ISPs and the public wild card. Telmex (owned by Carlos Slim and controlling 95 per cent of the Mexican Internet-access market) in particular, as COFETEL's Basurto remarks, has "a lot of power."[169] Given the political power of Telmex and Televisa (whose interests are more divided, since they have interests on both the content and network sides), the road to a deal on ISP liability goes through these businesses. Government-mediated talks between copyright holders and ISPs were undertaken in 2008 and 2009 with no progress, suggesting strongly that there is little natural ground between the two groups, and that government intervention will be required to remedy the situation.[170]

The other key player in realizing a deal on ISP liability is the Secretaría de Comunicaciones y Transportes, which regulates the telecommunications industry. The telecoms industry can be expected to fight any proposal that requires investments that could threaten their profitability.

ACTA and the Future of Mexican Copyright Law[171]

The Senate's 12 July 2011 unanimous rejection of the Anti-Counterfeiting Trade Agreement marks a watershed in Mexican copyright history. In only eight years the Senate went from making, with little debate, Mexico's copyright term the longest in the world to rejecting unanimously the latest attempt to strengthen copyright.

What happened? As in other countries, digital technology has complicated Mexican copyright politics, enabling the emergence of civil-society voices in favour of stronger user rights. Specifically, it was the work of a small network of about a dozen individuals, using Twitter and their institutional contacts. This "Stop ACTA" network, which was linked to the transnational anti-ACTA movement, engaged in symbolic and substantive bricolage, linking copyright protection to concerns about ACTA's effect on freedom of speech and the government economic-development objective of growing the Mexican information economy. Their work, combined with (at times) less prominent opposition from the telecoms industry and bureaucratic allies, helped to cement ACTA's fate, at least temporarily, in the Senate.

Signs that Congress was beginning to consider copyright in ways that would expand the debate from one primarily focused on maximizing authors' rights to one that examines its effect on the rest of the economy and society were evident even before this vote. In October 2008 the Senate Comisión de Ciencia y Tecnología (Science and Technology Committee) held a seminar on "copyright in the digital environment." Although this seminar did not deal directly with the WIPO Internet treaties, it addressed copyright in cultural and economic terms, and touched on access issues (such as the need for a national digital library).

Committee president Francisco Castellón Javier Fonseca – who would become a key player in the ACTA debate – argued in favour of considering regulating copyright to focus on both its cultural and economic effects, since it has the potential to generate as much or more revenues than industrial property (i.e., patents).[172]

Stop ACTA benefited from a combination of past experience, fortuitous timing (i.e., luck), and smart and superior organizing. Many of its members knew each other from a 2009 battle to prevent a 4 per cent luxury tax on the Internet. The subsequent social-media protest, organized around the hashtag #internetnecesario, was referred to by Spanish newspaper *El País* as "the first Twitter protest."[173] It demonstrated to those involved that they could successfully influence Mexican politics via social media. It also legitimized those involved as what Antonio Martínez Velázquez, a young lawyer with the UK-based human rights group Article 19, called "the usual suspects of the Internet."[174] The #internetnecesario protests also put these activists in touch with Castellón, a senator from the leftist Partido de la Revolución Democratica (Party of the Democratic Revolution, PRD), a firm believer in the importance of Internet access and one of the few senators who understood the importance of this issue.

Despite his demonstrated keen interest in Internet-freedom issues, Castellón only became aware of ACTA's existence following a meeting with Martínez and Geraldine Juárez, an artist and activist with a passionate interest in copyright issues. The government had not bothered to inform either Castellón, whose committee had jurisdiction in this area, or the Senate. This was not just a case of bad manners: it was illegal under a 2007 law that requires the government to notify, and keep informed, the Senate of any economic treaties it is negotiating.[175] It was only after he sent a formal request to the government that he and the Senate were officially notified of the government's involvement, with IMPI as the lead agency.[176] In the face of government responses that ranged from dismissive (its first response took four months to arrive)[177] to insulting,[178] the Senate repeatedly requested information on the treaty, only to be stonewalled. On 5 October 2010 the Senate unanimously called on the Executive to withdraw from the ACTA negotiations. A month later, Castellón, with all-party support, created a working group to examine ACTA (in Spanish, the Grupo Pural para dar seguimiento al proceso de Negociaciones del ACTA). The group's mandate called on it to

- follow the (then still-ongoing) ACTA negotiations in order to in-crease their transparency and to ensure that they are in line with the constitution; and
- hold public meetings with government officials, experts, and inter-ested members of the public to determine an alternative to ACTA that would address intellectual property, the Internet, and freedom of expression and privacy.

The working group's objective was not so much to analyse ACTA, but rather to give affected parties an opportunity to express their opin-ions, and for the working group to listen.[179] While the government ig-nored the working group's request that it suspend its participation in ACTA talks,[180] it did agree not to sign the treaty until the Senate had is-sued its final report.[181]

Over the next several months, the working group heard from repre-sentatives from business, civil society, and the government. Notably, COFETEL came out against the agreement, arguing that ACTA could negatively affect broadband penetration rates and the general evolu-tion of the Internet, thus compromising the government's ability to re-duce Mexico's digital divide.[182] The Asociación Mexicana de Internet (Mexican Internet Association, AMIPCI), a group representing such important players as Google and Telmex, argued that it would cost the industry US$675 million to implement ACTA in its first year.[183]

The government incurred two fatal blows emerging from its decision to keep the ACTA negotiations secret. First, failing to include civil society and politically and economically powerful interests such as the telecoms industry merely postponed a political reckoning. Second, and most im-portant, there is nothing that upsets politicians more than being ignored in an area over which they hold power. Illegally bypassing senators cost the government support even from potentially sympathetic members of the ruling party. The working group was the Senate's response. Although such committees are not wholly unusual in Mexican parliamentary poli-tics, treaties and laws are usually not subject either to examination by working groups or to such intense scrutiny by members of the public.

While ACTA contains several potentially controversial elements, the Stop ACTA network made a conscious decision to focus on its online section and to frame the debate in terms of ACTA's potential effect on online privacy, freedom of expression, and the importance of broad-band access to Mexico's future.[184] These concerns were all reflected in the working group's final report. Between 23 November 2010 and

12 July 2011, the working group held nine meetings, six of which were devoted to hearing from witnesses and three to organizational issues. The overall structure of the hearings reveals a great deal about the senators' intentions. They were the most open in Senate history, and were streamed online, resulting in briefs from some 600 citizens – many more witnesses than is typical for legislative hearings – and from beyond the copyright establishment. Civil-society groups were given pride of place in the hearings. Originally, the working group had planned to invite civil society to present at the second meeting (government officials had presented first, on 24 November). However, at the 2 February 2010 meeting, Senator Federico Döring Casar, who belongs to the same party as then-President Calderón, argued successfully that the hearings be opened and closed with sessions set aside for civil society.

The hearings pitted the copyright establishment versus everyone else. IMPI, INDAUTOR, most intellectual-property lawyers, collection societies, and content-industry representatives argued that ACTA was necessary to modernize Mexican IP law, to promote creativity, and to keep Mexico in line with international standards. Government officials also downplayed concerns about the treaty. IMPI head Jorge Amigo, for example, remarked that a "three strikes" approach to infringement was no longer required by the treaty. INDAUTOR director-general Manuel Guerra Zamarro contended that ACTA would not violate individuals' rights, did not include an obligation for ISPs to monitor user activity, and allowed member states to design their own policies.[185]

While the copyright establishment's response was largely defensive and concentrated on defending author's rights, ACTA critics – including civil-society groups and telecommunications and Internet representatives – framed their argument in terms of ACTA's constitutionality, and its negative effect on human rights and social and economic development. Critics also focused on the ambiguity in ACTA's Internet provisions, specifically articles 27.1, 27.2, and 27.4 dealing with ISP requirements to police their systems. For example, Telmex did not want the cost or hassle of having to monitor its customers' activities,[186] while human-rights groups objected to the monitoring on constitutional grounds. There was no business support for ACTA beyond the usual suspects: Telmex, Google (which had recently set up an office in Mexico), and the Internet industry, as well as the banking and tourism industries, were all against it.[187]

Throughout the six-plus months of hearings, social media kept the conversation going, and that conversation was almost unanimously anti-ACTA. Organizing largely around the Twitter hashtag #ACTA, as well as on blogs and other social media, activists shared information and planned strategies. The overall online response was very negative towards government officials, whom they saw as lying about ACTA.[188] Similarly, the Senate hearings were also almost completely one-sided. Representatives of the copyright establishment were, according to intellectual property lawyer and co-leader of the Mexican chapter of Creative Commons Mexico, León Felipe Sánchez Ambía, dismissive of the activists at the first meeting: "You could see the faces of these guys, they were just mocking us, they were just laughing at us, they were just like 'Okay, let's listen to these guys and everything will just pass by and we'll have our treaty.'"[189] The copyright establishment did not deviate from their initial reassurances. Neither did the Executive engage beyond using press releases, according to Jesús Ramírez Díaz, the technical secretary for the Senate Science and Technology Committee.[190] ACTA supporters were further undercut by critiques of ACTA by the federal telecommunications regulator, COFETEL, by the National Human Rights Commission, and by the Federal Institute of Access to Public Information. They also received little support from the traditional media, with critical stories and columns running in prominent publications like *El Economista* and *El Universal*.[191]

By the working group's final hearings in July 2011, it was clear that the copyright establishment had lost both the public opinion and policy battles, gaining no allies in the Senate or in the wider society. Throughout the hearings senators such as Beatriz Zavala from the ruling PAN (the president's party) echoed protestors' main argument that copyright protection must be balanced against the right to access to information, free expression, communication, and access to education and culture. Implicit throughout was senators' conviction that ACTA did not meet this test and their dissatisfaction with the copyright establishment's responses. The final – unanimous – report, released formally on 20 July 2011, covered all these points, and called for President Calderón not to sign ACTA, on the grounds that

- the government had broken the law in negotiating the treaty in secret;
- ACTA, if implemented, would violate Mexican law;
- ACTA's ambiguity would introduce ambiguity into Mexican law (in civil-law jurisdictions like Mexico, treaties become part of a country's law, below the constitution but above legislated law, upon ratification);

- ACTA could limit access to the Internet and worsen the "digital divide" in Mexico; and
- ACTA could lead to Internet censorship, restricting net neutrality and endangering the legitimate development of e-commerce, digital creativity, and the legitimate diffusion of culture.

One of the most interesting things to arise from the Senate's rejection of ACTA, beyond the fact that it happened in the first place, was that senators raised the concern that ACTA could lead to a restriction of on-line freedom and Internet usage, potentially broadening the digital divide and restricting the introduction of beneficial new technologies that would support the development of the information society. This ideational innovation – a form of bricolage, linking copyright to developmental concerns – is based on the Mexican government's Plan Nacional de Desarrollo 2007–2012 (National Development Plan), which called for both improved broadband service and for 60 per cent of all Mexicans to be online by 2012. In the Senate ACTA debate, the development imperative trumped calls for stronger copyright, a remarkable change for a country in which reflexive support for ever-strong copyright was very much the norm. In fact, the Senate's linking of copyright to development harkened back to the calls in the 1970s for a new international economic order that would focus on fulfilling the economic needs of developing countries.

The use of the paradigmatic idea of "development" to frame copyright and to challenge ACTA does not mean that Mexico will suddenly change its perspective on copyright. The pro-stronger-copyright groups mentioned above still exist, supported by and reinforcing both INDAUTOR and IMPI. In late 2011, the Senate passed legislation increasing INDAUTOR's and IMPI's powers, while a senator put forward an ISP liability bill that would fine individuals violating digital-copyright law, though not cut off their Internet access, although the bill did not proceed very far.[192] However, as Tourné's comments linking copyright reform with low levels of broadband penetration suggest, those wishing to implement stringent ISP requirements are in a race against time. As the proportion of Mexicans with broadband Internet access rises, it will become increasingly difficult to pass a law that does not take their interests into account, since they will likely protest if their service is disrupted or changed in a way not to their liking. Familiarity will breed awareness and concern, much as it has in Canada and the United States.

All this is not to say that Mexico will rebalance its copyright law to focus more on its dissemination/development aspects than on increasing copyright protection. Even though the Senate indicated decisively that it would reject ACTA, on 12 July 2012 Mexico's ambassador to Japan, Claude Heller Rouassant, signed the treaty on behalf of the Mexican government. This signature was controversial not only because it flew in the face of the Senate's unanimous vote, but also because it was signed by a lame-duck administration – Mexican presidents are constitutionally limited to serving one six-year term – less than two weeks following the 1 July 2012 presidential elections.

The signing was quickly condemned by many in Mexico, with legislators, academics, lawyers, human-rights activists, and other members of civil society calling on President Calderón to rescind his signature.[193] Both the House of Representatives and Senate passed resolutions to that effect.[194] Mexican critics, including Castellón, argued that ACTA contravened the most basic human-rights protections including the right of expression, and that it was counterproductive in encouraging surveillance of the Internet at a time when the government is under attack for censoring journalists.[195] The Senate's unanimous vote against ACTA does not guarantee that it would be rejected if it were submitted for ratification. The constitutional rule mandating that senators cannot serve consecutive terms means that the senators who voted against ACTA – including Castellón – concluded their terms after the 2012 elections, and it is unclear if the new senators will be as offended by the lack of consultation as those of the previous session.

The government's precise motives for signing are unclear – analysts speculated that it was a quid pro quo for US permission to enter into the Trans Pacific Partnership negotiations.[196] With the EU's support all but gone, Mexico's signature became that much more important in order to keep the agreement alive. Furthermore, despite the increased opposition to stronger copyright, as well as COFETEL's anti-ACTA position within the bureaucracy, the Executive overall has firmly and consistently supported ACTA. A 2007 US government cable released by WikiLeaks remarks: "Mexican IPR officials have been keen to highlight their increasingly active role in the international arena, stressing their willingness to join the Anti-Counterfeiting Trade Agreement (ACTA) negotiations and their push-back against Brazilian efforts to undermine IPR in international health organizations."[197]

After the Senate vote, on 2 April 2012 President Calderón reiterated his support for ACTA at a North American Leaders Summit. Calderón,

US President Barack Obama, and Canadian Prime Minister Stephen Harper expressed support for ACTA's objectives, Mexico committing "to work on a comprehensive reform to its legal system to achieve the high standards pursued under ACTA."[198] As of December 2013, it is unclear whether the current president, Enrique Peña Nieto, would submit the treaty to the Senate for ratification or continue ACTA talks within the TPP.

Focusing on the ins and outs of this ACTA signing debacle, including whether the newly configured post-election Senate would be more amenable to ACTA than the previous one, obscures the most remarkable aspect of this debate: that it happened. Such an uproar would have been unimaginable only two years earlier. The mere fact of ACTA's uncertain future shows how much the Mexican copyright policy debate has changed in under a decade. ACTA's future, like that of the Internet treaties, is unclear. What is clear is that Mexican copyright policymaking has been thrown into turmoil by the involvement of the telecoms and the public, and by the rediscovery of a paradigm – development and dissemination – that challenges the dominant protection view of copyright. The battle has been joined, with uncertain consequences.

Part 4: Conclusion

In line with Canada's experiences with copyright reform, this chapter has found that the Internet treaties have indeed served as the ideological parameters for the discussion of digital-copyright reform in Mexico. Regionally, there was also a significant US influence on Mexican copyright policy, both through the NAFTA copyright provisions and subsequent lobbying, itself constrained by NAFTA's guarantee of access to the US market. However, rather than being a completely exogenously imposed form of change, the move towards a more Anglo-American form of copyright was welcomed by at least some significant domestic copyright actors. This "new" form of copyright has been justified in part with reference to the traditional view of copyright that preceded it, notably in the justification of the maximization of Anglo-American economic copyright in terms of the more Continental moral rights approach. In other words, the nature and effects of this change can only be understood with reference to pre-existing domestic ideas, just as North America itself can only be understood through an exploration of domestic polities, with an eye for the linkages among the domestic, regional, and global where they exist.

Mexico's experience also reinforces the primacy of domestic forces on copyright-reform efforts. Mexico's decisions related to the implementation of the WIPO Internet treaties have been driven primarily by domestic politics, reshaped somewhat by NAFTA. Its non-implementation of key parts of these treaties can be explained through reference to domestic factors (level of technological development, relative influence of the relevant interest groups, and institutional structure of copyright policymaking). Its future decisions on the treaties will also be shaped by domestic considerations, with one large caveat that will be taken up in the final chapter. As in Canada, NAFTA has influenced Mexican copyright by acting as a region-wide restraint on the ability of the United States (acting as a global hegemon) to coerce directly Mexican policymakers. NAFTA has led to a significant reorientation of the Mexican *derecho de autor* regime towards a greater emphasis on copyright as an economic, owner's right, rather than an author's moral right. In doing so, it has recast Mexican domestic politics and set the stage for an implementation of the Internet treaties in a way that favours policy convergence on a US-style implementation of the treaties.

These observations echo more general observations about Mexican–American relations. As Camp remarks: "The United States continues to exercise considerable influence on Mexico's leadership, albeit usually implicit and indirect. In fact, if the United States were to attempt to influence Mexican political affairs directly, the effort would surely backfire. Nevertheless, the influence is obvious and many actors are involved."[199]

The extent to which traditional Mexican copyright elites accommodated the sweeping reforms initiated by NAFTA is striking. While small groups within these elites may have lost out on specific changes, overall they seem very comfortable with the maximization of rights and control that NAFTA delivers and that a US interpretation of the WIPO Internet treaties proposes. This symmetry of interests has reinforced existing biases in the law, in favour of the content industries and the *sociedades de gestión colectivas*. Looking forward, we can expect direct political pressure by individuals as they become more affected by digital technologies and academics fully engaging the issue of digital copyright in the upcoming legislative review; the telecoms industry has already begun to give voice to the dissemination/user side of copyright.

Policy Takers, on Their Own Terms

The outcome of the Mexican debate over the Internet treaties will have important consequences for the future development of Mexican copyright law and the terms on which its individuals and creators will be able to engage with digital technologies. It will reveal whether Mexican copyright law can adapt to serve users (which also includes creators) as well as the traditional copyright interest groups. User groups, which are traditionally underrepresented in the corporatist copyright-policymaking setup, have the most to lose from a maximalist-style copyright policy. That they are beginning to make themselves heard bodes well for the chances for future copyright reforms.

Mexico may be somewhat unusual as a developing country and a self-identified cultural superpower, but its experiences with digital-copyright reform hold important lessons for our greater understanding of the relationship of developing countries to international copyright treaties. Developing countries are usually seen as policy takers on copyright issues: they lack the resources to drive international negotiations and trade agreements and tend to value other issues, such as general market access, more highly. Mexico's policy decisions to date regarding the Internet treaties suggest that developing-country copyright-policy outcomes are as shaped by domestic policy processes and interest groups as those of any developed country. They may be policy takers in the sense of their ability to influence international copyright treaties, but decisions related to the implementation of these treaties are based on domestically oriented calculations; to the extent possible, they are takers on their own terms.

Conclusion:
The New Politics of Copyright
and the Potential for Variation

The battle over the negotiation and implementation of the Internet treaties, the opening salvo in the global digital copyfight, set the pattern for what to expect from the new politics of copyright. Some aspects of the debate were hardy perennials: copyright has always been a brittle law. It suffers from fundamental and irreconcilable internal contradictions – the protection/dissemination paradox. It requires continual reform every time someone popularizes a new communications technology, be it the piano roll, the photocopier, or the Internet.

Seen in this light, the Internet treaties were merely one more skirmish in the unending global copyright wars. Stopping there, however, would miss what has made these treaties central to this new era of copyright politics. Most importantly, copyright has become a subject of mass politics, increasingly politicized and increasingly complex politically. The history of copyright is littered with new groups that have been incorporated into copyright law, but this is the first time that individuals have become directly involved. The involvement of individual citizens in what was a previously a commercial law negotiated among large corporate actors has the potential to change the entire complexion of copyright law.

The future, however, is not a blank slate. It will continue to be shaped by the institutional and political contexts within which copyright battles occur, by interests that support the status quo, and by our ideas – rooted largely in a pre-digital age – about what copyright should do. Future battles over copyright will continue to take place at the global, regional, and domestic levels. They will be shaped not only by technological innovations but also by the characteristics of existing institutional regimes, the actors working through these regimes, and their ideas about what is possible and desirable.

The experiences of the United States, Canada, and Mexico – the copyright superpower, a small developed country, and a key developing country – offer an illustration of the interaction of domestic, regional, and global copyright policymaking, with each case highlighting different aspects of the debate. This book has offered three portraits of these three countries at different points in their experience with digital technology. In Mexico, digital technology is only beginning to affect meaningfully the making of copyright policy. The United States in 1996 and 1998 was only beginning to experience the full effect of digital technology on copyright policymaking. The Canadian debate, which benefited from the US example of the DMCA and almost a decade of experience with digital technologies and the Internet, provides a tantalizing picture of the future of copyright governance. The Internet treaties debate and subsequent events in the three countries demonstrate that copyright will continue to become an increasingly mainstream political issue as digital technology brings more individuals directly into contact with copyright law.

This book's historical-institutionalist approach to North America has painted a picture of a region in which all three countries continue to demonstrate significant degrees of policy autonomy in copyright policy, even though the implementation of the WIPO Internet treaties – the policy under investigation – occurred within an identifiable regional and international framework. The three national governments' responses to the WIPO Internet treaties have been shaped largely by domestic institutions, the particular constellation of interests that have grown up around them, and the domestic approaches to copyright that have developed over time in response to ideological and material pressures.

Chapters 4 through 6 discussed how in the United States the content industries were able to link their self-interested desire for stronger copyright protection to growing US concerns about declining economic dominance in the mid-1980s. Chapter 6 further detailed how the outcome of the Digital Millennium Copyright Act (DMCA) was shaped by pluralist-style inter-industry negotiations overseen by Congress, which privileged politically and economically important interests while relatively neglecting the interests of those groups that were underrepresented in the process or not invited to the table. The result was a maximalist approach to the legal protection of technological protection measures and a notice-and-takedown regime to limit the liability of Internet Service Providers for the actions of their customers. Both outcomes were in keeping with the political and economic influence of the

US-based content industries and the telecommunications industries, respectively. They were also in keeping with the relative weakness of user and individual interests, whose rights could be overridden by TPMs and whose interests are not well served by a presumed-guilty approach to ISP liability.[1]

Chapter 7 argued that the Canadian reluctance to implement the Internet treaties was rooted in the lack of a large domestic constituency for stronger copyright and Canada's status as a net importer of copyrighted works: stronger copyright always increases the country's trade deficit in royalties. Responsibility for copyright is divided between two government departments with diametrically opposed mandates, thus further complicating implementation of the Internet treaties, while the supreme role of the Prime Minister's Office introduces a bureaucratic wild card into copyright-policy outcomes. The prime minister's preferences matter for what type of copyright policy gets passed. With respect to interests, increasing public interest in copyright has forced the government to acknowledge the concerns of individuals, even if proposed consumer-friendly provisions would be overruled by legal protections for digital locks that would favour the content industries. Nonetheless, Canadian public interest in copyright will only grow stronger as people become ever more exposed to digital works (such as e-books, downloaded movies, and digital music) and thus to a copyright law that was not written with their best interests at heart. The ultimate legislation reflected a made-in-Canada consensus on ISP liability around a notice-and-notice regime that reflects the political and economic importance of the telecommunications industry and the difficulty of changing an already established institution (in this case, a court-approved informal process). On TPMs, the changing position of the Canadian government has been the result of the respective prime ministers' differing willingness to satisfy US interests, even in the face of strong public opposition to US-style TPM rules.

Finally, chapter 8 noted the influence that the traditional Mexican human-rights approach to copyright has had in reinforcing a post-NAFTA economic-rights approach to copyright. Far from being a passive policy taker on copyright, the Mexican government and those traditional interests represented in the policymaking process are largely in favour of US-style copyright reforms, a view that is partly reinforced by the view of Mexico as a cultural superpower. The ACTA debate has brought civil society, academics, and the telecommunications industry and their bureaucratic allies into the debate, scoring a historic victory in the Senate's unanimous rejection of ACTA, politicizing and complicating what was previously an apolitical technocratic arena dominated by Mexican collection societies.

Internationally, the Internet treaties, whose direction was largely determined by the United States, set the parameters for the overall digital-copyright debate. Regionally, NAFTA and, to a lesser extent, the US-identified content industries gave copyright a North American dimension. In particular, NAFTA's Chapter 17 copyright provisions reinforce the regional parameters for undertaking copyright law, institutionalizing an economic-focused, pro-owner copyright path for the three countries. Their effect has been most obvious in Mexico, where they required a complete overhaul of the existing Mexican copyright law, whereas Chapter 17 simply reinforced the existing direction of Canadian and US copyright laws.

If Chapter 17's setting of North American path dependence on copyright represents a force for convergence on a single (likely US) standard, the rest of NAFTA represents a potential force for divergence. By guaranteeing (more or less) access to the US market, NAFTA makes it harder for the United States to link copyright reform in its neighbours to improved access to its market. NAFTA thus places a constraint on US actions.[2] As a result, Canada, Mexico, and the United States not only retain formal political autonomy, but this autonomy may, in some cases, also be enhanced by the existence of a trade agreement.

Lessons from North America

Two related questions have driven this book. First, in a world where economic giants – the United States, the content industries – drive copyright reform, are smaller countries able to exercise copyright-policy autonomy? Second, and no less important, when it comes to making copyright policy, whose voices matter? Studying the experiences of these different but tightly interconnected countries for traces of policy convergence and divergence, and for institutional, actor, and ideational overlap, offers a useful way to think about how countries in general approach copyright policymaking. That copyright policies in all three countries are rooted in particular domestic socio-political contexts reinforces the general principle that copyright has a crucial domestic dimension that needs to be studied, and that copyright reform happens locally, not just globally. Furthermore, the intimate nature of the economic, political, and social linkages among Canada, Mexico, and the

United States make this North American case study incredibly useful to those concerned about whether smaller countries can exercise copyright-policy autonomy. If they can chart a copyright course independent of the United States, then other countries might be able to as well.

Small-Country Copyright-Policy Autonomy?
"Yes" with an "if," "no" with a "but"

DOMESTIC POLITICS MATTERS

Copyright politics in the three countries continues to be driven as much by domestic concerns as by international pressures and agreements. In the case of the United States, its dominance was the result of its position atop the global copyright policymaking world. For Canada and Mexico, the presence of NAFTA helped to ensure the primacy of domestic politics in copyright affairs. That Canada and Mexico actually had greater copyright policy autonomy *after* NAFTA is somewhat counterintuitive. During the NAFTA negotiations, Mexico in particular dramatically reformed its copyright regime in response to US demands, including implementing partial protection for digital locks applied to computer programs. Post-NAFTA, all three countries could be thought of having copyright regimes generally in the Anglo-American tradition. On the face of it, it would not be unexpected, given that all three countries were now on the same "path," if they took similar approaches to the implementation of the Internet treaties.

As we have seen, however, this was not the case. Mexico, as of October 2013, has yet to implement any ISP-liability regime or further protection for digital locks. Canada postponed even trying to implement the treaties for almost a decade after their conclusion. It then went its own way on ISP liability. Even on digital locks, the Liberal government's 2005 bill demonstrated a willingness to act differently than the United States. Combined with the Liberal decision, the subsequent Conservative reversal of the previous departmental consensus and flaunting of the Justice Department's concerns that the final bill's digital-lock provisions were unconstitutional suggests that this choice could easily have gone another way.

For smaller and developing countries, the main lesson is that the United States' copyright leverage *outside of wider trade negotiations* and once a trade pact has been concluded is actually quite limited. Rather, its influence largely takes the form of moral suasion via PR exercises like the Special 301 process – a type of naming-and-shaming – and other indirect exercises such as the training of justice and enforcement officials. Phrased more positively, outside trade negotiations, smaller states can have significant room to manoeuvre on copyright policy. Beyond implementing policies appropriate to their situation, governments can delay implementation, giving new actors time to make their case and challenge their (often better-funded) opponents. The exceptions for users included in the Conservatives' 2012 bill, for example, were stronger than those in their initial 2008 bill or the Liberals' 2005 bill. Delaying the bills, first through study, and then as a reaction to citizen protests, made these positive changes possible.

The variations highlighted in this study reinforce the need for scholars to pay as much attention to domestic as to global copyright politics. This book, echoing studies such as Deere's analysis of developing countries' implementation of TRIPS, serve as a reminder that most, if not all, international treaties provide signatories with significant leeway for deciding if and how to implement and enforce their international agreements.[3] Comparing the Canadian and Mexican experiences with the Internet treaties suggests that this is as true for smaller developed countries as for developing countries. From an analytical standpoint, distinguishing between developed and developing countries when it comes to analysing differences in treaty implementation may obscure more than it illuminates. Domestic factors matter for both types of country, both have some leeway in their international copyright relations, and both can be brought to heel with similar incentives (i.e., market access). Similarities are more important than differences. In particular, Mexico's experience with the Internet treaties and ACTA serves as a reminder that developing countries' domestic copyright politics can be as complex as those in a developed country like Canada or even the United States. Canada and Mexico do differ in some key respects: Mexico's lower average incomes, for example, make copyright a more important issue in terms of ensuring access to knowledge and culture for that country. However, this is a difference in degree, not in kind. Too-strong copyright protection represents a threat to access and development in both developed and developing countries.

Second, although it is not discussed directly in this book, domestic variations in copyright policy can potentially lead to reforms in other countries and in future international treaties, as governments seek to export their domestic policies or as citizens and policymakers look abroad for inspiration and policy ideas. As will be discussed below, this is not idle speculation.

THE PERILS OF TRADE AGREEMENTS:
THE TRANS-PACIFIC PARTNERSHIP

When it comes to questions of domestic policy autonomy, the key caveat is that it is largely possible only *outside of wider trade negotiations*. Far-reaching changes to a country's copyright laws are exponentially more likely when copyright is part of trade negotiations. Inserting copyright, and intellectual property generally, into international trade negotiations has allowed the United States to drive a tougher bargain regarding the international rules on copyright and IP than it could otherwise because it can trade off against different sectoral interests. In situations where countries care more about having preferred or guaranteed access to the US market, acquiescing to US copyright demands, as Mexico did in the NAFTA negotiations, becomes easier and more logical.

In a sense, this finding is good news for those interested in smaller countries' copyright-policy autonomy. Countries may be getting a bad deal on intellectual property in these agreements, but they are at least getting something in return. Such trade-offs are more difficult when negotiating parties are only discussing one issue. This was one of the reasons why Bruce Lehman was not able to get a maximalist agreement in 1996; it is also the reason why ACTA, discussed in chapters 6 and 8, was watered down significantly once the telecommunications industry was allowed into the secret talks. Both cases resulted in agreements that were more open than they would have been otherwise. Without something to trade, the United States' ability to influence even its closest neighbours became more difficult.

When faced with negative outcomes in one institutional context, states often engage in forum shopping, looking for an arena that might be more favourable to their interests. Since the conclusion of the Internet treaties, the United States has engaged in just such an exercise, seeking a forum that would allow it to better establish its interpretation of copyright law as the global standard. Initially, it attempted to bypass WIPO (dependent on consensus and thus open to manipulation by developing countries) in favour of the plurilateral ACTA, which included only like-minded developing countries, as well as Mexico and Morocco. ACTA itself ran afoul of the European explosion of public interest in copyright (on which more below), and as noted above was watered down once groups other than those representing the content industries were allowed in.

ACTA, however, was not the United States' only attempt to further its pursuit of global copyright reform. In 2008, it began negotiations for a Trans-Pacific Strategic Economic Partnership (or Trans-Pacific Partnership, TPP) with Brunei, Chile, Singapore, and New Zealand. Since then, seven other countries, including Canada and Mexico (who were invited by the United States in mid-2012), have also joined the negotiations.[4] Among its other provisions, the TPP includes an intellectual-property chapter. Although the text as of October 2013 remained officially secret, a leaked version suggests that the United States is attempting to use the TPP to pursue "many dramatic expansions of the international minimum standards on the scope and length of copyright protection, including provisions not reflected in current law," according to a report prepared by the American University's Program on Information Justice and Intellectual Property.[5] According to the trade journal *Inside U.S. Trade*, "a U.S. industry source said TPP is still an opportunity for the U.S. to lay out rights and obligations on IPR enforcement better than it did in ACTA."[6] Among other issues, it attempts to resurrect the idea, rejected explicitly in the Internet treaties, that temporary electronic copies should be eligible for copyright protection.[7]

Directly relevant to this project, the US proposal would require criminal punishment for individuals who circumvent digital locks "regardless of whether such circumvention is effected for a use that is itself protected by copyright." As Flynn notes, "By removing the link between illegal circumvention and copyright violation, the proposal goes far beyond the requirements of the WPPT, existing U.S. free trade agreements and the bounds of U.S. law."[8] Post-1998 US court rulings have more tightly linked the DMCA's anti-circumvention rules to copyright; the United States' TPP proposal would go beyond this, as well as negating "important limitations and exceptions included in a country's own law," potentially creating "an indefinite term of protection."[9] The TPP would also require that member countries implement a notice-and-takedown ISP-liability regime.[10]

Predicting negotiation outcomes is a mug's game. That said, all else being equal, past experience suggests that the larger scope for trade-offs afforded by general trade negotiations gives the United States a greater chance for realizing its copyright objectives. If the negotiating countries want access to the US and each other's markets enough, then copyright – which remains for most of these countries a secondary economic concern – could be compromised in exchange for movement in other areas. The Mexican government's decision in July 2012 to sign the ACTA, in spite of the Senate's and the European Parliament's rejections of ACTA, is perhaps an early sign of this trade-off in action; many people speculated that it was a US-imposed condition for acceptance into the talks.[11] If true, it would be another example of how the United States uses the carrot of enhanced market access to convince other countries to undertake copyright reform. Now that all three countries have signed ACTA, and given both governments' support for the US view of copyright, it will be very interesting to see the extent to which this translates into a common "North American" IP position in the talks. Whether this common approach, should it come to pass, translates into similar domestic laws when (if) the three implement the TPP, however, will continue to depend on the particularities of their domestic IP regimes. That said, should the talks not founder on some other point, the odds that Canada and Mexico will further reform their laws to fit US desires are higher inside the TPP negotiations than outside.

As the previous section and Mexico's NAFTA experience suggests, while the trade-copyright linkage is very powerful within the dynamics of a trade negotiation, it will not necessarily extend beyond the trade deal itself. Any trade agreement must still be ratified and implemented domestically. Furthermore, technological change has a way of rendering obsolete any given copyright law, to say nothing of actors exploiting institutional or ideational inconsistencies. What is settled in a trade agreement can be rendered moot by technological changes. The copyfight never ends.

Whose Voice Matters? The Rise of the Public Interest

These three countries' experience with the Internet treaties also provides an answer to this study's second question: When it comes to making copyright policy, whose voices matter? The digital-copyright debates provide ample evidence of the influence that corporate interests continue to have on copyright lawmaking, but they have also charted something new: the rising importance of individual users as a force for change, particularly at the domestic level. The 2007 Fair Copyright for Canada Facebook uprising provided the template by which previously isolated individuals could pool the influence represented in their right to vote to pressure politicians to adapt or change their policies. They did so by emphasizing the copyright's dissemination role over its protection role, and to great effect.

Digital technology gives individuals a direct stake in the copyright debate and allows them to organize more easily, and this organization will tend to lead to greater attention to individual users' rights in all three countries (and beyond). This increased politicization will not necessarily lead to stronger users' rights, or to increased attention to dissemination at the expense of protection. The degree and direction of copyright reform is shaped as much by the institutional context within which it occurs as by technological change. In Mexico, the Stop ACTA movement thwarted ACTA in the Senate, though term limits have meant that it is unclear whether the current Senate will consider itself bound by its predecessors' unanimous vote. In Canada, while the 2007–8 Facebook uprising forced a hostile government to acknowledge individuals' views and to implement some user-friendly copyright reforms, its unwavering position on the main bone of contention – digital locks – demonstrated the limitations of their power and influence. Absent the threat of an election, a Canadian majority government can pass almost any copyright law it desires. With time, individual users may come to be seen as equals with other accepted groups – and the ever-rising interest in copyright (as measured by participation in the 2001–2 and 2009 public consultations) suggests that they will – but prudence cautions against assuming their involvement in the debate will necessarily become highly effective overnight. The entrenched copyright interests have shown no desire to accommodate any group that might threaten their existing financial returns from copyright law.

Increased public engagement will, however, increase the political cost of concluding a copyright treaty or legal reform that ignores user rights. Public pressure on copyright may not be sufficient on its own to force the inclusion of strong user rights within the TPP or to thwart the ratification of any agreement that does not include these rights, but neither will governments be able to ignore these interests.

US COPYRIGHT IN PLAY: THE 2012 INTERNET BLACKOUT[12]

As noted earlier in this book, historical institutionalism holds that institutions are continually being remade through the purposeful actions of actors. Institutions may shape policy development, but they are not immune to change. Change, HI reminds us, is possible when actors – longstanding or newly formed – are able to exploit existing ideational or material resources, as well as changing external circumstances.

This is as true in the United States as anywhere. The United States has been pursuing ever-stronger global copyright policies since the mid-1980s, a result of some particularly effective lobbying by its intellectual-property industries. This decades-long pursuit of stronger copyright makes it easy to treat the US international-copyright position as a given, ignoring that it was politically constructed. What was politically made can be politically unmade. The continued genius of the US system of government is its openness to new and different actors and ideas, even in an area like copyright, dominated as it is by entrenched interests. Lobbying may be a dirty game, but companies like Google have finally realized that their business depends as much on Washington politics as on their ability to produce innovative products and services. In the first quarter of 2012, it spent $5.3 million on lobbying, about as much as it spent in 2010 as a whole.[13]

Washington's relatively open political system can be exploited in other ways. The Special 301 process, for example, was set up to support the IP industries' calls for stronger global intellectual-property protection. At the same time, its open-submissions policy means that not only content industries can use Special 301 to promote their interests, and groups like Public Knowledge, which tabled their first Special 301 submission in 2010, are doing just that. If one believes that the United States Trade Representative evaluates all submissions in an unbiased manner, then these submissions will help balance the final Special 301 report. If not, then the submissions can be used to put political pressure on the USTR on the question of why these submissions are not being heard.

Congress, however, may be the most likely source of dramatic change. The new politics of digital copyright roared into full view on 18 January 2012. Over the previous months, US legislators from both parties had been working on two pieces of legislation, the Stop Online Piracy Act (SOPA) in the House of Representatives and the Protect Intellectual Property Act (PIPA) in the Senate. The two bills had been roundly criticized by technology experts and user-rights groups as Draconian measures that could, if implemented as originally planned, "break the Internet" by "damaging the core functionality of the Domain Name Service (DNS) system" – the means by which website names are linked to underlying addresses – by requiring that ISPs maintain lists of sites that Americans would be forbidden from accessing, and that computers be redirected away from any forbidden sites.[14] In the run-up to the vote, activist groups like the Electronic Frontier Foundation worked to raise public awareness of the bills online, with great success.[15] In late December 2011, the bill was becoming contentious enough that Representative Lamar Smith, the Republican chair of the House Judiciary Committee, which was considering the bill, postponed its hearings until February 2012.[16]

In 1998, the lawyer activists behind the Digital Future Coalition had played a significant coordinating role in getting user groups to the table, but their success was nothing compared to what was about to happen. On 18 January 2012 Representatives, Senators, their aides, and anyone else who tried to use Wikipedia, that free and indispensable font of information on everything from the plots of *Community* episodes to nearly comprehensible descriptions of the Higgs boson, were greeted with a (very stylish) blacked-out page that read:

> *Imagine a World*
> *Without Free Knowledge*
> *For over a decade, we have spent millions of hours building the largest encyclopedia in human history. Right now, the U.S. Congress is considering legislation that could fatally damage the free and open internet. For 24 hours, to raise awareness, we are blacking out Wikipedia.*

Wikipedia and thousands of high- and low-profile websites were staging a 24-hour Internet "blackout," replacing their web pages with darkened screens that alerted readers to the imminent passage from committee of SOPA in the US House of Representatives. The bill's critics contended that in the name of cracking down on copyright violators, SOPA would fundamentally damage the Internet's infrastructure, set up a censorship regime, and compromise online security.[17] The websites, most notably the English-language Wikipedia pages, also provided individuals with directions on how to contact their elected representatives. The Wikipedia page[18] also included links to Facebook, Google+, and Twitter, allowing people to further spread the word.

Reactions to the protest were overwhelming and could be observed in real time. Students freaked out on Twitter over how they were now going to fail their papers, due that morning, because they couldn't do any research on Wikipedia – all because of something called "SOAP"? Educators received incontrovertible proof that a fair share of their students leave their assignments to the last minute and depend too heavily on Wikipedia for their research. And American voters let their representatives in Washington know that they were very displeased with "SOPA."

The numbers boggle the mind: Google collected more than seven million signatures for its anti-SOPA online petition, while more than 162 million people saw the Wikipedia blackout page. According to Wikipedia, more than eight million people looked up their elected representatives' contact information via Wikipedia, with so many people trying to contact their representatives that "the Senate's web site was unable to accommodate the number of citizens attempting to use its contact forms."[19]

Washington did not know what hit it, but the results speak for themselves. Legislators from both parties spent the day scrambling to get off the SOPA bandwagon. By the time the dust had settled, both the Senate and House bills had been withdrawn. The Internet blackout, and the activism underlying it, allowed user groups to hand the better-financed and connected pro-stronger-copyright forces their first major defeat in over three decades. If that wasn't enough, Benkler's network analysis strongly suggests that the following month's anti-ACTA protests in Europe were influenced by the anti-SOPA demonstrations.[20]

These protests marked the maturing of US digital-copyright politics that were inaugurated by the 1996 Internet treaties, demonstrating decisively how users could make their voices heard politically in the United States. Besides the scale of the protest, the 2012 Internet Blackout was remarkable for the completeness of the victory it delivered, slamming the brakes on two key pieces of legislation over the wishes of very powerful politicians in Congress and the Executive (Vice-President Joe Biden, President Barack Obama's point man on copyright issues, supported SOPA and PIPA).[21] To return to terms introduced in chapter 2, protestors engaged in both substantive and symbolic bricolage. Where the IP industries in the 1980s effectively linked intellectual property to trade policy while emphasizing the need for greater protection, the protestors were able to link copyright policy with technology and Internet policy in favour of dissemination principles that themselves were deeply linked to the openness that people have come to expect from the Internet itself. The SOPA battle has also spurred Internet-based companies to become more involved in Washington, where their influence and clout has traditionally not matched their economic importance. In September 2012, Google, Amazon, eBay, Facebook, and other Internet companies launched the Internet Association, to lobby Congress on Internet-related issues. According to the association's president and CEO, Michael Beckerman, a former House Energy and Commerce Committee deputy staff director, "It's the first time that the Internet is coming together as an industry here in Washington."[22] Greater involvement in Congressional politics by these companies cannot but help affect the future direction of copyright and other Internet-related issues in the United States.

This domestic upheaval may already be having significant effects on the future direction of global copyright reform. In mid-July 2012 the USTR committed, for the first time ever, to enshrining US fair-use limitations and exceptions in a trade agreement.[23] What this will mean in practice remains to be seen, but it is a clear acknowledgment of the new reality in US and international copyright politics, that user-rights advocates, including public-interest groups, civil society, and the telecoms industry, cannot be ignored. That said, support for the status quo remains deeply entrenched in the institutions and actors that dominate the US copyright debate. While the United States was making these conciliatory noises on fair use, it was continuing to press its TPP negotiating partners to accept ACTA-style rules, even as support for the treaty collapsed in the European Union.

While the future, as always, is cloudy, this much is certain: The default US position on copyright is much more vulnerable than it appears.

The Future of Copyright

This analysis of the negotiation and implementation of the Internet treaties has confirmed that copyright is a path-dependent process, its continuation more dependent on its longevity and embeddedness in the international political economy than on whether or not it actually promotes creation and distribution. Faced with revolutionary technological changes that put mass copying and distribution in the hands of individuals for the first time in history, negotiators at WIPO crafted a treaty that sought to import traditional copyright concepts into the digital age. Domestically, all three countries covered by this study adopted the Internet treaties as their template for digital-copyright reform.

This path dependence, a function of ideational and institutional constraints, as well as the interests of those involved in negotiating the treaties and the subsequent legislative projects, suggests that it will be an uphill battle for those advocating a wholesale overhaul of copyright law into something more appropriate to the digital age and to its stated goals of maximizing creative production and distribution.

This book has detailed individual users' initial attempts to promote their interest in a copyright debate that previously had not acknowledged their (legitimate) point of view. The North American experience with the Internet treaties suggests that copyright reform that takes these individuals' and groups' interests into account – a policy that promotes their ability to create and to benefit fully from the creations of others – can be achieved by a direct engagement with domestic political processes. The Internet blackout and the Mexican anti-ACTA vote demonstrate that these groups have the ability to block legislation. The

Canadian debate over Bill C-61 in 2007–8 further suggests that, with organization, these new groups can also influence legislation. What this means for the future of global copyright reform, and the next generation of domestic copyright policymaking, in light of the ACTA and SOPA debates, offers a fruitful area for future research.

More radical change could also come about through a change in the terms of the debate, by moving from debates over whether one is pro- or anti-copyright to a debate over what tools, of which copyright is only one, are best suited to promoting the creation and distribution of creative works. Such a focus would move the debate away from foundational Western themes like "property" and "individuality" and towards a more empirical, pragmatic basis for debate. This shift would require greater attention to the real effects of copyright on creation and distribution, and the generation of more empirical research on this subject than currently exists. It would also require coming to terms with the reality that there is a surprising lack of evidence showing that copyright is necessary for the production and dissemination of creative works.

As desirable as this evidence-based turn might be, there currently exists little to suggest that copyright's ideological hegemony will be challenged successfully in the near future. In all three case-study countries, support for copyright is the ticket for admission to the "serious" copyright-policy debate. Almost all opponents of stronger copyright tend to preface their critiques by affirming their support for copyright, if not in its present form, while defenders of stronger copyright accuse their critics of being completely anti-copyright.

The potential for wholesale copyright reform is also limited by regional and international treaties, particularly TRIPS and NAFTA Chapter 17, which commit signatories to a particular view of copyright. The likely difficulty of reforming these treaties suggests that the potential for a radical departure from the current copyright framework is negligible. Even within this framework, however, copyright can be made more responsive to the needs of individuals and creators, not least by the implementation of ISP liability rules such as notice-and-notice that do not assume that users are guilty until proven innocent, and by ensuring that TPM rules do not interfere with individuals' existing rights.

Path Dependence and the Potential for Variation

The significance of Canadian and Mexican decisions regarding the Internet treaties, particularly with respect to divergences (realized and potential) from the US position, should not be overstated. In neither case were underlying assumptions about copyright challenged. Furthermore, the debate in both countries unfolded within the parameters set directly by the Internet treaties and indirectly by the United States.

Given these overarching conditions, however, copyright policies remain under the democratic control of domestic governments, within the constraints of rules of NAFTA and TRIPS. Treaties may set boundaries, and larger states may have significant influence over these boundaries and their interpretation. Smaller states, however, can (and do) exercise agency in terms of if and how these treaties are implemented. Both convergence with and divergence from treaty norms must be explained in terms of domestic variables. Regionally, NAFTA's restraining characteristics have increased the possibility for copyright-policy autonomy in Canada and Mexico. Copyright policymaking in the two countries is shaped by the peculiarities of each country's political processes, within the context of NAFTA and the Internet treaties.

These are exciting times for copyright scholars and activists. Everything is up for grabs. The Internet and digital technologies have given individuals a direct stake in the debate and the tools to make themselves heard. In just over a decade, they have gone from copyright's silent, neglected partners to the driving force for copyright reform. The 2007 Canadian Facebook Uprising, the 2011 Mexican Stop ACTA triumph, the January 2012 anti-SOPA blackouts, and the highly successful February 2012 European anti-ACTA protests all have had a direct, possibly lasting, effect on global copyright policies, shaping the contentious politics of copyright that emerged following the 1996 Internet treaties. In each case, results were driven by domestic politics. People, working through their domestic political institutions, can affect national – and perhaps even global – copyright regimes.

To a significant extent, each North American government remains master of its own copyright policy. The governments of Canada and Mexico may choose to follow the US lead, and they may do so in response to US pressure (as in the Canadian Conservative government's case) or in response to a mixture of US influence and domestic interest-group preference (as in the case of Mexico). Neither case, however, takes away from the crucial point, from the perspective of those who value democratic decision-making. Policy convergence is a choice: it is not preordained.

Notes

1. A Most Unlikely Debate

1 The other main IP categories being patents, which cover industrial processes such as pharmaceuticals, trademarks (which protect phrases and symbols that identify goods or services), and trade secrets.

2 Canada and Mexico were also involved in the ACTA negotiations. Chapters 7 and 9 cover ACTA in greater detail.

3 This protest, against the Stop Online Piracy Act (SOPA) and the Protect Intellectual Property Act (PIPA), is addressed in chapter 9.

4 Sebastian Haunss and Kenneth C. Shadlen, "Introduction: Rethinking the Politics of Intellectual Property," in *Politics of Intellectual Property: Contestation over the Ownership, Use, and Control of Knowledge and Information*, ed. S. Haunss and K.C. Shadlen (Cheltenham: Edward Elgar, 2009), 2.

5 An important exception is Carolyn Deere, *The Implementation Game: The TRIPS Agreement and the Global Politics of Intellectual Property Reform in Developing Countries* (Oxford: Oxford University Press, 2009).

6 WIPO, *Survey on Implementation Provisions of the WCT and the WPPT* (25 April 2003), 2–12: http://www.wipo.int/meetings/en/doc_details .jsp?doc_id=16415. The following countries were surveyed: Albania, Argentina, Belarus, Bulgaria, Burkina Faso, Chile, Colombia, Costa Rica, Croatia, Czech Republic, Ecuador, El Salvador, Gabon, Georgia, Guatemala, Honduras, Hungary, Indonesia, Jamaica, Japan, Kyrgyzstan, Latvia, Lithuania, Mali, Mexico, Mongolia, Republic of Moldova, Nicaragua, Panama, Paraguay, Peru, Philippines, Romania, Saint Lucia, Senegal, Slovakia, Slovenia, Ukraine, and the United States.

7 Ibid., 3.

8 Ibid., 4.

9 Andrew Mertha, *The Politics of Piracy: Intellectual Property in Contemporary China* (Ithaca: Cornell University Press, 2005).

10 As chapter 8 will discuss, the 1994 North American Free Trade Agreement moved Mexico's copyright regime much closer to the commercial-focused Anglo-American model, although it retains significant Continental influences.

11 Thanks to Miranda Forsyth of the Regulatory Institutions Network at Australian National University for the Vanuatu example.

12 This book adopts Keohane's definition of hegemony as "a situation in which one state is powerful enough to maintain the essential rules governing interstate relations and willing to do so." (Robert O. Keohane, *After Hegemony: Cooperation and Discord in the World Political Economy* [Princeton: Princeton University Press, 2005], 34–5.) A hegemonic state must, as the United States does, possess a "preponderance of material resources," particularly "control over raw materials, control over sources of capital, control over markets and comparative advantages in the production of highly valued goods" and be willing to exploit these advantages (ibid., 32). A hegemonic power will also exploit "nonterritorial power" (or soft power) resources such as ideology (Peter J. Katzenstein, *A World of Regions: Asia and Europe in the American Imperium* [Ithaca: Cornell University Press, 2005], 2). The definition of hegemon is relational: at heart it implies only the possession of relative advantages in its dealings with other states. It does not imply the ability to control all situations, a key point for this book's argument.

13 Susan K. Sell, *Private Power, Public Law: The Globalization of Intellectual Property Rights* (Cambridge: Cambridge University Press, 2003).

14 A point made in great detail by Sell (ibid.), and by Peter Drahos and John Braithwaite, *Information Feudalism: Who Owns the Knowledge Economy?* (London: Earthscan Publications Ltd, 2002).

15 Drahos and Braithwaite, ibid.; Sell, ibid.

16 Stephen Clarkson, *Does North America Exist? Governing the Continent after NAFTA and 9/11* (Toronto and Washington: University of Toronto Press and Woodrow Wilson Center Press, 2008), 11.

17 Based on author's calculations from data in the World Trade Organization statistics database (http://stat.wto.org/StatisticalProgram/WSDBStatProgramHome.aspx?Language=E). See also Clarkson, ibid., 25–32.

18 North American trade patterns reveal that the regional relationship is not so much trilateral as it is a "hub and spoke" model focused on the United States (Robert Pastor, *Toward a North American Community: Lessons from the Old World for the New* [Washington, DC: Institute for International Economics, 2001]). While Canada and Mexico are both sources of a large proportion of

US imports and customer for its exports, Canada and Mexico do not trade much with each other.

19 Matthew Rimmer, "Robbery under Arms: Copyright Law and the Australia-United States Free Trade Agreement," *First Monday* 11.3 (2006): http://firstmonday.org/htbin/cgiwrap/bin/ojs/index.php/fm/article/view/1316/1236.

20 Graham Dutfield and Uma Suthersanen, *Global Intellectual Property Law* (Cheltenham: Edward Elgar, 2008), 63–4.

21 In brief, the Anglo-American tradition in copyright emphasizes economic rights in creative works. It stands in contrast to the Continental European tradition, which emphasizes copyright as an author's moral rights in his or her creation. This distinction is elaborated further in the next section.

22 Peter Drahos, *A Philosophy of Intellectual Property* (Aldershot: Dartmouth, 1996), 5.

23 Specifically, economic rights in copyright – the main subject of discussion in this book – are alienable. Moral rights in copyright are generally considered to be inalienable.

24 Dutfield and Suthersanen, *Global Intellectual Property Law*, vi.

25 Adam D. Moore, ed., *Intellectual Property: Moral, Legal, and International Dilemmas* (Lanham, MD: Rowman & Littlefield Publishers, Inc., 1997), 8.

26 Yochai Benkler, "A Political Economy of the Public Domain: Markets in Information Goods versus the Marketplace of Ideas," in *Expanding the Boundaries of Intellectual Property: Innovation Policy for the Knowledge Society*, ed. Rochelle Cooper Dreyfuss et al. (Oxford: Oxford University Press, 2001), 268.

27 G. Bruce Doern and Markus Sharaput, *Canadian Intellectual Property: The Politics of Innovating Institutions and Interests* (Toronto: University of Toronto Press, 2000).

28 Discussed further in chapter 3. Whether this assertion is empirically valid is a separate question.

29 For a discussion of the economic costs and benefits of copyright see William M. Landes and Richard A. Posner, *The Economic Structure of Intellectual Property Law* (Cambridge: Harvard University Press, 2003); and Landes and Posner, "An Economic Analysis of Copyright Law," *Journal of Legal Studies* 18.2 (1988).

30 This is not to say that the balance is always wisely chosen.

31 For a discussion and defence of the public domain, as well as for a wider critique of intellectual property laws, see James Boyle, *The Public Domain: Enclosing the Commons of the Mind* (New Haven: Yale University Press, 2008).

32 These terms are general; in certain cases, somewhat different terms apply.

33 NAFTA and TRIPS set member countries' term of protection at life of the author plus fifty years; countries are free to provide longer terms. As discussed in chapter 8, Mexico's term was extended in 2003 following lobbying by the collection societies that represent creators in the Mexican copyright law-making process.

34 Sunny Handa, *Copyright Law in Canada* (Markham: Butterworths Canada Ltd, 2002), 23.

35 As US copyright critic Lawrence Lessig notes, this right "boils down to 'the right to hire a lawyer,' to engage in protracted, costly and time-consuming litigation to defend one's right to speak" (cited in Neil Weinstock Netanel, *Copyright's Paradox* [Oxford: Oxford University Press, 2008], 66).

36 In 2012, the Canadian Supreme Court affirmed earlier rulings, such as *CCH v. Law Society of Upper Canada*, that effectively created or confirmed an explicit user's right in Canada (Laura J. Murray and Samuel E. Trosow, *Canadian Copyright: A Citizen's Guide* [Toronto: Between the Lines, 2007], 74; Bob Tarantino, "Five Cases That Shook the World: An Entertainment Lawyer's Guide to the Copyright Pentalogy," Heenan Blaikie LLP [17 July 2012], http://www.jdsupra.com/legalnews/five-cases-that-shook-the-world-an-ente-18513/).

37 Luis C. Schmidt, "Mexico's Fair Use Balancing Act," *Managing Intellectual Property – Supplement, Brand Management IP Focus 2009* (2009), http://www.managingip.com/Article.aspx?ArticleID=2192575.

38 Ruth Towse and Rudi Holzhauer, "Introduction," in *The Economics of Intellectual Property*, vol. 1, ed. R. Towse and R. Holzhauer (Cheltenham: Edward Elgar Publishing Ltd, 2002), xix.

39 Article 27 reads: "(1) Everyone has the right freely to participate in the cultural life of the community, to enjoy the arts and to share in scientific advancement and its benefits. (2) Everyone has the right to the protection of the moral and material interests resulting from any scientific, literary or artistic production of which he is the author."

40 Leo J. Raskind, "Copyright," in *The New Palgrave Dictionary of Economics and the Law*, vol. 1, ed. Peter Newman (London: Macmillan, 1998), 478.

41 Reynaldo Urtiaga Escobar, "Los sistemas de derechos de autor y copyright hoy," *Revista Mexicana del Derecho de Autor* 2.6 (2002).

42 Drahos and Braithwaite, *Information Feudalism*, 32–8.

43 Ibid., 31–2.

44 Ibid., 85.

45 Christopher May, *A Global Political Economy of Intellectual Property Rights* (New York: Routledge, 2000).

46 Alice Amsden emphasizes the importance of learning and information transfer for late-industrializing countries, in contrast to early industrializers, who developed their knowledge and processes "in house," as it were. As IP protection (especially patents, but also copyright) increases the cost of obtaining such information, strong IP protection places developing countries at a disadvantage, making it more expensive for them to develop (Alice H. Amsden, *The Rise of "The Rest": Challenges to the West from Late-Industrializing Economies* [Oxford: Oxford University Press, 2000]; *Asia's Next Giant: South Korea and Late Industrialization* [New York: Oxford University Press, 1989]).

47 Ha-Joon Chang, "Kicking away the Ladder," *post-autistic economics review* 15 (2002), http://www.btinternet.com/~pae_news/review/issue15.htm.

48 See Benkler, "A Political Economy of the Public Domain," for a discussion of how different groups (industry groups, individual creators, and so on) are affected by the strengthening of copyright protection.

49 http://www.wipo.int/treaties/en/ip/wct/trtdocs_wo033.html and www.wipo.int/treaties/en/ip/wppt/trtdocs_wo034.html.

50 "Internet treaties" and "WIPO Internet treaties" as used in this book refer to these two treaties.

51 As chapters 5 and 6 discuss, implementation of the Internet treaties was linked to this liability issue over the course of the US debate on digital-copyright reform.

52 Chapter 3 discusses in greater detail the importance of TRIPS for global copyright policymaking.

53 While the Internet treaties cover several other issues, this book focuses exclusively on the implementation of ISP liability and TPMs as proxies for the implementation of the treaties as a whole, in part because few, if any, WIPO member countries previously had enacted laws to address these issues directly.

54 Ian R. Kerr, Alana Maurushat, and Christian S. Tacit, "Technical Protection Measures: Tilting at Copyright's Windmill," *Ottawa Law Review* 34.1 (2002–3), 13.

55 Digital rights management systems are "technology systems facilitating the trusted, dynamic management of rights in any kind of digital information, throughout its lifecycle and wherever and however it is distributed" (Kerr, Maurushat, and Tacit, ibid., 25).

56 Ian Brown, "The Evolution of Anti-Circumvention Law," *International Review of Law and Computers* 20.3 (2006), 240.

57 Michael Geist, "Anti-circumvention Legislation and Competition Policy: Defining a Canadian Way?" in *In the Public Interest: The Future of Canadian Copyright Law*, ed. M. Geist (Toronto: Irwin Law 2005), 220.

58 Murray and Trosow, *Canadian Copyright*, 113, 18.
59 Kerr, Maurushat, and Tacit, "Technical Protection Measures," 31.
60 Jeremy de Beer, "Constitutional Jurisdiction over Paracopyright Laws," in *In the Public Interest*, ed. Geist, 98.
61 Christopher May, *The World Intellectual Property Organization: Resurgence and the Development Agenda* (New York: Routledge), 69.
62 Jeremy de Beer, "Copyright and Innovation in the Networked Information Economy," Conference Board of Canada working paper (2009), 5–6.
63 Kerr, Maurushat, and Tacit, "Technical Protection Measures," 42–3.
64 de Beer, "Constitutional Jurisdiction."
65 Murray and Trosow, *Canadian Copyright*, 111.
66 John Borland, "FAQ: Sony's 'Rootkit' CDs," CNET News, 10 November 2005, http://news.cnet.com/FAQ-Sonys-rootkit-CDs/2100-1029_3-5946760.html.
67 Bruce Schneier, "Real Story of the Rogue Rootkit," *Wired*, 17 November 2005, http://www.wired.com/politics/security/commentary/securitymatters/2005/11/69601.
68 The idea that "property rights" in general do not imply absolute rights for owners is discussed further in chapter 3.
69 May 2007, 71; de Beer 2009, 5.
70 de Beer, "Constitutional Jurisdiction."
71 Ibid., 8.
72 Daniel J. Gervais, "The Purpose of Copyright Law in Canada," *University of Ottawa Law and Technology Journal* 2.2 (2005), 327.
73 Jeremy de Beer and Christopher D. Clemmer, "Global Trends in Online Copyright Enforcement: The Role of Internet Intermediaries," *Jurimetrics* 49.4 (2009), 376; Joe Karaganis, "Disciplining Markets in the Digital Age," in *Structures of Participation in Digital Culture*, ed. J. Karaganis (New York: Social Science Research Council, 2007), 226.
74 de Beer, "Copyright and Innovation," 8.
75 Of course, if creators were rewarded otherwise than through the regulation of copy making, this "problem" would not be a problem at all.
76 de Beer and Clemmer, "Global Trends in Online Copyright Enforcement."
77 Josh Taylor, "France drops Hadopi three-strikes copyright law," *ZDNet*, 10 July 2013, http://www.zdnet.com/france-drops-hadopi-three-strikes-copyright-law-7000017857/.
78 Chapter 6 will discuss this development in greater detail.
79 Doern and Sharaput, *Canadian Intellectual Property*, 106.
80 The term "US-identified content industries" acknowledges that while several content-industry corporations, such as Sony Pictures, are non-

US-based (Sony, for example, originated in Japan), they tend to identify with the United States, while the US government treats them as US-based interests (e.g., treating the motion picture industry as "Hollywood").

81 Blayne Haggart, "Birth of a Movement: The Anti-Counterfeiting Trade Agreement and the Politicization of Mexican Copyright," *Policy & Internet*. Forthcoming, 2014.

82 In the Mexican political system, treaties do not come into force unless the Senate ratifies them. This vote essentially told the executive branch not to bother submitting ACTA for ratification. Despite this vote, the Mexican government signed ACTA in July 2012, further complicating the treaty's future. See chapter 8 for further details.

83 Orfeo Fioretos, "Historical Institutionalism in International Relations," *International Organization* 65.2 (2011).

84 E.g., Susan K. Sell, "The Rise and Rule of a Trade-based Strategy: Historical Institutionalism and the International Regulation of Intellectual Property," *Review of International Political Economy* 17.4 (2010), which deals explicitly with copyright.

85 Kathleen Thelen and Sven Steinmo, "Historical Institutionalism in Comparative Politics," in *Structuring Politics*, ed. Steinmo, Thelen, and Longstreth; Paul Pierson, "Increasing Returns, Path Dependence, and the Study of Politics," *American Political Science Review* 94.2 (2000).

86 Peter A. Hall, "Policy Paradigms, Social Learning, and the State: The Case of Economic Policymaking in Britain," *Comparative Politics* 25.3.

87 Keith Banting, George Hoberg, and Richard Simeon, "Introduction," in *Degrees of Freedom: Canada and the United States in a Changing World*, ed. K. Banting, G. Hoberg, and R. Simeon (Montreal: McGill-Queen's University Press, 1997).

88 Doern and Sharaput, *Canadian Intellectual Property*. For more on copyright's protection/dissemination function, see chapter 3.

2. A Historical-Institutionalist Framework for Analysing Copyright Policymaking

1 This chapter draws in part on Blayne Haggart, "Historical Institutionalism and the Politics of Intellectual Property," in *Intellectual Property Law for the 21st Century: Interdiscilinary Approaches to IP*, ed. Courtney B. Doagoo, Mistrale Goudreau, Madelaine Saginur, and Teresa Scassa (Toronto: Irwin Law, 2014), 160–81.

2 John L. Campbell, *Institutional Change and Governance* (Princeton: Princeton University Press, 2004), 23.

3 Peter A. Hall and Rosemary C.R. Taylor, "Political Science and the Three New Institutionalisms," *Political Studies* 44 (1996); James G. March and Johan P. Olsen, *Rediscovering Institutions: The Organizational Basis of Politics* (New York: The Free Press, 1989). The other new institutionalisms were rational-choice and sociological/organizational institutionalism. While all neo-institutionalisms agree on several points – the centrality of institutions in social life as structures that influence human behaviour and socio-political outcomes – and overlap in practice, they can be distinguished by their choice of subject matter, descriptions of how institutions influence behaviour, and how agents' preferences are formed. The 1992 edited volume by Sven Steinmo, Kathleen Thelen, and Frank Longstreth (*Structuring Politics: Historical Institutionalism in Comparative Analysis* [Cambridge: Cambridge University Press, 1992]) is generally identified as the first complete articulation of "new institutionalism" as it applies to historical institutionalism (B. Guy Peters, Jon Pierre, and Desmond S. King, "The Politics of Path Dependency: Political Conflict in Historical Institutionalism," *Journal of Politics* 67.4 [2005]). In sociology, Paul J. DiMaggio and Walter W. Powell ("Introduction," in *The New Institutionalism in Organizational Analysis*, ed. Walter W. Powell and Paul J. DiMaggio [Chicago: University of Chicago Press, 1991], 11) date the new institutionalism to 1977 and the publication of John Meyer's "The Effects of Education as an Institution" in the *American Journal of Sociology*. For a discussion of the rise of the new institutionalisms see Ira Katznelson, "Structure and Configuration in Comparative Politics," in *Comparative Politics*, ed. Mark I. Lichbach and Alan S. Zuckerman (Cambridge: Cambridge University Press, 1997).

4 Kathleen Thelen and Sven Steinmo, "Historical Institutionalism in Comparative Politics," in *Structuring Politics*, ed. Steinmo, Thelen, and Longstreth.

5 For an institutionalist, if not explicitly HI, analysis of Canadian IP policy-making, see Doern and Sharaput, *Canadian Intellectual Property*.

6 Ellen Immergut, cited in Katznelson, "Structure and Configuration," 104.

7 Hall and Taylor, "Political Science and the Three New Institutionalisms," 938.

8 Katznelson, "Structure and Configuration."

9 Herbert Kitschelt, Peter Lange, Gary Marks, and John D. Stephens, "Convergence and Divergence in Advanced Capitalist Democracies," in *Continuity and Change in Contemporary Capitalism*, ed. H. Kitschelt (London: Cambridge University Press, 1999), 440–1.

10 Thelen and Steinmo, "Historical Institutionalism," 11, 3.

11 Colin Hay, "Contemporary Capitalism, Globalization, Regionalization and the Persistence of National Variation," *Review of International Studies* 26 (2000), 512.

12 Frank R. Baumgartner and Bryan D. Jones, *Agendas and Instability in American Politics* (Chicago: University of Chicago Press, 1993), 9.

13 Sell, *Private Power, Public Law*, 5.

14 Colin Hay and Daniel Wincott, "Structure, Agency and Historical Institutionalism," *Political Studies* 46 (1998), 951.

15 Ira Katznelson, "Review: The Doleful Dance of Politics and Policy: Can Historical Institutionalism Make a Difference?" *American Political Science Review* 92 (1998), 196; Katznelson, "Structure and Configuration," 83.

16 Karen Orren and Stephen Skowronek, *The Search for American Political Development* (Cambridge: Cambridge University Press, 2004), 82.

17 James G. March and Johan P. Olsen, "The New Institutionalism: Organizational Factors in Political Life," *American Political Science Review* 78.3 (1984); Hall and Taylor, "Political Science."

18 Ira Katznelson, "Periodization and Preferences: Reflections on Purposive Action in Comparative Historical Social Science," in *Comparative Historical Analysis in the Social Sciences*, ed. James Mahoney and Dietrich Rueschemeyer (Cambridge: Cambridge University Press, 2003), 294.

19 Olsen, "Change and Continuity," 9.

20 Thelen and Steinmo, "Historical Institutionalism," 9.

21 Jonas Pontusson, "From Comparative Public Policy to Political Economy: Putting Political Institutions in Their Place and Taking Interests Seriously," *Comparative Political Studies* 28.1 (1995), 136.

22 Michele Boldrin and David K. Levine, *Against Intellectual Monopoly* (Cambridge: Cambridge University Press, 2008).

23 Hay and Wincott, "Structure, Agency and Historical Institutionalism."

24 John L. Campbell, *Institutional Change and Governance* (Princeton: Princeton University Press, 2004); Stephen Bell, "Do We Really Need a New 'Constructivist Institutionalism' to Explain Institutional Change?" *British Journal of Political Science* 41.4 (2011).

25 Campbell, *Institutional Change and Governance*.

26 Baumgartner and Jones, *Agendas and Instability in American Politics*, 7.

27 Ibid., 11, 24–5.

28 Katznelson, "Periodization and Preferences," 296.

29 Baumgartner and Jones, *Agendas and Instability in American Politics*, 11.

30 Ibid., 16.

31 Campbell, *Institutional Change and Governance*, 118.

32 See ibid., 94–110 for a particularly useful taxonomy of ideas.

33 Hay and Wincott, "Structure, Agency and Historical Institutionalism," 955.

34 Hall and Taylor, "Political Science."

35 Campbell, *Institutional Change and Governance*, 8.

36 Paul Pierson, "Increasing Returns, Path Dependence, and the Study of Politics," *American Political Science Review* 94 (2000), 251–2.

37 James Mahoney, "Path Dependence in Historical Sociology," *Theory and Society* 29.4 (2000); Pierson, "Increasing Returns, Path Dependence, and the Study of Politics," 252.

38 Pierson, "Increasing Returns," 251–2.

39 Pierson and Skocpol, "Historical Institutionalism in Contemporary Political Science," 700.

40 Pollack, "The New Institutionalisms and European Integration," 140.

41 Banting, Hoberg, and Simeon, "Introduction," 14–15.

42 Pierson, "The Limits of Design," 482.

43 Ibid., 492. See also North, *Institutions, Institutional Change, and Economic Performance*.

44 Stephen D. Krasner, "Sovereignty: An Institutional Perspective," *Comparative Political Studies* 21.1 (1988), 84.

45 Campbell, *Institutional Change and Governance*, 67; Mahoney, "Path Dependence," 517.

46 Kathleen Thelen, "Historical Institutionalism in Comparative Politics," *Annual Review of Political Science* 2 (1999), 391.

47 Arthur L. Stinchcombe, *Constructing Social Theories* (New York: Harcourt, Brace & World, 1968), 109.

48 Alan Story, "Burn Berne: Why the Leading International Copyright Convention Must Be Repealed," *Houston Law Review* 40.3 (2003).

49 Baumgartner and Jones, *Agendas and Instability in American Politics*, 9.

50 Marie-Laure Djelic and Sigrid Quack, "Overcoming Path Dependency: Path Generation in Open Systems," *Theoretical Sociology* 36 (2007), 163.

51 Rational-choice institutionalism can also yield a finding of historical inefficiency, given the assumption of unequal distribution of resources among actors involved in setting up the institution (North, *Institutions*).

52 Thelen, "Historical Institutionalism," 391.

53 Pollack, "The New Institutionalisms," 140.

54 Krasner, "Sovereignty," 74.

55 Thelen, "Historical Institutionalism," 397.

56 Baumgartner and Jones, *Agendas and Instability in American Politics*, 19.

57 Krasner, "Sovereignty," 66.

58 Thelen and Steinmo, "Historical Institutionalism," 15.

59 Campbell, *Institutional Change and Governance*, 8.

60 Mahoney, "Path Dependence," 511.

61 Streeck and Thelen, "Introduction," 8.

62 Paul Pierson, *Politics in Time: History, Institutions and Social Analysis* (Princeton: Princeton University Press, 2004).

63 Haydu, "Making Use of the Past," 354, 358.

64 Graham Dutfield and Uma Suthersanen, *Global Intellectual Property Law* (Cheltenham: Edward Elgar, 2008).

65 For example, the formal nature of the League of Nations, the predecessor of today's United Nations, could be argued to be a novel innovation. However, even this could perhaps be traced to the Council of Europe, a subject beyond the scope this study.

66 Olsen, "Change and Continuity," 11.

67 Thelen and Steinmo, "Historical Institutionalism," 16–17.

68 Djelic and Quack, "Overcoming Path Dependency," 182.

69 Orren and Skowronek, 2004, *The Search for American Political Development*. See also Archer, *Realist Social Theory*, 227; and Thelen, "Historical Institutionalism," 383.

70 Streeck and Thelen, "Introduction," 19.

71 Ibid., 19; Olsen, "Change and Continuity," 15.

72 Olsen, "Change and Continuity," 13.

73 Campbell, *Institutional Change and Governance*, 58.

74 Thelen, "Historical Institutionalism," 385.

75 Streeck and Thelen, "Introduction"; see also Steven Levitsky and María Victoria Murillo, "Variation in Institutional Strength," 12 *Annual Review of Political Science* 12 (2009), 115.

76 Levitsky and Murillo, "Variation in Institutional Strength," 115.

77 Campbell, *Institutional Change and Governance*, 69–73.

78 Baumgartner and Jones, *Agendas and Instability in American Politics*, 31–2.

79 Campbell, *Institutional Change and Governance*, 65.

80 Peter Drahos and John Braithwaite, *Information Feudalism: Who Owns the Knowledge Economy?* (London: Earthscan Publications Ltd, 2002). All IP owners, including patent and copyright holders, have exploited this trade-IP nexus.

81 T.R. Voss, "Institutions," in *International Encyclopedia of the Social and Behavioral Sciences* (Cambridge: Cambridge University Press, 2001), 7561.

3. The Political Economy of Copyright

1 Cited in Stan Liebowitz, "MP3s and Copyright Collectives: A Cure Worse than the Disease?" in *Developments in the Economics of Copyright: Research and Analysis*, ed. Lisa N. Takeyama, Wendy J. Gordon, and Ruth Towse (Cheltenham: Edward Elgar Publishing Ltd, 2005), 37.

2 A. Claire Cutler, "Gramsci, Law, and the Culture of Global Capitalism," *Critical Review of International Social and Political Philosophy* 8.4 (2005), 532.

3 Australia, Canada, the European Union, Japan, the Republic of Korea, Mexico, Morocco, New Zealand, Singapore, Switzerland, and the United States.

4 Its full title is "An Act for the Encouragement of Learning, by vesting the Copies of Printed Books in the Authors or purchasers of such Copies, during the Times therein mentioned." For accounts of the introduction of copyright in Great Britain, see Drahos, *A Philosophy of Intellectual Property*; Mark Rose, *Authors and Owners: The Invention of Copyright* (Cambridge: Harvard University Press, 1993); and Ronald V. Bettig, *Copyrighting Culture: The Political Economy of Intellectual Property*, (Boulder, CO: Westview Press, 1996), 14–22, among others.

5 Again, while the Statute of Anne typically is taken as the starting point for modern copyright laws, the statute itself emerged from a specific historical and material situation, as a response to the creation of the printing press and the popularization of Enlightenment ideals around individuality, shaped by the historically dominant role of publishers in Great Britain.

6 Christopher May, *Digital Rights Management: The Problem of Expanding Ownership Rights* (Oxford: Chandos Publishing, 2007), 27.

7 Jessica Litman, "The Public Domain," *Emory Law Journal* 39 (1990), http://www.law.duke.edu/pd/papers/Litman_background.pdf.

8 Dutfield and Suthersanen, *Global Intellectual Property Law*, 63–4. On the Romantic notion of the author, see Rose, *Authors and Owners*; Kembrew McLeod, *Owning Culture: Authorship, Ownership and Intellectual Property Law* (New York: Peter Lang, 2001); Henry C. Mitchell, Jr, *The Intellectual Commons: Toward an Ecology of Intellectual Property* (Lanham, MD: Lexington Books, 2005); Robert H. Rotstein, "Beyond Metaphor: Copyright Infringement and the Fiction of the Work," *Chicago-Kent Law Review* 68.2 (1993); Litman, "The Public Domain"; Joost Smiers, "The Abolition of Copyright: Better for Artists, the Third World, and the Public Domain," *International Communications Gazette* 62.5 (2000); and Drahos, *A Philosophy of Intellectual Property*.

9 Sell, *Private Power, Public Law*, 24. On this point, see also May, *A Global Political Economy of Intellectual Property Rights*, 53; and Rosemary J. Coombe, *The Cultural Life of Intellectual Properties: Authorship, Appropriation, and the Law* (Durham: Duke University Press, 1998).

10 Justin Hughes, "Notes on the Origin of 'Intellectual Property': Revised Conclusions and New Sources," Benjamin N. Cardozo School of Law, Jacob Burns Institute for Advanced Legal Studies working paper 265 (2009);

Justin Hughes, "Copyright and Incomplete Historiographies: Of Piracy, Propertization, and Thomas Jefferson," *Southern California Law Review* 79 (2006); Martin Kretschemer and Friedmann Kawohl, "The History and Philosophy of Copyright," in *Music and Copyright*, 2nd ed., ed. Simon Frith and Lee Marshall (Edinburgh: Edinburgh University Press, 2004); and May, *A Global Political Economy*.

11 Drahos, *A Philosophy of Intellectual Property*, 15.

12 For a discussion of the rhetoric of piracy, see chapter 2 of Drahos and Braithwaite, *Information Feudalism*; May, *A Global Political Economy*; Hughes 2006; Gervais 2005; and Jane C. Ginsburg, "Copyright and Control over New Technologies of Dissemination," *Columbia Law Review* 101 no. 7 (2001). For a discussion of property rhetoric see Hughes, "Copyright and Incomplete Historiographies" and Hughes 2009.

13 Rose, *Authors and Owners*, 142; May, *A Global Political Economy*, 178.

14 Notable exceptions in the literature include Boldrin and Levine, *Against Intellectual Monopoly*, from an economics perspective; Bettig, *Copyrighting Culture* from a Marxist perspective; and Story, "Burn Berne" and Smiers, "The Abolition of Copyright" from a developmental/social justice perspective.

15 Raymond Ku, Jiayang Sun, and Yiying Fan, "Does Copyright Law Promote Creativity? An Empirical Analysis of Copyright's Bounty," *Vanderbilt Law Review* 63 (2009); Ruth Towse, "Copyright and Economic Incentives: An Application to Performers' Rights in the Music Industry," *Kyklos* 52.3 (1999), 369.

16 Wendy J. Gordon and Robert G. Bone, "Copyright," in *Encyclopedia of Law and Economics*, vol. 2, chap. 1610, ed. Boudewijn Bouckaert and Gerrit De Geest (Cheltenham: Edward Elgar, 2000), 181.

17 William Patry, *Moral Panics and the Copyright Wars* (Oxford: Oxford University Press, 2010).

18 Drahos, *A Philosophy of Intellectual Property*, 123. *The Economics of Intellectual Property*, ed. Towse and Holzhauer, vol. 1, offers a useful survey of theoretical and empirical economic approaches to intellectual property and copyright.

19 J.S.G. Boggs, "Who Owns This?" *Chicago-Kent Law Review* 68.2 (1993); Robert M. Hurt and Robert M. Schuman, "The Economic Rationale of Copyright," *American Economic Review* 56, nos. 1–2 (1966), 425–6. For arguments against the need for copyright see Boldrin and Levine, *Against Intellectual Monopoly*; Michele Boldrin and David K. Levine, "The Case against Intellectual Property," *Research on Innovation* 2 (2002), http://www.researchoninnovation.org/tiip/archive/issue2003_2.html; Stanley M. Besen, "Intellectual Property," in

The New Palgrave Dictionary of Economics and the Law, vol. 2, ed. Peter New-man (London: Macmillan, 1998); and Lawrence Lessig, *The Future of Ideas: The Fate of the Commons in a Connected World* (New York: Random House, 2001). For discussions of intellectual production in the absence of copyright, also see Boldrin and Levine, *Against Intellectual Monopoly* and Boyle *The Public Domain*. For a list of conditions under which copyright would not be needed to limit copying see Landes and Posner, "An Economic Analysis of Copyright Law." Hurt and Schuman, "The Economic Rationale of Copy-right" offer a neoclassical economics argument against copyright under many circumstances. Even Kenneth Arrow, "Economic Welfare and the Allocation of Resources for Invention," in *The Rate and Direction of Inventive Activity: Economic and Social Factors* (Princeton: Princeton University Press, 1962), http://www.litagion.org/pubs/papers/2006/P1856.pdf, which pres-ents a defence of copyright as a necessary evil, somewhat surprisingly con-cludes with a call for further research into alternative commercial regimes that may be able to deliver creative works without copyright's pernicious monopoly effects.

20 Debora J. Halbert, *Resisting Intellectual Property* (New York: Routledge, 2005), 8.

21 May, *Digital Rights Management*, 27.

22 On all three, see Drahos, *A Philosophy of Intellectual Property* and May, *A Global Political Economy*. On "just deserts," see May, *A Global Political Economy*, 25; Hughes "The Philosophy of Intellectual Property"; Gordon, "An Inquiry into the Merits of Copyright"; Edwin C. Hettinger, "Justify-ing Intellectual Property," *Philosophy & Public Affairs* 18.1 (1989), 40–1; and Hurt and Schuman, "The Economic Rationale of Copyright," 424. On "per-sonality," see Justin Hughes, "The Philosophy of Intellectual Property," in *Intellectual Property: Moral, Legal, and International Dilemmas*, ed. Adam D. Moore (Lanham, MD: Rowman & Littlefield Publishers, 1997); originally published in *Georgetown Law Journal* 287 (1988). Against "just deserts," see Russell Hardin, "Valuing Intellectual Property," *Chicago-Kent Law Review* 68.2 (1993), 669–70. For a wide-ranging discussion of this issue, see the entirety of *Chicago-Kent Law Review* 68.2 (1993), 583–888.

23 Timothy J. Brennan, "Copyright, Property, and the Right to Deny," *Chicago-Kent Law Review* 68.2 (1993), 681.

24 Drahos, *A Philosophy of Intellectual Property*, 4.

25 Cited in May, *The World Intellectual Property Organization*, 36. See McLeod, *Owning Culture* for a discussion of the effects of the commodification of knowledge; Gordon, "An Inquiry into the Merits of Copyright" offers an interesting ahistorical/natural rights view of property.

26 May, *The World Intellectual Property Organization*, 21; McLeod, *Owning Culture*, 9.

27 Drahos, *A Philosophy of Intellectual Property*, 213–18.

28 Jeremy Waldron, "From Authors to Copiers: Individual Rights and Social Values in Intellectual Property," *Chicago-Kent Law Review* 68.2 (1993), 887.

29 Gervais, "The Purpose of Copyright Law in Canada," 324.

30 Dutfield and Suthersanen, *Global Intellectual Property Law*, 68.

31 Handa, *Copyright Law in Canada*, 43.

32 Drahos and Braithwaite, *Information Feudalism*, ix–x.

33 A historical example is offered by Michael W. Carroll, "The Struggle for Music Copyright," Villanova University School of Law working paper 31 (2005). He argues that British musicians were late to demand a performance right around the time of the Statute of Anne because "composers and publishers had not come to see the intangible musical work as the resource that could be the subject of property rights because they still had a more limited conception of printed music as the resource that appropriately could be the subject of exclusive rights." In other words, it was not clear to them that music was equivalent to books, and thus amenable to copyright.

34 See Reuben E. Slesinger, Robert W. Frase, and Armen A. Alchian. "Discussion," *American Economic Review* 56, nos. 1–2 (1966) for a defence of copyright along these lines; see Gordon, "An Inquiry into the Merits of Copyright" for a discussion of potential alternatives to copyright.

35 Stephen Breyer, "The Uneasy Case for Copyright: A Study of Copyright in Books, Photocopies, and Computer Programs," *Harvard Law Review* 84.2 (1970), 322.

36 For examples of various categorizations of interest groups, see Doern and Sharaput *Canadian Intellectual Property*; Benkler, "A Political Economy of the Public Domain"; and Teresa Scassa, "Interests in the Balance," in *In the Public Interest: The Future of Canadian Copyright Law*, ed. Michael Geist (Toronto: Irwin Law, 2005).

37 Sony Music Entertainment, Universal Music, Warner Music Group, and EMI.

38 Karaganis, "Disciplining Markets in the Digital Age," 224.

39 Sell, *Private Power, Public Law*; Drahos and Braithwaite, *Information Feudalism*.

40 ACPM, http://www.apcm.org.mx/index.php?item=menuapcm&contenido=main.

41 Drahos and Braithwaite, *Information Feudalism*, 175.

42 AMPROFON, http://www.amprofon.com.mx/amprofon.php?item=menuAmprofon&contenido=perfil.

43 Simon Doyle, *Prey to Thievery* (Ottawa: Simon Doyle, 2006), 17. In 2011 CRIA changed its name to Music Canada.

44 Sell, *Private Power, Public Law*, 82, 84.

45 John Sinclair, "Culture and Trade: Some Theoretical and Practical Considerations," in *Mass Media and Free Trade: NAFTA and the Cultural Industries*, ed. Emile G. McAnany and Kenton T. Wilkinson (Austin: University of Texas Press, 1996), 46.

46 Simon Frith and Lee Marshall, "Making Sense of Copyright," in *Music and Copyright*, 2nd ed., ed. S. Frith and L. Marshall (Edinburgh: Edinburgh University Press, 2004), 14.

47 F.M. Scherer, "The Innovation Lottery," in *Expanding the Boundaries of Intellectual Property: Innovation Policy for the Knowledge Society*, ed. Rochelle Cooper Dreyfuss, Diane Leenheer Zimmerman, and Harry First (Oxford: Oxford University Press, 2001), 22.

48 Benkler, "A Political Economy of the Public Domain," 279–84.

49 Arnold Plant, "The Economic Aspects of Copyright in Books," *Economica*, n.s., 1.2 (1934), 189.

50 Ibid., 189.

51 Boldrin and Levine, *Against Intellectual Monopoly*, 33.

52 Michael A. Carrier, "Copyright and Innovation: The Untold Story," *Wisconsin Law Review* (2012), 812.

53 de Beer, "Copyright and Innovation in the Networked Information Economy," 4.

54 Karaganis, "Disciplining Markets in the Digital Age," 224–5.

55 "Rip. Mix. Burn," *The Economist*, 2 July 2005.

56 Dutfield and Suthersanen, *Global Intellectual Property Law*, 234–5. It would actually be more accurate to say that the distribution of digital works "undermines the ability of creators and rights owners to derive profits from their own works" *under the existing copy-based business model.*

57 Laura J. Murray, "Copyright Talk: Patterns and Pitfalls in Canadian Policy Discourses," in *In the Public Interest*, ed. Geist, 26.

58 Tarleton Gillespie, "Price Discrimination and the Shape of the Digital Commodity," in *Structures of Participation in Digital Culture*, ed. Joe Karaganis (New York: Social Science Research Council, 2007), 249.

59 Paul Goldstein, *Copyright's Highway: From Gutenberg to the Celestial Jukebox* (Stanford: Stanford Law and Politics, 2003), 170.

60 Jessica Litman, *Digital Copyright* (Amherst, NY: Prometheus Books, 2006), 14.

61 Hurt and Schuman, "The Economic Rationale of Copyright," 425–6.

62 May, *The World Intellectual Property Organization*, 100. For specific examples of the creator/publisher imbalance under copyright, see Steve Albini, "The

Problem with Music," *Maximumrocknroll* 133 (1994), http://www
.arancidamoeba.com/mrr/problemwithmusic.html; and Boldrin and
Levine, *Against Intellectual Monopoly*, 106.

63 David Lowery, "Meet the New Boss, Worse than the Old Boss?"
The Trichordist, 15 April 2012, http://thetrichordist.wordpress.
com/2012/04/15/meet-the-new-boss-worse-than-the-old-boss-full-post/
offers a musician's critical take on the benefits of the old system versus the
current digital free-for-all.

64 Details available at http://www.kickstarter.com/projects/amandapalmer/
amanda-palmer-the-new-record-art-book-and-tour.

65 Details available at http://www.kickstarter.com/projects/breadpig/
to-be-or-not-to-be-that-is-the-adventure.

66 NPR staff, "Metric: A Rock Band Declares Independence," NPR, 30 June
2012, http://www.npr.org/2012/06/30/155968897/metric-a-rock-band-
declares-independence.

67 Jonathan Coulton, "Emily and David," blog post, 20 June 2012, http://
www.jonathancoulton.com/2012/06/20/emily-and-david/.

68 Benkler, "A Political Economy of the Public Domain."

69 Netanel, *Copyright's Paradox*.

70 Tarleton Gillespie, *Wired Shut: Copyright and the Shape of Digital Culture*
(Cambridge, MA: MIT Press, 2007).

71 Story, "Burn Berne," 800.

72 Knowledge Ecology International, "Timeline of Privileges regarding the
Commercialization and use of Knowledge. Part 2: 1980 to 1999," http://
keionline.org/timeline-from-2000.

73 Knowledge Ecology International, "Access to Medical Technologies,"
http://www.keionline.org/a2m.

74 CPTech, "Draft Treaty on Access to Knowledge," 9 May 2005, http://
www.cptech.org/a2k/a2k_treaty_may9.pdf. The draft treaty was actually
created by the Consumer Project on Technology (CPTech), whose staff and
work program were absorbed by the newly created Knowledge Ecology
International. Knowledge Ecology International, "KEI Mission," http://
www.keionline.org/node/15.

75 As discussed in chapter 8, until 2011 Mexico treated copyright as an apolitical, technical issue.

76 Geist, "Introduction," in *In the Public Interest*, ed. Geist, 10.

77 Litman, *Digital Copyright*, 19.

78 Greg Sandoval, "For RIAA, a Black Eye Comes with the Job," CNET News,
9 October 2007, http://news.cnet.com/For-RIAA,-a-black-eye-comes-
with-the-job/2100-1027_3-6212374.html.

79 Mike Masnick, "RIAA Spent $17.6 Million in Lawsuits … to Get $391,000 in Settlements?" Techdirt, 14 July 2010, http://www.techdirt.com/articles/20100713/17400810200.shtml.

80 Rick Burgess, "$222,000 Award Upheld in RIAA v. Jammie Thomas-Rasset Lawsuit," Techspot.com, 12 September 2012, http://www.techspot.com/news/50132-220000-award-upheld-in-riaa-v-jammie-thomas-rasset-lawsuit.html.

81 Geist, "Introduction," 1.

82 Karaganis, "Disciplining Markets in the Digital Age," 228.

83 Gervais, "The Purpose of Copyright Law in Canada," 329.

84 "A Fine Balance," *The Economist*, 25 January 2003.

85 Karaganis, "Disciplining Markets in the Digital Age," 224.

86 Ibid., 226.

87 de Beer, "Copyright and Innovation in the Networked Information Economy," 8.

88 Sell, *Private Power, Public Law*, 5.

89 Carsten Fink and Keith E. Maskus, "Why We Study Intellectual Property Rights and What We Have Learned," in *Intellectual Property and Development*, ed. C. Fink and K.E. Maskus (Washington: World Bank, 2005), 3, 5.

90 Chang, "Kicking away the Ladder."

91 Discussed later in this chapter and in chapter 4.

92 Sell, *Private Power, Public Law*, 9.

93 Drahos and Braithwaite, *Information Feudalism*, 75.

94 Keith E. Maskus, "Lessons from Studying the International Economics of Intellectual Property Rights," *Vanderbilt Law Review* (2000), 2221–2.

95 Cited in Dutfield and Suthersanen, *Global Intellectual Property Law*, 8.

96 Ibid., 5.

97 These data focus on intellectual property generally, not copyright. Furthermore, studies such as Fink and Maskus ("Why We Study Intellectual Property Rights"), and indeed most studies of "intellectual property" in developing countries, often concentrate on patents and treat copyright as an afterthought. An international comparison of the material and economic effects of copyright alone, while beyond the scope of this book, would be very useful. However, as Ku, Sun, and Fan ("Does Copyright Law Promote Creativity?") note, there has been very little study of the empirical effects of stronger or weaker copyright laws.

98 Rushton, "Economic Impact of WIPO Ratification," 8.

99 Boldrin and Levine (*Against Intellectual Monopoly*, 130) remark that "according to the RIAA, the value of all CDs, live presentations, music videos, and DVDs in 1998 in the U.S. was $13.72 billion. In 1998 the business

receipts of the computer and electronic product manufacturing including both hardware and software was $560.27 billion. In other words, the computer industry has an economic value over 40 times as large as that of the 'copyright' industry. Indeed, IBM's (worldwide) sales in 2000 alone were $88 billion – over six times the size of the entire U.S. 'copyright' market."

100 Doern and Sharaput, *Canadian Intellectual Property*, 20.

101 Steve Jones, "Mass Communication, Intellectual Property Rights, International Trade, and the Popular Music Industry," in *Mass Media and Free Trade: NAFTA and the Cultural Industries*, ed. Emile G. McAnany and Kenton T. Wilkinson (Austin: University of Texas Press, 1996), 345–6.

102 May, *A Global Political Economy*, 44.

103 Drahos and Braithwaite, *Information Feudalism*; Sell, *Private Power, Public Law*.

104 See Sam Ricketson and Jane C. Ginsburg, *International Copyright and Neighbouring Rights: The Berne Convention and Beyond*, 2nd ed., vols. 1 and 2 (Oxford: Oxford University Press, 2006), for a definitive history of the Berne Conventions and WIPO; see May, *The World Intellectual Property Organization* for a critical history of WIPO.

105 World Intellectual Property Organization (WIPO), "What Is WIPO?" (2009), http://www.wipo.int/about-wipo/en/what/.

106 World Intellectual Property Organization (WIPO), "Core Tasks of WIPO" (2009), http://www.wipo.int/about-wipo/en/what/core_tasks.html.

107 May, *The World Intellectual Property Organization*, 13.

108 Dave Laing, "Copyright, Politics and the International Music Industry," in *Music and Copyright*, 2nd ed., ed. Simon Frith and Lee Marshall (Edinburgh: Edinburgh University Press, 2004), 73.

109 Sell, *Private Power, Public Law*, 11.

110 Dutfield and Suthersanen, *Global Intellectual Property Law*, 26.

111 Ibid., 27.

112 Ibid., 26–7.

113 Myra J. Tawfik, "International Copyright Law: W[h]ither User Rights?" in *In the Public Interest*, ed. Geist, 73–5.

114 May, *The World Intellectual Property Organization*, 13.

115 Ibid., 74.

116 Ibid., 1.

117 Ibid., 75.

118 Ibid., 2.

119 Doern and Sharaput, *Canadian Intellectual Property*, 76. For an exhaustive discussion of the WIPO-administered treaties, see Ricketson and Ginsburg, *International Copyright and Neighbouring Rights*; see also Laing, "Copyright, Politics and the International Music Industry."

120 May, *The World Intellectual Property Organization*, 56.

121 ACTA is discussed in greater detail in chapter 6 and 8.

122 Sell, *Private Power, Public Law*, 5.

123 Chapter 4 will return to this issue in its domestic context.

124 Gigi Sohn, president and co-founder, Public Knowledge, interview by author, Washington, DC, 5 August 2008.

125 Sell, *Private Power, Public Law*, 13.

126 That is, those dependent on copyrights and patents, such as the pharmaceutical, software, and entertainment industries.

127 Drahos and Braithwaite, *Information Feudalism*, xi. Specifically, the Jackson-Vanik amendment applies to non-market economies such as the former Soviet Union and "requires compliance with its specific free-emigration criteria in order to receive certain economic benefits from the United States" (Vladimir Pregeli, "The Jackson-Vanik Amendment: A Survey," CRS Report for Congress 98-545 [Washington: Congressional Research Service, 1998], http://www.fas.org/sgp/crs/row/98-545.pdf). It also requires that a bilateral commercial agreement, including adequate protection of intellectual property rights, be concluded before such a country can be granted Most Favored Nation status (United States, "Most-favored-nation status – MFN," U.S. Department of State Dispatch [17 September 1990], http://findarticles.com/p/articles/mi_m1584/is_n3_v1/ai_9079866/).

128 Dutfield and Suthersanen, *Global Intellectual Property Law*, 32.

129 Sell, *Private Power, Public Law*, 37, 50.

130 Dutfield and Suthersanen, *Global Intellectual Property Law*, 32.

131 Cited in Drahos and Braithwaite, *Information Feudalism*, 61.

132 Sell, *Private Power, Public Law*, 1.

133 As of 1986, the IPC consisted of Bristol-Myers, CBS, Du Pont, General Electric, GM, Hewlett-Packard, IBM, Johnson & Johnson, Merck, Monsanto, and Pfizer (Sell, *Private Power, Public Law*, 2).

134 Drahos and Braithwaite, *Information Feudalism*, 10.

135 Peter Drahos, "The US, China and the G-77 in the Era of Responsive Patentability," in *Global Perspectives on Patent Law*, ed. Margo Bagley and Ruth Okediji (Oxford: Oxford University Press, 2012).

136 See, e.g., Keith E. Maskus, *Intellectual Property Rights in the Global Economy* (Washington: Institute for International Economics, 2000).

137 Data are from the US Census Bureau, US International Trade in Goods and Services, Annual revision for 2007, Exhibit 6 (10 June 2008).

138 Jonathan Band, Intellectual-property lawyer, interview by author, Washington, DC, 20 June 2008.

139 Drahos and Braithwaite, *Information Feudalism*, 87.

140 Sell, *Private Power, Public Law*, 190–1.

141 Drahos and Braithwaite, *Information Feudalism*, 88–9.

142 Ibid., 86, 90.

143 Maryse Robert, *Negotiating NAFTA: Explaining the Outcome in Culture, Textiles, Autos, and Pharmaceuticals* (Toronto: University of Toronto Press, 2001).

144 United States, "2010 Special 301 Report," Office of the United States Trade Representative, 30 April 2010, http://www.ustr.gov/webfm_send/1906, 47.

145 Stephen D. Cohen, Robert A. Blecker, and Peter D. Whitney, *Fundamentals of U.S. Foreign Trade Policy: Economics, Politics, Laws, and Issues*, 2nd ed. (Boulder: Westview Press, 2003), 175.

146 James A.R. Nafzinger, "NAFTA's Regime for Intellectual Property: In the Mainstream of Public International Law," *Houston Journal of International Law* 19 (Spring 1997), http://www.bibliojuridica.org/libros/2/950/25 .pdf.

147 Drahos and Braithwaite, *Information Feudalism*, 96–7.

148 Ibid., 107.

149 Ibid., 96–7.

150 Stan McCoy, Assistant US Trade Representative for Intellectual Property and Innovation, Office of the United States Trade Representative, interview by author, Washington, DC, 8 August 2008.

151 Drahos and Braithwaite, *Information Feudalism*, 97.

152 Computer and Communications Industry Association (CCIA), "Comments of the Computer and Communications Industry Association before the United States Trade Representative re 2010 Special 301 Review," Docket no. USTR-2010-0003, 2010, http://www.ccianet.org/CCIA/files/ccLibraryFiles/Filename/000000000321/CCIA-2010-Spec301-cmts.pdf, 3.

153 Sohn, interview.

154 Canada was joined on this list by Algeria, Argentina, Chile, China, India, Indonesia, Pakistan, Russia, Thailand, and Venezuela.

155 Mexico was joined on this list by Belarus, Bolivia, Brazil, Brunei, Colombia, Costa Rica, the Dominican Republic, Ecuador, Egypt, Finland, Greece, Guatemala, Italy, Jamaica, Kuwait, Lebanon, Malaysia, Norway, Peru, the Philippines, Romania, Spain, Tajikistan, Turkey, Turkmenistan, Ukraine, Uzbekistan, and Vietnam.

156 Drahos and Braithwaite, *Information Feudalism*, 11. Sell (*Private Power, Public Law*, 37) remarks that developing countries asked for, and received, the phase-out of the Multi-Fiber Agreement, which protected U.S. textile

interests, in return. For background on the concerns and objectives of developing and developed countries with respect to the TRIPS negotiations, see Nikolaus Thumm, *Intellectual Property Rights: National Systems and Harmonisation in Europe* (New York: Physica-Verlag, 2000), 63–4.

157 Dutfield and Suthersanen, *Global Intellectual Property Law*, 33.

158 Towse and Holzhauer, "Introduction," xviii.

159 Hughes, "The Philosophy of Intellectual Property"; Thumm, *Intellectual Property Rights*, 63–4.

160 Drahos and Braithwaite, *Information Feudalism*, 192–4.

161 Maskus, *Intellectual Property Rights in the Global Economy*, 16.

162 Doern and Sharaput, *Canadian Intellectual Property*, 10, 20. Dutfield and Suthersanen, *Global Intellectual Property Law*, 34, caution against seeing TRIPS as something that was simply imposed on the world. Europe and the United States disagreed on several parts of it, and developing countries "were much more involved in the drafting than they are often given credit for," getting concessions in 10 out of 73 articles.

163 Sell, *Private Power, Public Law*, 7–8.

164 Frith and Marshall, "Making Sense of Copyright," 13.

165 World Trade Organization, "Members and Observers," http://www.wto .org/english/thewto_e/whatis_e/tif_e/org6_e.htm.

166 Maskus, *Intellectual Property Rights in the Global Economy*, 18.

167 Kretschmer and Kawohl, "The History and Philosophy of Copyright," 41.

168 Tawfik, "International Copyright Law," 77–8.

169 Myra J. Tawfik, "Intellectual Property Laws in Harmony with NAFTA: The Courts as Mediators between the Global and the Local," *Canadian Journal of Law and Technology* 2.3 (2003), 213.

170 Handa, *Copyright Law in Canada*, 416.

171 Chapter 8 discusses Mexico's decision to accept US copyright demands.

172 Jones, "Mass Communication, Intellectual Property Rights."

173 Article 6bis of the 1971 text of the Berne Convention provides authors with inalienable moral rights.

174 As will be seen in chapter 5, Mexico also had a strong domestic lobby for copyright reform. This does not change the fact, however, that the reorientation of Mexican copyright law was a US demand.

175 Robert, *Negotiating NAFTA*, 52–3.

176 Keith Acheson and Christopher J. Maule, "Copyright, Contract, the Cultural Industries, and NAFTA," in *Mass Media and Free Trade: NAFTA and the Cultural Industries*, ed. Emile G. McAnany and Kenton T. Wilkinson (Austin: University of Texas Press, 1996), 369.

177 Doern and Sharaput, *Canadian Intellectual Property*, 106.

178 Jones, "Mass Communication, Intellectual Property Rights," 345–6.
179 Acheson and Maule, "Copyright, Contract, the Cultural Industries, and NAFTA," 369.
180 Gordon Mace, "Introduction," in *Regionalism and the State: NAFTA and Foreign Policy Convergence*, ed. G. Mace (Hampshire: Ashgate, 2008), 8.
181 Stephen Clarkson, *Uncle Sam and Us: Globalization, Neoconservatism, and the Canadian State* (Toronto: University of Toronto Press, 2002).
182 Blayne Haggart, "Analysis of the Security and Prosperity Partnership of North America's Report to Leaders" (Ottawa: Parliamentary Information and Research Service, 2005); Luiza Ch. Savage, "Meet NAFTA 2.0," *Maclean's*, 13 September 2006, http://www.macleans.ca/topstories/canada/article.jsp?content=20060911_133202_133202.
183 Email obtained under the Access to Information Act from Douglas George (DFAIT) to Bruce Stockfish (Canadian Heritage) and Susan Bincoletto (Industry Canada), "Canada's Proposed Commitments under SPP re. International Agreement," 27 May 2005; file no. ATIP PCH ATI 232-ATI-05/06-250, p. 712.
184 United States, "Security and Prosperity Partnership of North America (SPP) Intellectual Property Rights Action Strategy" (2007), http://www.spp.gov/pdf/spp_ip_strat_final.pdf.
185 See chapter 7.
186 Campbell, *Institutional Change and Governance*, 86.
187 Carroll, "The Struggle for Music Copyright," 910.
188 Gillespie, *Wired Shut*, 69.

4. The United States, the Internet Treaties, and the Setting of the Digital-Copyright Agenda

1 Sell, *Private Power, Public Law*, 5.
2 For a timeline of key revisions to US copyright law, see Association of Research Libraries, *Copyright Timeline: A History of Copyright in the United States*, http://www.arl.org/pp/ppcopyright/copyresources/copytimeline.shtml.
3 While copyright is a federal responsibility, some states legislate in this area. These cases, however, do not affect the overall direction of US copyright nor are they relevant for the implementation of the Internet treaties.
4 Gillespie, *Wired Shut*, 22.
5 As a reminder, bricolage refers to the recombination of "locally available institutional principles and practices in ways that yield change." It can be either "substantive" ("the recombination of already existing institutional

principles and practices to address [substantive] problems and thus follows a logic of instrumentality") or "symbolic," involving "the recombination of symbolic principles and practices" (Campbell, *Institutional Change and Governance*, 69). "Bricolage" shares many similarities with the "policy streams" view of policymaking in the American Political Development field (see especially John Kingdon, *Agendas, Alternatives, and Public Policies*, 2nd ed. [New York: Longman, 2003]). In this approach, identified problems, policies, and political considerations exist independently. Successful "policy entrepreneurs" (or actors) are able to get their preferred policies enacted by linking them to identified problems and political considerations.

6 Howard Knopf, "The Annual '301' Show – USTR Calls for Comment – 21 Reasons Why Canadian Copyright Law Is Already Stronger than USA's," *Excess Copyright*, 17 February 2010, http://excesscopyright.blogspot.com/2010/02/annual-301-parade-ustr-calls-for.html.

7 Sell, *Private Power, Public Law*, 60.

8 Ibid., 61.

9 Charles M. Cameron and Rebecca Morton, "Formal Theory Meets Data," in *Political Science: The State of the Discipline*, ed. Ira Katznelson and Helen V. Milner (New York: WW Norton & Co., 2002), 788. See also David Truman, *The Governmental Process* (New York: Knopf, 1951).

10 Orren and Skowronek, *The Search for American Political Development*, 18.

11 Litman, *Digital Copyright*.

12 Ibid., 36.

13 Chapter 3 examined those US institutions with a direct responsibility for US international copyright policy.

14 United States, "United States Copyright Office: A Brief Introduction and History," http://www.copyright.gov/circs/circ1a.html.

15 Ibid.

16 Patent and Trademark Office, "The U.S. PTO: Who We Are," http://www.uspto.gov/about/index.jsp.

17 On whom much more in chapters 5 and 6.

18 Seth Greenstein, lawyer, Constantine Cannon LLP, interview by author, Washington, DC, 9 July 2008.

19 Cited in Bill D. Herman and Oscar H. Gandy, Jr, "Catch 1201: A Legislative History and Content Analysis of the DMCA Exemption Proceedings," *Cardozo Arts & Entertainment Law Journal* 24 (2006), 138.

20 Jennifer Schneider, legislative counsel, Rep. Rick Boucher (D-VA), interview by author, Washington, DC, July 25, 2008.

21 Both Berman and Boucher were active in the DMCA debate. Rick Boucher was defeated in the 2010 mid-term elections.

22 Band, interview. Reverse engineering refers to the process of taking some-
    thing apart (hardware or software) in order to determine how it works. It
    is an important means to realize innovations and, in the case of computer
    programs, to allow for interoperability across computer systems.
23 Jeff Turner, intellectual property lawyer, Patton Boggs, interview by au-
    thor, Washington, DC, 2 July 2008.
24 Greenstein, interview.
25 Laing, "Copyright, Politics and the International Music Industry," 78.
26 Boldrin and Levine, *Against Intellectual Monopoly*, 251.
27 Mike Masnick, "Congress Brings Back Recently Removed 'IP Subcommit-
    tee' Now That Copyright Reformer Won't Lead It," *Techdirt*, 22 December
    2010, http://www.techdirt.com/articles/20101220/23143712353/
    congress-brings-back-recently-removed-ip-subcommittee-now-that-
    copyright-reformer-wont-lead-it.shtml.
28 Thanks to Michael Petricone, senior vice-president of government affairs,
    Consumer Electronics Association, interview by author, Washington, DC,
    14 August 2008, for the analogy.
29 Litman, *Digital Copyright*, 39–41.
30 Campbell, *Institutional Change and Governance*, 86.
31 Litman, *Digital Copyright*, 25.
32 Ibid., 47–8.
33 Ibid., 23.
34 Keith Kupferschmid, senior vice-president for intellectual property policy
    and enforcement, Software and Information Industry Association, inter-
    view by author, Washington, DC, 1 July 2008.
35 Gillespie, *Wired Shut*, 22.
36 Doern and Sharaput, *Canadian Intellectual Property*.
37 While more important in later years, the ESA was not active significantly
    in the run-up to the 1998 DMCA.
38 Kingdon, *Agendas, Alternatives, and Public Policies*, 46–53.
39 Defined as "those industries whose primary purpose is to create, produce,
    distribute or exhibit copyright materials. These industries include books,
    newspapers and periodicals, motion pictures, recorded music (including
    both music and sound recordings), radio and television broadcasting, and
    computer software (including both business applications and entertain-
    ment software) equipment whose function is primarily to facilitate the
    creation, production, or use of works of copyrighted matter" (Stephen E.
    Siweck, "Copyright Industries in the U.S. Economy: The 2011 Report,"
    Washington, International Intellectual Property Alliance, 2011, http://
    www.iipa.com/pdf/2011CopyrightIndustriesReport.PDF, 8). Because

· these data are produced by an interested industry organization, they should be taken with a healthy dose of scepticism. The Computer and Communications Industries Association ("Comments of the Computer & Communications Industry Association," 18) has fired back at the IIPA with its own statistics, claiming that in 2009 "fair use" industries – those that depend on limitations built into the Copyright Act rather than on copyright itself – contributed $4.5 trillion to the US economy ($2.5 trillion from "core" and $1.9 trillion from "non-core").

40 Siweck, "Copyright Industries in the U.S. Economy," 4. Total content industries are defined as the core industries plus "industries in which only some aspect or portion of the products that they create they can quality for copyright protection," which "range from fabric to jewellery to furniture to toys and games," and "industries that distribute both copyright and non-copyright protected materials to business and consumers. Examples here include transportation services, telecommunications and wholesale and retail trade … Only a portion of the total value added by these [latter] industries is considered to be part of the content industries" (ibid., 8). This definition is even more permissive than that of "core" industries, bringing in industries with only a peripheral relationship to copyright and whose views on copyright are not necessarily consistent with those of the traditional content industries.

41 Data from http://www.opensecrets.org.

42 Schneider, interview.

43 Motion-picture industry official, interview by author, Washington, DC, 18 July 2008.

44 Greenstein, interview.

45 Halbert, *Resisting Intellectual Property*, 8.

46 Patry, *Moral Panics and the Copyright Wars*.

47 Cited ibid., 145.

48 In terms of Kingdon's (*Agendas*) "policy streams" model, the content industries (policy entrepreneurs) were able to use their resources to link their preferred policy (stronger copyright protection) to a perceived problem (waning US economic competitiveness) and to exploit the national concern about economic competitiveness to convince Congress (the political "stream") to place strong copyright at the very heart of the US trade agenda. In Kingdon's jargon, concerns about declining US economic power opened a "policy window" that allowed these groups to promote successfully their preferred policy option.

49 All figures are current dollars.

50 Figures from US Census Bureau, *2010 Statistical Abstract*, http://www
    .census.gov/compendia/statab/cats/information_communications/
    telecommunications.html.

51 Figures from US Census Bureau, "Economic Census: Industry Snapshots,"
    http://www.census.gov/econ/census/snapshots/SNAP51.HTM.

52 Herman and Gandy, Jr, "Catch 1201," 135.

53 Litman, *Digital Copyright*, 126.

54 Gillespie, *Wired Shut*.

55 Band, interview.

56 Mancur Olson, *The Logic of Collective Action* (Cambridge: Harvard University Press, 1971).

57 Litman, *Digital Copyright*, 51–2.

58 Ibid., 52. These public-interest groups are the spiritual descendants of
    Ralph Nader's Public Citizen organization, created in 1971.

59 Greenstein, interview. While this group continues to exist, it was most
    active in the early 1990s and the Audio Home Recording Act.

5. 1993–1996: US Copyright Reform and the WIPO Internet Treaties

1 For accounts of this policy-laundering episode, see especially Litman, *Digital Copyright*; Pamela Samuelson, "The U.S. Digital Agenda at the World
   Intellectual Property Organization," monograph (1997), http://people
   .ischool.berkeley.edu/~pam/courses/cyberlaw97/docs/wipo.pdf; and
   Herman and Gandy, Jr, "Catch 1201."

2 Brown, "The Evolution of Anti-Circumvention Law," 245, who also notes
   that the EU Copyright Directive, which addresses the European Union's
   WIPO obligations, "has changed the direction of copyright law in the
   European Economic Area's 30-plus member and aspiring member states,
   affecting another half a billion citizens."

3 Litman, *Digital Copyright*, 134.

4 This part draws on chapters six and seven of Litman, ibid.

5 Ibid., 90. Lehman was also the first openly gay person to be confirmed by
   the US Senate.

6 Kupferschmid, interview.

7 Greenstein, interview.

8 Available at http://www.uspto.gov/web/offices/com/doc/ipnii/.

9 Department of Commerce, *Intellectual Property and the National Information
   Infrastructure: The Report of the Working Group on Intellectual Property Rights*
   (Washington: Department of Commerce, 1995), 2.

10 Litman, *Digital Copyright*, 90.
11 Ibid., 90.
12 See Samuelson 1997, 8, for a further list of the White Paper's most radical changes.
13 Ibid.
14 Litman, *Digital Copyright*, 122; Samuelson, "The U.S. Digital Agenda," 3. This legislation was introduced in December 1995 by Carlos Moorhead (Republican of California), Patricia Schroeder (Democrat of Colorado), and Howard Coble (Republican of North Carolina).
15 A current list of DFC members can be found at http://www.dfc.org/dfc1/Learning_Center/members.html.
16 Litman, *Digital Copyright*, 122–7.
17 Quoted in Goldstein, *Copyright's Highway*, 172.
18 Band, interview.
19 Samuelson, "The U.S. Digital Agenda," 42–3.
20 Band, interview.
21 Greenstein, interview.
22 May, *The World Intellectual Property Organization*, 56, 66, 68.
23 Ricketson and Ginsberg 2006, 148.
24 Emery Simon, counsellor, Business Software Alliance, interview by author, Washington, DC, 1 August 2008.
25 Mihály Ficsor, *The Law of Copyright and the Internet: The 1996 WIPO Treaties, Their Interpretation and Implementation* (Oxford: Oxford University Press, 2002).
26 Simon, interview.
27 Greenstein, interview.
28 Brown, "The Evolution of Anti-Circumvention Law," 240.
29 Neil Turkewitz, executive vice-president, Recording Industry Association of America, interview by author, Washington, DC, 17 July 2008.
30 Simon, interview; Greenstein, interview.
31 Ficsor, *The Law of Copyright and the Internet*, 51–2.
32 May, *The World Intellectual Property Organization*, 89.
33 As will be seen in the following chapter, the United States has learned its lesson on this score. The ACTA negotiations were held among a small group of like-minded countries outside the auspices of the more-representative United Nations, World Trade Organization, or WIPO. Similarly, the Trans-Pacific Partnership negotiations are also taking place among a smaller group of nations, although the end result of those talks is, as of this writing, unclear.
34 Ricketson and Ginsburg, *International Copyright and Neighbouring Rights*, 1: 150.
35 Kupferschmid, interview.

36 Graeme Dinwoodie, "The WIPO Copyright Treaty: A Transition to the Future of International Copyright Lawmaking?" *Case Western Reserve Law Review* 57.4 (2007), 752, http://ssrn.com/abstract=1601235.

37 Tawfik, "International Copyright Law," 80.

38 Samuelson, "The U.S. Digital Agenda," 28–9.

39 Ficsor, *The Law of Copyright and the Internet*, 72.

40 Ricketson and Ginsburg, *International Copyright and Neighbouring Rights*, 2: 1235.

41 Despite several attempts over an eight-month period, the author was unable to secure an interview with the head of the Mexican WIPO delegation.

42 Greenstein, interview.

43 Brown, "The Evolution of Anti-Circumvention Law," 24.

44 Ficsor, *The Law of Copyright and the Internet*, 544.

45 Ricketson and Ginsburg, *International Copyright and Neighbouring Rights*, 1: 152.

46 Samuelson, "The U.S. Digital Agenda," 31.

47 Ricketson and Ginsburg, *International Copyright and Neighbouring Rights*, 2: 968.

48 Samuelson, "The U.S. Digital Agenda," 33.

49 Ibid., 32.

50 Ricketson and Ginsburg, *International Copyright and Neighbouring Rights*, 2: 970–1.

51 Ficsor, *The Law of Copyright and the Internet*, 404.

52 WCT article 11 is often read alongside article 12, "Obligations concerning Rights Management Information" (article 19 in the WPPT), which prohibits the unauthorized removal or alteration of electronic "rights management information" of a work (i.e., "information which identifies the work, the author of the work, the owner of any right in the work, or information about the terms and conditions of use of the work, and any numbers or codes that represent such information"), or the traffic in "works or copies of works knowing that electronic rights management information has been removed or altered without authority." As with final WCT article 11, it also calls for "adequate and effective legal remedies." According to Ficsor, it was relatively uncontroversial during negotiations (Ficsor, *The Law of Copyright and the Internet*, 564).

53 Ricketson and Ginsburg, *International Copyright and Neighbouring Rights*, 2: 873.

54 Ibid., 2: 976; Ficsor, *The Law of Copyright and the Internet*, 550.

55 Geist 2005; Tawfik, "International Copyright Law."

56 Band, interview.

57 WIPO, *Survey on Implementation Provisions of the WCT and the WPPT* (25 April 2003), http://www.wipo.int/meetings/en/doc_details.jsp?doc_id=16415, 2. Canada was not included, as it had not yet implemented the treaties.

58 Strowel and Dussolier, "Workshop on Implementation Issues," 27.

59 An interesting point, given Canada's struggle with this issue, discussed in chapter 7.

60 Ficsor, *The Law of Copyright and the Internet*, 404.

61 Department of Commerce, *Intellectual Property and the National Information Infrastructure*, 28.

62 World Intellectual Property Organization (WIPO) Diplomatic Conference on Certain Copyright and Neighboring Rights Questions, "Memorandum Prepared by the Chairman of the Committee of Experts," CRNR/DC/4 (Geneva: WIPO, 1996), para. 7.05.

63 Litman, *Digital Copyright*, 147 n. 10.

64 Kupferschmid, interview.

65 Ficsor, *The Law of Copyright and the Internet*, 443–5.

66 Ricketson and Ginsburg, *International Copyright and Neighbouring Rights*, 2: 686–7.

67 Ficsor, *The Law of Copyright and the Internet*, 63. Agreed statements are designed to "provide guidance in the interpretation of particular treaty provisions," both past (in the case of Berne) and future (in the case of the WCT) (Ricketson and Ginsburg, *International Copyright and Neighbouring Rights*, 1: 151). As has been noted, the statement's lack of clarity has complicated this goal. There is also a question of its relevance, given the fact that the agreed statement attached to article 1(4) was not passed unanimously: a majority of delegates were either absent or abstained from voting (Samuelson, "The U.S. Digital Agenda," 15). Ficsor (*The Law of Copyright and the Internet*, 63) argues that under the Vienna Convention on the Law of Treaties consensus was not required, only that the agreed statements "be made between all the parties in connection with the conclusion of the treaty." Ricketson and Ginsburg disagree, arguing that the agreed statement cannot be used to interpret the WCT and the application of Berne article 9 because the Vienna Convention requires unanimous consent for it to be applied to all countries. Instead, they argue that, following Vienna Convention article 32, it "could clearly be regarded as forming part of 'the circumstances of [the treaty's] conclusion,'" though they note that not everyone agrees with this interpretation (Ricketson and Ginsburg, *International Copyright and Neighbouring Rights*, 1: 865). If Ficsor is correct, then all countries are required to provide protection to RAM copies; if not, then it need only be treated "as a supplementary aid to interpretation"

(ibid., 1: 866). Judging these two positions is beyond the scope of this project and the modest legal abilities of the author. Politically, however, it does not matter which side is right, since both make plausible claims. Opponents of extending copyright to temporary copies can point to the fact that Draft article 7 was explicitly excluded from the final WCT, and that the agreed statement is quite vague and "open to highly variable interpretation," and was passed under dubious circumstances. Proponents, meanwhile, can point to the presence of the agreed statement and combine it with a generous reading of Berne article 9.

68 Greenstein, interview.

69 Ficsor, *The Law of Copyright and the Internet*, 109–14, 133.

70 WIPO 1996, para. 7.05. The openness of these discussions offer a disheartening contrast to current copyright negotiations, namely, ACTA and the Trans-Pacific Partnership, both of which have been characterized by extreme secrecy, to the extent that official texts have not been released until after the negotiations have concluded. See chapters 6, 8, and 9 for further discussion of the two treaties.

71 Kupferschmid, interview.

72 Ricketson and Ginsburg, *International Copyright and Neighbouring Rights*, 1: 685.

73 Goldstein, *Copyright's Highway*, 174.

74 Greenstein, interview.

75 Litman, *Digital Copyright*, 129.

76 May, *The World Intellectual Property Organization*, 16–19.

77 Hatch wrote Lehman: "Surely you will not want to be in the position of negotiating final language on a treaty that as yet commands no clear support in the full Senate and which may not ultimately be retied. Congress will not wish to be in the position of having its hands tied by international developments on the basis of proposed legislation that has stalled precisely because it contains so many unresolved issues" (cited in Brown, "The Evolution of Anti-Circumvention Law," 242).

78 Samuelson, "The U.S. Digital Agenda," 46.

79 Ibid., 26.

80 Ibid., 40.

81 Greenstein, interview.

82 Ibid.

83 Simon, interview.

84 Thomas C. Vinje and Jonathan Band, "The WIPO Copyright Treaty: A New International Intellectual Property Framework for the Digital Age" (1997), 9, http://www.policybandwidth.com/doc/JBand-NewWIPO CopyrightTreaty.pdf.

85 Simon, interview.
86 Ibid.
87 Greenstein, interview.
88 Simon, interview.
89 Samuelson, "The U.S. Digital Agenda," 4.
90 Greenstein, interview.
91 Samuelson, "The U.S. Digital Agenda," 49.
92 Ibid., 48.

6. 1997–1998: The Digital Millennium Copyright Act

 1 While the most important parts of the DMCA centre on WIPO implemen-
    tation and the ISP liability limitation needed to make WIPO implementa-
    tion politically feasible, the bill also covers other copyright issues like hull
    design. This project restricts its analysis to titles 1 and 2 of the DMCA,
    which deal with WIPO-related issues.
 2 Litman, *Digital Copyright*, 130.
 3 Glazier would eventually go to work for the RIAA.
 4 Litman, *Digital Copyright*, 141.
 5 Ibid., 142.
 6 Ibid., 142.
 7 Ibid., 143.
 8 Ibid., 144–5.
 9 Band, interview; Brown "The Evolution of Anti-Circumvention Law," 246.
10 Greenstein, interview.
11 Goldstein, *Copyright's Highway*, 174.
12 Band, interview.
13 Ibid.
14 The analysis in this section is based mainly on Kerr, Maurushat, and Tacit,
    "Technical Protection Measures"; Kerr, "Technical Protection Measures:
    Part II"; and Copyright Office, *The Digital Millennium Copyright Act of 1998*.
15 Kerr, "Technical Protection Measures: Part II," 47.
16 Quoted in Goldstein, *Copyright's Highway*, 175.
17 Kerr, "Technical Protection Measures: Part II," 39.
18 Gillespie, *Wired Shut*, 179.
19 These are: non-profit library, archives, and educational institutions, to
    decide whether they wish to obtain authorized access to a work (s. 1201(d),
    an exception that Litman says was "un-asked-for and unwanted," and
    that implied "that ordinary citizens had no privilege to browse" [Litman,
    Digital Copyright, 136]); for the purposes of reverse-engineering computer

programs to ensure interoperability; for the purposes of encryption research; for the purposes of the protection of minors from harmful material
on the Internet; to protect personal privacy, when the TPM, or the work it
protects, can collect or disseminate private personal information; and to
test the security of computer networks (s. 1201(d–j)).

20 Kerr, Maurushat, and Tacit, "Technical Protection Measures," 68.
21 In paragraph 1201(a)(1)(C).
22 Litman, *Digital Copyright*, 144. This section requires the librarian to con-
    sider "the availability for use of copyrighted works; the availability for use
    of works for non-profit archival, preservation, and educational purposes;
    the impact that the prohibition on the circumvention of technological
    measures applied to copyrighted works has on criticism, comment, news
    reporting, teaching, scholarship, or research; the effect of circumvention of
    technological measures on the market for or value of copyrighted works;
    and such other factors as the Librarian considers appropriate."
23 Band, interview.
24 Ibid.
25 Kupferschmid, interview.
26 Brady Teufel, "Gauging the Influence of America's Legal Decisions regard-
    ing Intellectual Property on the World Wide Web," Master's diss. (Univer-
    sity of Missouri–Columbia, 2004), 37.
27 Copyright Office, *The Digital Millennium Copyright Act of 1998*, 12.
28 Litman, *Digital Copyright*, 143.
29 Electronic Frontier Foundation (EFF), "Chamberlain Group Inc. v. Skylink
    Technologies Inc," (2004): https://www.eff.org/cases/chamberlain-group-
    inc-v-skylink-technologies-inc. In *Chamberlain v. Skylink*, Chamberlain, a
    maker of garage-door openers, sued Skylink for reverse-engineering their
    (TPM-protected) garage-door-opening code and using this information in
    its own remote.
30 Band, interview.
31 Stevan Mitchell, vice-president, intellectual property policy, Entertainment
    Software Association, interview by author, Washington, DC, 8 July 2008.
32 Kerr, Maurushat, and Tacit, "Technical Protection Measures," 68.
33 Sohn, interview.
34 Glyn Moody, "Another Reason Why DRM Is Bad – for Publishers," *Techdirt*,
    16 April 2012, http://www.techdirt.com/articles/20120412/07212918466/
    another-reason-why-drm-is-bad-publishers.shtml.
35 Brown, "The Evolution of Anti-Circumvention Law," 253; Boldrin and
    Levine, *Against Intellectual Monopoly*, 109. For an in-depth critique of the
    DMCA's TPM provisions, see also Electronic Frontier Foundation (EFF),

"Unintended Consequences: Twelve Years under the DMCA," March 2010, http://www.eff.org/wp/unintended-consequences-under-dmca.

36 Petricone, interview.

37 Gillespie, *Wired Shut*, 181.

38 Michael Geist, "The U.S. DMCA vs. Bill C-32: Comparing the Digital Lock Exceptions," www.michaelgeist.ca, 27 July 2010, http://www.michaelgeist .ca/content/view/5229/125/.

39 Peter Jazi, "Worth the Wait – Installment #1." ©ollectanea blog, Center for Intellectual Property, 30 July 2010, http://chaucer.umuc.edu/blogcip/ collectanea/2010/07/worth_the_wait_-_installment_1.html.

40 Sohn, interview; Petricone, interview.

41 US government official, interview by author, Washington, DC, 1 July 2008.

42 Kupferschmid, interview.

43 Band, interview.

44 Center for Copyright Information, "What Is a Copyright Alert?"; http://www.copyrightinformation.org/the-copyright-alert-system/ what-is-a-copyright-alert/.

45 Ernesto, "AT&T Threatens Persistent Pirates with Account Termination," TorrentFreak, 13 September 2013, http://torrentfreak.com/att-threatens- persistent-pirates-with-account-termination-130913/.

46 Ibid.

47 Halbert, *Resisting Intellectual Property*, 3.

48 Turkewitz, interview.

49 Heather A. Sapp, "North American Anti-Circumvention: Implementation of the WIPO Internet Treaties in the United States, Mexico and Canada," *Computer Law Review and Technology Journal* 10 (2005), 18.

50 Simon, interview.

51 Turkewitz, interview.

52 US government official, interview.

53 Ann Chaitovitz, executive director, Future of Music Coalition, interview by author, Washington, DC, 22 July 2008.

54 The other involved countries were Australia, Morocco, New Zealand, Singapore, South Korea, and Switzerland. Mexico and Morocco were the only developing countries involved in the negotiations.

55 "WikiLeaks Cables Shine Light on ACTA History," La Quadrature du Net, 3 February 2011, http://www.laquadrature.net/en/wikileaks-cables- shine-light-on-acta-history.

56 Michael Geist, "U.S. Caves on Anti-Circumvention Rules in ACTA," www.michaelgeist.ca, 19 July 2010, http://www.michaelgeist.ca/content/ view/5210/125/.

57 Litman, *Digital Copyright*, 124.
58 Samuelson, "The U.S. Digital Agenda," 3–4, also credits these groups with moderating the White House's position at the negotiations.
59 The terms are from Clarkson, *Does North America Exist?*, 19.
60 In his highly detailed treatise on the treaties' negotiations, Ficsor (*The Law of Copyright and the Internet*) mentions Canada only a couple of times and Mexico hardly ever.

7. Canada and the Internet Treaties: Aborted Implementations

1 On 1 July.
2 While bills usually come into force upon receiving royal assent, Bill C-11 actually went into force a few months later, once its related regulatory process had been completed.
3 Handa, *Copyright Law in Canada*, 138.
4 de Beer, "Constitutional Jurisdiction over Paracopyright Laws," 90.
5 Handa, *Copyright Law in Canada*, 113.
6 Cited in Gervais, "The Purpose of Copyright Law in Canada," 315.
7 This statement declares that government copyright policy is guided by the objectives of "ensuring net gains for Canadians; maintaining the responsiveness of the [Copyright] Act to technological innovation and new business models; clarifying the law where it will reduce the risk of unnecessary litigation; and ensuring a direction for reform that takes into account, and helps shape, international trends" (Industry Canada and Canadian Heritage, *Supporting Culture and Innovation: Report on the Provisions and Operation of the Copyright Act* [2002], 41).
8 While Anglo-American and Continental European traditions are represented in Canadian law, the Copyright Act does not acknowledge the traditions of Canada's First Nations, namely, the aboriginal "concept of collective or communal intellectual property existing in perpetuity," with rights "often exercised by only one individual in each generation, sometimes through matrilineal descent" (Harry Hillman Chartrand, *The Compleat Canadian Copyright Act: Past, Present and Proposed Provisions 1921–2006* [Saskatoon: Compiler Press, 2006], xiv).
9 Handa, *Copyright Law in Canada*, 67–8.
10 Cultural Human Resources Council, *Cultural HR Study 2010: Labour Market Information for Canada's Cultural Sector Report* (Ottawa: Conference Board of Canada, 2010), 5.
11 Statistics Canada defines "culture" as: "creative artistic activity and the goods and services produced by it, and the preservation of human heritage"

(Vik Singh, "Economic Contribution of Culture in Canada," 81-595-MIE – no. 023 [Ottawa: Statistics Canada, 2008], 7). "Cultural activity" is divided into creation, production, manufacturing, distribution, and support (e.g., "copyright collectives, agents, managers, promoters") (ibid., 11).

12 Ibid., 9.

13 Statistics Canada, Table 1-3: Gross Domestic Product at Basic Prices, Overview – Annual (2006–11), http://www.statcan.gc.ca/pub/15-001-x/2012004/t003-eng.htm.

14 Statistics Canada, Employment by Industry, http://www.statcan.gc.ca/tables-tableaux/sum-som/l01/cst01/econ40-eng.htm. The Heritage Canada report's definition of the cultural sector means that some cultural production is covered by these categories, such as manufacturing.

15 For a "core" industry definition, see Connectus Consulting Inc., *The Economic Impact of Canadian Copyright Industries – Sectoral Analysis* (Ottawa: Copyright Policy Branch, Department of Canadian Heritage, 2006), 5–7. For some reason, the report does not define "non-core" industries.

16 Interestingly, given the fact that the music industry has been the main driver of the debate over Canadian WIPO implementation as a necessary ingredient to ensuring the continued production of music, the study found that the sound-recording industry's contribution to Canadian GDP actually rose to $387 million in 2004, from $243 million in 1997. Overall declines in product sales, industry consolidation, reduced employment, and the exit of inefficient firms from the industry allowed the industry as a whole to perform well, outperforming Canadian GDP between 1999 and 2004 (ibid., 13).

17 Ibid., 9. These figures are chained 1997 dollars.

18 Doern and Sharaput, *Canadian Intellectual Property*, 43.

19 The Department of Industry's predecessor department, it was responsible for copyright policy.

20 Sara Bannerman, "Canada and the Berne Convention, 1886–1971, PhD diss. (Carleton University, 2009), 258.

21 That few people today know what Telidon is provides us with a reminder both of how quickly information technologies evolve and of the problems and inefficiencies involved with reforming copyright laws to address specific technologies. These, however, are lessons that it seems few legislators and other interested parties have learned.

22 Bannerman, "Canada and the Berne Convention," 259.

23 Consumer and Corporate Affairs Canada and the Department of Communications, *From Gutenberg to Telidon: A White Paper on Copyright. Proposals for the Revision of the Canadian Copyright Act* (Ottawa: Supply and Services Canada, 1984), 87.

24 This white paper was adopted by the committee as a discussion paper.

25 Bannerman, "Canada and the Berne Convention," 260.

26 Sunny Handa, "A Review of Canada's International Copyright Obligations," *McGill Law Journal* 42 (1997), 970.

27 Handa, *Copyright Law in Canada*, 287.

28 See chapters 3–4 of Campbell's book *Institutional Change and Governance*.

29 Stephanie R. Golob, "Beyond the Policy Frontier: Canada, Mexico and the Ideological Origins of NAFTA," *World Politics* 55 (2003).

30 Cited in Doern and Sharaput, *Canadian Intellectual Property*, 195. Among other things, it provided copyright protection for computer programs and abolished compulsory licences for the reproduction of sound recordings. It also reformed the Copyright Appeal Board as the Copyright Board of Canada, which regulates the tariffs that Canada's collection societies can charge (ibid., 105).

31 Doyle, *Prey to Thievery*, 62–3.

32 Mexico provides an interesting parallel to the Canadian situation: its 1997 overhaul of the Ley Federal del Derecho de Autor was followed six years later by a bill of author-centric amendments.

33 Doyle, *Prey to Thievery*, 78.

34 NAFTA article 1701; Doern and Sharaput, *Canadian Intellectual Property*, 110–11.

35 Doern and Sharaput, *Canadian Intellectual Property*, 105. These include three under the Progressive Conservatives: the Canada-U.S. Free Trade Agreement Implementation Act (1988) and two minor amendments in 1993. Acts implementing NAFTA and the WTO/TRIPS agreement were passed by the Liberal government of Jean Chrétien. This division of labour further suggests the non-partisan nature of copyright in Canada at the time.

36 Doern and Sharaput, *Canadian Intellectual Property*, 106.

37 Janice Tibbetts, "Ottawa Tackles Movie Pirates," *Saskatoon Star Phoenix*, 2 June 2007, http://www.canada.com/saskatoonstarphoenix/news/national/story.html?id=83e4be8e-49ee-4ce1-b826-4850446ef4be.

38 Dominique Valiquet, "Bill C-59: An Act to Amend the Criminal Code (unauthorized recording of a movie)," LS-559E (legislative summary) (Ottawa: Library of Parliament, 2007).

39 Scassa, "Interests in the Balance," 45–7. The court case was *Théberge v. Galerie d'Art du Petit Champlain*.

40 See Gervais ("The Purpose of Copyright Law in Canada," 320–1). Although Warren Sheffer, "Writers' Rights Upheld: The Robertson Decision," *Copyright & New Media Law Newsletter* 10.4 (2006), argues that a 2006 Supreme Court ruling, (*Robertson v. Thompson Corp.*, concerning unauthorized and unpaid digital reproduction of freelancers' articles) revealed an

unwillingness by the court to reject an author-centric view of copyright in favour of a social-utility view.

41 See Tarantino, "Five Cases That Shook the World" for a discussion of these changes.

42 Sinclair, "Culture and Trade," 46.

43 See, e.g., Doyle, *Prey to Thievery*; for a historical perspective see Bannerman, "Canada and the Berne Convention."

44 The Department of Justice also has a role in vetting legislation to ensure that it is both constitutional and in line with Canada's treaty obligations. This is significant when one considers arguments that either the Liberals' or the Conservatives' very different bills to implement the Internet treaties do not fulfil Canada's obligations under the Internet treaties.

45 Doern and Sharaput, *Canadian Intellectual Property*, 101.

46 Ibid., 107.

47 Denis Gratton, former manager, copyright policy, Department of Canadian Heritage, interview by author, Ottawa, 7 February 2008.

48 Donald J. Savoie, *Court Government and the Collapse of Accountability in Canada and the United Kingdom* (Toronto: University of Toronto Press, 2008).

49 While other institutions also share influence over Canadian copyright policy, this study focuses only on those with a direct effect on the copyright law-making process.

50 Before 1993, the predecessor to Industry Canada, the Department of Consumer and Corporate Affairs, handled the file. The Department of Canadian Heritage is treated as a joint partner; in practice, the two departments must negotiate in order to bring forth copyright legislation.

51 Doern and Sharaput, *Canadian Intellectual Property*, 24. The dual nature of this relationship could be seen even before the reorganization: the 1985 white paper, *From Gutenberg to Telidon*, was published in the name of Consumer and Corporate Affairs and the Department of Communications, whose responsibility for culture would be given to Canadian Heritage in 1993 and whose technical responsibility for communications matters would be taken over by Industry Canada.

52 Doern and Sharaput, *Canadian Intellectual Property*, 107.

53 Ibid., 183; Murray, "Copyright Talk," 27.

54 Murray, "Copyright Talk," 18.

55 Michele Austin, former chief of staff, industry minister Maxime Bernier, interview by author, Ottawa, 30 April 2008.

56 Murray, "Copyright Talk," 18, 16n2.

57 Doern and Sharaput, *Canadian Intellectual Property*, 131, 24; Doyle, *Prey to Thievery*, 97.

58 Doyle, *Prey to Thievery*, 134; see also 109–11.

59 Austin, interview.

60 On this point see also Murray and Trosow, *Canadian Copyright*, 31.

61 Doyle, *Prey to Thievery*.

62 Austin, interview.

63 Savoie, *Court Government and the Collapse of Accountability*.

64 Doyle, *Prey to Thievery*, 73–4.

65 The May 2011 federal election, which occurred following most of the events discussed in this chapter, upended the Canadian federal political scene. The Bloc Québécois caucus was decimated and the Liberal party, once Canada's "natural governing party," was reduced to third-party status. As of October 2013, it is unclear whether the Liberals or Bloc Québécois can still be considered to be major political parties.

66 The BQ's decimation in the 2011 federal election reduces the importance of this point for the future, although it will be interesting to see if the NDP, which rose to Official Opposition status in 2011 on the strength of its Quebec vote, adopts the BQ's copyright position.

67 Doyle, *Prey to Thievery*. Despite its name, CRIA historically has been dominated by foreign record companies, which, since 2006, it has exclusively represented. CRIA has since renamed itself Music Canada. This book refers to it as CRIA as this was its moniker throughout most of this debate.

68 Bannerman, "Canada and the Berne Convention."

69 Robert, *Negotiating NAFTA*, 65.

70 Murray and Trosow, *Canadian Copyright*, 30.

71 Bannerman, "Canada and the Berne Convention," esp. 178–81.

72 Royal Commission on Patents, Copyright, Trade Marks and Industrial Designs (Ilsley Commission), *Report on Copyright* (Ottawa: Queen's Printer and Controller of Stationary, 1957), 8–10.

73 Murray and Trosow, *Canadian Copyright*, 27.

74 Ibid., 28.

75 Cited in Scassa, "Interests in the Balance," 79n44.

76 Ilsley Commission, *Report on Copyright*, 16. The influence of the United States on Canadian copyright thinking can also be seen in the Ilsley commission's remark that in the drafting of their report, they gave "full consideration" to US "copyright legislation, its governing principles and its importance in relation to the Canadian economy" (ibid., 8).

77 Doern and Sharaput, *Canadian Intellectual Property*, 8.

78 Austin, interview.

79 Michael Geist, "How the U.S. Got Its Canadian Copyright Bill," *Toronto Star*, 16 June 2008.

80 David Wilkins, speech to Public Policy Forum, "Intellectual Property Reform: Innovation and the Economy," sound recording, Ottawa, 28 April 2008. On file with the author.
81 Michael Shapiro, speech to Public Policy Forum, sound recording, Ottawa, 28 April 2008. On file with the author.
82 Michael Geist, "Behind the Scenes of Canada's Movie Piracy Bill," www.michaelgeist.ca, 11 June 2007, http://www.michaelgeist.ca/content/view/2016/275/.
83 This downgrade was partly a response to the passage of the 2012 Copyright Modernization Act (United States. "2013 Special 301 Report," Office of the United States Trade Representative," May 2013, 59).
84 Yannick Mondy, first secretary, trade policy, Embassy of Canada in the United States, interview by author, Washington, 6 August 2008.
85 Nancy Segal, Testimony (edited) before Standing Committee on Public Safety and National Security. House of Commons, 1st Session, 39th Parliament. Ottawa, 27 March 2007.
86 Doyle, *Prey to Thievery*, 9.
87 Ibid., 1.
88 For an account of how the CRIA lobbied the government in pursuit of its copyright objectives, see Doyle, *Prey to Thievery*.
89 Michael Geist, professor of law, University of Ottawa, interview by author, Ottawa, 14 May 2008.
90 Canadian Recording Industry Association, "News," 2006, http://www.cria.ca/news/020306a_n.php.
91 Canadian Recording Industry Association, "About CRIA," http://www.cria.ca/about.php.
92 In 2006, several Canadian record labels left CRIA, arguing that the association was only representing the interests of the "Big Four" foreign record labels ("Indie Labels Break with CRIA over Commercial Radio Proposal," CBC News, 13 April 2006, http://www.cbc.ca/arts/story/2006/04/13/cria-indie-crtc.html#ixzz19eiHs9pl).
93 Canadian Media Production Association, *Profile 2011: An Economic Report on the Screen-based Production Industry in Canada* (Ottawa: Canadian Media Production Association, Association des producteurs de films et de télévision du Québec, and the Department of Canadian Heritage 2011), http://www.cftpa.ca/newsroom/pdf/profile/Profile2011Eng.pdf.
94 Its predecessor made a submission to the 2004 "Bulte report," discussed below, but was too new to have done anything else.
95 Jason Kee, director of policy and legal affairs, ESAC, interview by author, Ottawa, 10 February 2008.
96 Doern and Sharaput, *Canadian Intellectual Property*, 130.

97 Doyle, *Prey to Thievery*, 7.
98 The Alliance of Canadian Cinema, Television and Radio Artists (ACTRA), for example, works internationally through the International Federation of Actors, and was deeply involved through the FIA in the negotiations that led to the WPPT (Garry Neil, policy adviser, ACTRA, interview by author, Toronto, 19 May 2008).
99 Keith Serry, communications director, CMCC, interview by author, digital recording. Montreal, 13 May 2008.
100 Steve Wills, manager, legal affairs, AUCC, interview by author, Ottawa, 10 February 2009. Wills further notes that the AUCC has always emphasized that it represents both creators and users of copyright materials and seeks a balanced approach to copyright reforms.
101 Wills, interview.
102 While telecommunications companies are the main Canadian ISPs, universities also function as ISPs, giving the AUCC an interest in the issue; it supports a formalization of the notice-and-notice regime (Wills, interview by author, February 10, 2009).
103 Tom Copeland, chair, Canadian Association of Internet Providers, phone interview by author, Ontario, 24 June 2010.
104 Ibid.
105 Ibid.
106 Doyle, *Prey to Thievery*, 85. While this comment refers specifically to the 2005 copyright bill, it also applies to Canadian copyright politics generally.
107 Sara Bannerman, "Canadian Copyright Reform: Consulting with Copyright's Changing Public," *Intellectual Property Journal* 19.2 (2006); Doyle, *Prey to Thievery*.
108 CIPPIC is now known as the Glushko-Samuelson Canadian Internet Policy and Public Interest Clinic, named after US technology innovator and entrepreneur Dr. Robert Glushko and his wife, law professor Pamela Samuelson, who made a "large donation" to the clinic in 2007. This funding is an example of US material linkages to Canadian user-oriented advocacy groups.
109 Industry Canada and Canadian Heritage, *A Framework for Copyright Reform* (Ottawa, 2001), http://strategis.ic.gc.ca/eic/site/crp-prda.nsf/eng/rp01101.html.
110 Industry Canada and Canadian Heritage, *Consultation Paper on Digital Copyright Issues* (Ottawa, 2002), http://strategis.gc.ca/eic/site/crp-prda.nsf/eng/h_rp01102.html.
111 Industry Canada and Canadian Heritage, *Consultation Paper on the Application of the Copyright Act's Compulsory Retransmission Licence to the Internet* (Ottawa, 2002), http://www.ic.gc.ca/eic/site/crp-prda.nsf/eng/rp00008.html.

112 Bannerman, "Canadian Copyright Reform."

113 Industry Canada and Department of Canadian Heritage, *Consultation Paper on Digital Copyright Issues*, 13–15.

114 Doyle, *Prey to Thievery*, 36.

115 Industry Canada and Department of Canadian Heritage, *Consultation Paper on Digital Copyright Issues*, 24.

116 Industry Canada and Canadian Heritage, *Supporting Culture and Innovation.*

117 In contrast to these charmingly optimistic timelines, the Department of Canadian Heritage's internal estimates were more accurate: they calculated that, despite the fact that the treaties were a high priority for the content industries, it would take five to ten years to implement short-term reforms, and eight to twenty years to implement fully the WIPO Internet treaties (Doyle, *Prey to Thievery*, 100).

118 Gervais, "The Purpose of Copyright Law in Canada," 339–40.

119 Industry Canada and Canadian Heritage, *Supporting Culture and Innovation*, 43–4, 22 (TPMs), 28 (ISP liability). Rights Management Information refers to the protection of the bibliographic or identifying data attached to a digital work, such as author and copyright owner. A making-available right is the right to forbid others from making a copyrighted work available over the Internet or other means of telecommunications.

120 The departments received 670 written submissions (of which 234 were closely modelled on a form letter produced by the US-based EFF; Doyle, *Prey to Thievery*, 95; Geist, "Anti-circumvention Legislation," 2). The diversity of opinions, and the lack of clarity in many submissions about who the individual represented – as well as the fact that the consultations were aimed at traditional copyright experts, not laypeople (Bannerman, "Canadian Copyright Reform") – made it difficult to summarize their input.

121 See Bannerman, ibid., for a discussion.

122 Russell McOrmond, independent software producer, interview by author, Ottawa, 18 January 2008.

123 Doyle, *Prey to Thievery*, 85, 86, 94.

124 Ibid., 85.

125 Ministers of Canadian Heritage and Industry, "Status Report on Copyright Reform," submitted to the House of Commons Standing Committee on Canadian Heritage (2005), http://www.ic.gc.ca/eic/site/crp-prda.nsf/eng/rp01133.html.

126 As de Beer and Clemmer ("Global Trends in Online Copyright Enforcement," 379) note: "In its analysis in *Society of Composers, Authors and Music Publishers of Canada v. Canadian Association of Internet Providers*, Canada's

Supreme Court held that the *Copyright Act* specifies that only neutral intermediaries enjoy immunity from liability. This immunity is to be enjoyed "so long as an Internet intermediary does not itself engage in acts that relate to the content of the communication, *i.e.*, whose participation is content neutral, but confines itself to providing 'a conduit' for information communicated by others." Supreme Court Justice Ian Binnie reiterated this principle, reinforcing that "to the extent [that ISPs] act as innocent disseminators, they are protected by §2.4(1)(*b*) of the Act." He drew an analogy to a case that held the owners of telephone wires, who were "utterly ignorant of the nature of the message," were not responsible for the content of the transmissions" (citations omitted).

127 "Under this arrangement, ... CRIA first notifies a CAIP- or CCTA-member ISP in writing when an alleged infringement of CRIA's copyrights by a customer of the ISP is taking place; the ISP then notifies its customer of the allegation, again in writing, and sends a written confirmation that it has done so back to CRIA" (CAIP, "Submission from Canadian Association of Internet Providers," Copyright Reform Process, 18 September 2001, http://www.ic.gc.ca/eic/site/crp-prda.nsf/eng/rp00314.html).

128 Doyle, *Prey to Thievery*, 117.

129 Ibid., 138.

130 Ibid., 107, 109.

131 Ibid., 87.

132 Ibid., 96.

133 Ibid., 140.

134 Ibid., 84.

135 CRIA, "Submission of the Canadian Recording Industry Association in Respect of Consultation Paper on Digital Copyright Issues" (2001), http://www.ic.gc.ca/eic/site/crp-prda.nsf/eng/rp00249.html.

136 Doyle, *Prey to Thievery*, 126.

137 Ibid., 127.

138 Ibid., 121.

139 Ibid., 122–3. Following Copps's departure in 2003, Heritage Minister Helene Scherrer took a similar approach.

140 Ibid., 138.

141 House of Commons Standing Committee on Canadian Heritage, *Interim Report on Copyright Reform* (Ottawa: House of Commons, 2004).

142 Doyle, *Prey to Thievery*, 125.

143 Murray, "Copyright Talk," 22.

144 Tawfik, "International Copyright Law," 70–1.

145 Murray, "Copyright Talk," 22.

146 "Liberal MP Takes Flak for Fundraiser by Copyright Lobbyists," CBC News, 6 January 2006, http://www.cbc.ca/news/story/2006/01/06/elxn-bulte-fundraiser.html.

147 Doyle, *Prey to Thievery*, 136–7.

148 For a full summary of the bill see Sam Banks and Andrew Kitching, *Bill C-60: An Act to Amend the Copyright Act, Legislative Summary,* LS-512-E (Ottawa: Library of Parliament, 2005).

149 Michael Geist, "Bill C-60 User Guide: The ISPs and Search Engines," www.michaelgeist.ca, June 2005, http://www.michaelgeist.ca/content/view/824/125/.

150 Doyle, *Prey to Thievery*, 146–7.

151 Ibid., 117.

152 Also discussed ibid., 116, 118–19.

153 Ibid., 156–8.

154 As Kingdon, *Agendas, Alternatives, and Public Policies*, 57, notes, good policy must also be good politics in order to be implemented.

155 Savoie, *Court Government and the Collapse of Accountability*.

156 David Fewer, director, Canadian Internet Policy and Public Interest Clinic, interview by author, Ottawa, 7 February 2008.

157 Austin, interview.

158 Fewer, interview.

159 "This is the mandate letter to Bernier," reads Austin: "'It is important that you and [Canadian Heritage] Minister [Bev] Oda proceed with work ensuring that our intellectual property regime is modernized and among the best in the world. Any delays on this file may put Canada's international reputation at risk. In particular, I ask that you and your colleague [Minister Oda] focus on developing amendments to the copyright act that will bring the 1996 WIPO Internet treaties into force.'" Oda's letter read: "'You should jointly lead with the Minister of Industry a review of bill C-60, *An Act to Amend the* Copyright Act' [and]'ensure that any new act provides reasonable access to copyrighted work for learning for teachers while promoting educational policy goals'" (Austin, interview).

160 Ibid.

161 Ibid.

162 Ibid.

163 Margaret Kopala, "Softwood Deal Tears a Hole in NAFTA," *Ottawa Citizen*, 26 August 2006: http://www.canada.com/ottawacitizen/news/opinion/story.html?id=ce0dbe37-c91c-4305-ade6-58dbd68a5925.

164 Austin, interview.

165 Robert O. Keohane and Joseph S. Nye, *Power and Interdependence*, 2nd ed. (Glenview, IL: Scott, Foresman/Little Brown, 1989).

166 Geist, "How the U.S. Got Its Canadian Copyright Bill."

167 Austin, interview.

168 The following sections draw on Blayne Haggart, "Fair Copyright for Canada: Lessons from Canada's First Facebook Uprising," forthcoming.

169 Canada, "2007 Speech from the Throne," 17 October 2007.

170 Bill C-59, the 2007 bill that outlawed camcording at the request of the United States and its motion-picture industry, was an early indicator of the Conservative government's tendencies on this file.

171 See http://www.facebook.com/group.php?gid=6315846683.

172 Michael Geist, "Copyright's 10K," michaelgeist.ca, 9 December 2007, http://www.michaelgeist.ca/content/view/2453/99999/.

173 Jennifer Earl et al., "Changing the World One Webpage at a Time: Conceptualizing and Explaining Internet Activism," *Mobilization: An International Journal* 15 (2010), 429.

174 Kempton Lam, copyright blogger, interview by author, Calgary, 16 April 2008; available at www.facebook.com/events/7365003311/.

175 Lam's blog, which contains further details of his meet-up with the industry minister, is available at http://kempton.wordpress.com/.

176 Austin, interview.

177 Rob Hyndman, technology lawyer, interview by author, Toronto, 22 April 2008.

178 Jean-Sébastien Rioux, chief of staff to former industry minister Jim Prentice, interview by author, Calgary, 26 February 2009.

179 Fewer, interview.

180 Kee, interview.

181 Canadian Intellectual Property Council (IP Council), "Business Coalition Stresses Need for Better Protection of Intellectual Property rights," 2008, http://www.ipcouncil.ca/uploads/ReleaseIPCoalitionLaunch260508.pdf.

182 BCBC, "A Balanced 'Package' Approach for a Strong Canadian Copyright Regime," February 2008, http://static.googleusercontent.com/external_content/untrusted_dlcp/services.google.com/en//blog_resources/google_bcbc_position_paper.pdf.

183 Jacob Glick, policy counsel, Google Canada, interview by author, Ottawa, 21 April 2008.

184 Rioux, interview.

185 Ibid.

186 Industry Canada, "Government of Canada Proposes Update to Copy-
     right Law: Balanced Approach to Truly Benefit Canadians," news release,
     12 June 2008, http://www.ic.gc.ca/eic/site/ic1.nsf/eng/04204.html.
187 Rioux, interview.
188 The exemptions allowed for under Bill C-61 are for law-enforcement or
     national-security purposes, or encryption research; to make computers
     interoperable; for people with perceptual disabilities; in cases where the
     user is not informed that his/her personal information will be transmit-
     ted to a third party; and, for broadcasters (in certain cases), to "fix" an
     ephemeral reproduction of a work.
189 Discussed in chapter 6.
190 Jeremy de Beer, "Jeremy de Beer on Canada's Copyright Bill: Win-win
     or Spin-spin?" *National Post*, 13 June 2008, http://network.nationalpost.
     com/np/blogs/fullcomment/archive/2008/06/13/174920.aspx.
191 It supported the principle of copyright reform, but was disappointed by
     the bill's lack of a levy on ISPs that would go to rights holders (Writers
     Guild of Canada, "Copyright Balance Can Be Struck with Levies on Tech-
     nologies and Distribution Platforms," news release, 12 June 2008, http://
     www.wgc.ca/files/WGC%20on%20Copyright%20June%2012.pdf).
192 This last group argued that, for visual and media artists, C-61 simply rep-
     resented the "status quo" (CARFAC Ontario, "Copyright Bill Represents
     Status Quo for Visual and Media Artists," news release, 26 June 2008,
     www.carfacontario.ca/images/C-61_Release.pdf).
193 Christian Paradis replaced Clement as minister of industry in May 2011.
194 Submissions can be read at http://www.ic.gc.ca/eic/site/008.nsf/eng/
     home.
195 Michael Geist, "The 2009 Copyright Consultation: Setting the Record
     Straight," www.michaelgeist.ca, 20 April 2010, http://www.michaelgeist
     .ca/content/view/4971/125/. Calculations are by the author, from a 2010
     Copyright Consultations submissions database, http://www.ic.gc.ca/
     eic/site/008.nsf/eng/h_00001.html.
196 Michael Geist, "The Final Copyright Consultation Numbers: No Repeat
     of Bill C-61," www.michaelgeist.ca, 9 April 2010, http://www.michael-
     geist.ca/content/view/4946/125/.
197 DRM, or Digital Rights Management, refers to electronic systems that
     manage access to content; many work by using TPMs.
198 Michael Geist, "The Battle over C-11 Concludes: How Thousands of
     Canadians Changed the Copyright Debate," www.michaelgeist.ca,
     18 June 2012, http://www.michaelgeist.ca/content/view/6544/125/.
199 Ibid.

200 Cited in Michael Geist, "The Missing Copyright Docs, Pt 1: Justice Dept Warned about Constitutionality of Digital Lock Rules," www.michaelgeist .ca, 25 June 2012, http://www.michaelgeist.ca/content/view/6557/125/.
201 Banting, Hoberg, and Simeon, "Introduction," 15.
202 Michael Geist, "Government Launches Consultation on Rules for ISP Notice-and-Notice System Amid Shift in Priorities," www.michaelgeist.ca, 10 October 2013, http://www.michaelgeist.ca/content/view/6967/125/.
203 In terms of public policy, inaction and delay are also outcomes.
204 Campbell, *Institutional Change and Governance*, 65.
205 For example, when the author contacted the Canadian embassy in Mexico in 2008 for their views on the Mexican copyright debate, they declined to participate, saying it was not an issue that the embassy followed.

8. Mexico and the Internet Treaties, 1996–2010: International Pressure, Domestic Politics

1 Figures are from http://wiki.stoppacta-protest.info/INT:Teilnehmerzahlen.
2 Charles Arthur, "Acta Criticised after Thousands Protest in Europe," *The Guardian*, 13 February 2012, http://www.guardian.co.uk/technology/2012/feb/13/acta-protests-europe.
3 Amnesty International, "EU Urged to Reject International Anti-Counterfeiting Pact," news release, 10 February 2012, https://www .amnesty.org/en/news/eu-urged-reject-international-anti-counterfeiting-pact-2012-02-10.
4 Ernesto, "Copyright Lobby Hires Pro-ACTA Demonstrators," TorrentFreak, 24 April 2012, http://torrentfreak.com/copyright-lobby-hires-pro-acta-demonstators-120424/.
5 Ana Ramalho, "Murder They Wrote – the Dutch Kill ACTA," Kluwer Copyright Blog, 30 May 2012, http://kluwercopyrightblog.com/2012/05/30/murder-they-wrote-%E2%80%93-the-dutch-kill-acta/.
6 Glyn Moody, "European Parliament Declares Its Independence from the European Commission with a Massive Rejection of ACTA. Now What?" Techdirt, 4 July 2012, http://www.techdirt.com/articles/20120704/07533019579/european-parliament-declares-its-independence-european-commission-with-massive-rejection-acta-now-what.shtml.
7 Senate of Mexico, Grupo plural de trabajo para dar seguimiento a las negociaciones del acuerdo commercial anti-falsificaciones (Working Group Following the Anti-Counterfeiting Trade Agreement Negotiations), Report, 20 July 2011, http://www.senado.gob.mx/comisiones/LX/grupo_acta/content/docs/20julio11.pdf.

8 As will be discussed later in the chapter, the Executive nonetheless signed the treaty on 12 July 2012, possibly setting up a showdown with the Senate and Mexico's anti-ACTA forces.

9 Mike Masnick, "Debunking the Faulty Premises of the Pirate Bay Criminalization Treaty," *Techdirt*, 23 May 2009, http://www.techdirt.com/articles/20080523/1203101212.shtml.

10 Alfredo Tourné Guerrero, director of protection, INDAUTOR, interview by author, Mexico City, 24 and 29 September 2009.

11 John C. Cross, "Mexico," in *Media Piracy in Emerging Economies*, ed. Joe Karaganis (New York: Social Science Research Council, 2011), 307.

12 See, e.g., Story, "Burn Berne."

13 That is, rights related to, but not directly involved in, the creative process, such as those of broadcasters and record producers.

14 See Robert, *Negotiating NAFTA* for a detailed accounting of the specific nature of these changes.

15 See, e.g., Drahos and Braithwaite, *Information Feudalism*; Sell, *Private Power, Public Law*.

16 Pedro Carrillo, *El derecho intellectual en México* (Mexicali: Universidad Autónoma de Baja California, 2002), 26. See the discussion of moral rights in chapter 3.

17 For a review of Mexican copyright law through to the 1997 law see Fernando Serrano Migallón, *Marco jurídico del derecho de autor en México*, 2nd ed. (Mexico City: Editorial Porrúa, 2008), 29-49.

18 Translation by author. The article also exempts patents, as well as establishing a monopoly over Mexico's energy sector. It was maintained under NAFTA and continues to be a source of irritation in the Mexico–US relationship.

19 Serrano Migallón, *Marco jurídico del derecho de autor*, 38. For example, an author's right to attribution does not expire after a certain period, while an author's right to determine who can copy her work expires after a set time, currently the life of the author plus 100 years in Mexico.

20 J. Ramón Obón León, "La actualidad del derecho de autor en México," presentation to WIPO conference "El derecho de autor: Un valor estratégico para el futuro," Museo Nacional de Antropología e Historia, 28 June 2003, 10–11. On file with the author.

21 And, recall, unlike Canadian law, which provides no explicit guidance on the purpose of copyright.

22 Serrano Migallón, *Marco jurídico*, xvii, author's translation.

23 Kamil Idirs, "Preface," in Serrano Migallón, *Marco jurídico*, xv.

24 Serrano Migallón, *Marco jurídico*, 4, author's translation.

25 Author's translation.

26 Luis Malpica De Lamadrid, *La influencia del derecho internacional en el derecho Mexicano: La apertura de modelo de desarrollo de México* (Mexico, D.F.: Editorial Limusa, 2002), 197.

27 The subject remains woefully understudied even by Mexican legal academics; Eduardo Nivón Bolán, "Propiedad intelectual y política cultural: Una perspectiva desde la situación Mexicana," in *Propiedad intelectual, nuevas tecnologías y libre acceso a la cultura*, ed. Alberto López Cuenca and Eduardo Ramírez Pedrajo (Puebla: Universidad de las Américas Puebla / Centro Cultural de España México, 2009), 62; María del Carmen Arteaga Alvarado, legal scholar and former legal director, INDAUTOR (2000–8), interview by author, Mexico City, 19 October 2009; Alberto López Cuenca, professor of philosophy and contemporary art theory and coordinator of the doctoral program on cultural creation and theories at the Universidad de las Américas (Puebla, Mexico), interview by author, Puebla, 18 September 2009. The truth of this observation – voiced unanimously by every interview subject with whom the issue was raised – came home to the author during a visit to the legal studies bookstore of UNAM, Mexico's largest university. There, texts on copyright took up all of one small section of one small shelf, vastly outnumbered by books on every other legal subject.

28 See, e.g., J. Ramón Obón León, "El orden público y el interés social en la nueva Ley Federal del Derecho De Autor." In *Estudios de derecho intelectual en homenaje al Profesor David Rangel Medina*, ed. Manuel Becerra Ramírez (Mexico: UNAM, 1998), 118.

29 See, e.g., Serrano Migallón, *Marco jurídico*; Obón León, "La actualidad del derecho de autor en México."

30 Serrano Migallón, *Marco jurídico*, 33, 36.

31 1971 revisions, ratified in 1975.

32 The Berne Convention entered into force in Mexico in 1967; Mexico ratified the 1971 Paris revision to the Berne Convention in 1974.

33 Malpica De Lamadrid, *La influencia del derecho internacional en el derecho Mexicano*, 193–6.

34 "False Friends," *The Economist*, 13 January 1996, 66; Barry Appleton, *Navigating NAFTA: A Concise User's Guide to the North American Free Trade Agreement* (Scarborough, ON: Carswell, 1994); Robert, *Negotiating NAFTA*.

35 Carrillo, *El derecho intellectual en México*, 27; Serrano Migallón, *Marco jurídico*, 49; Billboard magazine, cited in Jones, "Mass Communication, Intellectual Property Rights," 338. Changes in 1982 were also made to address international requirements (Carrillo, *El Derecho intellectual en México*, 27).

36 Cesar Benedicto Callejas, director, patents and trademarks, National Autonomous University of Mexico (UNAM), interview by author, Mexico City, 26 October 2009.

37 Manuel Morante Soria, copyright lawyer, Arochi, Marroquín & Linder, S.C., interview by author, Mexico City, 3 December 2009.

38 Arteaga, interview.

39 Serrano Migallón, *Marco jurídico*, 147.

40 That is, they do not base their judgments on precedents, as in common-law jurisdictions.

41 "False Friends," *The Economist*, 66. Tobias Schonwetter et al., "Copyright and Education: Lessons on African Copyright and Access to Knowledge," *African Journal of Information and Communication* 10 (2010), http://ifap-is-observatory.ittk.hu/node/470, note a similar paradox in African countries.

42 Tourné, interview. INDAUTOR's role is discussed further below.

43 Ernesto Piedras Feria, *¿Cuánto vale la cultura? Contribución económica de las industrias protegidas por los derechos de autor en México* (México: CONACULTA/SACM/SOGEM, 2004), 150. For a list of included industries see ibid., 46–51, one of the main reports that frames the Mexican copyright debate. While these numbers may be a bit out of date, there is little reason to believe that the overall trend has changed much. This chapter cites them not just as evidence of Mexico's actual economic situation, but because they are cited by *all* Mexican experts when discussing copyright policy.

44 Ernesto Piedras Feria, "Industrias culturales en México: Una actualización de los cálculos al 2003," 2007, http://www.odai.org/biblioteca/biblioteca1/10.pdf. Mechanical royalties refer to royalties from the sale of audio recordings.

45 Tourné, interview.

46 Simon, interview.

47 Sinclair, "Culture and Trade," 46.

48 Chappell H. Lawson, *Building the Fourth Estate: Democratization and the Rise of a Free Press in Mexico* (Berkeley: University of California Press, 2002), 29.

49 Ibid., 5.

50 Ibid., 29.

51 World Intellectual Property Organization, "List of Participants" (WIPO Internet treaties) (1996), http://www.wipo.int/meetings/en/html.jsp?file=/redocs/mdocs/mdocs/en/db_im/db_im_6-annex1.html.

52 Cited in Sinclair, "Culture and Trade," 46; see also Robert, *Negotiating NAFTA*.

53 Victor Carlos García Moreno, "El capítulo XVII del TLCAN y su influencia en la nueva ley Mexicana del derecho de autor," in *Estudios de derecho intelectual en homenaje al Profesor David Rangel Medina*, ed. Manuel Becerra Ramírez (Mexico: UNAM, 1998), 106–7.

54 Robert, *Negotiating NAFTA*, 50

55 Available at http://www.coneval.gob.mx/cmsconeval/rw/pages/index.en.do.

56 Mauricio Jalife Daher, "El nuevo escquema antipiratería," in *Legislación de Derechos de Autor*, 2006 ed. (Mexico: Editorial Sista, 2006), xxix. See also José Ángel Quintanilla, "Algunos puntos sobre la piratería editorial en México," *Pensar el Libro* 2 (2005), http://www.cerlalc.org/Revista_Pirateria/pdf/n_art04.pdf.

57 Cross "Mexico," 305.

58 Ibid., 306; Julia Preston, "As Piracy Grows in Mexico, U.S. Companies Shout Foul," *New York Times*, 20 April 1996, 1. Cross ("Mexico") also provides a fascinating overview of the organization of these illegal markets, including the infamous Tepito market.

59 Joe Karaganis, "Rethinking Piracy," in *Media Piracy in Emerging Economies*, ed. Joe Karaganis (New York: Social Science Research Council, 2011), 25.

60 Callejas, interview.

61 "False Friends," *The Economist*, 66.

62 Marco González, Javier Torres Medina, and Omar Jiménez, *La república informal: El ambulantaje en la ciudad de México* (Mexico City: Editions Porrúa, 2008), 10.

63 Karaganis, "Rethinking Piracy."

64 Coldplay may have their fans, but this price seems unreasonably high.

65 Karaganis, "Rethinking Piracy," 57.

66 Arteaga, interview.

67 Golob, "Beyond the Policy Frontier"; Gabriel Garcia, "Economic Development and the Course of Intellectual Property Protection in Mexico," *Texas International Law Journal* 27 (1992).

68 Claraluz Aguilar, directora juridica, Asociación Mexicana de Productores de Fonogramas y Videogramas, A.C., interview by author, Mexico City, 3 February 2010.

69 Obón León, "La actualidad del derecho de autor en México," 11–12.

70 Ibid., 15.

71 Arteaga, interview; Callejas, interview.

72 Serrano Migallón, *Marco jurídico*, xvii, xix, translation by the author. For an account of the passage of the bill see ibid., 51 and 255–6.

73 José Luis Caballero Leal and Mauricio Jalife Daher, "Comentarios a la Ley Federal de Derecho de Autor," in *Legislación de derechos de autor*, 2006 ed. (Mexico: Editorial Sista, 2006), i.

74 Horacio Rangel Ortiz, "La usurpación de derechos en la nueva ley autoral Mexicana y su reforma," in *Estudios de derecho intelectual en homenaje al Profesor David Rangel Medina*, ed. Manuel Becerra Ramírez (Mexico: UNAM, 1998), 381.

75 Robert, *Negotiating NAFTA*, 47, explains NAFTA outcomes for all three countries in terms of tactics used and resources available. While Robert

focuses mainly on analyses of Canadian outcomes, she notes that Mexico was able to use resources such as its adherence to the Rome Convention to exempt itself from the national treatment of sound recordings. This exemption was useful to the United States in that it allowed the United States to ensure that NAFTA did not require the United States to implement Berne article 6bis, on moral rights.

76 Frederick M. Abbott, *Law and Policy of Regional Integration: The NAFTA and Western Hemispheric Integration in the World Trade Organization System* (Boston: Martinus Nijhoff Publishers, 1995), 93–4. Abbot contends that NAFTA's effect was more significant on Mexico's patent regime, an issue beyond the scope of this study.

77 García Moreno, "El capítulo XVII del TLCAN," 115–16, translation by the author.

78 Maxwell A. Cameron and Brian W. Tomlin, *The Making of NAFTA: How the Deal Was Done* (Ithaca: Cornell University Press, 2000), 98.

79 Acheson and Maule, "Copyright, Contract, the Cultural Industries, and NAFTA," 368–9; see also Appleton, *Navigating NAFTA*, 124–8.

80 Serrano Migallón, *Marco jurídico*, 51. This lack of conflict over copyright would carry over from this undemocratic period: copyright reforms in 2003 were just as uncontroversial.

81 Roderic Ai Camp, *Politics in Mexico: The Democratic Consolidation*, 5th ed. (New York: Oxford University Press, 2007), 137.

82 Ibid., 136.

83 Ibid., 136–7.

84 Ibid., 162.

85 Callejas, interview.

86 Eduardo De la Parra Trujillo, "Comentarios a las reformas a la Ley Federal del Derecho de Autor," *Revista de Derecho Privado* 3.8 (2004), 96.

87 Aguilar, interview. Camp notes that lobbyists have been paying attention to members of Congress since 1997 (Camp, *Politics in Mexico*, 186), although according to copyright lawyer Manuel Morante, Mexican politicians are still getting used to a system in which Congress has a fair share of power, and in their grasp of responsibility are like "teenagers discovering life" (Morante, interview).

88 While these committees are the main ones for copyright matters, copyright issues can also come up in the context of other issues, in which case other committees and departments would be consulted.

89 Tourné, interview.

90 Serrano Migallón, *Marco jurídico*, 336.

91 González, Torres, and Jiménez, *La república informal*.

92 Cross, "Mexico," 313.
93 Camp, *Politics in Mexico*, 180.
94 Aguilar, interview.
95 Carlos Viñamata Paschkes, *La propiedad intelectual*, 3rd ed. (Mexico: Trillas, 2005), 77.
96 Serrano Migallón, *Marco jurídico*, 164.
97 Viñamata, *La propiedad intelectual*, 77.
98 Tourné, interview.
99 Also on the committee were two representatives of the Mexican embassy in Geneva, a representative of the Mexican foreign ministry, and – representing the private sector – a vice-president from Televisa.
100 Callejas, interview.
101 Viñamata, *La propiedad intelectual*, 77; translation by the author.
102 Carolyn Deere-Birkbeck, "The Politics of Intellectual Property Reform in Developing Countries," in *Intellectual Property and Sustainable Development: Development Agendas in a Changing World*, ed. Pedro Roffe (Oxford: Edward Elgar Press, 2009), http://papers.ssrn.com/sol3/papers.cfm?abstract_id=1325044.
103 Available under "Mexico" at http://www.iipa.com/countryreports.html.
104 See, for example, article 14 of Telmex's "Terms and Conditions of Internet Use" (available at http://www.telmex.com/mx/hogar/pdf/pt_descarga.jsp?a=Terminosycondiciones_Infinitum.pdf, and on file with the author).
105 Available (in Spanish) at http://pnd.presidencia.gob.mx/.
106 See http://pnd.calderon.presidencia.gob.mx/igualdad-de-oportunidades/cultura-arte-deporte-y-recreacion.html.
107 Translation by the author.
108 Jorge Basurto Hernández, Comisión Federal de Telécomunicaciones, director de servicios de valor agregado, interview by author, Mexico City, 29 January 2010.
109 Eduardo Vicente Nivón Bólan, professor of anthropology, Universidad Autónoma Metropolitana, interview by author, Mexico City, 9 October 2009.
110 Serrano Migallón, *Marco jurídico*, 71.
111 LFDA, art. 192.
112 Serrano Migallón, *Marco jurídico*, 153.
113 José Ramón Cárdeno Shaadi, general coordinator of legal affairs, SACM, interview by author, Mexico City, 10 November 2009.
114 Serrano Migallón, *Marco jurídico*, 154.
115 Ibid., 47–8.
116 Eric Alba, "Mafias controlan el pago de derechos de autor a compositores en México," *La Jornada Michoacán*, 23 May 2009, http://www

.lajornadamichoacan.com.mx/2009/05/23/index.php?section=cultura& article=016n1cul; Viñamata, *La propiedad intelectual*, 71–2; Angelina Cue Bolaños, "La Sociedad General de Escritores de México, SOGEM," *Revista Mexicana del Derecho de Autor* 1.2 (1990), 72–3.

117 Callejas, interview.

118 Serrano Migallón, *Marco jurídico*, 280; International Intellectual Property Alliance, "IIPA Letter on Copyright Enforcement and Pending Legislative Reform in Mexico" (2003), http://www.iipa.com/countryreports.html.

119 De la Parra Trujillo, "Comentarios a las reformas a la Ley Federal del Derecho de Autor," 107.

120 Alba, "Mafias controlan el pago de derechos de autor."

121 Callejas, interview.

122 Asociación Protectora de Cine y Música, "¿Quiénes somos?" http://www.apcm.org.mx/apcm.php?item=menuapcm&contenido=qsomos.

123 International Intellectual Property Alliance, "Special 301 Report: Mexico," 2007, http://www.iipa.com/countryreports.html.

124 Appleton, *Navigating NAFTA*, 126, 124.

125 García Moreno, "El capítulo XVII del TLCAN," 111.

126 A "three-strikes" policy would restrict then remove a user's Internet access for repeat copyright offences.

127 Aguilar, interview.

128 Morante, interview.

129 Mitchell, interview.

130 Tourné, interview.

131 Website: http://www.uspto.gov/ip/training/.

132 United States Patent and Trademark Office, "The Global Intellectual Policy Academy," http://www.uspto.gov/ip/training/.

133 Information from http://www.uspto.gov/ip/training/schedule_2009 .jsp.

134 Basurto, interview.

135 Mike Margáin, vice-president, American Chamber of Commerce Mexico, Intellectual Property Committee, interview by author, Mexico City, 27 April 2010.

136 Cross, "Mexico," 319.

137 Cathy Blacklock and Laura Macdonald, "Human Rights and Citizenship in Guatemala and Mexico: From 'Strategic' to 'New' Universalism?" *Social Politics* 5.2 (1998), 146–7.

138 *Propiedad intelectual, nuevas tecnologías y libre acceso a la cultura*, available at http://www.ccemx.org/img_act_x_tipo/propiedadint.pdf.

139 Callejas, interview.

140 As for practical interest in the issue of copyright, Callejas remarks that many academics depend on royalties for part of their income (interview).

141 Aguilar, interview; Callejas, interview.

142 Nivón, "Propiedad intelectual y política cultural," 62.

143 Diplomatic official, interview by author, Washington, DC, 13 August 2008.

144 Luis Schmidt, "Digital Millenium [sic] 'a la Mexicaine': Internet and Other Digital Technologies Examined in Light of the Mexican Copyright Law," *Copyright World Magazine* (January 1, 2001), http://74.125.95.132/search?q=cache:ePbeMjjMeuIJ:www.olivares.com.mx/formatos/lsr/digital.pdf+Digital+Millenium+%27a+la+Mexicaine%27&cd=1&hl=en&ct=clnk.

145 Article 27 II (c) of the LFDA.

146 Article 17 III of the LFDA.

147 The law also protects temporary or ephemeral digital copies, anticipating – incorrectly, it turns out – that it would be required by the final text of the Internet treaties.

148 A "non-paper," in international relations, is a paper circulated without attribution for comment. It does not represent an organization's official position.

149 INDAUTOR, "Internet & Technology Provisions: Questions for Discussion," non-paper for discussion at WIPO (2008). On file with the author.

150 Gabriela Barrios Garrido, "Internet y lo que falta en la nueva Ley Federal del Derecho de Autor," in *Estudios de Derecho Intelectual en Homenaje al Profesor David Rangel Medina*, ed. Manuel Becerra Ramírez (México: UNAM, 1998), 372. The only Internet-specific laws Mexico has on its books are related to e-commerce (Adriana Hernández Arzate, *Delimitación del contenido del derecho de autor en Internet*, tesis, Licenciado en Derecho [Toluca: Universidad Autónoma del Estado de México, 2006], 117).

151 Luis Schmidt, "The New Digital Agenda," *Copyright World*, 23 February 2009.

152 Ibid.

153 Serrano Migallón, *Marco jurídico*, 280; International Intellectual Property Alliance, "IIPA Letter on Copyright Enforcement."

154 International Intellectual Property Alliance, "Special 301 Report: Mexico" (2005), http://www.iipa.com/countryreports.html.

155 Serrano Migallón, *Marco jurídico*, 336.

156 International Intellectual Property Alliance, "Special 301 Report: Mexico," 2005–10, http://www.iipa.com/countryreports.html; Office of the United States Trade Representative (USTR), "Special 301 Report," reports dating back to 1989, http://www.keionline.org/ustr/special301.

157 As already noted, the US government, particularly the PTO, have provided training to Mexican copyright officials over the past decade.

158 Enforcement in the post–1997 law period was also the main issue, as the US government claimed to be satisfied with Mexico's laws.

159 Available at http://www.iipa.com/countryreports.html.

160 For a biography of Guerra Zamarro, see http://www.pglmg.com/home .php?seccion=socios&subSeccion=guerrazamarro.

161 Morante, interview.

162 Aguilar, interview; Morante, interview; Tourné, interview. For example, he was apparently working to get the Internet treaties officially published. Although ratified in 2003, parts of the treaties (some agreed statements) were never published fully, a result of human error. Since treaties in Mexico are not formally part of the law of the land until they are published, this is a technical issue of some importance (Morante, interview; Margáin, interview), although it is unclear to the author how much effect it has on the actual conduct of copyright policy and the ongoing debate about what implementation of the Internet treaties should look like with respect to TPMs and ISP liability.

163 Aguilar, interview.

164 US government official, interview.

165 Tourné, interview.

166 "Nace coalición en defensa del acceso legal a la cultura," *El Universal*, 19 November 2009, http://www.eluniversal.com.mx/notas/641091.html.

167 Aguilar, interview; Jose Miranda, gerente legal, Sociedad Mexicana de Productores de Fonogramas, interview by author, Mexico City, 25 November 2009.

168 The coalition's potential could be seen in early 2010, when the government announced that it would give government officials ex officio authority to deal with copyright infringement (that is, they would not have to wait for a complaint in order to begin an investigation) ("Diputados aprueban ley contra piratería," *El Universal*, 6 April 2010, http://www .eluniversal.com.mx/notas/670994.html). This was one of the Coalición's initial demands, one for which members had been lobbying for three years (Margáin, interview). Whether this will actually have any effect on copyright infringement, given Mexico's resource constraints and history of weak enforcement of strong copyright laws, remains to be seen.

169 Basurto, interview.

170 IIPA 2010. While the two positions are not necessarily irreconcilable, neither will Telmex's privileged position in the Mexican political economy

necessarily trump that of the content industries. Televisa, also an important Mexican economic player, has both ISP and content interests, for example.

171 This section draws on Blayne Haggart, "Birth of a Movement: The Anti-Counterfeiting Trade Agreement and the Politicization of Mexican Copyright," *Policy & Internet*, forthcoming 2014.

172 Comisión de Ciencia y Tecnología del Senado de México, "B-0564 Seminario: 'Derecho de autor en el entorno digital'" (2008), http://comunicacion .senado.gob.mx/index.php?option=com_content&task=view&id=7856& Itemid=163.

173 As cited by Ricardo Zamora, "Internet necesario: Crónica de un pequeño gran cambio," in *Ciudadanos.mx: Twitter y el cambio político en México*, ed. Ana Vega and José Merino (Mexico City: Random House Mondadori, 2010), 26.

174 Antonio Martínez Velázquez, Communications and digital content officer, Article 19 Mexico. Interview by author, Mexico City, 18 February 2013.

175 The Ley sobre la Aprobación de Tratados en Materia Económica.

176 Francisco Javier Castellón Fonseca, former senator, PRD, interview by author, Mexico City, 20 February 2013.

177 Castellón, interview.

178 At his 9 March 2010 appearance before the Science and Technology Commission, IMPI head Jorge Amigo dismissed critics as "clueless people who believe that ACTA will destroy the Internet" (Francisco Javier Castellón, "En respuesta ACTA y #ACTA en la conciencia legislativa," in *Ciudadanos.mx*, 86, author's translation).

179 Grupo Plural, testimony, 23 November 2010, 25. Available at http:// www.senado.gob.mx/comisiones/LX/grupo_acta/content/reu.htm.

180 Grupo Plural, "Documento de conclusiones" (Final report), 20 July 2011, 1, http://www.senado.gob.mx/comisiones/LX/grupo_acta/content/ docs/20julio11.pdf.

181 Grupo Plural, testimony, 12 July 2011, 23.

182 Comisión Federal de Telecomunicaciones, "Emite COFETEL consideraciones sobre el ACTA," Comunicado de prensa no. 65/2010, 24 November 2010, http://www.cft.gob.mx/swb/Cofetel_2008/652010.

183 Asociación Mexicana de Internet, "Postura de la Asociación Mexicana de Internet A.C. (AMIPCI) sobre la sección del ámbito digital del Acuerdo commercial anti-falsificaciones, ACTA," 12 July 2012, http://amipci.org .mx/?P=articulo&Article=103.

184 Martínez, interview.

185 Grupo Plural, testimony, 24 November 2010.

186 Castellón, interview; Pepe Flores, blogger,interview by author via Skype, 19 February 2013.

187 Jesús Ramírez Díaz, technical secretary, Mexican Senate Committee on Science and Technology, interview by author, Mexico City, 21 February 2013.

188 Ramírez, interview.

189 León Felipe Sánchez Ambía, intellectual property lawyer, interview by author, Mexico City, 19 February 2013.

190 Ramírez, interview.

191 Martínez, interview; Ramírez, interview.

192 Geraldine Juárez, "Senado Mexicano se postra a los pies de la industria del copyright," alt1040.com, 16 December 2011), http://alt1040.com/2011/12/senado-mexicano-se-postra-a-los-pies-de-la-industria-del-copyright.

193 Pepe Flores, "Legisladores y ciudadanos piden a Felipe Calderón retirar la firma de ACTA." alt1040.com, 18 July 2012, http://alt1040.com/2012/07/senado-acta-calderon.

194 Mike Palmedo, "Mexican Legislature Passes Two Resolutions Opposing the Executive's Signing of ACTA," infojustice.org, 19 July 2012, http://infojustice.org/archives/26624. The resolutions are available at http://www.senado.gob.mx/index.php?ver=sp&mn=2&sm=2&id=15792&lg=61 (Senate) and http://www.senado.gob.mx/index.php?ver=sp&mn=2&sm=2&id=15776&lg=61 (House).

195 Flores, "Legisladores."

196 Discussed in the following chapter. Mike Masnick, "Mexico's IP Office Surprised Its Congress by Signing ACTA, and Now Hopes to Win Their Support," Techdirt, 16 July 2012, http://www.techdirt.com/articles/20120716/03505519709/mexicos-ip-office-surprised-its-congress-signing-acta-now-hopes-to-win-their-support.shtml.

197 Cable from US embassy in Mexico City, 19 December 2007, Wikileaks cable 07MEXICO6229.

198 United States, "Joint Statement by North American Leaders," the White House, 2 April 2012, http://www.whitehouse.gov/the-press-office/2012/04/02/joint-statement-north-american-leaders.

199 Camp, *Politics in Mexico: The Democratic Consolidation*, 295.

Conclusion: The New Politics of Copyright and the Potential for Variation

1 Recall that under a notice-and-takedown regime, material that has been alleged to infringe on a copyright must be taken down. Only then can

the user file a counter-notice if he or she believes no copyright has been infringed.

2 As noted in the introduction, guaranteed market access makes it harder for any one NAFTA country to convince the other to change its policies. However, this effect is likely to be most pronounced when the United States, the largest economic power in the region, is the one doing the offering.

3 Deere, "The Politics of Intellectual Property Reform in Developing Countries."

4 The other countries involved as of October 2013 are Australia, Japan, Malaysia, Peru, and Vietnam.

5 Sean Flynn, "Public Interest Analysis of Articles 1 and 4 of the US TPP Proposal for an IP Chapter," draft version 1.0 (Washington, DC: Program on Information Justice and International Property, American University Washington College of Law, 2012), 8–9.

6 "USTR Seeks to Enact ACTA This Year, but TPP Seen as Key New Venue," *Inside U.S. Trade*, 13 July 2012.

7 Flynn, "Public Interest Analysis," 9.

8 Ibid., 25–6.

9 Ibid., 26–7.

10 Carrie Ellen Sager, "TPP's Effects on the IP Law of Canada and Mexico," Infojustice.org, 11 April 2012, http://infojustice.org/archives/9508.

11 Geist, "Mexico signs ACTA."

12 This section draws on Blayne Haggart, "Fair Copyright for Canada: Lessons from Canada's First Facebook Uprising," *Canadian Journal of Political Science*, forthcoming.

13 Nicole Pelroth, "Under Scrutiny, Google Spends Record Amount on Lobbying," *New York Times* Bits blog, 23 April 2012, http://bits.blogs.nytimes.com/2012/04/23/under-scrutiny-google-spends-record-amount-on-lobbying/.

14 Joel Hruska, "How SOPA Could Actually Break the Internet," Extreme Tech, 19 December 2011, http://www.extremetech.com/computing/109533-how-sopa-could-actually-break-the-internet/2.

15 Yochai Benkler, "'The networked public sphere': Framing the Public Discourse of the SOPA/PIPA Debate," *The Guardian*, 15 May 2012, http://www.guardian.co.uk/media-network/video/2012/may/15/yochai-benkler-networked-public-sphere-sopa-pipa.

16 Mike Masnick, "Lamar Smith Says 'Just Joking …' about Tomorrow; SOPA Markup Postponed," Techdirt, 20 December 2011, http://www.techdirt.com/articles/20111220/11175317144/lamar-smith-says-just-joking-about-tomorrow-sopa-markup-postponed.shtml.

17 Center for Democracy and Technology, "The Stop Online Piracy Act: Summary, Problems & Implications" (2012), https://www.cdt.org/files/pdfs/SOPA%202-pager%20final.pdf.

18 A copy of which can be seen at http://en.wikipedia.org/wiki/File:Wikipedia_Blackout_Screen.jpg.

19 Wikipedia, "SOPA Initiative/Learn More," 4 May 2012, http://en.wikipedia.org/wiki/Wikipedia:SOPA_initiative/Learn_more.

20 Benkler, "'The Networked Public Sphere.'"

21 Mike Masnick, "Joe Biden on the Internet: 'If it ain't broke, don't fix it… unless Hollywood asks you to," Techdirt, 3 November 2011, http://www.techdirt.com/articles/20111102/11450816604/joe-biden-internet-if-it-aint-broke-dont-fix-it-unless-hollywood-asks-you-to.shtml.

22 Chris Frates, "Exclusive: New Internet Industry Trade Association to Launch," *National Journal*, 25 July 2012, http://influencealley.nationaljournal.com/2012/07/exclusive-new-internet-industr-1.php.

23 Cyrus Farivar, "For the First Time Ever, U.S. Seeking International Limits on Copyright," ars technical, 3 July 2012, http://arstechnica.com/tech-policy/2012/07/us-proposes-new-copyright-provision-in-major-international-treaty/.

References

Interview Subjects

United States

Band, Jonathan. Intellectual property lawyer. Interview by author, digital recording. Washington, DC. 20 June 2008.

Biette, David. Director, Canada Institute, Woodrow Wilson International Center for Scholars. Interview by author, digital recording. Washington. 27 June 2008.

Chaitovitz, Ann. Executive director, Future of Music Coalition. Interview by author, digital recording. Washington. 22 July 2008.

Consumer-electronics lawyer. Interview by author, digital recording. Washington. 2 July 2008.

Greenstein, Seth. Lawyer, Constantine Cannon LLP. Interview by author, digital recording. Washington. 9 July 2008.

Kupferschmid, Keith. Senior vice-president for intellectual property policy and enforcement, Software and Information Industry Association. Interview by author, digital recording. Washington. 1 July 2008.

McCoy, Stan. Assistant US trade representative for intellectual property and innovation, Office of the United States Trade Representative. Interview by author, digital recording. Washington. 8 August 2008.

Metalitz, Steven. Counsel, International Intellectual Property Alliance. Interview by author, digital recording. Washington. 30 July 2008.

Mexican diplomatic official. Interview by author, digital recording. Washington. 13 August 2008.

Mitchell, Stevan. Vice-president, intellectual property policy, Entertainment Software Association. Interview by author, digital recording. Washington. 8 July 2008.

Mondy, Yannick. First secretary, trade policy, Embassy of Canada in the United States. Interview by author, digital recording. Washington. 6 August 2008.

Motion-picture industry official. Interview by author, digital recording. Washington. 18 July 2008.

Papovich, Joseph. Senior vice-president, International, Recording Industry Association of America. Interview by author, digital recording. Washington. 17 July 2008.

Petricone, Michael. Senior vice-president of government affairs, Consumer Electronics Association. Interview by author, digital recording. Washington. 14 August 2008.

Sands, Christopher. Senior fellow, Hudson Institute. Interview by author, digital recording. Washington. 17 June 2008.

Schneider, Jennifer. Legislative counsel, Rep. Rick Boucher (D-VA). Interview by author, digital recording. Washington. 25 July 2008.

Simon, Emery. Counsellor, Business Software Alliance. Washington. 1 August 2008.

Sohn, Gigi. President and co-founder, Public Knowledge. Interview by author, digital recording. Washington. 5 August 2008.

Strong, Maria. Representative, International Intellectual Property Alliance. Interview by author, digital recording. Washington. 30 July 2008.

Turkewitz, Neil. Executive vice-president, Recording Industry Association of America. Interview by author, digital recording. Washington. 17 July 2008.

Turner, Jeff. Intellectual property lawyer, Patton Boggs. Interview by author, digital recording. Washington. 2 July 2008.

US government official. Interview by author, digital recording. Washington. 1 July 2008.

Canada

Angus, Charlie. New Democratic Party Member of Parliament, musician, former critic for the Department of Canadian Heritage. Interview by author, digital recording. Ottawa, ON. 14 April 2008.

Austin, Michele. Former chief of staff, Industry Minister Maxime Bernier. Interview by author, digital recording. Ottawa. 30 April 2008.

Copeland, Tom. Chair, Canadian Association of Internet Providers. Interview by author, digital recording, via telephone. Ontario. 24 June 2010.

Fewer, David. Director, Canadian Internet Policy and Public Interest Clinic. Interview by author, digital recording. Ottawa. 7 February 2008.

Geist, Michael. Professor of law, University of Ottawa. Interview by author, digital recording. Ottawa. 14 May 2008.

Glick, Jacob. Policy counsel, Google Canada. Interview by author, digital recording. Ottawa. 21 April 2008.

Gratton, Denis. Former manager, copyright policy, Department of Canadian Heritage. Interview by author, digital recording. Ottawa. 7 February 2008.

Hume, Kim. Director, public policy and communications, Alliance of Canadian Cinema, Television and Radio Artists. Interview by author, digital recording, via telephone. Toronto, ON. 19 May 2008.

Hyndman, Rob. Technology lawyer. Interview by author, digital recording, via telephone. Toronto. 22 April 2008.

Jones, Paul. Professional officer, Canadian Association of University Teachers. Interview by author, digital recording, via telephone. Ottawa. 5 February 2009.

Kee, Jason. Director of policy and legal affairs, Entertainment Software Association of Canada. Interview by author, digital recording. Ottawa. 10 February 2008.

Lam, Kempton. Copyright blogger. Interview by author, digital recording, via telephone. Calgary, AB. 16 April 2008.

McOrmond, Russell. Independent software producer. Interview by author, digital recording. Ottawa. 18 January 2008.

Mirella, Loris. Senior project leader, Copyright Policy Branch, Department of Canadian Heritage. Interview by author, digital recording. Ottawa. 7 February 2008.

Neil, Garry. Policy adviser, Alliance of Canadian Cinema, Television and Radio Artists. Interview by author, digital recording, via telephone. Toronto. 19 May 2008.

Rioux, Jean-Sébastien. Chief of staff to former Industry Minister Jim Prentice. Interview by author, digital recording, via telephone. Calgary. 26 February 2009.

Serry, Keith. Communications director, Canadian Music Creators Coalition. Interview by author, digital recording. Montreal, QC. 13 May 2008.

Wills, Steve. Manager, legal affairs, Association of Universities and Colleges of Canada. Interview by author, digital recording. Ottawa. 10 February 2009.

Mexico

Aguilar, Claraluz. Directora Juridica, Asociación Mexicana de Productores de Fonogramas y Videogramas, A.C. Interview by author, digital recording. Mexico City. 3 February 2010.

Arteaga Alvarado, María del Carmen. Legal scholar; Former legal director, INDAUTOR (2000–8). Interview by author, digital recording. Mexico City. 19 October 2009.

Basurto Hernández, Jorge. Comisión Federal de Telécomunicaciones, director de servicios de valor agregado. Interview by author, digital recording. Mexico City. 29 January 2010.

Callejas, Cesar Benedicto. Director, patents and trademarks, National Autonomous University of Mexico (UNAM). Interview by author, digital recording. Mexico City. 26 October 2009.

Cárdeno Shaadi, José Ramón. General coordinator of legal affairs, Sociedad de Autores y Compositores de México (SACM). Interview by author, digital recording. Mexico City. 10 November 2009.

Castellón Fonseca, Francisco Javier. Former senator, PRD. Interview by author, digital recording. Mexico City. 20 February 2013.

Flores, Pepe. Blogger. Interview by author via Skype. 19 February 2013.

López Cuenca, Alberto. Professor of philosophy and contemporary art theory and coordinator of the doctoral program on cultural creation and theories at the Universidad de las Américas (Puebla, Mexico). Interview by author, digital recording. Puebla. 18 September 2009.

Margáin, Mike. Vice-president, American Chamber of Commerce of Mexico Intellectual Property Committee. Interview by author, digital recording. Mexico City. 27 April 2010.

Martínez Velázquez, Antonio. Communications and digital content officer, Article 19 Mexico. Interview by author, digital recording. Mexico City. 18 February 2013.

Miranda, Jose. Gerente legal, Sociedad Mexicana de Productores de Fonogramas. Interview by author, digital recording. Mexico City. 25 November 2009.

Morante Soria, Manuel. Copyright lawyer, Arochi, Marroquín & Linder, S.C. Interview by author, digital recording. Mexico City. 3 December 2009.

Nivón Bólan, Eduardo Vicente. Professor of anthropology, Universidad Autónoma Metropolitana. Interview by author, digital recording and written notes. Mexico City. 9 October 2009.

Ramírez Díaz, Jesús. Technical secretary, Mexican Senate Committee on Science and Technology. Interview by author, digital recording. Mexico City. 21 February 2013.

Sánchez Ambía, León Felipe. Intellectual property lawyer. Interview by author, digital recording. Mexico City. 19 February 2013.

Tourné Guerrero, Alfredo. Director of protection, INDAUTOR. Interview by author, digital recording. Mexico City. 24 and 29 September 2009.

Bibliography

Abbott, Frederick M. *Law and Policy of Regional Integration: The NAFTA and Western Hemispheric Integration in the World Trade Organization System.* Boston: Martinus Nijhoff Publishers, 1995.

Acheson, Keith, and Christopher J. Maule. "Copyright, Contract, the Cultural Industries, and NAFTA." In *Mass Media and Free Trade: NAFTA and the Cultural Industries,* ed. Emile G. McAnany and Kenton T. Wilkinson, 351–82. Austin: University of Texas Press, 1996.

Alba, Eric. "Mafias controlan el pago de derechos de autor a compositores en México." *La Jornada Michoacán,* 23 May 2009. http://www.lajornadamichoacan.com.mx/2009/05/23/index.php?section=cultura&article=016n1cul.

Albini, Steve. "The Problem with Music." *Maximumrocknroll* 133 (1994). Excerpted from *The Baffler* 5. http://www.arancidamoeba.com/mrr/problemwithmusic.html.

Amnesty International. "EU Urged to Reject International Anti-Counterfeiting Pact." News release, 10 February 2012. https://www.amnesty.org/en/news/eu-urged-reject-international-anti-counterfeiting-pact-2012-02-10.

Amsden, Alice H. *Asia's Next Giant: South Korea and Late Industrialization.* New York: Oxford University Press, 1989.

Amsden, Alice H. *The Rise of "The Rest": Challenges to the West from Late-Industrializing Economies.* Oxford: Oxford University Press, 2000.

Ángel Quintanilla, José. "Algunos puntos sobre la piratería editorial en México." *Pensar el Libro* 2 (2005). http://www.cerlalc.org/Revista_Pirateria/pdf/n_art04.pdf.

Appleton, Barry. *Navigating NAFTA: A Concise User's Guide to the North American Free Trade Agreement.* Scarborough, ON: Carswell, 1994.

Archer, Margaret S. *Realist Social Theory: The Morphogenetic Approach.* Cambridge, UK: Cambridge University Press, 1995.

Armstrong, Kenneth, and Simon Bulmer. *The Governance of the Single European Market.* Manchester: Manchester University Press, 1998.

Arrow, Kenneth. "Economic Welfare and the Allocation of Resources for Invention." In *The Rate and Direction of Inventive Activity: Economic and Social Factors.* Princeton: Princeton University Press, 1962. http://www.litagion.org/pubs/papers/2006/P1856.pdf.

Arthur, Charles. "Acta Criticised after Thousands Protest in Europe." *The Guardian,* 13 February 2012. http://www.guardian.co.uk/technology/2012/feb/13/acta-protests-europe.

Asociación Mexicana de Internet. "Postura de la Asociación Mexicana de Internet A.C. (AMIPCI) sobre la sección del ámbito digital del Acuerdo

commercial anti-falsificaciones, ACTA." 12 July 2012. http://amipci.org
.mx/?P=articulo&Article=103.

Banks, Sam, and Andrew Kitching. *Bill C-60: An Act to Amend the Copyright
Act, Legislative Summary*. LS-512-E. Ottawa: Library of Parliament, 2005.

Bannerman, Sara. "Canada and the Berne Convention, 1886–1971." PhD diss.
Carleton University, Ottawa, 2009.

Bannerman, Sara. "Canadian Copyright Reform: Consulting with Copyright's
Changing Public." *Intellectual Property Journal* 19.2 (2006): 271–97.

Banting, Keith, George Hoberg, and Richard Simeon. "Introduction." In *Degrees of
Freedom: Canada and the United States in a Changing World*, ed. K. Banting, G.
Hoberg and R. Simeon, 1–19. Montreal: McGill-Queen's University Press, 1997.

Barrios Garrido, Gabriela. "Internet y lo que falta en la nueva Ley Federal del
Derecho de Autor." In *Estudios de derecho intelectual en homenaje al Profesor
David Rangel Medina*, ed. Manuel Becerra Ramírez. Mexico: UNAM, 1998.
http://www.bibliojuridica.org/libros/1/164/21.pdf.

Baumgartner, Frank R., and Bryan D. Jones. *Agendas and Instability in American
Politics*. Chicago: University of Chicago Press, 1993.

Bell, Stephen. "Do We Really Need a New 'Constructivist Institutionalism' to
Explain Institutional Change?" *British Journal of Political Science* 41.4 (2011):
883–906.

Benkler, Yochai. "'The Networked Public Sphere': Framing the Public Discourse of the SOPA/PIPA Debate." *The Guardian*, 15 May 2012. http://
www.guardian.co.uk/media-network/video/2012/may/15/yochai-
benkler-networked-public-sphere-sopa-pipa.

Benkler, Yochai. "A Political Economy of the Public Domain: Markets in
Information Goods versus the Marketplace of Ideas." In *Expanding the
Boundaries of Intellectual Property: Innovation Policy for the Knowledge Society*,
ed. Rochelle Cooper Dreyfuss, Diane Leenheer Zimmerman, and Harry
First, 267–92. Oxford: Oxford University Press, 2001.

Bennett, Colin J. "What Is Policy Convergence and What Causes It?" *British
Journal of Political Science* 21.2 (1991): 215–33.

Besen, Stanley M. "Intellectual Property." In *The New Palgrave Dictionary of
Economics and the Law*, vol. 2, ed. Peter Newman, 348–52. London: Macmillan, 1998.

Bettig, Ronald V. *Copyrighting Culture: The Political Economy of Intellectual
Property*. Boulder, CO: Westview Press, 1996.

Blacklock, Cathy, and Laura Macdonald. "Human Rights and Citizenship in
Guatemala and Mexico: From 'Strategic' to 'New' Universalism?" *Social
Politics* 5.2 (1998): 132–57.

Boggs, J.S.G. "Who Owns This?" *Chicago-Kent Law Review* 68.2 (1993): 889–910.

Boldrin, Michele, and David K. Levine. *Against Intellectual Monopoly*. Cambridge: Cambridge University Press, 2008.

Boldrin, Michele, and David K. Levine. "The Case against Intellectual Property." *Research on Innovation* 2 (2002). http://www.researchoninnovation.org/tiip/archive/issue2003_2.html.

Borland, John. "FAQ: Sony's 'Rootkit' CDs." CNET News, 10 November 2005. http://news.cnet.com/FAQ-Sonys-rootkit-CDs/2100-1029_3-5946760.html.

Boyle, James. *The Public Domain: Enclosing the Commons of the Mind*. New Haven: Yale University Press, 2008.

Brennan, Timothy J. "Copyright, Property, and the Right to Deny." *Chicago-Kent Law Review* 68.2 (1993): 675–715.

Breyer, Stephen. "The Uneasy Case for Copyright: A Study of Copyright in Books, Photocopies, and Computer Programs." *Harvard Law Review* 84.2 (1970): 281–351.

Brown, Ian. "The Evolution of Anti-Circumvention Law." *International Review of Law and Computers* 20.3 (2006): 239–60.

Burgess, Rick. "$222,000 Award Upheld in RIAA v. Jammie Thomas-Rasset Lawsuit." Techspot.com, 12 September 2012. http://www.techspot.com/news/50132-220000-award-upheld-in-riaa-v-jammie-thomas-rasset-lawsuit.html.

Business Coalition for Balanced Copyright. "A Balanced 'Package' Approach for a Strong Canadian Copyright Regime." February 2008. http://static.googleusercontent.com/external_content/untrusted_dlcp/services.google.com/en//blog_resources/google_bcbc_position_paper.pdf.

Caballero Leal, José Luis, and Mauricio Jalife Daher. "Comentarios a la Ley Federal de Derecho de Autor." In *Legislación de Derechos de Autor*, 2006 edition, i–xxvii. Mexico: Editorial Sista, 2006.

Cameron, Charles M., and Rebecca Morton. "Formal Theory Meets Data." In *Political Science: The State of the Discipline*, ed. Ira Katznelson and Helen V. Milner, 784–804. New York: WW Norton & Co., 2002.

Cameron, Maxwell A., and Brian W. Tomlin. *The Making of NAFTA: How the Deal Was Done*. Ithaca: Cornell University Press, 2000.

Camp, Roderic Ai. *Politics in Mexico: The Democratic Consolidation*. 5th ed. New York: Oxford University Press, 2007.

Campbell, John L. *Institutional Change and Governance*. Princeton: Princeton University Press, 2004.

Canadian Association of Internet Providers (CAIP). "Submission from Canadian Association of Internet Providers." Copyright reform process, 18 September 2001. http://www.ic.gc.ca/eic/site/crp-prda.nsf/eng/rp00314.html.

Canadian Intellectual Property Council (IP Council). "Business Coalition Stresses Need for Better Protection of Intellectual Property Rights." 2008. http://www.ipcouncil.ca/uploads/ReleaseIPCoalitionLaunch260508.pdf.

Canadian Media Production Association. *Profile 2011: An Economic Report on the Screen-based Production Industry in Canada*. Ottawa: Canadian Media Production Association, Association des producteurs de films et de télévision du Québec, and the Department of Canadian Heritage, 2011. http://www.cftpa.ca/newsroom/pdf/profile/Profile2011Eng.pdf.

Canadian Recording Industry Association (CRIA). "News." 2006. http://www.cria.ca/news/020306a_n.php.

Canadian Recording Industry Association (CRIA). "Submission of the Canadian Recording Industry Association in Respect of Consultation Paper on Digital Copyright Issues." 2001. http://www.ic.gc.ca/eic/site/crp-prda.nsf/eng/rp00249.html.

CARFAC Ontario. "Copyright Bill Represents Status Quo for Visual and Media Artists." News release, 26 June 2008. www.carfacontario.ca/images/C-61_Release.pdf.

Carrier, Michael A. "Copyright and Innovation: The Untold Story." *Wisconsin Law Review*, 2012, no. 4. http://ssrn.com/abstract=2099876.

Carrillo, Pedro. *El derecho intellectual en México*. Mexicali: Universidad Autónoma de Baja California, 2002.

Carroll, Michael W. "The Struggle for Music Copyright." *Villanova University School of Law Working Paper Series* 31 (2005): 908–61.

Castellón, Francisco Javier. "En respuesta ACTA y #ACTA en la conciencia legislativa." In *Ciudadanos.mx: Twitter y el cambio politico en México*, ed. Ana Vega and José Merino, 83–7. Mexico City: Random House Mondadori, 2010.

Center for Democracy and Technology. "The Stop Online Piracy Act: Summary, Problems & Implications." 2012. https://www.cdt.org/files/pdfs/SOPA%202-pager%20final.pdf.

Chang, Ha-Joon. "Kicking away the Ladder." *post-autistic economics review* 15 (2002). http://www.btinternet.com/~pae_news/review/issue15.htm.

Chartrand, Harry Hillman. *The Compleat Canadian Copyright Act: Past, Present and Proposed Provisions 1921–2006*. Saskatoon: Compiler Press, 2006.

Clarkson, Stephen. *Does North America Exist? Governing the Continent after NAFTA and 9/11*. Toronto and Washington: University of Toronto Press and Woodrow Wilson Center Press, 2008.

Clarkson, Stephen. *Uncle Sam and Us: Globalization, Neoconservatism, and the Canadian State*. Toronto: University of Toronto Press, 2002.

Cohen, Stephen D., Robert A. Blecker, and Peter D. Whitney. *Fundamentals of U.S. Foreign Trade Policy: Economics Politics, Laws, and Issues*. 2nd ed. Boulder: Westview Press, 2003.

Computer and Communications Industry Association (CCIA). "Comments of the Computer & Communications Industry Association before the United States Trade Representative re 2010 Special 301 Review." Docket no. USTR-2010-0003, 2010. http://www.ccianet.org/CCIA/files/ccLibraryFiles/Filename/000000000321/CCIA-2010-Spec301-cmts.pdf.

Connectus Consulting Inc. *The Economic Impact of Canadian Copyright Industries – Sectoral Analysis*. Ottawa: Copyright Policy Branch, Department of Canadian Heritage, 2006.

Coombe, Rosemary J. *The Cultural Life of Intellectual Properties: Authorship, Appropriation, and the Law*. Durham: Duke University Press, 1998.

Cross, John C. "Mexico." In *Media Piracy in Emerging Economies*, ed. Joe Karaganis, 305–26. New York: Social Science Research Council, 2011.

Cue Bolaños, Angelina. "La Sociedad General de Escritores de México, SOGEM." *Revista Mexicana del Derecho de Autor* 1.2 (1990): 21–9.

Cultural Human Resources Council. *Cultural HR Study 2010: Labour Market Information for Canada's Cultural Sector Report*. Ottawa: Conference Board of Canada, 2010.

Cutler, A. Claire. "Gramsci, Law, and the Culture of Global Capitalism." *Critical Review of International Social and Political Philosophy* 8.4 (2005): 527–42.

de Beer, Jeremy. "Constitutional Jurisdiction over Paracopyright Laws." In *In the Public Interest: The Future of Canadian Copyright Law*, ed. Michael Geist, 89–124. Toronto: Irwin Law, 2005.

de Beer, Jeremy. "Copyright and Innovation in the Networked Information Economy." Conference Board of Canada Working Paper. 2009.

de Beer, Jeremy. "Jeremy de Beer on Canada's Copyright Bill: Win-win or Spin-spin?" *National Post*, 13 June 2008. http://network.nationalpost.com/np/blogs/fullcomment/archive/2008/06/13/174920.aspx.

de Beer, Jeremy, and Christopher D. Clemmer. "Global Trends in Online Copyright Enforcement: The Role of Internet Intermediaries." *Jurimetrics* 49.4 (2009). http://ssrn.com/abstract=1529722.

Deere, Carolyn. "The Politics of Intellectual Property Reform in Developing Countries." In *Intellectual Property and Sustainable Development: Development Agendas in a Changing World*, ed. Pedro Roffe. Oxford: Edward Elgar Press, 2009. http://papers.ssrn.com/sol3/papers.cfm?abstract_id=1325044.

Deere-Birkbeck, Carolyn. *The Implementation Game: The TRIPS Agreement and the Global Politics of Intellectual Property Reform in Developing Countries*. Oxford: Oxford University Press, 2009.

De la Parra Trujillo, Eduardo. "Comentarios a las reformas a la Ley Federal del Derecho de Autor." *Revista de Derecho Privado* 3.8 (2004): 95–110.

DiMaggio, Paul J., and Walter W. Powell. "Introduction." In *The New Institutionalism in Organizational Analysis*, ed. W.W. Powell and P.J. DiMaggio, 1–38. Chicago: University of Chicago Press, 1991.

Dinwoodie, Graeme. "The WIPO Copyright Treaty: A Transition to the Future of International Copyright Lawmaking?" *Case Western Reserve Law Review* 57.4 (2007): 751–66. http://ssrn.com/abstract=1601235.

Djelic, Marie-Laure, and Sigrid Quack. "Overcoming Path Dependency: Path Generation in Open Systems." *Theoretical Sociology* 36 (2007): 161–86.

Doern, G. Bruce, and Markus Sharaput. *Canadian Intellectual Property: The Politics of Innovating Institutions and Interests*. Toronto: University of Toronto Press, 2000.

Doyle, Simon. *Prey to Thievery*. Ottawa: Simon Doyle, 2006.

Drahos, Peter. *A Philosophy of Intellectual Property*. Aldershot: Dartmouth, 1996.

Drahos, Peter. "The US, China and the G-77 in the Era of Responsive Patentability." In *Global Perspectives on Patent Law*, ed. Margo Bagley and Ruth Okediji. Oxford: Oxford University Press, 2012.

Drahos, Peter, with John Braithwaite. *Information Feudalism: Who Owns the Knowledge Economy?* London: Earthscan Publications Ltd, 2002.

Dutfield, Graham, and Uma Suthersanen. *Global Intellectual Property Law*. Cheltenham: Edward Elgar, 2008.

Earl, Jennifer, Katrina Kimport, Greg Prieto, Carly Rush, and Kimberly Reynoso. "Changing the World One Webpage at a Time: Conceptualizing and Explaining Internet Activism." *Mobilization: An International Journal* 15 (2010): 425–46.

Economic Council of Canada. *Report on Intellectual and Industrial Property*. Ottawa: Economic Council of Canada, 1971.

The Economist. "False Friends." 13 January 1996, 66.

Electronic Frontier Foundation (EFF). "Chamberlain Group Inc. v. Skylink Technologies Inc." 2004. https://www.eff.org/cases/chamberlain-group-inc-v-skylink-technologies-inc.

Electronic Frontier Foundation (EFF). "Unintended Consequences: Twelve Years under the DMCA." March 2010. http://www.eff.org/wp/unintended-consequences-under-dmca.

El Universal. "Diputados aprueban ley contra piratería." 6 April 2010. http://www.eluniversal.com.mx/notas/670994.html.

El Universal. "Nace coalición en defensa del acceso legal a la cultura." 19 November 2009. http://www.eluniversal.com.mx/notas/641091.html.

Ernesto. "AT&T Threatens Persistent Pirates with Account Termination." TorrentFreak, 13 September 2013. http://torrentfreak.com/att-threatens-persistent-pirates-with-account-termination-130913/.

Ernesto. "Copyright lobby hires pro-ACTA demonstrators." TorrentFreak, 24 April 2012. http://torrentfreak.com/copyright-lobby-hires-pro-acta-demonstators-120424/.

Escobar, Reynaldo Urtiaga. "Los sistemas de derechos de autor y copyright hoy." *Revista Mexicana del Derecho de Autor* Año 2.6 (2002): 11–15.

Farivar, Cyrus. "For the First Time Ever, U.S. Seeking International Limits on Copyright." *ars technica*, 3 July 2012. http://arstechnica.com/tech-policy/2012/07/us-proposes-new-copyright-provision-in-major-international-treaty/.

Ficsor, Mihály. *The Law of Copyright and the Internet: The 1996 WIPO Treaties, Their Interpretation and Implementation.* Oxford: Oxford University Press, 2002.

Fink, Carsten, and Keith E. Maskus. "Why We Study Intellectual Property Rights and What We Have Learned." In *Intellectual Property and Development*, ed. C. Fink and K.E. Maskus, 1–15. Washington: World Bank, 2005.

Fioretos, Orfeo. "Historical Institutionalism in International Relations. *International Organization* 65.2 (2011): 367–99.

Flores, Pepe. "Legisladores y ciudadanos piden a Felipe Calderón retirar la firma de ACTA." alt1040.com, 18 July 2012. http://alt1040.com/2012/07/senado-acta-calderon.

Flynn, Sean. "Public Interest Analysis of Articles 1 and 4 of the US TPP Proposal for an IP Chapter." Draft version 1.0. Program on Information Justice and International Property, American University Washington College of Law. 2012.

Frates, Chris. "Exclusive: New Internet Industry Trade Association to Launch." *National Journal*, 25 July 2012. http://influencealley.national journal.com/2012/07/exclusive-new-internet-industr-1.php.

Frith, Simon, and Lee Marshall. "Making Sense of Copyright." In *Music and Copyright*, 2nd ed., ed. S. Frith and L. Marshall, 1–20. Edinburgh: Edinburgh University Press, 2004.

Garcia, Gabriel. "Economic Development and the Course of Intellectual Property Protection in Mexico." *Texas International Law Journal* 27 (1992): 703–53.

García Moreno, Victor Carlos. "El capítulo XVII del TLCAN y su influencia en la nueva ley Mexicana del derecho de autor." In *Estudios de derecho intelectual en homenaje al Profesor David Rangel Medina*, ed. Manuel Becerra Ramírez, 103–16. Mexico: UNAM, 1998.

Geist, Michael. "Anti-circumvention Legislation and Competition Policy: Defining a Canadian Way?" In *In the Public Interest: The Future of Canadian Copyright Law*, ed. M. Geist, 211–50. Toronto: Irwin Law, 2005.

Geist, Michael. "Government Launches Consultation on Rules for ISP Notice-and-Notice System amid Shift in Priorities." www.michaelgeist.ca, 10 October 2013. http://www.michaelgeist.ca/content/view/6967/125/.

Geist, Michael. "The Battle over C-11 Concludes: How Thousands of Canadians Changed the Copyright Debate." www.michaelgeist.ca, 18 June 2012. http://www.michaelgeist.ca/content/view/6544/125/.

Geist, Michael. "Behind the Scenes of Canada's Movie Piracy Bill." www.michaelgeist.ca, 11 June 2007. http://www.michaelgeist.ca/content/view/2016/275/.

Geist, Michael. "Bill C-60 User Guide: The ISPs and Search Engines." www.michaelgeist.ca, June 2005. http://www.michaelgeist.ca/content/view/824/125/.

Geist, Michael. "Copyright's 10K." www.michaelgeist.ca, 9 December 2007. http://www.michaelgeist.ca/content/view/2453/99999/.

Geist, Michael. "The Final Copyright Consultation Numbers: No Repeat of Bill C-61." www.michaelgeist.ca, 9 April 2010. http://www.michaelgeist.ca/content/view/4946/125/.

Geist, Michael. "How the U.S. Got Its Canadian Copyright Bill." *Toronto Star*, 16 June 2008.

Geist, Michael. "Introduction." In *In the Public Interest: The Future of Canadian Copyright Law*, ed. M. Geist, 1–12. Toronto: Irwin Law, 2005.

Geist, Michael. "Mexico signs ACTA amid speculation it was price of TPP admission." michaelgeist.ca, 12 July 2012. http://www.michaelgeist.ca/content/view/6586/196/.

Geist, Michael. "The Missing Copyright Docs, Pt 1: Justice Dept Warned about Constitutionality of Digital Lock Rules." www.michaelgeist.ca, 25 June 2012. http://www.michaelgeist.ca/content/view/6557/125/.

Geist, Michael. "The 2009 Copyright Consultation: Setting the Record Straight." www.michaelgeist.ca, 20 April 2010. http://www.michaelgeist.ca/content/view/4971/125/.

Geist, Michael. "U.S. Caves on Anti-Circumvention Rules in ACTA." www.michaelgeist.ca, 19 July 2010. http://www.michaelgeist.ca/content/view/5210/125/.

Geist, Michael. "The U.S. DMCA vs. Bill C-32: Comparing the Digital Lock Exceptions." www.michaelgeist.ca, 27 July 2010. http://www.michaelgeist.ca/content/view/5229/125/.

Gervais, Daniel J. "The Purpose of Copyright Law in Canada." *University of Ottawa Law and Technology Journal* 2.2 (2005): 315–56.

Gillespie, Tarleton. "Price Discrimination and the Shape of the Digital Commodity." In *Structures of Participation in Digital Culture*, ed. Joe Karaganis, 246–55. New York: Social Science Research Council, 2007.

Gillespie, Tarleton. *Wired Shut: Copyright and the Shape of Digital Culture.* Cambridge, MA: MIT Press, 2007.

Ginsburg, Jane C. "Copyright and Control over New Technologies of Dissemination." *Columbia Law Review* 101.7 (2001): 1612–47.

Goldstein, Paul. *Copyright's Highway: From Gutenberg to the Celestial Jukebox.* Stanford: Stanford Law and Politics, 2003.

Golob, Stephanie R. "Beyond the Policy Frontier: Canada, Mexico and the Ideological Origins of NAFTA." *World Politics* 55 (2003): 361–98.

González, Marco, Javier Torres Medina, and Omar Jiménez. *La república informal: El ambulantaje en la ciudad de México.* Mexico City: Editions Porrúa, 2008.

Gordon, Wendy J. "An Inquiry into the Merits of Copyright: The Challenges of Consistency, Consent, and Encouragement Theory." *Stanford Law Review* 41 (1989): 1343–1469.

Gordon, Wendy J., and Robert G. Bone. "Copyright." In *Encyclopedia of Law and Economics*, vol. 2, chap. 1610, ed. Boudewijn Bouckaert and Gerrit De Geest, 189–215. Cheltenham: Edward Elgar, 2000.

Haggart, Blayne. "Historical Institutionalism and the Politics of Intellectual Property." In *Intellectual Property Law for the 21st Century: Interdisciplinary Approaches to IP*, ed. Courtney B. Doagoo, Mistrale Goudreau, Madelaine Saginur, and Teresa Scassa, 160–81. Toronto: Irwin Law, 2014.

Haggart, Blayne. "Birth of a Movement: The Anti-Counterfeiting Trade Agreement and the Politicization of Mexican Copyright." *Policy & Internet* (2014): forthcoming.

Haggart, Blayne. "Fair Copyright for Canada: Lessons from Canada's First Facebook Uprising." *Canadian Journal of Political Science* (2014): forthcoming.

Haggart, Blayne. "Analysis of the Security and Prosperity Partnership of North America's Report to Leaders." Ottawa: Parliamentary Information and Research Service. Confidential document prepared for Mr.. Peter Julian, MP, 2005. On file with the author. Released with permission.

Halbert, Debora J. *Resisting Intellectual Property.* New York: Routledge, 2005.

Hall, Peter A. "Policy Paradigms, Social Learning, and the State: The Case of Economic Policymaking in Britain." *Comparative Politics* 25.3 (1993): 275–96.

Hall, Peter A., and Rosemary C.R. Taylor. "Political Science and the Three New Institutionalisms." *Political Studies* 44.5 (1996): 936–57.

Handa, Sunny. *Copyright Law in Canada.* Markham: Butterworths Canada Ltd, 2002.

Handa, Sunny. "A Review of Canada's International Copyright Obligations." *McGill Law Journal* 42 (1997): 961–90.

Hardin, Russell. "Valuing Intellectual Property." *Chicago-Kent Law Review* 68.2 (1993): 659–75.

Haunss, Sebastian, and Kenneth C. Shadlen. "Introduction: Rethinking the Politics of Intellectual Property." In *Politics of Intellectual Property: Contestation over the Ownership, Use, and Control of Knowledge and Information*, ed. S. Haunss and K.C. Shadlen, 1–12. Cheltenham: Edward Elgar, 2009.

Hay, Colin. "Contemporary Capitalism, Globalization, Regionalization and the Persistence of National Variation." *Review of International Studies* 26 (2000): 509–31.

Hay, Colin, and Daniel Wincott. "Structure, Agency and Historical Institutionalism." *Political Studies* 46 (1998): 951–7.

Haydu, Jeffrey. "Making Use of the Past: Time Periods as Cases to Compare and as Sequences of Problem Solving." *American Journal of Sociology* 104.2 (1998): 339–71.

Heichel, Stephan, Jessica Pape, and Thomas Sommerer. "Is There Convergence in Convergence Research? An Overview of Empirical Studies on Policy Convergence." *Journal of European Public Policy* 12.5 (2005): 817–40.

Herman, Bill D., and Oscar H. Gandy, Jr. "Catch 1201: A Legislative History and Content Analysis of the DMCA Exemption Proceedings." *Cardozo Arts & Entertainment Law Journal* 24 (2006): 121–90.

Hernández Arzate, Adriana. "Delimitación del contenido del derecho de autor en Internet." Thesis, Licenciado en Derecho (law degree). Toluca: Universidad Autónoma del Estado de México, 2006.

Hettinger, Edwin C. "Justifying Intellectual Property." *Philosophy & Public Affairs* 18.1 (1989): 31–52.

Holzinger, Katharina. "Methodological Pitfalls of Convergence Analysis." *European Union Politics* 7.2 (2006): 271–87.

Holzinger, Katharina, and Christoph Knill. "Causes and Conditions of Cross-National Policy Convergence." *Journal of European Public Policy* 12.5 (2005): 775–96.

Hruska, Joel. "How SOPA Could Actually Break the Internet." ExtremeTech, 19 December 2011. http://www.extremetech.com/computing/109533-how-sopa-could-actually-break-the-internet/2.

Hughes, Justin. "Notes on the Origin of 'Intellectual Property': Revised Conclusions and New Sources," Benjamin N. Cardozo School of Law, Jacob Burns Institute for Advanced Legal Studies working paper 265 (2009).

Hughes, Justin. "Copyright and Incomplete Historiographies: Of Piracy, Propertization, and Thomas Jefferson." *Southern California Law Review* 79 (2006): 993–1084.

Hughes, Justin. "The Philosophy of Intellectual Property." In *Intellectual Property: Moral, Legal, and International Dilemmas*, ed. Adam D. Moore,

107–77. Lanham, MD: Rowman & Littlefield Publishers, 1997. Originally published in *Georgetown Law Journal* 287 (1988).

Hurt, Robert M., and Robert M. Schuman. "The Economic Rationale of Copyright." *American Economic Review* 56.1–2 (1966): 421–32.

Idirs, Kamil. "Preface." In Fernando Serrano Migallón, *Marco jurídico del derecho de autor en México*, 2nd ed. Mexico City: Editorial Porrúa, 2008.

Immergut, Ellen M. "The Theoretical Core of the New Institutionalism." *Politics and Society* 26.5 (1998): 5–34.

Inside U.S. Trade. "USTR Seeks to Enact ACTA This Year, but TPP Seen as Key New Venue." 13 July 2012.

International Intellectual Property Alliance. "IIPA Letter on Copyright Enforcement and Pending Legislative Reform in Mexico." 2003. http://www.iipa.com/countryreports.html.

International Intellectual Property Alliance. "Special 301 Report: Mexico." 2005–10. http://www.iipa.com/countryreports.html.

Jalife Daher, Mauricio. "El nuevo escquema antipiratería," In *Legislación de Derechos de Autor*, 2006 edition, xxix–xxx. Mexico: Editorial Sista, 2006.

Jazi, Peter. "Worth the Wait – Installment #1." ©ollectanea blog, Center for Intellectual Property, 30 July 2010. http://chaucer.umuc.edu/blogcip/collectanea/2010/07/worth_the_wait_-_installment_1.html.

Jenson, Jane. "Converging, Diverging or Shifting?" Social Architecture in an Era of Change." Prepared for the Canadian Political Science Association, Halifax, May 2003.

Jones, Steve. "Mass Communication, Intellectual Property Rights, International Trade, and the Popular Music Industry." In *Mass Media and Free Trade: NAFTA and the Cultural Industries*, ed. Emile G. McAnany and Kenton T. Wilkinson, 331–50. Austin: University of Texas Press, 1996.

Juárez, Geraldine. "Senado Mexicano se postra a los pies de la industria del copyright." alt1040.com, 16 December 2011. http://alt1040.com/2011/12/senado-mexicano-se-postra-a-los-pies-de-la-industria-del-copyright.

Karaganis, Joe. "Disciplining Markets in the Digital Age." In *Structures of Participation in Digital Culture*, ed. J. Karaganis, 222–45. New York: Social Science Research Council, 2007.

Karaganis, Joe. "Rethinking Piracy." In *Media Piracy in Emerging Economies*, ed. J. Karaganis, 1–74. New York: Social Science Research Council, 2011.

Katzenstein, Peter J. *A World of Regions: Asia and Europe in the American Imperium*. Ithaca: Cornell University Press, 2005.

Katznelson, Ira. "Periodization and Preferences: Reflections on Purposive Action in Comparative Historical Social Science." In *Comparative Historical*

Analysis in the Social Sciences, ed. James Mahoney and Dietrich Rueschemeyer, 270–301. Cambridge: Cambridge University Press, 2003.

Katznelson, Ira. "Review: The Doleful Dance of Politics and Policy: Can Historical Institutionalism Make a Difference?" *American Political Science Review* 92.1 (1998): 191–7.

Katznelson, Ira. "Structure and Configuration in Comparative Politics," In *Comparative Politics*, ed. Mark I. Lichbach and Alan S. Zuckerman, 81–112. Cambridge: Cambridge University Press, 1997.

Keohane, Robert O. *After Hegemony: Cooperation and Discord in the World Political Economy*. Princeton: Princeton University Press, 2005.

Keohane, Robert O., and Joseph S. Nye. *Power and Interdependence*. 2nd ed. Glenview, IL: Scott, Foresman/Little Brown, 1989.

Kerr, Ian. "Technical Protection Measures: Part II – The Legal Protection of TPMs." Ottawa: Department of Canadian Heritage, 2004. http://www.pch.gc.ca/progs/ac-ca/progs/pda-cpb/pubs/protectionII/tdm_e.cfm.

Kerr, Ian R., Alana Maurushat, and Christian S. Tacit. "Technical Protection Measures: Tilting at Copyright's Windmill." *Ottawa Law Review* 34.1 (2002–3): 6–80.

Keyes, A.A., and C. Brunet. *Copyright in Canada: Proposals for a Revision of the Law*. Ottawa: Consumer and Corporate Affairs Canada, 1977.

Kingdon, John. *Agendas, Alternatives, and Public Policies*. 2nd ed. New York: Longman, 2003.

Kitschelt, Herbert, Peter Lange, Gary Marks, and John D. Stephens. "Convergence and Divergence in Advanced Capitalist Democracies." In *Continuity and Change in Contemporary Capitalism*, ed. H. Kitschelt, 427–60. London: Cambridge University Press, 1999.

Knopf, Howard. "The Annual '301' Show – USTR Calls for Comment – 21 Reasons Why Canadian Copyright Law Is Already Stronger than USA's." *Excess Copyright*, 17 February 2010. http://excesscopyright.blogspot.com/2010/02/annual-301-parade-ustr-calls-for.html.

Kopala, Margaret. "Softwood Deal Tears a Hole in NAFTA." *Ottawa Citizen*, 26 August 2006. http://www.canada.com/ottawacitizen/news/opinion/story.html?id=ce0dbe37-c91c-4305-ade6-58dbd68a5925.

Krasner, Stephen D. "Sovereignty: An Institutional Perspective." *Comparative Political Studies* 21.1 (1988): 66–94.

Kretschmer, Martin, and Friedmann Kawohl. "The History and Philosophy of Copyright." In *Music and Copyright*, 2nd ed., ed. Simon Frith and Lee Marshall, 21–53. Edinburgh: Edinburgh University Press, 2004.

Ku, Raymond, Jiayang Sun, and Yiying Fan. "Does Copyright Law Promote Creativity? An Empirical Analysis of Copyright's Bounty." *Vanderbilt Law Review* 63 (2009): 1669–746.

Laing, Dave. "Copyright, Politics and the International Music Industry." In *Music and Copyright*, 2nd ed., ed. Simon Frith and Lee Marshall, 70–86. Edinburgh: Edinburgh University Press, 2004.

Landes, William M., and Richard A. Posner. "An Economic Analysis of Copyright Law." *Journal of Legal Studies* 18.2 (1988): 325–63.

Landes, William M., and Richard A. Posner. *The Economic Structure of Intellectual Property Law*. Cambridge, MA: Harvard University Press, 2003.

Lawson, Chappell H. *Building the Fourth Estate: Democratization and the Rise of a Free Press in Mexico*. Berkeley: University of California Press, 2002.

Lessig, Lawrence. *The Future of Ideas: The Fate of the Commons in a Connected World*. New York: Random House, 2001.

Levitsky, Steven, and María Victoria Murillo. "Variation in Institutional Strength." *Annual Review of Political Science* 12 (2009): 115–33.

Liebowitz, Stan. "MP3s and Copyright Collectives: A Cure Worse than the Disease?" In *Developments in the Economics of Copyright: Research and Analysis*, ed. Lisa N. Takeyama, Wendy J. Gordon, and Ruth Towse, 37–59. Cheltenham: Edward Elgar Publishing, 2005.

Litman, Jessica. *Digital Copyright*. Amherst, NY: Prometheus Books, 2006.

Litman, Jessica. "The Public Domain." *Emory Law Journal* 39 (1990): 965–1023. http://www.law.duke.edu/pd/papers/Litman_background.pdf.

Lowery, David. "Meet the New Boss, Worse than the Old Boss?" *The Trichordist*, 15 April 2012. http://thetrichordist.wordpress.com/2012/04/15/meet-the-new-boss-worse-than-the-old-boss-full-post/.

Mace, Gordon. "Introduction." In *Regionalism and the State: NAFTA and Foreign Policy Convergence*, ed. G. Mace, 1–11. Hampshire: Ashgate, 2008.

Mahoney, James. "Path Dependence in Historical Sociology." *Theory and Society* 29.4 (2000): 507–48.

Malpica De Lamadrid, Luis. *La influencia del derecho internacional en el derecho mexicano: La apertura de modelo de desarrollo de México*. Mexico, D.F.: Editorial Limusa, 2002.

March, James G., and Johan P. Olsen. "The New Institutionalism: Organizational Factors in Political Life." *American Political Science Review* 78.3 (1984): 734–49.

Maskus, Keith E. "Lessons from Studying the International Economics of Intellectual Property Rights," *Vanderbilt Law Review* 53.6 (2000): 2219–39.

Maskus, Keith E. *Intellectual Property Rights in the Global Economy*. Washington: Institute for International Economics, 2000.

Masnick, Mike. "Congress Brings Back Recently Removed 'IP Subcommittee' Now That Copyright Reformer Won't Lead It." Techdirt, 22 December 2010. http://www.techdirt.com/articles/20101220/23143712353/congress-brings-back-recently-removed-ip-subcommittee-now-that-copyright-reformer-wont-lead-it.shtml.

Masnick, Mike. "Debunking the Faulty Premises of the Pirate Bay Criminalization Treaty." Techdirt, 23 May 2009. http://www.techdirt.com/articles/
20080523/1203101212.shtml.

Masnick, Mike. "Joe Biden on the Internet: 'If it ain't broke, don't fix it …
unless Hollywood asks you to." Techdirt, 3 November 2011.
http://www.techdirt.com/articles/20111102/11450816604/joe-biden-
internet-if-it-aint-broke-dont-fix-it-unless-hollywood-asks-you-to.shtml.

Masnick, Mike. "Lamar Smith Says 'Just joking …' about Tomorrow; SOPA
Markup Postponed." Techdirt, 20 December 2011. http://www.techdirt
.com/articles/20111220/11175317144/lamar-smith-says-just-joking-about-
tomorrow-sopa-markup-postponed.shtml.

Masnick, Mike. "Mexico's IP Office Surprised Its Congress by Signing ACTA,
and Now Hopes to Win Their Support." Techdirt, 16 July 2012.
http://www.techdirt.com/articles/20120716/03505519709/
mexicos-ip-office-surprised-its-congress-signing-acta-now-hopes-to-win-
their-support.shtml.

Masnick, Mike. "Organization Overseeing Six Strikes Agreement between
Labels and ISPs Includes Advisory Board to Try to Keep Tech Folks Happy."
Techdirt, 2 April 2012. http://www.techdirt.com/articles/20120402/
18015918339/organization-overseeing-six-strikes-agreement-between-
labels-isps-includes-advisory-board-to-try-to-keep-tech-folks-happy.shtml.

Masnick, Mike. "RIAA Spent $17.6 Million in Lawsuits … to Get $391,000
in Settlements." Techdirt, 14 July 2010. http://www.techdirt.com/articles/
20100713/17400810200.shtml.

May, Christopher. Digital Rights Management: The Problem of Expanding
Ownership Rights. Oxford: Chandos Publishing, 2007.

May, Christopher. A Global Political Economy of Intellectual Property Rights. New
York: Routledge, 2000.

May, Christopher. The World Intellectual Property Organization: Resurgence and
the Development Agenda. New York: Routledge, 2007.

McLeod, Kembrew. Owning Culture: Authorship, Ownership and Intellectual
Property Law. New York: Peter Lang, 2001.

Mitchell, Henry C., Jr. The Intellectual Commons: Toward an Ecology of Intellectual
Property. Lanham, MD: Lexington Books, 2005.

Moody, Glyn. "Another Reason Why DRM Is Bad – for Publishers." Techdirt,
16 April 2012. http://www.techdirt.com/articles/20120412/07212918466/
another-reason-why-drm-is-bad-publishers.shtml.

Moody, Glyn. "European Parliament Declares Its Independence from the
European Commission with a Massive Rejection of ACTA. Now What?"
Techdirt, 4 July 2012. http://www.techdirt.com/articles/20120704/.

07533019579/european-parliament-declares-its-independence-european-
commission-with-massive-rejection-acta-now-what.shtml.

Moore, Adam D., ed. *Intellectual Property: Moral, Legal, and International
Dilemmas.* Lanham, MD: Rowman & Littlefield Publishers, Inc., 1997.

Murray, Laura J. "Copyright Talk: Patterns and Pitfalls in Canadian Policy
Discourses," In *In the Public Interest: The Future of Canadian Copyright Law,*
ed. Michael Geist, 15–40. Toronto: Irwin Law, 2005.

Murray, Laura J., and Samuel E. Trosow. *Canadian Copyright: A Citizen's Guide.*
Toronto: Between the Lines, 2007.

Nafzinger, James A.R. "NAFTA's Regime for Intellectual Property: In the
Mainstream of Public International Law." *Houston Journal of International
Law* 19 (Spring 1997): http://www.bibliojuridica.org/libros/2/950/25.pdf.

Netanel, Neil Weinstock. *Copyright's Paradox.* Oxford: Oxford University Press,
2008.

Nivón Bolán, Eduardo. "Propiedad intelectual y política cultural: Una
perspectiva desde la situación mexicana." In *Propiedad intelectual, nuevas
tecnologías y libre acceso a la cultura,* ed. Alberto López Cuenca and Eduardo
Ramírez Pedrajo, 43–72. Puebla: Universidad de las Américas Puebla /
Centro Cultural de España México, 2009. http://www.ccemx.org/
img_act_x_tipo/propiedadint.pdf.

North, Douglass C. *Institutions, Institutional Change, and Economic Performance.*
Cambridge: Cambridge University Press, 1990.

Obón León, J. Ramón. "La actualidad del derecho de autor en México."
Presentation to WIPO conference "El derecho de autor: Un valor estratégico
para el futuro." Museo Nacional de Antropología e Historia, 28 June 2003.
On file with the author.

Obón León, J. Ramón. "El orden público y el interés social en la nueva Ley
Federal del Derecho de Autor." In *Estudios de derecho intelectual en homenaje
al Profesor David Rangel Medina,* ed. Manuel Becerra Ramírez, 117–33.
Mexico: UNAM, 1998.

Olsen, Johan P. "Change and Continuity: An Institutional Approach to
Institutions of Democratic Government." *European Political Science Review*
1.1 (2009): 3–32.

Olson, Mancur. *The Logic of Collective Action.* Cambridge, MA: Harvard
University Press, 1971.

Orren, Karen, and Stephen Skowronek. *The Search for American Political
Development.* Cambridge: Cambridge University Press, 2004.

Palmedo, Mike. "Mexican Legislature Passes Two Resolutions Opposing
the Executive's Signing of ACTA." infojustice.org, 19 July 2012. http://
infojustice.org/archives/26624.

Pastor, Robert. *Toward a North American Community: Lessons from the Old World for the New.* Washington: Institute for International Economics, 2001.

Patry, William. *Moral Panics and the Copyright Wars.* Oxford: Oxford University Press, 2010.

Pelroth, Nicole. "Under Scrutiny, Google Spends Record Amount on Lobbying." *New York Times*, Bits blog, 23 April 2012. http://bits.blogs.nytimes.com/2012/04/23/under-scrutiny-google-spends-record-amount-on-lobbying/.

Peters, B. Guy. "Institutional Theory: Problems and Prospects." In *Debating Institutionalism*, ed. Jon Pierre, B.G. Peters, and Gerry Stoker, 1–21. New York: Manchester University Press, 2008.

Peters, B. Guy, Jon Pierre, and Desmond S. King. "The Politics of Path Dependency: Political Conflict in Historical Institutionalism." *Journal of Politics* 67.4 (2005): 1275–1300.

Piedras Feria, Ernesto. *¿Cuánto vale la cultura? Contribución económica de las industrias protegidas por los derechos de autor en México.* Mexico: CONACULTA/SACM/SOGEM, 2004.

Piedras Feria, Ernesto. "Industrias culturales en México: Una actualización de los cálculos al 2003." 2007. http://www.odai.org/biblioteca/biblioteca1/10.pdf.

Pierson, Paul. "Increasing Returns, Path Dependence, and the Study of Politics." *American Political Science Review* 94.2 (2000): 251–67.

Pierson, Paul. "The Limits of Design: Explaining Institutional Origin and Change." *Governance: An International Journal of Policy and Administration* 13.4 (2000): 475–99.

Pierson, Paul. "Not Just What, but *When*: Timing and Sequence in Political Processes." *Studies in American Political Development* 14 (2000): 72–92.

Pierson, Paul. *Politics in Time: History, Institutions and Social Analysis.* Princeton: Princeton University Press, 2004.

Pierson, Paul, and Theda Skocpol. "Historical Institutionalism in Contemporary Political Science." In *Political Science: The State of the Discipline*, ed. Ira Katznelson and Helen V. Milner, 693–721. New York: WW Norton & Co., 2002.

Plant, Arnold. "The Economic Aspects of Copyright in Books." *Economica*, n.s., 1.2 (1934): 167–95.

Pollack, Mark A. "The New Institutionalisms and European Integration." In *European Integration Theory*, ed. Antje Wiener and Thomas Diez, 137–56. Oxford: Oxford University Press, 2004.

Pontusson, Jonas. "From Comparative Public Policy to Political Economy: Putting Political Institutions in Their Place and Taking Interests Seriously." *Comparative Political Studies* 28.1 (1995): 117–47.

Pregeli, Vladimir. "The Jackson-Vanik Amendment: A Survey." CRS Report for Congress 98-545. Washington: Congressional Research Service, 1998. http://www.fas.org/sgp/crs/row/98-545.pdf.

Preston, Julia. "As Piracy Grows in Mexico, U.S. Companies Shout Foul." *New York Times*, 20 April 1996, 1.

Ramalho, Ana. "Murder They Wrote – The Dutch Kill ACTA." Kluwer Copyright Blog, 30 May 2012. http://kluwercopyrightblog.com/2012/05/30/murder-they-wrote-%E2%80%93-the-dutch-kill-acta/.

Rangel Ortiz, Horacio. "La usurpación de derechos en la nueva ley autoral Mexicana y su reforma." In *Estudios de derecho intelectual en homenaje al Profesor David Rangel Medina*, ed. Manuel Becerra Ramírez, 377–95. Mexico: UNAM, 1998.

Raskind, Leo J. "Copyright." In *The New Palgrave Dictionary of Economics and the Law*, vol. 1, ed. Peter Newman, 478–83. London: Macmillan, 1998.

Rhodes, R.A.W., Sarah Binder, and Bert A. Rockman, eds. "Preface." In *The Oxford Handbook of Political Institutions*, xii–xvii. Oxford: Oxford University Press.

Richardson, Jeremy. "Government, Interest Groups and Policy Change." *Political Studies* 48 (2000): 1006–25.

Ricketson, Sam, and Jane C. Ginsburg. *International Copyright and Neighbouring Rights: The Berne Convention and Beyond*, 2nd ed., vols. 1 and 2. Oxford: Oxford University Press, 2006.

Rimmer, Matthew. "Robbery Under Arms: Copyright Law and the Australia–United States Free Trade Agreement." *First Monday* 11.3 (2006). http://firstmonday.org/htbin/cgiwrap/bin/ojs/index.php/fm/article/view/1316/1236.

Robert, Maryse. *Negotiating NAFTA: Explaining the Outcome in Culture, Textiles, Autos, and Pharmaceuticals*. Toronto: University of Toronto Press, 2001.

Rose, Mark. *Authors and Owners: The Invention of Copyright*. Cambridge: Harvard University Press, 1993.

Rotstein, Robert H. "Beyond Metaphor: Copyright Infringement and the Fiction of the Work." *Chicago-Kent Law Review* 68.2 (1993): 725–804.

Sager, Carrie Ellen. "TPP's Effects on the IP Law of Canada and Mexico." Infojustice.org, 11 April 2012. http://infojustice.org/archives/9508.

Samuelson, Pamela. "The U.S. Digital Agenda at the World Intellectual Property Organization." Monograph (1997). http://people.ischool.berkeley.edu/~pam/courses/cyberlaw97/docs/wipo.pdf.

Sandoval, Greg. "For RIAA, a Black Eye Comes with the Job." CNET News, 9 October 2007. http://news.cnet.com/For-RIAA,-a-black-eye-comes-with-the-job/2100-1027_3-6212374.html.

Sapp, Heather A. "North American Anti-Circumvention: Implementation of the WIPO Internet Treaties in the United States, Mexico and Canada." *Computer Law Review and Technology Journal* 10 (2005): 1–39.

Savage, Luiza Ch. "Meet NAFTA 2.0." *Maclean's*, 13 September 2006. http://www.macleans.ca/topstories/canada/article.jsp?content=20060911_133202_133202.

Savoie, Donald J. *Court Government and the Collapse of Accountability in Canada and the United Kingdom*. Toronto: University of Toronto Press, 2008.

Scassa, Teresa. "Interests in the Balance." In *In the Public Interest: The Future of Canadian Copyright Law*, ed. Michael Geist, 41–65. Toronto: Irwin Law, 2005.

Scherer, F.M. "The Innovation Lottery." In *Expanding the Boundaries of Intellectual Property: Innovation Policy for the Knowledge Society*, ed. Rochelle Cooper Dreyfuss, Diane Leenheer Zimmerman, and Harry First, 3–21. Oxford: Oxford University Press, 2001.

Schmidt, Luis. "Digital Millenium [*sic*] 'a la Mexicaine': Internet and Other Digital Technologies Examined in Light of the Mexican Copyright Law." *Copyright World Magazine*, 1 January 2001. http://74.125.95.132/search?q=cache:ePbeMjjMeuIJ:www.olivares.com.mx/formatos/lsr/digital.pdf+Digital+Millenium+%27a+la+Mexicaine%27&cd=1&hl=en&ct=clnk.

Schmidt, Luis. "Mexico's Fair Use Balancing Act." Managing Intellectual Property (2009). http://www.managingip.com/Article.aspx?ArticleID=2192575.

Schmidt, Luis. "The New Digital Agenda." *Copyright World*, 23 February 2009.

Schneier, Bruc. "Real Story of the Rogue Rootkit." *Wired*, 17 November 2005. http://www.wired.com/politics/security/commentary/securitymatters/2005/11/69601.

Schonwetter, Tobias, Jeremy de Beer, Dick Kawooya, and Achal Prabhala. "Copyright and Education: Lessons on African Copyright and Access to Knowledge." *African Journal of Information and Communication* 10 (2010): 37–52. http://ifap-is-observatory.ittk.hu/node/470.

Seeliger, Robert. "Conceptualizing and Researching Policy Convergence. *Policy Studies Journal* 24.2 (1996): 287–306.

Segal, Nancy. Testimony (edited) before Standing Committee on Public Safety and National Security. House of Commons, 1st Session, 39th Parliament. Ottawa, 27 March 2007.

Sell, Susan K. *Private Power, Public Law: The Globalization of Intellectual Property Rights*. Cambridge: Cambridge University Press, 2003.

Sell, Susan K. "The Rise and Rule of a Trade-Based Strategy: Historical Institutionalism and the International Regulation of Intellectual Property." *Review of International Political Economy* 17.4 (2010): 762–90.

Serrano Migallón, Fernando. *Marco jurídico del derecho de autor en México*. 2nd ed. Mexico City: Editorial Porrúa, 2008.

Shapiro, Michael. Speech to Public Policy Forum "Intellectual Property Reform: Innovation and the Economy." Sound recording. Ottawa, ON, 28 April 2008. On file with the author.

Sheffer, Warren. "Writers' Rights Upheld: The Robertson Decision." *Copyright & New Media Law Newsletter* 10.4 (2006): 8–9.

Sinclair, John. "Culture and Trade: Some Theoretical and Practical Considerations." In *Mass Media and Free Trade: NAFTA and the Cultural Industries*, ed. Emile G. McAnany and Kenton T. Wilkinson, 30–60. Austin: University of Texas Press, 1996.

Singh, Vik. "Economic Contribution of Culture in Canada." 81-595-MIE – no. 023. Ottawa: Statistics Canada, 2008.

Siweck, Stephen E. "Copyright Industries in the U.S. Economy: The 2011 Report." Washington: International Intellectual Property Alliance, 2011. http://www.iipa.com/pdf/2011CopyrightIndustriesReport.PDF.

Slesinger, Reuben E., Robert W. Frase, and Armen A. Alchian. "Discussion." *American Economic Review* 56.1–2 (1966): 433–9.

Smiers, Joost. "The Abolition of Copyright: Better for Artists, the Third World, and the Public Domain." *International Communications Gazette* 62.5 (2000): 379–406.

Steinmo, Sven, Kathleen Thelen, and Frank Longstreth, eds. *Structuring Politics: Historical Institutionalism in Comparative Analysis*. Cambridge: Cambridge University Press, 1992.

Stinchcombe, Arthur L. *Constructing Social Theories*. New York: Harcourt, Brace & World, 1968.

Story, Alan. "Burn Berne: Why the Leading International Copyright Convention Must Be Repealed." *Houston Law Review* 40.3 (2003): 763–801.

Streeck, Wolfgang, and Kathleen Thelen. "Introduction: Institutional Change in Advanced Political Economies." In *Beyond Continuity: Institutional Change in Advanced Political Economies*, ed. W. Streeck and K. Thelen, 1–39. Oxford: Oxford University Press. 2005.

Strowel, Alain, and Séverine Dussolier. "Workshop on Implementation Issues of the WIPO Copyright Treaty (WCT) and the WIPO Performances and Phonograms Treaty (WPPT): Legal Protection of Technological Systems." WCT-WPPT/IMP/2. Geneva: WIPO, 1999. http://www.wipo.int/edocs/mdocs/copyright/en/wct_wppt_imp/wct_wppt_imp_2.doc.

Tarantino, Bob. "Five Cases That Shook the World: An Entertainment Lawyer's Guide to the Copyright Pentalogy." Heenan Blaikie LLP, 17 July 2012.

http://www.jdsupra.com/legalnews/five-cases-that-shook-the-world-an-ente-18513/.

Tawfik, Myra J. "Intellectual Property Laws in Harmony with NAFTA: The Courts as Mediators between the Global and the Local." *Canadian Journal of Law and Technology* 2.3 (2003): 213–21.

Tawfik, Myra J. "International Copyright Law: W[h]ither User Rights?" In *In the Public Interest: The Future of Canadian Copyright Law*, ed. Michael Geist, 66–85. Toronto: Irwin Law, 2005.

Taylor, Josh. "France Drops Hadopi Three-Strikes Copyright Law." *ZDNet*, 10 July 2013. http://www.zdnet.com/france-drops-hadopi-three-strikes-copyright-law-7000017857/.

Teufel, Brady. "Gauging the Influence of America's Legal Decisions regarding Intellectual Property on the World Wide Web." Master's dissertation, University of Missouri–Columbia, 2004.

Thelen, Kathleen. "Historical Institutionalism in Comparative Politics." *Annual Review of Political Science* 2 (1999): 369–404.

Thelen, Kathleen, and Sven Steinmo. "Historical Institutionalism in Comparative Politics." In *Structuring Politics: Historical Institutionalism in Comparative Analysis*, ed. S. Steinmo, K. Thelen, and Frank Longstreth, 1–32. Cambridge: Cambridge University Press, 1992.

Thumm, Nikolaus. *Intellectual Property Rights: National Systems and Harmonisation in Europe*. New York: Physica-Verlag, 2000.

Tibbetts, Janice. "Ottawa Tackles Movie Pirates." Saskatoon *StarPhoenix*, 2 June 2007. http://www.canada.com/saskatoonstarphoenix/news/national/story.html?id=83e4be8e-49ee-4ce1-b826-4850446ef4be.

Towse, Ruth. "Copyright and Economic Incentives: An Application to Performers' Rights in the Music Industry." *Kyklos* 52.3 (1999): 369–90.

Towse, Ruth, and Rudi Holzhauer. "Introduction." In *The Economics of Intellectual Property*, vol. 1, ed. R. Towse, and R. Holzhauer, ix–xxxii. Cheltenham: Edward Elgar Publishing, 2002.

Truman, David. *The Governmental Process*. New York: Knopf, 1951.

Valiquet, Dominique. "Bill C-59: An Act to Amend the Criminal Code (unauthorized recording of a movie)." LS-559E. Legislative summary. Ottawa: Library of Parliament, 2007. http://www2.parl.gc.ca/Sites/LOP/LegislativeSummaries/Bills_ls.asp?lang=E&ls=c59&source=library_prb&Parl=39&Ses=1.

Viñamata Paschkes, Carlos. *La propiedad intelectual*. 3rd ed. Mexico: Trillas, 2005.

Vinje, Thomas C., and Jonathan Band. "The WIPO Copyright Treaty: A New International Intellectual Property Framework for the Digital Age."

policybandwidth.com. 1997. http://www.policybandwidth.com/publications/JBand-NewWIPOCopyrightTreaty.pdf.

Voss, T.R. "Institutions." In *International Encyclopedia of the Social & Behavioral Sciences*. Cambridge: Cambridge University Press, 2001.

Waldron, Jeremy. "From Authors to Copiers: Individual Rights and Social Values in Intellectual Property." *Chicago-Kent Law Review* 68.2 (1993): 841–87.

Wikipedia. "SOPA Initiative." http://en.wikipedia.org/wiki/Wikipedia:SOPA_initiative.

Wilkins, David. Speech to Public Policy Forum "Intellectual Property Reform: Innovation and the Economy." Sound recording. Ottawa, ON, 28 April 2008. On file with the author.

Writers Guild of Canada. "Copyright Balance Can Be Struck with Levies on Technologies and Distribution Platforms." News release, 12 June 2008. http://www.wgc.ca/files/WGC%20on%20Copyright%20June%2012.pdf.

Writers Union of Canada. "Writers' Union Says Copyright Act 'Still Needs Work.'" News release, 17 June 2007. http://web.archive.org/web/20111103205801/http://www.writersunion.ca/av_pr061708.asp.

Wu, Tim. *The Master Switch: The Rise and Fall of Information Empires*. New York: Alfred A. Knopf, 2010.

Zamora, Ricardo. "Internet necesario: Crónica de un pequeño gran cambio." In *Ciudadanos.mx: Twitter y el cambio politico en México*, ed. Ana Vega and José Merino, 18–29. Mexico City: Random House Mondadori, 2010.

Government and International Organization Documents Cited

World Intellectual Property Organization (WIPO)

World Intellectual Property Organization (WIPO). "Core Tasks of WIPO." 2009. http://www.wipo.int/about-wipo/en/what/core_tasks.html.

World Intellectual Property Organization. *Survey on Implementation Provisions of the WCT and the WPPT*, 25 April 2003. http://www.wipo.int/meetings/en/doc_details.jsp?doc_id=16415.

World Intellectual Property Organization. "What Is WIPO?" 2009. http://www.wipo.int/about-wipo/en/what/.

United States

Copyright Office. *The Digital Millennium Copyright Act of 1998*. Copyright Office summary. Washington, DC: Copyright Office, 1998. http://www.copyright.gov/legislation/dmca.pdf.

Department of Commerce. *Intellectual Property and the National Information Infrastructure: The Report of the Working Group on Intellectual Property Rights.* Washington, DC: Department of Commerce, 1995.

United States. "Joint Statement by North American Leaders." The White House, 2 April 2012. http://www.whitehouse.gov/the-press-office/2012/04/02/joint-statement-north-american-leaders.

United States. "Most-Favored-Nation Status – MFN." U.S. Department of State dispatch, 17 September 1990. http://findarticles.com/p/articles/mi_m1584/is_n3_v1/ai_9079866/.

United States. "Security and Prosperity Partnership of North America (SPP) Intellectual Property Rights Action Strategy." 2007. http://www.spp.gov/pdf/spp_ip_strat_final.pdf.

United States. "2013 Special 301 Report." Office of the United States Trade Representative. May 2013. http://www.ustr.gov/sites/default/files/05012013%202013%20Special%20301%20Report.pdf.

United States. "2010 Special 301 Report. Office of the United States Trade Representative." 30 April 2010. http://www.ustr.gov/webfm_send/1906.

Canada

Canada. "2007 Speech from the Throne." 17 October 2007.

Consumer and Corporate Affairs Canada, and Department of Communications. *From Gutenberg to Telidon: A White Paper on Copyright. Proposals for the Revision of the Canadian Copyright Act.* Ottawa: Supply and Services Canada, 1984.

Foreign Affairs and International Trade Canada. "Anti-Counterfeiting Trade Agreement – Fact Sheet." 2010. http://www.international.gc.ca/trade-agreements-accords-commerciaux/fo/IP-factsheet-fiche.aspx?lang=en.

House of Commons Standing Committee on Canadian Heritage. *Interim Report on Copyright Reform.* Ottawa: House of Commons, 2004.

House of Commons Standing Committee on Communications and Culture. *A Charter of Rights for Creators.* Ottawa: House of Commons, 1985.

Industry Canada. "Government of Canada Proposes Update to Copyright Law: Balanced Approach to Truly Benefit Canadians." News release, 12 June 2008. http://www.ic.gc.ca/eic/site/ic1.nsf/eng/04204.html.

Industry Canada and Canadian Heritage. *Consultation Paper on the Application of the Copyright Act's Compulsory Retransmission Licence to the Internet.* Ottawa, 2002. http://www.ic.gc.ca/eic/site/crp-prda.nsf/eng/rp00008.html.

Industry Canada and Canadian Heritage. *Consultation Paper on Digital Copyright Issues.* Ottawa, 2002. http://strategis.gc.ca/eic/site/crp-prda.nsf/eng/h_rp01102.html.

Industry Canada and Canadian Heritage. *A Framework for Copyright Reform.* Ottawa, 2001. http://strategis.ic.gc.ca/eic/site/crp-prda.nsf/eng/rp01101 .html.

Industry Canada and Canadian Heritage. *Supporting Culture and Innovation: Report on the Provisions and Operation of the Copyright Act.* 2002. http://www .ic.gc.ca/eic/site/crp-prda.nsf/eng/rp00863.html.

Ministers of Canadian Heritage and Industry. "Status Report on Copyright Reform." Submitted to the House of Commons Standing Committee on Canadian Heritage. 2005. http://www.ic.gc.ca/eic/site/crp-prda.nsf/eng/ rp01133.html.

Royal Commission on Patents, Copyright, Trade Marks and Industrial Designs (Ilsley Commission). *Report on Copyright.* Ottawa: Queen's Printer and Controller of Stationary, 1957. http://epe.lac-bac.gc.ca/100/200/301/ pco-bcp/commissions-ef/ilsley1957a-eng/ilsley1957a-eng.htm.

Mexico

Comisión de Ciencia y Tecnología del Senado de México. "B-0564 Seminario: 'Derecho de autor en el entorno digital.'" 2008. http://comunicacion.senado .gob.mx/index.php?option=com_content&task=view&id=7856&Itemid=163.

Comisión Federal de Telecomunicaciones. "Emite COFETEL consideraciones sobre el ACTA." Comunicado de prensa, no. 65/2010, 24 November 2010. http://www.cft.gob.mx/swb/Cofetel_2008/652010.

Senate of Mexico. Report from *Grupo plural de trabajo para dar seguimiento a las negociaciones del Acuerdo Comercial Anti-Falsificaciones* [Working group following the Anti-Counterfeiting Trade Agreement negotiations], 20 July 2011. http://www.senado.gob.mx/comisiones/LX/grupo_acta/content/ docs/20julio11.pdf.

Senate of Mexico. ACTA Working Group. Testimony and documents. http:// www.senado.gob.mx/comisiones/LX/grupo_acta/content/reu.htm.

Instituto Nacional del Derecho de Autor (INDAUTOR). "Internet & Technology Provisions: Questions for Discussion." Non-paper for discussion at WIPO. 2008. On file with the author.

Instituto Nacional del Derecho de Autor (INDAUTOR). "Internet & Technology Provisions: Questions for Discussion," 2008. On file with the author.

International Treaties

Anti-Counterfeiting Trade Agreement. http://www.dfat.gov.au/trade/acta/Final-ACTA-text-following-legal- verification.pdf&pli=1.

Canada–United States Free Trade Agreement (Articles 2004–6).
    http://www.worldtradelaw.net/nafta/CUSFTA.pdf.
North American Free Trade Agreement, Chapter 17: Intellectual Property.
    http://www.nafta-sec-alena.org/en/view.aspx?conID=590&mtpiID=149.
North American Free Trade Agreement, Chapter 20: Exceptions (Article 2106:
    Cultural Industries).
    http://www.nafta-sec-alena.org/en/view.aspx?conID=590&mtpiID=155#A2106.
World Intellectual Property Organization Copyright Treaty.
    http://www.wipo.int/treaties/en/ip/wct/trtdocs_wo033.html.
World Intellectual Property Organization Performances and Phonograms Treaty.
    http://www.wipo.int/treaties/en/ip/wppt/trtdocs_wo034.html.

Domestic Legislation

United States

United States. Copyright Act (17 U.S.C.): http://www.law.cornell.edu/
    uscode/html/uscode17/usc_sup_01_17.html.
United States. "Digital Millennium Copyright Act 1998." http://www
    .copyright.gov/legislation/hr2281.pdf.
United States. "NII Copyright Protection Act of 1995." http://thomas.loc
    .gov/cgi-bin/query/z?c104:H.R.2441.
United States. "Sonny Bono Copyright Term Extension Act." 1998. www
    .copyright.gov/legislation/s505.pdf.
United States. Trade Act of 1974 (19 U.S.C. Chapter 12. http://www.law
    .cornell.edu/uscode/19/usc_sup_01_19_10_12.html.
Wikileaks. Cable 07MEXICO6229, from US Embassy in Mexico City, 19 De-
    cember 2007.

Canada

Canada. An Act Respecting Copyright, (1985) R.S., 1985, c. C-42.
Canada. Parliament. House of Commons. "An Act to Amend the *Copyright
    Act.*" Bill C-32, 35th Parliament, 2nd Session, 1996–7. Ottawa: Public Works
    and Government Services Canada. Assented to 25 April 1997.
Canada. Parliament. House of Commons. "An Act to Amend the *Copyright
    Act.*" Bill C-60, 38th Parliament, 1st Session, 2004–5. Ottawa: Public Works
    and Government Services Canada. 1st reading, 20 June 2005.
Canada. Parliament. House of Commons. "An Act to Amend the *Copyright
    Act.*" Bill C-61, 39th Parliament, 2nd Session, 2007–8. Ottawa: Public Works
    and Government Services Canada. 1st reading, 12 June 2008.

Canada. Parliament. House of Commons. "An Act to amend the *Criminal Code* (unauthorized recording of a movie)." Bill C-59, 39th Parliament, 1st Session, 2006–7. Ottawa: Public Works and Government Services Canada. Assented to 22 June 2007.

Canada. Parliament. House of Commons. The Copyright Modernization Act. Bill C-11, 41st Parliament, 1st Session, 2011–12. Ottawa: Public Works and Government Services Canada. Assented to 29 June 2012.

Canada. Parliament. House of Commons. The Copyright Modernization Act. Bill C-32, 40th Parliament, 3rd Session, 2010–11. Ottawa: Public Works and Government Services Canada. 2nd 5eading, 5 November 2010.

Mexico

México. Ley Federal del Derecho de Autor. 1997. http://www.sice.oas.org/int_prop/nat_leg/mexico/lcra.asp.

Index

Studies in Comparative Political Economy and Public Policy